Rethinking International Skilled Migration

In today's global knowledge economy, competition for the best and brightest workers has intensified. Highly skilled workers are an asset to companies, knowledge institutions, cities, and regions as they contribute to knowledge creation, innovation, and economic growth and development. Skilled migrants cross, and many times straddle, international borders to pursue professional opportunities. These spatial relocations provide opportunities and challenges for migrants and the cities and regions they inhabit.

How have international skilled migratory flows been formed, sustained, and transformed over multiple spaces and scales? How have these processes affected cities and regions? And how have multiple stakeholders responded to these processes? The contributors to this book bring together perspectives from economic, social, urban, and population geography in order to address these questions from a myriad of angles. Empirical case studies from different regions illuminate the multiscaled processes of international skilled migration. In particular, the contributions rethink skilled migration theories and provide insights into: the experiences of highly skilled labor migrants and international students; issues related to transnational activities and return migration; and policy implications for both immigrant source and destination countries. It also charts a future research agenda for international skilled migration research.

Rethinking International Skilled Migration provides a comparative perspective on the experiences of skilled migrants across the local, regional, national, and/or global scale, paying particular attention to spatial and place-based dimensions of international skilled migration. It will be of interest to scholars and professionals in international migration, regional and national development policymakers, international businesses, and NGOs.

Micheline van Riemsdijk is J. Harrison and Robbie C. Livingston Associate Professor of Population Geography at the University of Tennessee, USA.

Qingfang Wang is an Associate Professor of Geography and Public Policy at the University of California Riverside, USA.

Regional Studies Association

THE GLOBAL FORUM FOR CITY AND REGIONAL RESEARCH, DEVELOPMENT AND POLICY

Routledge
Taylor & Francis Group

Regions and Cities

Series Editor in Chief

Susan M. Christopherson, *Cornell University, USA*

Editors

Maryann Feldman, *University of Georgia, USA*
Gernot Grabher, *HafenCity University Hamburg, Germany*
Ron Martin, *University of Cambridge, UK*
Kieran P. Donaghy, *Cornell University, USA*

In today's globalised, knowledge-driven and networked world, regions and cities have assumed heightened significance as the interconnected nodes of economic, social and cultural production, and as sites of new modes of economic and territorial governance and policy experimentation. This book series brings together incisive and critically engaged international and interdisciplinary research on this resurgence of regions and cities, and should be of interest to geographers, economists, sociologists, political scientists and cultural scholars, as well as to policy-makers involved in regional and urban development.

For more information on the Regional Studies Association visit www.regional-studies.org

109 Rethinking International Skilled Migration
Edited by Micheline van Riemsdijk and Qingfang Wang

108 The EU's New Borderland
Cross-border relations and regional development
Andrzej Jakubowski, Andrzej Miszczuk, Bogdan Kawałko, Tomasz Komornicki, and Roman Szul

107 **Entrepreneurship in a Regional Context**
Edited by Michael Fritsch and David J. Storey

106 **Governing Smart Specialisation**
Edited by Dimitrios Kyriakou, Manuel Palazuelos Martínez, Inmaculada Periáñez-Forte, and Alessandro Rainoldi

105 **Innovation, Regional Development and the Life Sciences**
Beyond clusters
Kean Birch

104 **Unfolding Cluster Evolution**
Edited by Fiorenza Belussi and Jose Luis Hervás-Olivier

103 **Place-based Economic Development and the New EU Cohesion Policy**
Edited by Philip McCann and Attila Varga

102 **Transformation of Resource Towns and Peripheries**
Political economy perspectives
Edited by Greg Halseth

101 **Approaches to Economic Geography**
Towards a geographical political economy
Ray Hudson

100 **Secondary Cities and Development**
Edited by Lochner Marais, Etienne Nel and Ronnie Donaldson

99 **Technology and the City**
Systems, applications and implications
Tan Yigitcanlar

98 **Smaller Cities in a World of Competitiveness**
Peter Karl Kresl and Daniele Ietri

97 **Code and the City**
Edited by Rob Kitchin and Sung-Yueh Perng

96 **The UK Regional–National Economic Problem**
Geography, globalisation and governance
Philip McCann

95 **Skills and Cities**
Edited by Sako Musterd, Marco Bontje and Jan Rouwendal

94 **Higher Education and the Creative Economy**
Beyond the campus
Edited by Roberta Comunian and Abigail Gilmore

93 **Making Cultural Cities in Asia**
Mobility, assemblage, and the politics of aspirational urbanism
Edited by Jun Wang, Tim Oakes and Yang Yang

92 **Leadership and the City**
Power, strategy and networks in the making of knowledge cities
Markku Sotarauta

91 **Evolutionary Economic Geography**
Theoretical and empirical progress
Edited by Dieter Kogler

90 Cities in Crisis
Socio-spatial impacts of the economic crisis in Southern European cities
Edited by Jörg Knieling and Frank Othengrafen

89 Socio-Economic Segregation in European Capital Cities
East meets West
Edited by Tiit Tammaru, Szymon Marcińczak, Maarten van Ham, Sako Musterd

88 People, Places and Policy
Knowing contemporary Wales through new localities
Edited by Martin Jones, Scott Orford and Victoria Macfarlane

87 The London Olympics and Urban Development
The mega-event city
Edited by Gavin Poynter, Valerie Viehoff and Yang Li

86 Making 21st Century Knowledge Complexes
Technopoles of the world revisited
Edited by Julie Tian Miao, Paul Benneworth and Nicholas A. Phelps

85 Soft Spaces in Europe
Re-negotiating governance, boundaries and borders
Edited by Philip Allmendinger, Graham Haughton, Jörg Knieling and Frank Othengrafen

84 Regional Worlds: Advancing the Geography of Regions
Edited by Martin Jones and Anssi Paasi

83 Place-making and Urban Development
New challenges for contemporary planning and design
Pier Carlo Palermo and Davide Ponzini

82 Knowledge, Networks and Policy
Regional studies in postwar Britain and beyond
James Hopkins

81 Dynamics of Economic Spaces in the Global Knowledge-based Economy
Theory and East Asian cases
Sam Ock Park

80 Urban Competitiveness
Theory and practice
Daniele Letri and Peter Kresl

79 Smart Specialisation
Opportunities and challenges for regional innovation policy
Dominique Foray

78 The Age of Intelligent Cities
Smart environments and innovation-for-all strategies
Nicos Komninos

77 Space and Place in Central and Eastern Europe
Historical trends and perspectives
Gyula Horváth

76 Territorial Cohesion in Rural Europe
The relational turn in rural development
Edited by Andrew Copus and Philomena de Lima

75 The Global Competitiveness of Regions
Robert Huggins, Hiro Izushi, Daniel Prokop and Piers Thompson

74 The Social Dynamics of Innovation Networks
Edited by Roel Rutten, Paul Benneworth, Dessy Irawati and Frans Boekema

73 The European Territory
From historical roots to global challenges
Jacques Robert

72 Urban Innovation Systems
What makes them tick?
Willem van Winden, Erik Braun, Alexander Otgaar and Jan-Jelle Witte

71 Shrinking Cities
A global perspective
Edited by Harry W. Richardson and Chang Woon Nam

70 Cities, State and Globalization
City-regional governance
Tassilo Herrschel

69 The Creative Class Goes Global
Edited by Charlotta Mellander, Richard Florida, Bjørn Asheim and Meric Gertler

68 Entrepreneurial Knowledge, Technology and the Transformation of Regions
Edited by Charlie Karlsson, Börje Johansson and Roger Stough

67 The Economic Geography of the IT Industry in the Asia Pacific Region
Edited by Philip Cooke, Glen Searle and Kevin O'Connor

66 Working Regions
Reconnecting innovation and production in the knowledge economy
Jennifer Clark

65 Europe's Changing Geography
The impact of inter-regional networks
Edited by Nicola Bellini and Ulrich Hilpert

64 The Value of Arts and Culture for Regional Development
A Scandinavian perspective
Edited by Lisbeth Lindeborg and Lars Lindkvist

63 The University and the City
John Goddard and Paul Vallance

62 Re-framing Regional Development
Evolution, innovation and transition
Edited by Philip Cooke

61 Networking Regionalised Innovative Labour Markets
Edited by Ulrich Hilpert and Helen Lawton Smith

60 Leadership and Change in Sustainable Regional Development
Edited by Markku Sotarauta, Ina Horlings and Joyce Liddle

59 **Regional Development Agencies: The Next Generation?**
Networking, knowledge and regional policies
Edited by Nicola Bellini, Mike Danson and Henrik Halkier

58 **Community-based Entrepreneurship and Rural Development**
Creating favourable conditions for small businesses in Central Europe
Matthias Fink, Stephan Loidl and Richard Lang

57 **Creative Industries and Innovation in Europe**
Concepts, measures and comparative case studies
Edited by Luciana Lazzeretti

56 **Innovation Governance in an Open Economy**
Shaping regional nodes in a globalized world
Edited by Annika Rickne, Staffan Laestadius and Henry Etzkowitz

55 **Complex Adaptive Innovation Systems**
Relatedness and transversality in the evolving region
Philip Cooke

54 **Creating Knowledge Locations in Cities**
Innovation and integration challenges
Willem van Winden, Luis de Carvalho, Erwin van Tujil, Jeroen van Haaren and Leo van den Berg

53 **Regional Development in Northern Europe**
Peripherality, marginality and border issues
Edited by Mike Danson and Peter De Souza

52 **Promoting Silicon Valleys in Latin America**
Luciano Ciravegna

51 **Industrial Policy Beyond the Crisis**
Regional, national and international perspectives
Edited by David Bailey, Helena Lenihan and Josep-Maria Arauzo-Carod

50 **Just Growth**
Inclusion and prosperity in America's metropolitan regions
Chris Benner and Manuel Pastor

49 **Cultural Political Economy of Small Cities**
Edited by Anne Lorentzen and Bas van Heur

48 **The Recession and Beyond**
Local and regional responses to the downturn
Edited by David Bailey and Caroline Chapain

47 **Beyond Territory**
Edited by Harald Bathelt, Maryann Feldman and Dieter F. Kogler

46 **Leadership and Place**
Edited by Chris Collinge, John Gibney and Chris Mabey

45 **Migration in the 21st Century**
Rights, outcomes, and policy
Kim Korinek and Thomas Maloney

44 **The Futures of the City Region**
Edited by Michael Neuman and Angela Hull

43 **The Impacts of Automotive Plant Closures**
A tale of two cities
Edited by Andrew Beer and Holli Evans

42 **Manufacturing in the New Urban Economy**
Willem van Winden, Leo van den Berg, Luis de Carvalho and Erwin van Tuijl

41 **Globalizing Regional Development in East Asia**
Production networks, clusters, and entrepreneurship
Edited by Henry Wai-chung Yeung

40 **China and Europe**
The implications of the rise of China as a global economic power for Europe
Edited by Klaus Kunzmann, Willy A Schmid and Martina Koll-Schretzenmayr

39 **Business Networks in Clusters and Industrial Districts**
The governance of the global value chain
Edited by Fiorenza Belussi and Alessia Sammarra

38 **Whither Regional Studies?**
Edited by Andy Pike

37 **Intelligent Cities and Globalisation of Innovation Networks**
Nicos Komninos

36 **Devolution, Regionalism and Regional Development**
The UK experience
Edited by Jonathan Bradbury

35 **Creative Regions**
Technology, culture and knowledge entrepreneurship
Edited by Philip Cooke and Dafna Schwartz

34 **European Cohesion Policy**
Willem Molle

33 **Geographies of the New Economy**
Critical reflections
Edited by Peter W. Daniels, Andrew Leyshon, Michael J. Bradshaw and Jonathan Beaverstock

32 **The Rise of the English Regions?**
Edited by Irene Hardill, Paul Benneworth, Mark Baker and Leslie Budd

31 **Regional Development in the Knowledge Economy**
Edited by Philip Cooke and Andrea Piccaluga

30 **Regional Competitiveness**
Edited by Ron Martin, Michael Kitson and Peter Tyler

29 **Clusters and Regional Development**
Critical reflections and explorations
Edited by Bjørn Asheim, Philip Cooke and Ron Martin

28 Regions, Spatial Strategies and Sustainable Development
David Counsell and Graham Haughton

27 Sustainable Cities
Graham Haughton and Colin Hunter

26 Geographies of Labour Market Inequality
Edited by Ron Martin and Philip S. Morrison

25 Regional Innovation Strategies
The challenge for less-favoured regions
Edited by Kevin Morgan and Claire Nauwelaers

24 Out of the Ashes?
The social impact of industrial contraction and regeneration on Britain's mining communities
Chas Critcher, Bella Dicks, David Parry and David Waddington

23 Restructuring Industry and Territory
The experience of Europe's regions
Edited by Anna Giunta, Arnoud Lagendijk and Andy Pike

22 Foreign Direct Investment and the Global Economy
Corporate and institutional dynamics of global-localisation
Edited by Jeremy Alden and Nicholas F. Phelps

21 Community Economic Development
Edited by Graham Haughton

20 Regional Development Agencies in Europe
Edited by Charlotte Damborg, Mike Danson and Henrik Halkier

19 Social Exclusion in European Cities
Processes, experiences and responses
Edited by Judith Allen, Goran Cars and Ali Madanipour

18 Metropolitan Planning in Britain
A comparative study
Edited by Peter Roberts, Kevin Thomas and Gwyndaf Williams

17 Unemployment and Social Exclusion
Landscapes of labour inequality and social exclusion
Edited by Sally Hardy, Paul Lawless and Ron Martin

16 Multinationals and European Integration
Trade, investment and regional development
Edited by Nicholas A. Phelps

15 The Coherence of EU Regional Policy
Contrasting perspectives on the structural funds
Edited by John Bachtler and Ivan Turok

14 New Institutional Spaces
TECs and the remaking of economic governance
Martin Jones, Foreword by Jamie Peck

13 Regional Policy in Europe
S. S. Artobolevskiy

12 **Innovation Networks and Learning Regions?**
James Simmie

11 **British Regionalism and Devolution**
The challenges of state reform and European integration
Edited by Jonathan Bradbury and John Mawson

10 **Regional Development Strategies**
A European perspective
Edited by Jeremy Alden and Philip Boland

9 **Union Retreat and the Regions**
The shrinking landscape of organised labour
Ron Martin, Peter Sunley and Jane Wills

8 **The Regional Dimension of Transformation in Central Europe**
Grzegorz Gorzelak

7 **The Determinants of Small Firm Growth**
An inter-regional study in the United Kingdom 1986–90
Richard Barkham, Graham Gudgin, Mark Hart and Eric Hanvey

6 **The Regional Imperative**
Regional planning and governance in Britain, Europe and the United States
Urlan A. Wannop

5 **An Enlarged Europe**
Regions in competition?
Edited by Louis Albrechts, Sally Hardy, Mark Hart and Anastasios Katos

4 **Spatial Policy in a Divided Nation**
Edited by Richard T. Harrison and Mark Hart

3 **Regional Development in the 1990s**
The British Isles in transition
Edited by Ron Martin and Peter Townroe

2 **Retreat from the Regions**
Corporate change and the closure of factories
Stephen Fothergill and Nigel Guy

1 **Beyond Green Belts**
Managing urban growth in the 21st century
Edited by John Herington

Rethinking International Skilled Migration

Edited by Micheline van Riemsdijk and Qingfang Wang

Routledge
Taylor & Francis Group
LONDON AND NEW YORK

First published 2017
by Routledge
2 Park Square, Milton Park, Abingdon, Oxon OX14 4RN

and by Routledge
711 Third Avenue, New York, NY 10017

Routledge is an imprint of the Taylor & Francis Group, an informa business

British Library Cataloguing in Publication Data
A catalogue record for this book is available from the British Library

Library of Congress Cataloging in Publication Data
Names: Riemsdijk, Françoise Micheline van, editor.
Title: Rethinking international skilled migration / edited by Micheline van Riemsdijk and Qingfang Wang.
Description: New York : Routledge, [2017] | Includes index.
Identifiers: LCCN 2016020601| ISBN 9781138918726 (hardback) | ISBN 9781315688312 (ebook)
Subjects: LCSH: Professional employees. | Students, Foreign. | Emigration and immigration.
Classification: LCC HD8038.A1 .R47 2017 | DDC 378.1/982691–dc23
LC record available at https://lccn.loc.gov/2016020601

ISBN: 978-1-138-91872-6 (hbk)
ISBN: 978-1-315-68831-2 (ebk)

Typeset in Times New Roman
by Cenveo Publisher Services

Contents

Figures

Tables

Contributors

Heike Alberts is a Professor of Geography at the University of Wisconsin Oshkosh. She came to the United States as an international student after completing her Master's degree at the Free University of Berlin in Germany and obtained her Ph.D. from the University of Minnesota. Her research focuses on highly skilled migrations; she is particularly interested in the migration intentions and decisions of international students and faculty.

Scott Basford received a Master's degree in Geography from the University of Tennessee in 2014. His research interests include international student migration, governmentality, and globalization. More specifically, his work qualitatively examines the role of both public and private institutions as brokers of the student migrant experience. He plans to pursue a doctorate in Geography in the near future.

Harald Bauder is a Professor in the Department of Geography and the Director of the Graduate Program for Immigration and Settlement Studies (ISS) at Ryerson University in Toronto, Canada. From 2011 and 2015 he served as the founding Academic Director of the Ryerson Centre for Immigration and Settlement (RCIS). In 2015 he received the Konrad Adenauer Research Award from the Royal Society of Canada and the Alexander von Humboldt Foundation in recognition for his outstanding scholarly lifetime contribution to the Social Sciences. His latest book is titled *Migration Borders Freedom*, published by Routledge. Among his previous books are *Immigration Dialectic: Imagining Community, Economy, and Nation* (Toronto: University of Toronto Press, 2011), and *Labor Movement: How Migration Regulates Labor Markets* (New York: Oxford University Press, 2006).

Jonathan V. Beaverstock is Professor of International Management in the School of Economics, Finance and Management at the University of Bristol, UK. A geographer by training, he has held Chairs in Economic Geography at the University of Nottingham and Loughborough University, UK. He is a world-leading expert on highly skilled international labor migration and work-related mobilities, and the City of London, and has published widely in

Business and Management, Geography and Migration, and Urban Studies. Jonathan is a Fellow of the Academy of Social Sciences and Royal Society of the Arts, Manufacture and Commerce.

Elizabeth Chacko is Professor of Geography and International Affairs at the George Washington University (GWU) in Washington, DC. She is also the Associate Dean for Undergraduate Studies in the Columbian College of Arts and Sciences at GWU. Elizabeth is currently engaged in research on immigration from Ethiopia and India to the United States and Singapore and on the return migration of Asian Indian professionals to India, and the effects of these flows on identities, inclusion, cities, and neighborhoods. She has worked on these and related research projects on migration and mobility in India, Singapore, Malaysia, Ethiopia, and the United States.

Ryan Dicce is a Ph.D. student at Texas A&M University with a research focus on the geographies of finance and the human capital elements of financial centers in the global economy. As a research assistant, he has worked on a US National Science Foundation project examining the emergence of Islamic financial centers in Bahrain and Malaysia. More recently, he has expanded this work to include the development and circulation of human capital necessary for the creation of Islamic finance in centers of traditional banking, such as New York. Prior to Texas A&M, Ryan was a Global Academic Fellow for New York University Abu Dhabi.

Michael C. Ewers's research examines the human capital dimensions of international economic development. More specifically, he studies how places attract and utilize global human capital and foreign knowledge through migration, trade, and investment as means to generate local development capacity. While all his research is situated in a global context, he specializes on regional economic development in the Middle East. Ewers's work on human capital formation and global talent mobility has been published in numerous international journals, such as *Geoforum, Progress in Human Geography,* and *The Geographical Journal*. His research has also been funded by several prestigious grants and fellowships, including the US National Science Foundation, Fulbright-Hays, and the Social Science Research Council.

Allan Findlay is Professor of Geography at the University of St Andrews. Between 1994 and 2011 he was Professor of Geography at the University of Dundee, and has also held visiting positions at the International Labour Office in Geneva, the Chinese University of Hong Kong, and the University of Umeå. He is interested in all aspects of human mobility and has worked especially on highly skilled migration, brain drain issues, student mobility, and on the relationship between environmental change and human mobility. He is strand leader of the New Mobilities theme of the UK's *ESRC's Centre for Population Change*. He also directs *ESRC's Census and Administrative Longitudinal Studies Hub*. He was founder (1995) and editor of the journal *Population Space and Place* from 2003 to 2016.

Ashley Gunter is Chair of the Department of Geography at the University of South Africa. He has published on issues of urban development, but having begun his academic career at a branch campus is interested in the neoliberal state of education in the post-apartheid South African system. He is a council member of the South African Geographical Society and on the editorial board of *InterEspaço: Revista de Geografia e Interdisciplinaridade*. The inception of this chapter was begun while he was a visiting research fellow at the Centre for African studies at the University of Edinburgh.

William S. Harvey is Director of the Public Policy Research Cluster, Director of Research and Senior Lecturer in Organization Studies at the University of Exeter Business School, and an Honorary Senior Lecturer at the University of Sydney. William's research focuses on the mobility, economic impact, and social networks of talented workers; reputation and leadership within professional service firms; practical challenges with fieldwork and interviewing business and political elites. William has published articles in a wide range of journals in business and management, sociology, geography, migration, and industrial relations.

Russell King is Professor of Geography at the University of Sussex and also Visiting Professor of Migration Studies at Malmö University. He has directed major research projects on international retirement migration, international student migration, and return migration. He was editor of the *Journal of Ethnic and Migration Studies* between 2000 and 2013. Among his recent books are *The atlas of human migration* (Earthscan 2010), *Remittances, gender and development* (I. B. Tauris 2011) and *Counter-diaspora: The Greek second generation returns "home"* (Harvard University Press 2014), all co-authored. In recent years he has published papers in many of the major journals in geography and migration studies, including *Transactions of the Institute of British Geographers*; *Geoforum*; *Population, Space and Place*; *Gender, Place and Culture*; *Global Networks*; *Diaspora*; *Mobilities*; *International Migration*; and *Ethnic and Racial Studies*.

Huiping Li is an Associate Professor at the School of Public Economics and Administration of Shanghai University of Finance and Economics. Her research includes urban/regional development, residential segregation, and local government. She has published in journals such as *Social Forces*; *Urban Studies*; *Population, Place and Space;* and *Habitat International*.

Jon Mulholland is an Associate Professor in Sociology, and Associate Head of Sociology and Criminology, at the University of the West of England, Bristol, following a position as Associate Professor in Sociology at Middlesex University, London. Jon has recently held grants with the Economic and Social Research Council and the British Academy, and researches in fields of "race," ethnicity, nation, and migration, in addition to gender and sexuality. With Professor Louise Ryan, Jon has published the findings of the ESRC-funded French Capital project in leading international journals, including

Sociology; Global Networks; Ethnic and Migration Studies; International Migration; and *Sociological Research Online*. Emerging from his British Academy-funded project on women's support for the nationalist Right in the UK, Jon (along with Erin Sanders-McDonagh and Nicola Montagna) is the editor of a forthcoming book, *Gendering nationalism: Intersections of nation, gender and sexuality in the 21st century* (Palgrave Press).

Jörg Plöger holds a Ph.D. in Geography and is a Senior Researcher at the ILS (Institute for Regional and Urban Development) in Dortmund, Germany. His current research focuses on how migrants relate to places. In this contribution he draws from qualitative empirical work about high-skilled migrant professionals in Manchester and Dortmund. In his work he seeks to understand how this group negotiates a balance between mobility and fixity in their practices and how these contribute to the transformation of urban space. He has published his work in a range of journals and edited volumes.

Parvati Raghuram is Professor in Geography and Migration at the Open University. She has published widely on gender, migration and development and on postcolonial theory. Her most recent ESRC funded project is titled Gender, skilled migration and the IT sector: a comparative study of India and the UK. She has co-authored *Gender, migration and social reproduction* (Palgrave), *The practice of cultural studies* (Sage), *Gender and international migration in Europe* (Routledge) and co-edited *South Asian women in the diaspora* (Berg) and *Tracing Indian diaspora: Contexts, memories, representations* (Sage). Parvati has written for policy audiences having co-authored research papers for a number of think-tanks such as IPPR, UNRISD, the Hamburg Institute of International Economics, Heinrich Böll Stiftung, IPPR, and UNRISD and co-edited a special issue of the journal *Diversities* for UNESCO. She co-edits the journal *South Asian Diaspora* with the Centre for Study of Diaspora, Hyderabad and the Palgrave Pivot series *Mobility and politics* with Martin Geiger and William Walters both at Ottawa.

Louise Ryan, Ph.D., formerly of Middlesex University, is now a Professorial Fellow at the University of Sheffield. She has published widely on Intra-EU migration including several highly cited papers in *Sociology*; *Sociological Review*; and *Journal of Ethnic and Migration Studies*. She also has an interest in research methods, and has taught and published on research design and analysis. Her two most recent books reflect these key interests: Louise Ryan, Umut Erel, and Alessio D'Angelo (2015) *Migrant capital: Networks, identities and strategies*. Palgrave; Linda McKie and Louise Ryan (2016) *An end to the crisis of empirical sociology? Trends and challenges in social research*. Routledge.

Alexandra Stam is a senior researcher at the Swiss Centre of Expertise in the Social Sciences (FORS) since 2009. She is currently leading the 2016–2017 Swiss Federal Survey of Adolescents (ch-x), which will investigate geographical mobility among young people. Trained as a geographer, her research interests are on new forms of migration, particularly student mobility and marriage migration.

Li Tang is a Professor of Public Policy at the School of International Relations and Public Affairs of Fudan University, China. Her research interests include science, technology, and innovation policy, policy and program evaluation, and knowledge management. She has (co)authored over forty articles and consulting reports including publications in leading international journals such as *Journal of the Association for Information Science and Technology; Research Policy;* and *Journal of Technology Transfer*.

Christof Van Mol is senior researcher at the Netherlands Interdisciplinary Demographic Institute (NIDI, the Hague). He has an MA in history from the University of Antwerp, Belgium; an international MA in migration studies from the University of Valencia, Spain, and Lille Catholic University, France; and a Ph.D. in Sociology from the University of Antwerp. He is interested in the broad field of migration studies with a particular focus on different forms and patterns of intra-European mobility and migration. He extensively published on the topic in leading journals such as *European Union Politics, Global Networks*, and *Population, Space and Place*.

Micheline van Riemsdijk is J. Harrison and Robbie C. Livingston Associate Professor of Population Geography at the University of Tennessee. Her research is situated in migration studies, labor geographies, and international migration governance. Micheline's research focuses on skilled migration policymaking, valuation of skills, the recognition and transfer of professional qualifications, and the sociocultural incorporation of skilled migrants. She has conducted fieldwork research in Norway, Poland, Belgium, and India, and published in journals in geography, migration studies, and legal studies.

Margaret Walton-Roberts is a professor at Wilfrid Laurier University and a human geographer with research interests in gender and migration, transnational networks, and immigrant settlement. Her current research focuses on gender and the international migration of health care professionals in the context of India. She has been awarded several external grants for her research, and has co-edited three books on migration, diaspora and citizenship issues, published over 18 book chapters, and more than 20 journal articles.

Qingfang Wang is an Associate Professor of Geography and Public Policy at the University of California Riverside. She is interested in how place, as both work site and residential location, interacts with race, ethnicity, immigration status, and gender in shaping individual labor market experiences and other factors of socioeconomic well-being. Using both quantitative and qualitative research methods, she is currently conducting projects on immigrant, ethnic minority, and female entrepreneurship and development, with a particular interest in the sector of higher education.

Wan Yu is Assistant Professor in the Department of Geography at Binghamton University. Her research interests include ethnic geography, urban geography, migration, and Asian Americans.

Acknowledgments

This book project grew out of a three-part paper session that explored conceptual challenges in international skilled migration research, held at the annual meeting of the Association of American Geographers in Tampa, Florida, in April 2014. We thank all presenters and the discussants Kavita Pandit, Emily Skop, and Harald Bauder. We are grateful to the latter for leading the roundtable discussion at the Tampa meeting and summarizing the main themes for this book (Chapter 16). We thank all session participants and the audience for their comments and suggestions, and all book authors for their contributions. We appreciate the assistance of the editors of Routledge's Regions and Cities series Emily Kindleysides and Robert Langham, and we especially thank Elanor Best for guiding us through this project.

Micheline would like to thank Rachel Silvey, Marte Hult, and Louis Becker for their teachings in the art of editing, Henri Grissino-Mayer and Derek Alderman for their helpful advice on book-related issues, and Kevin Durand for unwavering support and encouragement. Qingfang Wang would like to thank Micheline for her patience and tireless efforts, the inspiring, long phone calls over the year, and the blocked AAG sessions for the last push on this book project. As her first edited book volume, and an educational and productive process, Qingfang thanks all the participants and colleagues who have made it happen. She would also like to thank Kavita and Wei for their guidance, Li and Huiping for their support to start the first project on this topic, and her husband and children to tolerate her numerous absences from family time and occasional "tantrums."

Micheline van Riemsdijk and Qingfang Wang
April 2016

1 Introduction: Rethinking International Skilled Migration

A Place-based and Spatial Perspective

Micheline van Riemsdijk and Qingfang Wang

In 2012, the company Blueseed announced a plan that would enable foreign-born entrepreneurs to work in the United States without a work visa. The entrepreneurs would live and work on a converted cruise ship, docked in international waters twelve nautical miles off the California coast. The residents would be transported to land in small ferries with easy access to Silicon Valley. The entrepreneurs could travel up to 180 days a year on a temporary business or tourist visa (B1/B2), but could not earn money on the US mainland. This solution was Blueseed's answer to the shortage of H-1B temporary work visas for skilled migrants in the United States. In the year 2012, the cap of 85,000 H-1B visas was reached within ten weeks, compared to thirty-three weeks in 2011. Over 1,500 entrepreneurs have expressed interest, and Blueseed is currently trying to raise US$31 million to launch the project (Blueseed; Gustin 2012). While critics have derided the Blueseed plan as a publicity stunt, it raises interesting questions about the politics and practicalities of international skilled migration.

The Blueseed plan illustrates key roles of place and spatial relations in international skilled migration. The cruise ship's location in international waters is beyond the jurisdiction of US immigration law, enabling the foreign-born entrepreneurs to work on American projects offshore. The residents abide by the regulations of US law as long as they do not perform paid work onshore and hold a valid business or tourist visa (which are easier to obtain than H-1B permits). Interestingly, the "seastead," or floating city, would have authority to create its own labor, migration, and taxation laws. At the same time, the close proximity to Silicon Valley would enable the entrepreneurs to meet face-to-face with venture capitalists and build a network with US-based workers. Geographical proximity to and the place attractiveness of Silicon Valley are key factors in the appeal of the Blueseed project, because the physical co-presence (Ryan and Mulholland 2014) of information technology specialists can facilitate knowledge transfer and innovation.

Discussions about the Blueseed project seemingly centered on the shortcomings of the H-1B visa program. However, they reflect larger concerns about the uneven spatial relations between high-, middle-, and low-income countries. These concerns have sparked larger debates about the ethics of international talent recruitment, the objectives of skilled migration policies, and the effects on migrants themselves, the companies, and migrant sending and receiving places. The flexibility in residence and employment of the Blueseed entrepreneurs also reflects the increasingly fluid and transient nature of international migration, prompting King (2002) to argue that it is more accurate to label today's international flows as mobilities rather than migration. Although merely a thought experiment at this point, the Blueseed project raises key questions about the roles of space and place in international skilled migration. In particular, it problematizes traditional conceptualizations of sending and receiving countries, understandings of (national) belonging and inclusion, and the objectives and outcomes of skilled migration laws.

Aim and Scope

To more fully understand the entire process of international skilled migration, this book investigates international student migration, the experiences of skilled migrants in cities and regions, and the transnational experiences of returned migrants. It aims to rethink international skilled migration theories and perspectives from a place-based and spatial perspective. Traditional migration theories, which have predominantly focused on low-skilled migrants and refugees, do not fully explain international skilled migration processes and outcomes. While scholars have made important contributions to understandings of skilled migration, a coherent theoretical framework is missing to study the spatial dimension and place-embeddedness of this process. This book contributes to theory development in international skilled migration through a wide variety of empirical cases, examining how policymaking practices, migrant experiences, international recruitment, and uneven spatial relationships between sending and receiving countries shape international skilled migration at various geographical scales.

Within Geography, economic geographers have predominantly studied the global knowledge economy from company, regional, or (inter)national economic perspectives. However, these studies have not paid sufficient attention to the social actors of the global knowledge economy—namely, the migrants who make migration and settlement decisions based on individual, household, and institutional factors in sending and receiving states. Significant gaps of knowledge still exist with regard to the experiences of skilled migrants and their place-based behaviors: How have international skilled migratory flows been formed, sustained, and transformed over multiple spaces and scales? How have these processes affected cities and regions? And how have multiple stakeholders responded to these processes? These are the questions to be addressed in this book.

While addressing these questions through studies of various professions across different states and regions, we particularly emphasize how actors and institutions in international skilled migration are embedded in places, transforming and being transformed through spatial interactions. In the following sections we discuss such interactions at various stages of migration and at multiple scales, as expressed through daily lives in the city and region.

The Roles of Place and Space in International Skilled Migration

Delineating the factors and forces from the decision-making stage to settlement and possible onward or return migration is fundamental to understanding the relationship between place, space, and international migration. We address four aspects of these stages in the following sections. First, we discuss the individual characteristics and factors that inform the decision-making for migration and the post-migration experiences of skilled migrants. Second, we address the interactions between individuals and place, examining how the socioeconomic, cultural, and political environment in cities and regions shape the experiences of skilled migrants, and how migrants shape places through their interaction (Glick Schiller and Çağlar 2009, 2011). Third, we examine the national and international policy regimes that have fundamental impacts on international skilled migration flows. Fourth, we shortly discuss the spatial and place-based aspects of the "brain drain," "brain gain," and "brain circulation" debate in the skilled migration literature.

Personal Experiences of Skilled Migrants

While this book foregrounds the roles of place and space in international skilled migration, it is still important to pay attention to the factors at the individual and household level that shape the migration experience. These factors inform the decision to migrate, coping strategies after arrival, experiences in the workplace, and the decision to stay, return, or move to another destination. In addition, migrants' personal characteristics influence the hiring decisions of employers and the valuation of skills, which we discuss in more detail below.

The traditional neoclassical economic perspectives explicitly view international migration as a result from individual cost-benefit analyses to maximize expected income through movement across country borders. Since the rate of return of human capital differs between the high- and low-skilled labor force, the high-skilled respond to wage differences differently from the low-skilled, and thus, have different flow patterns (Lewis 1954; Borjas 1990). In making the decision whether to migrate or not, and when and where to migrate, personal characteristics, human capital, social conditions, personal preferences, a migrant's stage in the life course, and availability of technologies have all played significant roles (Massey et al. 1993).

Migrants in relationships additionally take household considerations into account, such as professional opportunities for a spouse, the quality of local schools, healthcare, and the general well-being of the family (Silvanto and Ryan 2014). Some parents decide to return to the home country because they want their children to grow up in the country of origin, or when they have to care for aging parents (Favell, Feldblum, and Smith 2006). In fact, the "new economics of migration" perspective has long argued that migration is a collective decision made in a family, household, or "other culturally defined units of production and consumption" to minimize risk to income or to maximize expected benefits (Massey et al. 1993, 439; see also Stark and Bloom 1985).

Employers, recruitment agents, and other actors also shape the personal experiences of skilled migrants through their valuation of migrants' skills and expertise. These actors often have stereotypical assumptions about the educational qualifications from a migrant's country of origin, which can determine the starting salary, assignment of tasks, and opportunities for promotion (van Riemsdijk 2013; for low-skilled migrants, see Pratt 2004; Findlay et al. 2013), and result in the underemployment of skilled migrants (Bauder 2003). The valuation of skill is time- and place-specific (Kuvik 2012), and depends on the actor, location, and sociocultural and political context within which a migrant's skills and competencies are evaluated (van Riemsdijk 2013). The negative outcomes of the devaluation of skills are likely to diminish over time as migrants accumulate place-specific social and cultural capital.

A related aspect of the uneven geography of international skilled migration is a lack of language proficiency and knowledge of cultural codes in the place of destination. For example, Batalova, Fix, and Creticos (2008) find that high-skilled immigrants who have limited English proficiency are twice more likely to work in low-skilled jobs than those who speak English fluently. Chiswick and Taengnoi (2007) also argue that highly educated immigrants who do not speak English fluently tend to concentrate in social service occupations that often require little English proficiency. Accordingly, Wang and Lysenko (2014) find that the foreign-born labor force, particularly the highly educated, are more likely to be underemployed than US-born workers when other conditions are held constant. Other factors, such as job-searching strategies, immigrants' unfamiliarity with host country labor regulations, nontransferable education credentials, and other economic and cultural differences between source and destination countries have all contributed to the imperfect transferability of human capital across borders (Boyd and Thomas 2001; Piracha and Vadean 2012).

These obstacles show that skilled migrants do not seamlessly integrate into the host society. This warrants more attention in both research and practice. First, highly skilled migrants are not homogeneously "privileged." Important differences exist among skilled migrants in terms of country of origin, marital status, age, race/ethnicity, and other personal characteristics that intersect in various ways. Some of these differences have been highlighted in critiques of the study of "elite"—predominantly male—migrants (Kofman 2000; Raghuram 2000; Conradson and Latham 2005) and the identity politics of skilled migrants (Nagel 2005; Scott 2006). More research is needed to understand how these personal characteristics shape the experiences of skilled migrants and their migration outcomes. Second, in practice, immigrant integration initiatives have been focused on low-skilled migrants and refugees. Although some cities have developed programs to recruit and welcome skilled migrants, there remains a lack of attention to their long-term integration. This oversight may reflect the assumption that these "privileged" migrants will easily adapt to their new environment. The personal and institutional integration difficulties highlighted above, however, indicate a need for more study to better understand this process.

Interactions between Place and Individuals at the Local Scale

The demand and supply in the local labor markets directly influence the opportunity structure and quality of jobs for highly skilled migrants. For example, previous studies have found that unemployment rate, economic structure, income level, and the resource base are all relevant for the labor market experiences of highly skilled migrants (Stiles and Galbraith 2004; Storper and Scott 2009). In addition to economic factors, place-based amenities, diversity, and tolerance have an especially potent effect on the migration patterns of individuals endowed with high levels of human capital (Florida 2005; Glaeser and Gottlieb 2006).

Public attitudes and local migration policies can also influence the experiences of skilled migrants. For example, the classic visibility-discrimination hypothesis argues that increases in the number of visible minorities will heighten the perceived economic and political threat posed to the majority. This threat may provoke discrimination by the latter, contributing to a greater earnings gap between the two groups (Cohen 1998; Huffman and Cohen 2004; Wang 2010). When job markets tighten, anti-immigration sentiment may increase. For instance, economic recessions generally spark nativist concerns about the local economy and the welfare state, which can negatively affect skilled migrants as well (Hainmueller and Hiscox 2010).

Cities are shaped by the international migration of the highly skilled. Talents (those endowed with high level of human capital) can significantly contribute to knowledge creation, innovation, and regional economic development (Florida 2005; Glaeser and Gottlieb 2006; Storper and Scott 2009). Further, skilled immigrants can enhance the prestige of a city through their employment contributions and transnational connections with institutions, colleagues, and friends. And, thus, international migration of the highly skilled can help improve the position of a city in international and global hierarchies through the linking of migration pathways, global restructuring processes, and place (Glick Schiller and Çağlar 2009, 2011). Indeed, the majority of scholarship in international skilled migration has studied global cities, immigrant gateways, and regions of innovation as they have drawn the majority of highly skilled migrants. Migrants in these places have established businesses (Saxenian 2002), recruited colleagues and friends through their transnational professional networks (Brettell 2005), and have contributed to knowledge exchange and innovative practices in the cities and regions in which they live and work (Williams and Baláž 2008).

It is not surprising that many cities and regions profile themselves as attractive destinations for skilled migrants, showcasing their amenities and professional opportunities. They also try to attract domestic and international skilled migrants through city branding and welcome initiatives. For example, the German cities Bonn, Cologne and Aachen created a "welcome culture" to attract skilled migrants with English-language websites, television commercials, and attractive housing and cultural amenities (Föbker, Temme, and Wiegandt 2014). These policy initiatives and practices reflect the increasing importance of international skilled migration for urban and regional economic development.

Reflecting upon the existing literature, we identify two gaps in current knowledge on interactions between places and individual migrants that warrant further research: first, economic geographers have highlighted the key roles of regions in knowledge creation, innovation, and knowledge transfer, including the attraction of human capital and businesses. These studies, however, conceptualize human capital as an input factor in business rather than studying the individuals that embody this knowledge. Various chapters in this book aim to add a "human face" to international skilled migration (Smith and Favell 2006) through empirical case studies of the lived experiences of skilled migrants in various cities and regions. Second, since highly skilled immigrants tend to concentrate in global cities and immigration gateway cities, our knowledge of them is mainly based on these places. As immigrants become more spatially dispersed, we still know little about the experiences of skilled migrants in lesser known destinations. Therefore, we argue that it is important to study less iconic destinations to broaden our understanding of the meanings of place and space in international skilled migration.

National and International Skilled Migration Policy Regimes

National policy regimes govern the spatial movement of foreign-born workers and define the legal context for social and economic relations. "Traditional" countries of immigration (the United Kingdom, the United States, Canada, and Australia) developed policies to attract skilled migrants in the early 1990s, followed by other high-income countries. These measures include a fast-track system for residential permits and assessment of professional qualifications, and tax breaks for highly skilled migrants. Most high-income countries have now liberalized their skilled migration policies in an attempt to attract more skilled workers and international students. For example, Australia relaxed its rules on student visas and Canada now offers three-year work visas to foreign students who graduated in the country with a master's degree (*The Economist* 2012). These policy measures aim to attract more skilled migrants, but institutional and personal obstacles remain, as we have discussed above.

Several middle-income states have developed talent programs to entice their citizens to return, often offering attractive employment benefits and career opportunities. For example, China's Thousand Talent Program recruits overseas-educated Chinese skilled migrants (Wang, Tang, and Li 2014), and the Colombian government offers financial incentives and a reintegration program under the *Colombia Nos Une* program (OECD 2012). High-income states have implemented similar programs like the European Commission's Marie Curie reintegration scheme, devised to lure European Union citizens back to universities in its member states. These initiatives underline the high value placed on return skilled migrants who have acquired professional experience abroad.

While most states have liberalized their skilled migration policies, some states are restricting access to their skilled labor markets. For example, the UK government tightened its policies for foreign students in response to the global financial crisis and rising domestic unemployment. Students used to have the right to remain in the United Kingdom for two years after their graduation to gain work experience. In 2012, it was decided that they have to find a sponsor within a few months and earn at least £20,000 per year (*Economist* 2012). A minimum income requirement has now been extended to all non-EU skilled migrants in the United Kingdom. Since April 2016, the UK government has enforced a £35,000 minimum salary for non-EU citizens, excluding skilled migrants in Ph.D.-level occupations and recognized shortage occupations such as nursing. The minimum salary requirement was developed to encourage employers to train domestic workers instead of importing migrant labor (*The Guardian* 2016). The restrictions on visas for non-EU students and skilled workers illustrate the difficulty of balancing the need for human capital and calls for tougher migration regulations and border control, especially in a time of increasing public concerns about rising immigration.

Impacts of High-skilled International Migration and Concerns

The recruitment of skilled migrants from lower income to higher income countries raises concerns about "brain drain," or the loss of highly educated workers from countries with a low level of human capital. At the same time, skilled migrants can transfer their knowledge and professional expertise to people in their home countries through "brain circulation." When these migrants return to their country of origin to take up high-level positions, the initial loss of human capital can be turned into "brain gain" (Chacko 2007). While the extent of gain or loss of human capital continues to be debated by migration scholars, it is important to take the ethical aspects of international skilled migration into consideration (Saxenian 2005; Tejada et al. 2014; Findlay and Cranston 2015).

The brain drain debate has focused on the ethical recruitment of skilled migrant workers, particularly in the healthcare sector. Hospitals increasingly recruit workers from abroad to fill labor shortages, particularly from lower income states. This practice has become an ethical concern, especially if workers are recruited from states that need these workers, and the home government has funded their education (also see Raghuram 2009). In an effort to curb the negative impact of brain drain, the World Health Organization has developed a Global Code of Practice on the International Recruitment of Health Personnel. According to this code, "Member States should discourage active recruitment of health personnel from developing countries facing critical shortages of health workers" (World Health Organization 2010). Even if healthcare employers in high-income states would not engage in active recruitment, this migration will continue as these workers are attracted by higher pay, better working conditions, and more professional development opportunities (Buchan et al. 2014).

The skilled migration and development debate has become more complex as states in the Global South are turning into knowledge-based economies, particularly some Gulf countries, Malaysia, and South Africa. New destinations for skilled migrants are also emerging in the BRIC countries, and some countries in Africa and Latin America (International Organization of Migration 2008). The recent financial crisis in the Global North coupled with an increased demand for skilled workers in the Global South contributed to an increase in North–South migration (ibid.). These changes in directions of skilled migration flows warrant more attention to these migrants' impacts in the Global South, transnational connections between skilled migrants in the Global North and the Global South, and South–South migration flows.

It is evident from the discussions above that skilled migration policy has largely been developed within a national framework, paying most attention to the national political and economic interests of host societies. However, these studies do not provide insights into the impact of individuals on workplaces and cities, and the social, cultural and political outcomes in origin and destination countries. In addition, how do skilled migrants influence and transform the demographics, culture, and politics in the receiving society? Answering these questions require a more nuanced approach to the connections between individual migrants and the places where they live and work (see Meier 2015), and the various scales at which these migration processes occur. To a certain extent, various chapters in this book pay attention to the local aspects of international skilled migration, and relations between the local, regional, national, and international scale in the governance of international skilled migration (see also Menz 2009). Still, more efforts are needed to bring a multiscalar, place-based, and spatial perspective to international skilled migration research.

An Agenda for International Skilled Migration Research

To sum up our reflections on the existing studies, we outline a four-point research agenda to address the identified research gaps in the international skilled migration literature. We hope that this agenda will contribute to a more coherent theoretical framework to study international skilled migration, enhancing knowledge about the drivers and outcomes of international skilled migration flows and the personal experiences of skilled migrants.

First, we call for more research on the ways in which the personal characteristics of skilled migrants shape the migration experience. For example, gender, nationality, race, age, and stage in the lifecycle can intersect in various ways depending on geographic location. The examples discussed above and in subsequent book chapters indicate that skilled migrants are differentially positioned in local and regional labor markets according to their personal characteristics and their interactions with places at various geographic scales. As most immigrant integration initiatives at the city and local scale have targeted low-skilled and/or undocumented immigrants, it is important to abandon the explicit or inexplicit assumption of highly skilled immigrants as a "no-problem" and "privileged" homogeneous group.

Second, we propose a multiscalar and interactive perspective on the impacts of highly skilled migration. As discussed earlier, existing literature of impacts of highly skilled migration is mainly focused on the national scale. Even though the recruitment of skilled migrants operates at the regional and local scale, there is a lack of systematic studies of impacts from highly skilled migration. At the local and neighborhood level, most research is about the experiences of immigrants, but not necessarily about the specific impacts that they are making. How do these migrants generate economic growth? What are the impacts across different geographic scales? How can these impacts be identified and measured? And what are the mechanisms through which international highly skilled migrants and migration influence the region, city, and local communities? To answer these questions, we believe that a broader, multiscaled, and multidimensional perspective will be necessary. Building on Glick Schiller and Çağlar (2009, 2011), we have previously argued for a two-way interactive process between migrants and their (sending and receiving) places. These impacts should be examined as part of this interactive process to gain insights into the collaborations and tensions among stakeholders in international skilled migration, and the forces that drive international skilled migration, the post-migration experience, and the outcomes of these migration flows.

Third, we recommend more research on skilled migration to second- and third-tier cities. Taking the United States as an example, immigration is no longer limited to a few states and cities with long-established migration histories. As new immigrants are settling in areas that have traditionally welcomed few immigrants, new challenges of incorporation and integration emerge in smaller cities unaccustomed to substantial minority and immigrant populations (National Academies of Sciences, Engineering, and Medicine 2015). As most studies have examined global and gateway cities, we know little about these less iconic places. It is necessary for both research and practice purposes to examine how skilled migrants make impacts on these new destinations and contribute to the repositioning of cities in the regional, national, and even global hierarchy (Glick Schiller and Çağlar 2011).

Fourth, the skilled migration literature has been dominated by the mobility of migrant *bodies*, paying less attention to migrant *minds*. The economic geography literature has made important contributions to our understanding of knowledge transfer between companies (Williams and Baláž 2008; Trippl 2013), but has focused little on the knowledge that individual migrants bring to workplaces, companies, and cities. We call for more research on the mobility of knowledge as part of highly skilled international migration, studying how knowledge is transferred through transnational and local networks. We expect that both the bodies and knowledge of international migrants have been and will continue to transform places and spaces; and thus, it will be fruitful to examine the impacts on place as knowledge is created and exchanged through international migration.

Themes in this Book

Bringing together perspectives from economic, social, and population geography, this book investigates the experiences of international knowledge migrants and rethinks established skilled migration theories through empirical case studies of various regions. Covering a variety of industries and occupational sectors in the new knowledge economy, the multiscaled processes of international skilled migration are also examined from different stages of migration (e.g. from decision-making to moving, integration, and return—or remigration). Beyond the traditional focus on professional migrants, chapters in this book also provide insights into the experiences of international students, issues related to transnational activities and return migration, and policy implications for both immigrant source and destination countries.

In particular, the book's contributors take a spatial approach to understand the process of international skilled migration, foregrounding the role of place and space in international skilled migration. Through the lens of the spatial relationships between migrants and their surrounding places, such as their communities, cities, regions, and nations, these studies examine international skilled migration as multiscalar, transient, and place-based processes that interact with individual migrants (and their families), institutions, employers, and other actors in global knowledge production. Specifically, this book addresses these key dimensions in three thematic parts: "International Student Migration," "Transforming Cities, Transforming Lives," and "Transnational and Return Migration."

Part I: International Student Migration. The first theme examines the factors that shape international student mobility, their status after migration, the job search and career prospects, and their experiences transitioning from student to skilled worker. The case studies in this part examine the individual experiences of students, higher education providers, formal and informal institutions, historical legacies of institutions of higher education, and current migration policies. In these studies, the migration process is deeply entrenched in global geopolitical power relationships, the sociospatial interaction between students and their sending and receiving states, and their decision to stay or return based on their personal experiences, institutional environments, local labor markets, and local communities.

Findlay, King, and Stam (Chapter 2) argue that providers of higher education have considerable influence on international student mobility through their marketing and recruitment activities. Based on interviews with university staff in the United States, Australia, Germany, France, Ireland, and the Czech Republic, the chapter demonstrates the importance of the "market-place" in shaping student mobility.

In Chapter 3, Heike Alberts examines migration decision-making and return intentions of international students in the state of Wisconsin. She presents the professional, personal, and contextual factors (in states, cities, and universities within the United States) that students consider in their decision to migrate to the United States, and whether to remain in the United States, return home, or migrate to a third country after obtaining their university degrees in the United

States. She argues for a holistic perspective on international student migration that pays attention to migrant characteristics and contexts of reception.

In Chapter 4, Christof Van Mol examines the ways in which the study abroad experience of European exchange (Erasmus) students can shape their future migration aspirations. He argues that Erasmus students increase their human and social capital when they live abroad, developing place-based local and transnational social networks that are maintained after completion of the study abroad program. These transnational friendship networks can provide information about future destinations, and lower the cost of repeat migration.

In Chapter 5, Scott Basford examines the mental health challenges faced by students from low-income countries who receive scholarships to pursue a graduate degree in Norway. He finds that the four primary categorical sources of stress for these students are acculturation, finances, distance from home and family, and bureaucratic constraints. While the mental health status of international students is seldom studied, findings from this study call attention to the overall health situation of international students.

Using the case of Chinese students in the United States, Wan Yu (Chapter 6) focuses on a unique stage of international student migration: transitioning from student (right around graduation) to skilled labor migrant (once the student finds a job and stays in the host country). The chapter finds that the students' final decisions have been subtly, but strongly shaped by changes in US immigration policy (such as the annual H-1B visa cap and qualifications), the US social and economic context (evident in the recent economic downturn), and their home country situation (economic development and policy implementations).

Moving away from immigrant receiving countries, Ashley Gunter and Parvati Raghuram (Chapter 7) examine the evolving landscapes of higher education in South Africa, a regional hub for international student migration in the Global South. This chapter examines how national legacies, particularly the history of apartheid and attempts to address politics of race, shape international student migration and the broader landscape of higher education in South Africa.

Part II: Transforming Cities, Transforming Lives. Skilled migrants influence the cities in which they live and work, and these cities simultaneously shape the lives of these migrants. The second part thus examines the interaction between international skilled migrants and the places where they live and work. The empirical cases study the roles of cities in immigrant incorporation, as well as conceptualize migrants as actors who actively shape urban spaces and places through their day-to-day practices. At the same time, some states and governments, in partnership with employers and local organizations, have purposely utilized skilled migration as a tool for regional development.

Jon Mulholland and Louise Ryan in Chapter 8 explore the nature and dynamics of French highly skilled migrants' "sense of place" in London. The chapter examines the ways in which moral geographies of place are constructed through playscapes (pubs, parks), the city's "buzz," and participation in cultural events. They conclude that skilled migrants actively produce a sense of belonging through these place-making activities in the city.

In Chapter 9, Jörg Plöger analyzes the role of housing in the formation of local ties of international mobile professionals in Dortmund, a large post-industrial German city. The findings suggest that housing is a critical part of the incorporation process; and thus, access to adequate housing matters for an urban economic development agenda aimed at attracting migrant professionals.

In Chapter 10, Micheline van Riemsdijk investigates how Stavanger and Kongsberg, two Norwegian cities known for their petroleum-related industries, try to attract highly skilled migrants through city-branding strategies. She argues that these cities' relocation guides project a homogenized image of "Norwegianness," and they are used as integration tools to help create the "good migrant" who adopts Norwegian ways of life.

Using the case of Dubai (Chapter 11), Michael Ewers and Ryan Dicce examine how foreign and local companies in this city attract and incorporate expatriate knowledge workers through (mostly local) recruitment strategies. It argues that company employment practices intersect with state regulatory frameworks and local development contexts in shaping skilled migration flows.

Part III: Transnational Lives and Return Migration. The third part investigates the transnational and return migration experiences of international skilled migrants. A growing number of developing countries have invested heavily in international talent recruitment, including programs to attract citizens who have gained professional experience abroad. Taking these emerging powers and ever-changing global geopolitical hierarchies into account, studies in this part provide a deeper understanding of the spatial relationships between sending and receiving countries and the lived experiences of return migrants.

In Chapter 12, Elizabeth Chacko analyzes the return migration of first-generation skilled Indian migrants who worked in the United States, the United Kingdom, Australia, Malaysia, and Singapore. In particular, she studies how contextual, place-based factors in sending states and India shape the return experiences of these skilled migrants. She finds that the reason to return significantly shapes the return experience of Indian workers, especially whether the return migration was voluntary.

Margaret Walton-Roberts (Chapter 13) examines the relationships between place (in this case Punjab) and Canadian immigration policy in order to understand the effect of skilled immigration policy on sending regions. Using a longer historical frame of analysis she reminds us that skilled migration policy is part of a longer continuum of labor mobility policies that are constructed to service the receiving states' needs. Immigration policy change is matched by the responsiveness of the communities and institutions invested in this long term connection between places.

In Chapter 14, Wang, Tang, and Li examine the experiences of returnees from overseas in a national highly ranked Chinese university. They find that in addition to personal characteristics and preferences, professional practices in academia, universities' activities to purse "world-class university" status, China's national and regional development agenda, and the uneven global system of higher education system have all forged the social relationships between individual migrants and their interacted places.

In Chapter 15, William Harvey and Jonathan Beaverstock analyze the work and social networks of British migrants working in Singapore, Vancouver, and Boston. This chapter shows that their experiences of working and networking with other migrants varied markedly, despite the fact that they had similar education, professional, and social backgrounds. The findings suggest that governments and organizations can play a more effective role to attract, retain, and engage with highly skilled migrants.

Chapter 16, written by Harald Bauder, discusses insights from a roundtable discussion after three paper sessions on international skilled migration, held at the annual meeting of the Association of American Geographers in Tampa, Florida, in April 2014. The chapter concludes with the suggestions for reconceptualizing and retheorizing international skilled migration.

References

Batalova, J., M. Fix, and P. A. Creticos. 2008. *Uneven progress: The employment pathways of skilled immigrants in the United States*. Washington, DC: Migration Policy Institute.

Bauder, H. 2003. "Brain abuse," or the devaluation of immigrant labour in Canada. *Antipode* 35 (4): 699–717.

Blueseed. http://blueseed.com (last accessed March 25, 2015).

Borjas, G. 1990. *Friends or strangers: The impact of immigrants on the U.S. economy*. York: Basic Books.

Boyd, M., and D. Thomas. 2001. Match or mismatch? The employment of immigrant engineers in Canada's labor force. *Population, Research and Policy Review* 20: 107–133.

Brettell, C. B. 2005. The spatial, social, and political incorporation of Asian Indian immigrants in Dallas, Texas. *Urban Anthropology and Studies of Cultural Systems and World Economic Development* 34 (2/3): 247–280.

Buchan, J., M. Wismar, I. A. Glinos, and J. Bremner. 2014. Health professional mobility in a changing Europe: New dynamics, mobile individuals and diverse responses. Copenhagen: World Health Organization.

Chacko, E. 2007. From brain drain to brain gain: Reverse migration to Bangalore and Hyderabad, India's globalizing high tech cities. *GeoJournal* 68: 131–140.

Chiswick, B. R., and S. Taengnoi. 2007. Occupational choice of high skilled immigrants in the United States. *International Migration* 45 (5): 3–34.

Cohen, P. N. 1998. Black concentration effects on black–white and gender inequality: Multilevel analysis for US metropolitan areas. *Social Forces* 77 (1): 207–229.

Conradson, D., and A. Latham 2005. Transnational urbanism: Attending to everyday practices and mobilities. *Journal of Ethnic and Migration Studies* 31 (2): 227–233.

Economist, The 2012. Immigration and business: A harder road. *The Economist* October 20.

Favell, A., M. Feldblum, and M. P. Smith 2006. The human face of global mobility: A research agenda. In *The human face of global mobility*, eds. M. P. Smith and A. Favell, 1–25. New Brunswick, NJ: Transaction Publishers.

Findlay, A. M., and S. Cranston 2015. What's in a research agenda? An evaluation of research developments in the arena of skilled international migration. *International Development Planning Review* 37 (1): 17–31.

Findlay, A., D. McCollum, S. Shubin, E. Apsite, and Z. Krisjane. 2013. The role of recruitment agencies in imagining and producing the 'good' migrant. *Social and Cultural Geography* 14 (2): 145–167.

Florida, R. 2005. *The flight of the creative class*. New York, HarperCollins.

Föbker, S., D. Temme, and C. C. Wiegandt 2014. A warm welcome to highly-skilled migrants: How can municipal administrations play their part? *Tijdschrift voor Economische en Sociale Geografie* 105 (5): 542–557.

Glaeser, E. L., and J. D. Gottlieb 2006. Urban resurgence and the consumer city. Cambridge, MA: Harvard Institute of Economic Research Discussion Paper 2109.

Glick Schiller, N., and A. Çağlar 2009. Towards a comparative theory of locality in migration studies: Migrant incorporation and city scale. *Journal of Ethnic and Migration Studies* 35: 177–202.

Glick Schiller, N., and A. Çağlar, eds. 2011. Locating migration: Rescaling cities and migrants. Ithaca, New York: Cornell University Press.

Guardian, The 2016. The non-EU workers who'll be deported for earning less than £35,000. *The Guardian*, March 12 (last accessed April 20, 2016).

Gustin, S. 2012. Blueseed 'Googleplex of the sea' highlights need for visa reform. *Time* July 9.

Hainmueller, J., and M. J. Hiscox 2010. Attitudes toward highly skilled and low-skilled immigration: Evidence from a survey experiment. *American Political Science Review* 104 (01): 61–84.

Huffman, M. L., and P. N. Cohen. 2004. Racial wage inequality: Job segregation and devaluation across US labor markets. *American Journal of Sociology* 109 (4): 902–936.

International Organization of Migration (2008). World Migration Report 2008: Managing labour mobility in the evolving global economy. Geneva: International Organization of Migration.

King, R. 2002. Towards a new map of European migration. *International Journal of Population Geography* 8 (2): 89–106.

Kofman, E. 2000. The invisibility of skilled female migrants and gender relations in studies of skilled migration in Europe. *International Journal of Population Geography* 6 (1): 45–59.

Kuvik, A. 2012. Skilled migration in Europe and beyond: Recent developments and theoretical considerations. In *An introduction to international migration studies: European perspectives*, eds. M. Martiniello and J. Rath, 211–235. Amsterdam: Amsterdam University Press.

Lewis, W. A. 1954. Economic development with unlimited supplies of labour. *The Manchester School* 22 (2): 139–191.

Massey, D. S., J. Arango, G. Hugo, A. Kouaouci, A. Pellegrino, and J. E. Taylor. 1993. Theories of international migration: A review and appraisal. *Population and Development Review* 431–466.

Meier, L., ed. 2015. *Migrant professionals in the city: Local encounters, identities, and inequalities*. New York: Routledge.

Menz, G. 2009. *The political economy of managed migration*. Oxford: Oxford University Press.

Nagel, C. 2005. Skilled migration in global cities from 'Other' perspectives: British Arabs, identity politics, and local embededdness. *Geoforum* 36 (2): 197–210.

National Academies of Sciences, Engineering, and Medicine. 2015. *The integration of immigrants into American society*. Washington, DC: The National Academies Press.

OECD 2012. Harnessing the skills of migrants and diasporas to foster development: Policy options. Paris: Organization for Economic Cooperation and Development/French Ministry of Foreign Affairs.

Piracha, M., and F. Vadean. 2013. Migrant educational mismatch and the labor market. *The international handbook on the economics of migration* 9: 176–192.

Pratt, G. 2004. *Working feminism*. Philadelphia, PA: Temple University Press.

Raghuram, P. 2000. Gendering skilled migratory streams: Implications for conceptualising migration. *Asian and Pacific Migration Journal* 9 (4): 429–457.

Raghuram, P. 2009. Caring about 'brain drain' migration in a postcolonial world. *Geoforum* 40: 25–33.

Ryan, L., and J. Mulholland 2014. French connections: The networking strategies of French highly skilled migrants in London. *Global Networks* 14 (2): 148–166.

Saxenian, A. 2002. Silicon Valley's new immigrant high-growth entrepreneurs. *Economic Development Quarterly* 16 (1): 20–31.

Saxenian, A. 2005. From brain drain to brain circulation: Transnational communities and regional upgrading in India and China. *Studies in Comparative International Development* 40 (2): 35–61.

Scott, S. 2006. The community morphology of skilled migration: The changing role of voluntary and community organisations (VCOs) in the grounding of British migrant identities in Paris (France). *Geoforum* 38: 655–676.

Silvanto, S., and J. Ryan 2014. Relocation branding: A strategic framework for attracting talent from abroad. *Journal of Global Mobility* 2 (1): 102–120.

Smith, M. P., and A. Favell 2006. *The human face of global mobility: International highly skilled migration in Europe, North America and the Asia–Pacific*. New Brunswick, NJ: Transaction Publishers.

Stark, O. and Bloom, D.E., 1985. The new economics of labor migration. *The American Economic Review* 75(2): 173–178.

Stiles, C. H., and C. S. Galbraith. 2004. Ethnic entrepreneurship: Structure and process. Oxford: Elsevier.

Storper, M., and A. J. Scott. 2009. Rethinking human capital, creativity and urban growth. *Journal of Economic Geography* 9 (2): 147–167.

Tejada, G., U. Bhattacharya, B. Khadria, and C. Kuptsch, Eds. 2014. *Indian skilled migration and development: To Europe and back*. Berlin: Springer.

Trippl, M. 2013. Scientific mobility and knowledge transfer at the interregional and intraregional level. *Regional Studies* 47 (10): 1653–1667.

van Riemsdijk, M. 2013. Everyday geopolitics and the valuation of labor: International migration and socio-political hierarchies of skill. *Journal of Ethnic and Migration Studies* 39 (3): 373–390.

Walton-Roberts, M. W. 2011. Immigration, the university and the welcoming second tier city. *Journal of International Migration and Integration* 12 (4): 453–473.

Wang, Q. 2010. The earnings effect of ethnic labor market concentration under multi-racial metropolitan contexts in the United States. *Tijdschrift voor Economische en Sociale Geografie* 101(2): 161–176.

Wang, Q., and T. Lysenko. 2014. Underemployment of immigrants in the United States: From a spatial perspective. *Urban Studies* 51 (10): 220–2218.

Wang, Q., L. Tang, and H. Li 2014. Return migration of the highly skilled in higher education institutions: A Chinese University Case. *Population, Space and Place* 21 (8): 771–787.

Williams, A. M., and V. Baláž 2008. *International migration and knowledge*. New York: Routledge.

World Health Organization 2010. The WHO global code of practice on the international recruitment of health personnel. WHO: Geneva, Switzerland.

Part I

International Student Migration

2 Producing International Student Migration

An Exploration of the Role of Marketization in Shaping International Study Opportunities

Allan Findlay, Russell King, and Alexandra Stam

Introduction

The growth of international student mobility has been extraordinary. According to the International Institute for Education (IIE 2015), international student numbers rose from 2.1 to 4.5 million between 2001 and 2014. The trend can be interpreted in relation to the diverse drivers underpinning the rapid globalization of higher education. Research has shown that the production of international student mobility is both complex and geographically nuanced (Alberts and Hazen 2013; Bilicen 2014; Brooks and Waters 2011a; Gerard and Uebelmesser 2014; King and Raghuram 2013). This chapter explores one aspect of this important topic: the role of marketization in shaping international student flows. By the term "marketization" we guide the reader to reflect on the contested idea of higher education as an international market-place (Scott 2015), with many stakeholders seeking to "sell" opportunities for international study.

The chapter seeks to make several original contributions. First, it rebalances the international student migration literature that has given too much emphasis to students and their families as the overriding explanation driving the pattern of demand for international study. This dominant position tends to uphold a view of individual decision-making as highly significant. By paying attention to the other side of the higher education market (that is, to the supply side of those that provide and sell study opportunities), the chapter highlights many new and understudied drivers of student mobility. Linked to this is the contribution of the "place" dimension of the notion of "market-place." While economists have written about the financial structures shaping the globalized higher education market in different countries (Gerard and Uebelmesser 2014), these accounts fail to recognize how uneven the market is in spatial terms. Not only is there spatial variation between states in policies on international student immigration (Felbermayr and Reczkowski 2014), but there are often wide variations between universities operating within the same country in terms of their strategies and capacities to engage with international students. It is to this latter aspect of the supply of higher education that this chapter seeks to make a particular contribution from a geographical perspective. This in turn contributes to the wider reconceptualization of international student mobility argued for by King and Raghuram (2013).

We open the chapter with a brief summary of the international student migration literature. We then discuss the research methods that were used to capture the voices of key stakeholders, before introducing some themes emerging from our primary research. The chapter argues that there is significant potential to deepen understanding of the power of "marketization" through, first, evaluating how those supplying higher education, such as universities and other higher education institutions (HEIs), understand the global market for their products. Second, we explore how differences in the working environments of HEIs influence their approach to recruiting and nourishing international study opportunities. By changes in the working environment we mean policies implemented by governments regarding visa regimes for incoming students, regulatory mechanisms for quality control, and the governance structure determining how universities can operate and compete for (international) students.

Student Mobility Choices in a Structured Higher Education Market-place

Existing research has tended to focus on the drivers encouraging students to move to another country as well as reporting their experiences following migration. Many authors emphasize the processes by which students make choices about their international trajectories (Hazen and Alberts 2006). This perspective leads to a focus on individual motivations for mobility and on how individual sociodemographic characteristics can offer some explanation of who moves for international study and who is constrained, perhaps financially or politically, from taking up opportunities for international study.

Other researchers recognize that the social and economic values underpinning migration "choices" are far from being "individual." They point instead to the wider social meanings attributed to international student mobility and to the power of social class in producing uneven student geographies (Brooks and Waters 2011b; Findlay and King 2006; Holdsworth 2006). In particular, researchers have argued that the accumulation of cultural capital is a key driver explaining why middle-class families in many parts of the world, notably in the emerging economies, encourage and finance their children to study internationally (Brooks and Waters 2011a; Waters 2006).

The need to contextualize research informed by Bourdieu's (1986) propositions about the role of cultural capital has led geographers and others to explore in more depth the evolving, uneven nature of the international higher education system. It has been recognized that national higher education systems have increasingly been affected by international forces. Examples include the Bologna process and its attempt to standardize degree structures, the influence of international organizations in demanding metrics to judge the equivalence of degrees from different countries, and cultural shifts in favor of English becoming the international language of research and training in advanced education institutions in many countries. These trends have all facilitated flows and exchanges between the higher education systems of different countries.

If globalization has resulted in increasing similarities between formerly distinctive national higher education systems, it has also paradoxically produced "difference." This has manifested itself both horizontally and vertically. For universities and other higher education institutions, vertical differences have emerged because of their uneven capacities, statuses, and resources. These dimensions have always been important in differentiating higher education as a "field of power" (Bourdieu 1984; Bourdieu and Passeron 1997). Horizontal differences between universities of similar academic standing have emerged in terms of their degree of discipline specialization, as well as in relation to economic segmentation between state and private universities, and features such as the language of instruction or the academic culture. The potential significance of these differentiating features in geographical terms is very evident when one reflects on the empirics of international student mobility. For example, analysis of the destinations of international students shows that, in the USA, institutions in the top ten states hosted 61 percent of all international students in the country (IIE 2015). The cultural-capital explanation of this geographical concentration can be explained by the symbolic significance attributed by students, their families and the global elite to holding academic credentials from a "world-class" university (Brooks and Waters 2011b; Findlay et al. 2012). In contrast, the supply-side argument would be that, on the one hand, the significant wealth of top universities such as those in the Ivy League makes it possible to offer significant numbers of scholarships to selectively recruited international students, while on the other hand the pattern of international student flows is shaped by the practices of these universities competing against each other as global educational players to attract the best and the brightest from around the world. The supply-side perspective therefore leads to specific explanations of the geographical concentration of international student flows on certain host HEIs. In terms of vertical differentiation it suggests that there should be a numerical clustering of international students in the most powerful HEIs because these universities not only have the academic standing but also the financial resources to engage very actively in recruiting students from other countries (Findlay et al. 2012). Horizontal differentiation of universities by contrast should produce a selective flow (that is, a qualitative distinction by type) of international students in relation to the effectiveness of HEIs in marketing their specializations on the global educational market. And what is true at the level of individual universities is also true at the level of national higher education systems, with some countries marketing their higher education credentials through state-sponsored agencies (such as the British Council), resulting in them capturing a greater "market share" and a distinctive student demographic.

A key feature of globalization has been that universities have increasingly acted in competition with one another, not only within a country, but also on a global stage (Sadlak and Cai 2007). This being the case, those managing universities have come to be recognized as key actors in promoting the value of studying in one university rather than another and in marketing the attributes that differentiate one degree from another (Beech 2014). This opens up recognition of the importance of researching the power of the key stakeholders that shape international study opportunities. It is an approach which does not restrict analysis of student mobility to the "choices" of students in an undifferentiated educational landscape (Gulson and Symes 2007), but instead directs research to consider the "sites" and "actors" in the global educational market-place that disseminate information about international study opportunities and that channel potential international students to a select set of "world-class" universities. The "sites" include international education fairs, satellite campuses of international universities offering students preparatory courses for entry to the sponsoring institution, and the offices of intermediary actors such as educational recruitment agents engaged in the business of assisting prospective applicants to make applications to study abroad and to gain study visas from the destination country. Other key "actors" are, of course, the international offices of HEIs. Their staff identify the educational products that they see as having a niche or comparative advantage in the global market-place. They design university web pages to boost awareness of their university's distinctive brand and they spend much time traveling the world to recruit students at fairs and through site visits to "target" schools.

While this chapter focuses on the marketing of international study opportunities, we acknowledge that there are many other important narratives about international student mobility that have been developed by researchers. Raghuram (2013), for example, has argued that there is great merit in studying "knowledge migration" as opposed to student migration, and in a related but different vein Jöns (2015) has located student movement within the wider analysis of the circulation of many different types of people (university staff, postgraduate researchers, etc.) involved in knowledge mobility. These are valuable new avenues for research, but in this chapter we set these interesting ideas to one side, so that we can explore in more depth one particular issue relating to international student flows—marketization.

Marketization signifies that important economic processes are at work within the higher education market-place. Not only is it necessary to recognize that international students engage in a globalized higher education market where study opportunities have a cost that is determined by the intersection of the interests of those buying and selling study places; it is also necessary to recognize that the geography of the market-place is a "social field" in which power asymmetries are evident at the sites of study and in the patterning of the networks of student flows between countries. On the supply side these economic processes determine that some universities are more powerful than others in their ability to attract students. This is reflected in the resources they can call on, and in the efficacy of the marketing tools that they use in recruiting international students. The fundamental contention of the chapter is therefore that international study opportunities do not simply exist in a neutral space of globalized higher education. Instead, they are "marketed" by a range of stakeholders. The practices of these stakeholders in positioning the product of international education are important in understanding the geography of international student flows. The objective of the chapter is therefore to open up new insights into how one group of stakeholders—the international offices of universities—participate in reproducing geographical variations in the map of student mobility.

Definitions, Survey, and Methods

A key distinction that we wish to make from the outset is between international degree mobility and credit mobility. Degree mobility involves a student enrolling for their entire degree at a university in another country, while credit mobility involves the popular option of studying for part of a degree in another university but transferring credits from this spell of international study for inclusion in a degree in their country of origin (such as occurs within the EU Erasmus program). In this study the data we draw on relates to the international degree mobility of UK students. We examined degree mobility for all levels of study from undergraduate courses such as the Bachelor's degree through to Ph.D. programs.

The research reported here was commissioned by the United Kingdom's Department for Business, Innovation and Skills, and involved a questionnaire survey of 560 UK students enrolled abroad, interviews with the various personnel in the international offices of universities, and analysis of secondary data sources relating to international student mobility. The primary research was conducted over an 18-month period in 2008 and 2009, and the initial reports designed for a policy audience were published in 2010 (Findlay et al. 2010a, 2010b). In this chapter we report on the international office interview element of the project that has not previously been analyzed for an academic audience. Interviews were also held with course directors of programs oriented to international students as well as with representatives of national agencies charged with promoting higher education study opportunities. The interviews (twenty-one in all) took place with university staff in sixteen international offices in the United States, Australia, Ireland, France, Germany, and the Czech Republic as well as five other in-depth interviews with staff in para-state organizations promoting international student mobility. The offices were selected after a preliminary analysis of secondary data on the number of UK students in each of the six countries. In each country universities were targeted in relation to two criteria. First, we searched for universities where the largest number of UK students were enrolled. Second, we strived for efficiency in terms of the researchers' time, so that some universities located within the same city as the most popular university were chosen for international office interviews. Further details on the methodology have been published in the researchers' report to their principal funder (Findlay et al. 2010b). Interviews were also conducted with other stakeholders, such as para-state agencies promoting national strategies to export higher education opportunities, as well as agencies operating on behalf of one or more groups of universities. Some quotes from meetings with these other non-university stakeholders are included here, but the focus is on the practices reported by the international offices of universities.

The empirical material reported in this chapter was originally conceived within the conceptual framework laid out in Findlay et al. (2012). This schema suggested that international student flows reflect more than the choices of individual students, and are nested within a socially and geographically uneven education system. The schema noted that not only is secondary education structured unevenly—for example, with major differences evident between state schools and private schools in terms of the opportunities for international study that are presented to pupils (King and Raghuram 2013)—but also in relation to structural divisions in higher education. These divisions might be evident vertically in terms of the distinction between what might be considered world-class, high-esteem institutions and other less well-known universities, or horizontally between, for example, traditional universities recruiting international students to their home campus, and higher education institutions with satellite branch campuses in other countries (Waters and Leung 2013). This complex and variegated system of higher education provides one reason why it is pertinent to research the mechanisms used by universities to differentiate themselves in the international higher education market-place. As is evident in the empirical evidence that we report later, universities not only brand themselves in a variety of distinctive ways, but they also perceive that there are many different types of international student and that they need to position themselves strategically in relation to the multiple niches that they wish to "serve." Interviewees were left to define their perceptions of "student types" to discover whether all respondents followed the same classification and similar labels such as undergraduates, students on postgraduate taught courses, research students, international students enrolling in courses to gain global "credentials," students seeking to earn points to facilitate subsequent settlement, or students intending to use their international degrees to access an international career trajectory.

The interview schedule had four main sections, seeking to identify a) how the globalization of higher education was interpreted, b) the tools used to market international study opportunities, c) how student types are understood, and d) how future trends in student mobility are envisioned. Interviews lasted between one and two hours, and were usually held in the office of the interviewee. Interviews were transcribed and analyzed to identify the multiple meanings associated with international student recruitment as well as the social practices and performances of those involved in marketing and recruitment. The analysis was designed to identify the goals of key stakeholders shaping the patterning of international student migration and an understanding of the actions that these people took to achieve their goals. All interviewees have been given pseudonyms and the names of the institutions where we conducted the research have also been removed. The list of institutions is given in the original report to the funders of the research (Findlay et al. 2010b, 52).

Set alongside the findings reported in the remainder of this chapter are the papers produced by the research team relating to the motives reported by students for engaging in international study (Findlay et al. 2012; King and Raghuram 2013). Despite having access to high-quality UK universities of international standing, the students appeared to be mainly driven by a desire to access a world-class university in another country. This was perceived to be a means of accruing social and cultural capital, differentiating them from nonmobile students as well as helping them to attain an international mobility trajectory in harmony with the respondents' wider life-course aspirations for mobility (for instance, to enter international career pathways or to emigrate for permanent settlement in another country). The geography of these moves was argued to illustrate that, although Bourdieu's (1984) ideas about the importance of education in producing distinction have some purchase, they are limited in the depth of understanding that they offer to geographers seeking to achieve a more satisfying understanding of the patterning of international student flows. Their value lies in conceptualizing how social demand for international education structures the pattern of who leaves a country in response to uneven opportunities for secondary education (with the privileged middle classes often channeling their children through private schooling and onwards to a highly differentiated global university system (King et al. 2011)). The limitations of Bourdieu's approach are twofold. First, previous work has failed to fully valorize the power of place and mobility as differentiators in the production of the destination patterns of student mobility (Findlay et al. 2012). Second, most other work on student migration fails to recognize the strength of the forces responsible for shaping the supply of higher education opportunities (Findlay 2011). It is to this second agenda that we now turn.

The International Business of Student Mobility

Drivers of International Student Recruitment

From the perspective of those in charge of the international business of student mobility, competition for international students between states and between institutions is a driver of the "intentional" actions of those marketing higher education (UUK 2014). These key gatekeepers therefore act strategically. Not only do they recruit students to "their" country or "their" university, but they also engage in practices designed to maintain the market share of the interest groups that they represent. They also seek to ensure a good match between the diverse range of potential international students seeking a place to enroll for study and the particular educational niches offered by those who fund the activities of the stakeholders.

Of course, all universities want to attract foreign students because of the monetary rewards associated with earning international fees, but they are also concerned with the credentials that flow to educational institutions from establishing a reputation (both for their "home" and "international" students) as a leading world educational hub (Findlay 2011). Inevitably, some universities were more open than others in declaring to us information about the economic benefits of earning international student fees. National bodies responsible for promoting international study opportunities are less circumspect. Universities UK (2014) has estimated that students from outside the EU contribute more than £7 billion to the economy; in Canada, international student expenditure in 2014 was reported to be worth $16 billion, while in the USA, IIE (2015) reports the economic impact to be US$27 billion. Meanwhile, Australia proudly declares earnings from international students as the country's third largest export earner.

Turning from national economic impacts to the scale of individual universities, it is not hard to show from university accounts just how important overseas earnings are to their financial well-being (Tindal et al. 2014). Here we limit our evidence to the voices of those we interviewed. One example must suffice to represent the power of financial drivers in motivating the recruitment of international students. We have selected a Czech university with twenty years' experience of marketing its courses to English-language students to illustrate the relationship between an institution's motives for "internationalization" and the social performances and practices that follow from these motives. Any number of interviewees from universities around the world might have given a similar message:

> There were three main aims for the program. First, and almost without need for discussion, the program brings significant financial means (…) Almost all British students attend the English version of the program (which is organized as a separate course). While the program in Czech is free, there are quite high fees for the English program. The second reason to open the English program (in discipline W) was to create international links between the faculty and the world (…) The third reason is related to the previous as there is a will to create an internationally wide community of students …. As a result, there is a deliberate effort to outsource activities of the faculty in the countries where there was no previous connection.
>
> (Dusan, international course coordinator at a Czech university with over 100 UK students)

So, if earnings from selling the product of an English-language program were critical to Dusan's university in explaining why they had engaged in setting up and sustaining a degree, these commercial motivations were mixed with more academic aspirations such as establishing international academic links and the internationalization of the study environment. Dusan then went on to report the practices used to promote the product of an international education and to attract particular types of student to his program.

We switch to another country to illustrate the widespread nature of the marketization discourse that we encountered in our fieldwork. An interviewee from an Australian university describes the practices that flow from a desire to market higher education opportunities:

> One of my colleagues is going to Germany next week. And we go to Asia—I just came back from Korea, Hong Kong, China. I have a colleague in Malaysia, another colleague in India. We have just gone back from Canada and the US, another colleague just went to Latin American countries …. We either

> do a broad show with a lot of the Australian universities together, sometimes we do independent broad shows where we go out and we advertise and meet students in a hotel. Sometimes we do things with agents, we have recruitment agencies overseas and we do recruitment missions with them or that agent will act on our behalf.
>
> (John, international office of an Australian university, with about 100 UK students)

Dusan and John therefore present a picture of a higher education system where international students are paying customers in a higher education market-place. They refer to "sites" of activity such as international fairs or "broad shows" where opportunities for study are presented to interested students, as well as the use of intermediary actors such as recruitment agencies. In contrast to the literature on student "choices," these quotes begin to map a world of "shows" and "advertising" that requires a rethinking of the context within which student migration decisions are taken. The "product" of an international degree is being sold not only by universities themselves, but also by other actors such as recruitment agents and government intermediaries, with actors actively engaged in "advertising" the opportunities for international study. The same narrative was found in nearly all the interviews that we conducted in relation to the motives and the marketing of higher education products. Interviewees revealed a distinct set of countries that they visited, with most stakeholders going to those locations where they felt there was a lucrative market that they could tap into (most notably China and India). Despite the global reach of the stakeholders' activities, the localized "sites" of recruitment were at the same time largely limited to places where there was the potential for engagement with students and parents from wealthier and middle-income families.

In summary, the evidence presented above provides an insight into the complex map of the global higher education market-place. International student mobility is no longer set against the backdrop of demand-side actors such as the middle-class family seeking opportunities to invest in their children's cultural capital (cf. Waters 2006). Instead, the market-place is being shaped by university actors and other stakeholders such as recruitment agents who are motivated by the financial and other gains that result from attracting international students.

Differentiating the Product of International Higher Education

Not surprisingly, the competitiveness of the global higher education market-place led our interviewees to explain how they differentiated their product from the mass education market. Steven, a member of the international office of an Irish university, explains how branding is just as important in selling opportunities to international students as it would be true in any other market-place:

> On the one hand you have an element of mass marketing and profile generation. And on the other hand you need an extremely targeted approach to

> individual high schools. … Now … a lot of people assume that because the UK is next door and there is Ryanair that it would be a very cheap place to recruit students. But … (our university) doesn't have a brand all over the UK; we'd be competing within the extremely competitive UK sector.

Targeting particular schools was referred to by several interviewees, as code not only for the development of personalized networks of student mobility, but also for a desire to recruit from well-ranked private schools from outside the EU where applicants would be more likely to be able to afford to pay "international fees." Akin to retail demographics, our interviewees also hinted at different types of international student and explained how they mapped their differentiated products to these student types. For example, it was noted that Indian students were more likely than others to want to come for a one-year taught postgraduate degree, with a desire if possible to gain work experience in a Western economy as part of the credentials they hoped to achieve during their time abroad. This contrasted with students from other origin countries who wanted to use international study to achieve access to an international career and whose choice of courses and places of study was likely to be very different from students wanting a degree from a top-ranked university and having the intention of returning home upon graduation. Differentiation of the product varied of course from university to university, with some seeking to brand the authenticity of their educational excellence in terms of the age and standing of the university. Others stressed the international academic specializations that made their university distinctive or perhaps the study-lifestyle opportunities of their location. And this branding and differentiation was evident at many different levels (the state, the university, the degree program). Consider, for example, the voice of a top executive of a para-state organization promoting international education opportunities at the national level:

> (We are) looking for the best and brightest. Far more students come in than go out. … Over the last few years the concept of a mobility culture developed … Why would UK students study in Australia? I think it is a lifestyle consideration. As a growing person, why not do it? Of course we stress the quality of the qualification (offered by Australian universities). But we also use the strapline "Live, Learn, Grow" (to promote study in Australia). When you come from India, then the "learn" is the most important … The British may come for the climate. Some (UK students) go on a gap year and then stay on—love, lifestyle … we need to be a globally competitive industry.
>
> (Karen, employee of a para-state organization promoting the attractions of studying in Australia)

Karen's understanding of why Australia seeks to recruit students internationally is couched in terms of the business of international talent attraction, recognizing the internationally competitive global market and the attempt by states and para-state organizations to attract "the best and the brightest" in a sophisticated manner. This involved marketing and branding the education product at a national level in an effort to promote a greater awareness not only of the quality of education that is available at top universities, but also of other factors that differentiate Australia's niche market from other study destinations. Thus she represents Australia as being attractive not just for "learning" but also for "lifestyle" and she notes the connectedness of student mobility with a wider "mobility culture." Interviews carried out with representatives of organizations promoting study in other countries told similar stories, although each country emphasized different niches which they wished to fill, and with each making authenticity claims about what their HEIs could offer in relation to their self-defined metrics of distinction.

One strand to the marketing strategy raised by several interviewees in different countries was the importance of attracting students from a diversity of countries of origin. The significance of diversity to university marketing strategies was explained in several different ways:

> You have to focus on what does it mean educationally? Does this diversity of students really enhance the educational value of the university experience?
>
> (James, international office, US university, around 130 UK students)

It was noted, for example, that while the financial benefits for universities recruiting students in the mass markets of China and India were very great, there were also problems, as one Australian university official noted:

> To us diversity is very important and we don't want students to feel they are just in a China town, basically where there are just Chinese students. And you know going in E's (city) universities some students may feel like that.
>
> (Gareth, international office, Australian university, around 100 UK students)

According to many of the international recruitment staff interviewed in the United States and Australia, the search for diversity was an additional reason why universities were eager to recruit UK and other European students—namely, to satisfy the mass market expectations of Asian students of studying in an academically, ethnically and gender-diverse environment.

The geography of international recruitment was also informed by concerns about global economic swings and over-dependence on recruitment from only one or two origin countries. Over-dependence on India and China as dominant source countries was a particular concern. Set against this, interviewees discussed the apparent futility of trying to recruit from countries where the standard of living was very low, since students and their families would not be able to afford the cost of international fees. To quote James again:

> How many resources should you put into (recruiting) in a region where people cannot afford to come … Who do you recruit? Can they stay? Financially are they going to be able to make it?

Actions in relation to this kind of concern were set out particularly formally in Australia where national policy informed universities of the relative risks of international students from different origins not meeting their financial commitments. This was done through periodically issuing a list with a fivefold classification of sending countries rated by a student's ability to pay. The details of which countries were classified as desirable and which were seen as risky are not discussed here. What matters is the bigger picture that James points to, which is that intermediary stakeholders shape the pattern of international student recruitment through the specificity of their practices. Student flows do not simply reflect "demand" for study abroad but are shaped by "supply-side" actors who decide which places in the global educational market-place they should target for recruiting foreign students.

For world-class universities, the international business of recruiting global student talent was more complex than for HEIs lower in the global hierarchy. Some noted how they used satellite campuses or special bilateral arrangements with foreign universities as a means of pre-selecting the best students at point of origin to feed into their courses. Above all, financial concerns were overridden by the desire to remain at the apex of the university hierarchy by attracting the very best students in the world. Brad, working in the international office of a prestigious American university, describes the positioning of his HEI in targeting particular students who might otherwise enroll in what he considered to be competitor world-class universities:

> The university is already internationalized … we have students from all across the globe (yet) it was very intentional on the part of the university to increase our international undergraduate population … If you let the marketplace drive your (international student) growth you will get a disproportionate number of Asian students … If a student is capable enough to get into (this university), they will also be capable of getting into Harvard, MIT, Stanford. So we look at Stanford and see what they are offering their students when we prepare our financial package, because these are the students we are competing for.
>
> (Brad, international office, world-class American university, around 100 UK students)

Like many top North American universities, Brad therefore saw fellowship/scholarship programs as the key device for attracting the kind of international students who fitted the university's elite profile, leaving other universities to accept students allocated to them by "the market-place." The important distinction made by Brad in what he describes as "intentional" actions reflects the financial power of those universities with large endowments to "command and control" their position in the marketized higher education system. At this level the global brand of the university is marked out by the quality of the educational product and the quality of the student "clients," something that can be perpetuated through the power of the scholarship system. This stands in contrast with the way that Brad perceives some other universities who "let the market-place drive … growth." Thus, one arrives at a recognition that not only is it illusory to imagine that international students choose their places of study in a free and open educational market, but that universities too are engaged in an even market-place, where some have access to resources that they draw on to position themselves to good effect, while others are less able to stand against the ebb and flow of global market forces.

Some top US universities listed specific independent schools in the UK that they would target in diffusing information about scholarships, while others emphasized that there was no need to actively recruit and that the "intentional" aspect of their strategy lay in allocating scholarships selectively to attract students of the highest academic caliber.

To summarize, insights from a range of institutional actors have been introduced above to extend understanding of the patterning of flows of international students. It is clear that it is not just social differences in terms of class and school type in countries of origin that matter in explaining the structuring of international student flows (King and Raghuram 2013). This section of the chapter has provided evidence that goes beyond the threefold schema discussed by Findlay et al. (2012) which mapped international student flows only in relation to a school education system divided between private and state-funded schools, and a university system differentiated between world-class universities and lower-ranked HEIs. In this section of the chapter evidence has been presented that points to the insights that come from considering the practices of universities, para-state organizations promoting international student flows, and a range of intermediary stakeholders such as student recruitment agencies. In particular it has been argued that the spatial patterning of international student flows has been shaped by the competitive practices of nation-states and HEIs in their recruitment behavior (e.g. in avoiding countries where students are unlikely to be able to pay international student fees). At the same time the significantly greater financial power of some universities to offer scholarships to recruit foreign students helps one understand why the international composition of the student population of some universities is rather different from those HEIs whose recruitment patterns reflect the vagaries of market-driven growth in student numbers.

Discussion and Conclusions

This chapter has opened up a debate on the marketization of higher education within the context of international student flows. We have intentionally restricted our comments to those dimensions that are readily illustrated by our evidence base. This points to the importance of complicating the literature on the choices of students seeking to move internationally (Brooks and Everett 2008) by recognizing that the market-place for higher education is to some extent shaped by those who seek to market the products associated with international study opportunities. Those promoting the products have a range of motivations for their actions, with raising finance a primary driver in most instances (Findlay 2011).

Competitiveness in what is a highly lucrative market-place is sought through differentiating the products on sale. This is done both through developing strategies to match educational products (for example, taught Masters involving workplace experience) to particular student types, and through fostering distinctive market niches (Gulson and Symes 2007) such as courses directed to students who are more interested in achieving global career citizenship through their studies (Lewin 2009) than earning points under a specific immigration policy to permit them local settlement rights following graduation. Furthermore, the branding of the educational products that are on sale is important not only in terms of understanding what is offered in particular universities, but also more broadly in terms of the wider educational brands that are linked to national and international opportunities located outside the immediate study environment. This all contributes to recognizing that the "imaginative geographies" of potential international students (Beech 2014) involves the multiple geographical scales of the global market-place.

We conclude by making two propositions, based on the evidence presented in this chapter. First, it seems evident that international study opportunities are produced not only by the sociocultural forces that drive young people from more fortunate backgrounds to seek the cultural and symbolic capital that comes from international study. The "opportunities" are also produced by higher education providers seeking to fulfil their specified goals. For some universities this may simply be the significant financial gains that arise from earning international student tuition fees, but most universities also recognize more ethereal objectives such as the accreditation and prestige they felt were associated with being a desired destination for international students. This was in some way considered evidence of their global international standing. For nation-states, international students' fees were also important, but with other objectives also identified as important including in some cases the potential of acquiring and retaining future global talent by encouraging the best international students to stay beyond their studies and to contribute to national economic growth. A marketization perspective therefore places a focus on the educational product and the ways in which those that supply the product understand their motives for recruiting students.

Second, the chapter has illustrated some of the ways in which those who sell higher education seek to differentiate themselves in the international marketplace. Not only was there recognition of the varied types of educational product on offer, which had to be matched to a differentiated range of international students with different desires and objectives; there was also the recognition that marketing strategies and the way in which students might be reached could establish niches in the global patterning of student flows. At the same time universities talked about the "market" risk of being over-dependent on any one country of origin and discussed their strategies and motivations for diversification in relation to the students they recruited and for what purposes.

The dominant focus in this chapter has been on the evidence concerning international student recruitment provided by university international offices. This has allowed us to illustrate some distinctive spatialities associated with international student mobility. It is important to note, however, that other geographies would emerge from evidence gleaned from states about their policies on retaining or re-exporting international students. Thus, while some countries (such as Norway, see Chapter 5, and Sweden) encourage the return migration of as many international students as possible in order to contribute to international development and to prevent a "brain drain," others such as the USA favor the maximum retention of international students as a means of recruiting global talent and adding to the stock of highly skilled workers. The distinctive geography of the relation between international student mobility and skilled migration is therefore very interesting (Felbermayr and Reczkowski 2014), especially in light of the emergence of a third category of study location such as the UK. In the UK, both the state and universities make great efforts to recruit international students, but maintain very strict policies discouraging settlement after graduation. This import–export model of international student mobility does not, however, lead in most cases to a geography of return migration but rather to a pattern of onward skilled migration to a third country (Packwood et al. 2015). Much therefore remains to be explored of the complex relation between student mobility and skilled migration.

Inevitably, this chapter has only identified a limited number of aspects of the "supply side" mechanisms that are relevant to the study of international student mobility (Findlay 2011). One of the key questions awaiting further research is how universities located within countries with negative immigration policies market study opportunities to international students when there is little prospect of the students remaining after graduation. Other questions include asking how educational products pitched at different educational levels (e.g. undergraduate degrees, Master's courses and Ph.D. programs) serve different mobility markets in terms of students moving for study, compared with those using education as a trampoline to extend their lifetime aspirations for international migration and relocation (Li et al. 1996).

The key principle underpinning this chapter has been that limiting the analysis of student mobility to the motivations and choices of individuals is to miss many of the profound forces shaping international student flows. Cultural and symbolic capital are certainly important (Brooks and Waters 2011a), but so too are the structuring influences of those who seek to market higher education opportunities for financial and other gains.

Acknowledgments

We are very grateful to the UK's Department for Business, Innovation and Skills for funding the original research on which this chapter is based. We also owe a huge debt to Jill Ahrens, Matej Blazek, Alistair Geddes, Asayo Ohba, Fiona Smith, and Ron Skeldon. They helped extensively in conducting the interviews and questionnaire surveys. We are also indebted to the editors of this volume, whose insightful comments have greatly added to our understanding of the topic.

References

Alberts, H., and H. Hazen Eds. 2013. *International students and scholars in the United States*. Basingstoke: Palgrave Macmillan.

Beech, S. 2014. Why place matters. *Area* 46, 170–177.

Bilicen, B. 2014. *International student mobility and transnational friendships*. Basingstoke: Palgrave Macmillan.

Bourdieu, P. 1984. *Distinction*. Cambridge, MA: Harvard University Press.

Bourdieu, P. 1986. The forms of capital. In *Handbook of theory and research for the sociology of education*, ed. H. G. Richardson, 241–258. London: Greenwood.

Bourdieu, P., and J. Passeron. 1997. *Reproduction in education, society and culture*. London: Sage.

Brooks, R., and G. Everett. 2008. The prevalence of life planning: Evidence from UK graduates. *British Journal of Sociology Education* 29, 325–337.

Brooks, R., and J. Waters. 2011a. 'Vive la différence?' The international experiences of UK students overseas. *Population, Space and Place* 17, 567–578.

Brooks, R., and J. Waters. 2011b. *Student mobilities: Migration and the internationalization of higher education*. Basingstoke: Palgrave Macmillan.

Felbermayr, G., and I. Reczkowski. 2014. In search of evidence: Mobility of students and highly skilled workers interrelated. In *The mobility of students and the highly skilled*, eds. M. Gerard and S. Uebelmesser, 15–55. Cambridge: MIT Press.

Findlay, A. 2011. An assessment of supply and demand-side theorizations of international student mobility. *International Migration* 42, 162–189.

Findlay, A., R. King, E. Ruiz-Gelices, and A. Stam, 2006. Ever-reluctant Europeans. *European Urban and Regional Studies* 13, 291–318.

Findlay, A., A. Geddes, and F. Smith. 2010a. Motivations and experiences of UK students studying abroad. Statistical sources, *BIS Research Paper* 8a. London: Department for Business, Innovation and Skills.

Findlay, A., R. King, A. Geddes, F. Smith, A. Stam, M. Dunne, R. Skeldon, and J. Ahrens. 2010b. Motivations and experiences of UK students studying abroad, *BIS Research Paper* 8. Available at: http://webarchive.nationalarchives.gov.uk/20121212135622/http://www.bis.gov.uk/assets/biscore/corporate/migratedD/publications/B/BIS-RP-008 London: Department for Business, Innovation and Skills (accessed March 21, 2016).

Findlay, A., R. King, F. Smith, A. Geddes, and R. Skeldon. 2012. World class? An investigation of globalisation, difference and international student mobility. *Transactions of the Institute of British Geographers* 37, 118–131.

Gerard, M., and S. Uebelmesser Eds. 2014. *The mobility of students and the highly skilled*. Cambridge, MA: MIT Press.

Gulson, K., and C. Symes. 2007. Knowing one's place. In *Spatial theories of education*, eds. K. Gulson and C. Symes, 1–16. London: Routledge.

Hazen, H., and H. Alberts. 2006. Visitors or immigrants? *Population, Space and Place* 12, 201–216.

Holdsworth, C. 2006. Don't you think you are missing out living at home? *Sociological Review* 54, 495–513.

IIE (International Institute of Education). 2015. *Open Doors 2014*. New York: Institute for International Education.

Jöns, H. 2015. Talent mobility and the shifting geographies of Latourian knowledge hubs. *Population, Space and Place* 21, 372–389.

King, R., and P. Raghuram. 2013. International student migration. *Population, Space and Place* 19, 127–137.

King, R., A. Findlay, and J. Ahrens. 2010. *International student mobility literature review*. Report to HEFCE, British Council and UK National Agency for Erasmus.

King, R., A. Findlay, J. Ahrens, and M. Dunne. 2011. Reproducing advantage: The perspective of English school-leavers on studying abroad. *Globalisation, Societies and Education* 9, 161–181.

Lewin, R. 2009. The quest for global citizenship through study abroad. In *The handbook of practice and research in study abroad*, ed. R. Lewin, xiii–xxii. Abingdon: Routledge.

Li, L., A. Findlay, A. Jowett, and R. Skeldon. 1996. Migrating to learn and learning to migrate. *International Journal of Population Geography* 2, 51–67.

Packwood, H., A. Findlay, and D. McCollum. 2015. International study for an international career. *Centre for Population Change Briefing Paper 27*. Southampton: Centre for Population Change.

Raghuram, P. 2013. Theorising the spaces of student migration. *Population, Space and Place* 19, 138–154.

Sadlak, J., and L. Cai Eds. 2007. *The world class university and ranking: Aiming beyond status*. Bucharest: Unesco-Cepes.

Scott, P. 2015. There is a third way that universities could take, between state and market. *The Guardian* 9 July.

Tindal, S., A. Findlay, and R. Wright. 2014. The changing significance of EU and international student participation in Scottish higher education. *Centre for population change working paper* 49. Southampton: Centre for Population Change.

UUK (Universities UK). 2014. *International students in higher education: The UK and its competition*. London: Universities UK.

Waters, J. 2006. Geographies of cultural capital: Education, international migration and family strategies between Hong Kong and Canada. *Transactions of the Institute of British Geographers* 31, 179–192.

Waters, J., and M. Leung. 2013. Immobile transnationalisms? *Urban Studies* 50, 606–620.

3 Complex Decisions

Factors Determining International Students' Migrations

Heike Alberts

Making migration decisions is often difficult. Many international students face the decision twice: when they decide to get a university degree abroad, and when they ponder whether or not they should return to their home countries after graduation or stay in their host countries. For many students, the second decision is a lot more complex than the first, as they are now familiar with both countries and have ties in both places. As a result, they consider a large number of factors in their migration decisions that often pull them into different directions.

This chapter builds on and updates earlier work on the factors international students consider in their migration decisions (Alberts and Hazen 2005; Hazen and Alberts 2006, 2013), but expands it in several different ways. First, rather than focusing on a single host institution in the United States, this study examines international students at different types of institutions (research universities and teaching-intensive institutions) throughout the state of Wisconsin. Second, because the competition for talent among different countries has increased, this study explores whether international students consider other destination countries both initially and after graduation. Third, this study also delves into international students' preferences regarding where they study within the host country (region, state, city, and institution). A better understanding of the complexities of the decision-making process is important to provide students with the support they need at every step of their migration journey. Furthermore, in the climate of competition for global talent, this information may also allow hosts to better target their recruitment efforts.

Conceptually, this study demonstrates that a complex issue like a migration decision cannot be reduced to a few factors operating in isolation. Rather, a wide range of factors has to be considered, how these factors are weighted, how they change over time, and how they interact with one another. Furthermore, it shows the importance of studying students with different personal characteristics as well as from different countries of origin together, because only then can we begin to understand how personal migration decisions are embedded in and shaped by a wide variety of external circumstances.

Background

The literature on international students and other academic migrants has been growing significantly in recent times. One reason is that international student numbers worldwide have continued to increase, and countries and institutions actively compete with one another to reap the benefits of international student migrations. Furthermore, international students are an important component of the globalized knowledge economy. As a result, the topic of international student migrations cuts across three major areas of both public and academic concern: education, migration, and globalization (especially the globalization of higher education; King and Raghuram 2013).

The literature on international students in education and related fields (e.g. psychology, counseling) largely deals with international students' adjustment difficulties and other problems they encounter abroad. For example, some scholars have revealed that international students of color are often confronted with racism, both overt racism as well as more subtle forms such as low expectations of their academic performance because of their skin color, national origin, or accent (Lee 2007). Other scholars have examined international students' adjustment difficulties and culture shock more broadly, and found that students' adjustment problems increase with greater cultural differences between the home and host countries. For example, students from collectivist cultures often struggle with adjusting to the more individualistic culture in the United States (Sümer, Poyrazl, and Grahame 2008). Still other scholars have focused on academic issues, such as international students' challenges with adapting to very different classroom cultures, interactions with their professors, writing styles, plagiarism rules, and more generally different academic expectations (Eland and Thomas 2013). While the present study does not examine international students' adjustment issues, some of the insights from this body of literature are relevant, such as the experiences international students had during their studies, how strongly they perceive the cultural differences between their home and host countries, and how comfortable they feel in the United States, and whether these factors influence their decision to stay in the United States for a longer period of time after their graduation.

In the migration literature, international students have received less attention than other groups of international migrants (King and Raghuram 2013), but the number of studies has been increasing. In the early years of the 21st century, the literature on international students focused on the changes brought about by the terrorist attacks of September 11, 2001. While a small number of authors discussed international students as potential security risks (e.g. Borjas 2002), the majority of publications of this time focused on the difficulties international students faced because of tightened visa regulations as well as legislation like the Patriot Act[1] which disproportionally affected international students from Muslim countries (e.g. Rizvi 2004; Florida 2005). Several publications at that time warned of the potential costs of restricting international student migrations such as lost revenue from a smaller market share of international students, shortages of skilled labor and associated decline in global competitiveness, and reduced opportunities for the internationalization of American higher education, and made concrete recommendations for maintaining the United States' competitiveness on the international higher education market (e.g. NAFSA 2003).

Since then, the migration literature has returned to examining migration intentions and decisions. Several scholars have examined why international students go abroad. While many students study in other countries to gain experiences abroad or improve their career chances, their decisions are not taken in a vacuum. For example, their migration decisions may be influenced by their parents' migration history as well as their own experiences with other forms of mobility such as travel (Van Mol and Timmermann 2013) or by family ties (e.g. the need to return home to take care of ageing parents, or the desire to be with a partner; Raghuram 2012). In some cases, political or economic circumstances can motivate students to go abroad (King and Raghuram 2013). Social networks and the media can also play a role, as they shape the perceptions of places of destination prospective international students develop (Beech 2014).

A few studies have focused on factors that influence where students go to study. Distance from the home country, the language spoken in the host country, colonial linkages, per capita income, pre-existing migrant stocks, cost of living, and climate have been identified as important considerations in studies that examine international student migrations among a large number of countries across the world (Perkins and Neumeyer 2014).

Most studies about particular groups of students to date have focused on students from countries with less developed systems of higher education to those with high prestige (vertical migration). As a consequence, less is known about students who migrate horizontally, such as from Western Europe to North America (Brooks and Waters 2011). However, some research has been published on British students, arguing that they place a lot of value on attending a world-class university (King et al. 2013) and experience fewer adjustment problems as they do not have to adjust to radically different environments (Brooks and Waters 2011).

While several scholars have examined the reasons why students choose to study abroad, less is known about their decision to stay in the host country or return to their home countries. Alberts and Hazen (2005) and Hazen and Alberts (2006, 2013) examined the factors that international students consider when pondering their migration trajectories after graduating from United States universities. Broadly speaking, they argued that students consider a wide range of personal, societal, and professional reasons in their decisions. The importance attached to each group of factors or individual factor depends on the individual circumstances of the student (e.g. whether the student is married or in a committed relationship) as well as conditions in the home country.

Lu, Zong, and Schissel (2009) conducted a similar study with international students in Canada, and found that family status, friends, and gender were important factors in shaping migration decisions, but also identified students' academic performance and their experience abroad as significant factors. Men in their sample tended to prioritize professional factors, while women's intentions were often based on what they called emotional and relational factors.

Soon (2012) found that for international students contemplating returning from New Zealand family support, discipline of study, and perceived opportunities to use the knowledge and skills acquired abroad also mattered. Mosneaga and Winther (2013) concluded that ultimately it is the strength of attachment students have formed to the host country that determines whether a student will stay or leave; however, they also point to the difficulty of getting visas or finding an appropriate job as constraining the choices. Geddie (2013) emphasized the importance of personal ties in shaping migration decisions, such as caring for ageing parents or children or negotiating dual career partnerships.

Hardly any studies exist about returnees (Bevis and Lucas 2007). One of the few exceptions is Butcher (2004), who examined the experiences of East Asian students after their return from New Zealand, and found that a considerable percentage experienced reverse culture shock and had difficulty readjusting to their home countries. Data about returnees are also limited (Bevis and Lucas 2007). Based on tax records, Finn (2010) calculated that about 60 percent of international Ph.D. recipients stay in the United States. He also discovered that stay rates varied significantly among different nationalities and disciplines, with Chinese and Indians as well as engineering and computer science graduates being particularly likely to stay in the United States. Because of the difficulties of accurately determining return rates, many academic studies use return intentions as a useful indicator, even though it is acknowledged that intentions do not always translate into actions given the number of constraints people encounter. The present study examines both initial migration decisions as well as return migration intentions. It considers a wide range of different factors that shape migration intentions, but also looks at the possibility of migration to a third country.

While the two bodies of literature discussed above mostly focus on the students themselves, the literature on internationalization of higher education and globalization examines the broader impact of international student migrations. Many studies list the contributions that international students make to the host country as well as their host institutions, such as financial benefits through paying high tuition fees, enhancing the reputation of academic institutions, and contributing to internationalization agendas (e.g. Childress 2009). Especially in an era when countries and institutions are competing against one another, international students are seen as a valuable asset; therefore the competition for talent has become another topic of study. In order to remain competitive in attracting international students, it is argued that it is necessary to offer financial support to students, have clear and easy visa procedures, and make it possible for people to stay after graduation (Florida 2005; Bevis and Lucas 2007; Wadhwa 2012).

In earlier writings on international students and other skilled people more generally, it was often argued that the migrations to another country would result in a permanent brain drain for the country of origin. However, by now this somewhat simplistic notion has largely been replaced by understandings of these migrations as leading to brain exchanges, brain circulation, or other forms of knowledge transfers (Gaillard and Gaillard 1997; Brooks and Waters 2011). Brain exchange or circulation can be realized through return migration. Some researchers now prefer the term mobility rather than migration to emphasize the temporary nature of the migrations of many highly skilled people (Brooks and Waters 2011). Knowledge exchange can also be accomplished through building up networks from abroad that are facilitated by the increasing globalization of research activities as well as new forms of communication (Gaillard and Gaillard 1997).

Despite the large number of studies now available on international students, some notable gaps remain. The vast majority of studies focus on international students from a particular country or region of origin, but relatively few look across the entire spectrum of international students, including those from countries of different levels of development. Similarly, many studies on migration examine graduate students, but pay less attention to undergraduate students, and have been carried out at prestigious research institutions. As a consequence, relatively little is known about students at universities that are focused on teaching, not internationally known, and have small numbers of international students. This study is designed to begin to address these gaps.

Methods

In order to uncover the factors that international students consider in their migration decisions, I designed an online survey in Qualtrics. The survey contained mostly closed questions, with some asking students to choose the answer that most closely described their situation and others allowing multiple responses to allow students to mark all the factors that they considered in their decisions. The first part of the survey covered general background information such as country of origin, age, field of study, relationship status, self-reported English proficiency, and level of education. The second segment asked international students about the reasons for coming to the United States, whether they considered other countries as possible destinations, and what factors led them to choose their city or institution. The final part of the survey asked respondents to consider the advantages and disadvantages of staying in the United States or returning to their home countries. In addition to the closed questions (with answer categories derived from the literature), I also included a small number of open-ended questions to allow students to list which other countries they considered and why.

One of the goals of my study was to survey students at different types of institutions and at different levels of study (an approach that has rarely been used to date) in order to see how the experiences of students vary in these different contexts. I contacted the international offices of the twelve universities that are part of the University of Wisconsin system in spring of 2014. Eight universities agreed to send out information about my study to their international students, either via email or included in a newsletter for international students. Partly because of the survey distribution method (which did not allow any follow-up messages or reminders to increase participation), only 124 students responded to my survey. The number of responses varied among institutions, with proportionally more students responding from those institutions where an email was sent encouraging them to participate as opposed to those that mentioned the survey in a newsletter. Several of the international offices who cooperated commented that recently international students had been sent several surveys from different organizations to complete, providing a possible explanation why only a small percentage of international students took the time to respond to the survey.

Despite the relatively small number of responses, the survey was completed by a good cross-section of international students (Table 3.1). The sample was almost evenly split between men and women, as well as those studying at research universities and teaching-intensive institutions. Respondents included people of different ages, from all major world regions except Oceania, from diverse fields of study, and with varying levels of English proficiency (as reported by the students, so these data are a reflection of how the students judge their own proficiency). It is worth noting that almost two-thirds of the respondents were undergraduate students. Less than half (39.2 percent) described themselves as being in a long-term relationship, and 8.1 percent had children. Finally, it is important to point out that almost half (49.2 percent) had never been to the United States before coming as international students. As will be discussed later, these characteristics influence how international students take their migration decisions.

In this book, I almost exclusively report the summary data obtained from the survey. The data were downloaded from Qualtrics and processed in SPSS. In some cases, data had to be recoded or recategorized as the number of responses to some answer choices was too low to allow any meaningful statements. Unless otherwise noted, the number of students who responded to each question was over 120; percentages given always refer to the actual number of respondents and ignore those who chose not to respond to a particular question.

Initial Plans for Study Abroad

Studying in another country is not an easy decision. As opportunities for studying abroad have significantly expanded over time, potential international students can now choose among a number of different host countries and institutions. Among the students in my sample, 44.6 percent only considered the United States as a possible destination, reflecting the country's preeminent status as a destination for international students. A further 41.3 percent considered other host countries, but ultimately decided to go to the United States. Some students—5.8 percent—actually would have preferred to study in another country, but ended up in the United States as plans to study elsewhere did not work out. A further 8.3 percent would have preferred to stay in their home countries, but ended up going to the United States regardless. Taken together, these results clearly indicate that for many students, the United States is still the most desirable destination to study abroad. However, it is important to note that almost half of the international students surveyed considered other destinations, indicating that the United States must be proactive in ensuring that it does not fall behind in the race for global

Table 3.1 Characteristics of Survey Respondents

Characteristic	*Number*	*Percentage*
Gender		
Male	62	50.4
Female	61	49.6
Age		
Under 21 years of age	26	22.4
Between 21 and 29	73	62.9
30 and over	17	14.7
Region of Origin		
North America	2	1.7
Latin America	21	17.5
Europe	18	15.0
Africa	9	7.5
Asia	56	46.7
Middle East	14	11.7
Level of Study		
Undergraduate	79	64.8
Graduate (Master's)	16	13.1
Graduate (Ph.D.)	26	21.3
Type of University		
Research university	60	48.4
Teaching-intensive institution	64	51.6
Field of Study		
Languages	10	8.1
Humanities	3	2.4
Social Science	14	11.4
Natural Science	17	13.8
Business/Economics	27	22.0
Health	13	10.6
Engineering	26	21.1
Other	13	10.6
Relationship Status		
Single or in a short-term relationship	73	60.8
Stable relationship with someone from home country	30	25.0
Stable relationship with some from the United States	11	9.2
Stable relationship with someone from elsewhere	6	5.0
Children	10	8.1
English Proficiency		
Native speaker of English	9	7.3
Fluent speaker of English	30	24.4
Good English skills	41	33.3
Satisfactory English skills	41	33.3
Limited English skills	2	1.6
Previous Experience in the United States		
Been to the United States as a tourist before	35	28.2
Studied or worked in the United States before	40	32.2
In the United States for the first time	61	49.2

talent as other host countries become more attractive and recruit actively. More research is needed to uncover exactly how students decide which country to go to. For example, what information did they have available when they thought about where to study and why did they ultimately choose the United States over other countries?

Among those students (N = 52) who listed which country or countries they considered in addition to the United States, other English-speaking countries featured prominently: 40.1 percent considered going to the UK, 25.0 percent thought about studying in Canada, and 13.5 percent checked out Australia as a possible destination. This preference list clearly reflects the overall popularity of these countries for international students and other migrants as well as the fact that English is the most widely spoken second language. Some students also considered non-English-speaking countries, such as France and Japan (both marked by 9.6 percent of respondents) as well as Germany and Italy (7.7 percent each). In addition, respondents listed a wide variety of other European countries (Austria, Belgium, Greece, Ireland, the Netherlands, Norway, Poland, Sweden, Switzerland, Turkey) as possible destinations, as well as a few countries in other world regions (Dubai, Egypt, South Africa, South Korea, Thailand). In most cases, the countries considered were neighboring countries (e.g. French students considering Italy or German students considering the Netherlands), regional leaders (e.g. South Africa for African students), or countries that share the same or similar languages (e.g. Austrian or Swiss students considering Germany or West African students considering France). This clearly indicates that for students pondering studying in non-English-speaking destination countries, geographic proximity and linguistic similarities are important considerations.

When reporting these data by world region rather than individual country, a strong preference for European countries becomes visible, as Europe was chosen by 90.4 percent of all respondents in my sample as a possible alternative to studying in the United States. One quarter considered North America (i.e. Canada), 17.3 percent Asia, and 15.4 percent Oceania (i.e. Australia and New Zealand). The proportion of students selecting African or Latin American destinations was very small, indicating that these regions are not yet attractive as study abroad destinations. The results from this study clearly confirm the preeminence of North America, Western Europe, and Oceania as well as of English-speaking countries as desirable destinations for international students. This is also reflected in research, as few studies exist about international students in other host countries (see also Basford's study of international students in Norway in Chapter 5).

Choosing a Country and University

As mentioned above, over 80 percent of the students in my sample either only considered the United States as a destination, or eventually chose it as the host country after checking out opportunities in other potential host countries. Student respondents were given a list of answer choices derived from the literature and asked to mark all the reasons they considered in their decision. By far the most popular reason for students to choose the United States was the perceived "quality of a US education," marked by 73.4 percent of respondents. Roughly two-thirds of all respondents chose "desire to improve English" (64.5 percent), "desire to gain international experiences" (64.5 percent), as well as the "desire to experience another culture" (62.9 percent). Around half of the respondents were attracted by the "reputation of a US degree" (52.4 percent), and the "belief that a US degree would enhance career prospects in the home country" (47.6 percent).

Among the top six factors, three refer to the quality of the US education system. The broadest, the overall quality of a US education, was the most popular choice. For about half of the students obtaining a US degree held promise, showing that there is a strong belief that studying in the United States will be a quality experience and enhance career prospects at home. Among the top six answers, three are not strictly speaking academic motivations and could presumably be fulfilled by studying in another (English-speaking) host country: the more general reasons of wanting to improve language skills, gaining international experience, and experiencing another culture.

In the literature it has been argued that international students do not take their migration decisions in a vacuum, but are influenced by their families or friendship networks. Among my respondents, 31.5 percent reported that they were encouraged by their families to study abroad, but friends played a smaller role, with less than 15 percent of respondents reporting that friends had encouraged them to go. A similar percentage (11.4 percent) wanted to join friends who were already in the United States. Only a few students became international students because they accompanied a family member (4.8 percent), so the vast majority migrated independently from their families.

Finally, it has often been argued that the availability of funding and the quality of research facilities are major factors drawing international students to the United States. In my sample, only 29.0 percent marked the "quality of research facilities," and 23.4 percent the "availability of funding" as factors considered. However, it has to be kept in mind that about two thirds of my sample are undergraduate students; the quality of research facilities is likely not as critical for them as for graduate students who do their own research. Otherwise the findings reported above largely mirror those in other studies on the reasons why international students choose the United States as a destination country. However, very few other studies have looked at what factors international students consider when choosing a destination *within* the United States.

About half of my respondents (48.3 percent) did not care where in the United States they would study. Since many students simply want to gain experiences abroad, seek to improve their English skills, or are more generally attracted to the US education system, this is perhaps unsurprising. Some 15.8 percent wanted to study elsewhere in the United States, but ended up in Wisconsin as other opportunities did not work out. By contrast, one fifth of the respondents had a regional preference, with 10.8 percent stating that they wanted to study in the Midwest, and 9.2 more specifically in the state of Wisconsin. Unfortunately this study cannot answer the question what attracted them to the region or the state specifically. However, it needs to be remembered that about 15 percent of the respondents had reported that they were joining friends or family members in the United States, so the locational preference was likely shaped by what they learned from the people they know. This may be even more so the case for those who wanted to study in the city they are currently living in (6.7 percent), or the university they are currently at (9.2 percent). Taken together, 35.0 percent of the respondents had specific ideas where they wanted to be.

These findings are important for two reasons: first, for a significant proportion of the students, all that counts is being in the United States, and they do not really care where they are. This is in line with the earlier observation that many want a study abroad experience that includes being exposed to a different culture and language, and gaining international experience, so the exact location does not really matter. Second, about a third of the students had more concrete ideas regarding their destination, which can be explained by prior knowledge about these places (whether a specific state, city, or university) on which they based their decision. Since the majority of my respondents reported that they had never been to the United States before becoming international students or only visited as tourists, it is unlikely that they had access to large amounts of first-hand information. This, in turn, suggests the importance of networks, but also means that states, cities, or universities could potentially influence international student flows through information and marketing campaigns. Clearly, more research on this issue is necessary.

While my study did not delve deeper into why prospective students chose a specific place (at the scale of the region, state, or city), I asked what reasons they had for choosing the specific university they are at. The top two reasons were connected to the perceived quality of the university, with 33.1 percent marking the "quality of the department" and 29.0 percent the "reputation of the university." A further 15.3 percent indicated that they chose the university to "work with a specific professor," and 8.1 to use "specific research facilities." As expected, factors related to the quality of the experience were more important for graduate students and those at research universities, while factors such as recommendations and knowing people already at this institution mattered more for those at teaching-intensive institutions and undergraduates.

More research is needed to uncover on what information international students base their evaluation. For example, do they consult global ranking tables? How do they find out about the quality or reputation of a university that is not included in global rankings (for example, because it is a teaching-focused institution)? One answer may be that information flows along social networks. For example, a quarter of all respondents (26.6 percent) marked "people I know attended this university and recommended it." In addition, 12.1 percent noted that "people at home recommended this university" and 10.5 percent "joined other people (e.g. friend, sibling) who were already there." While there is possibly some overlap among the students marking these categories (e.g. the person who recommended the university could be the same person the student is joining now), the results indicate that networks may play an important role in determining university choices for some students. Especially when the main motivations are to gain experience abroad and experience another culture (as opposed to academic or career-enhancement reasons), positive reports from people who have been or are at that specific university could play a large role. This, in turn, suggests that making sure that international students have a good experience is not just important for the students themselves, but could indirectly have an influence on international student recruitment.

Future Plans

Just as coming to the United States was a big decision, the question of whether to stay in the United States for a longer period of time or returning to the home country after graduation is also difficult for many international students. Correspondingly, 19.2 percent of the international students in my sample do not know yet what they will do after graduation. While a few students (1.7 percent) want to leave as soon as they can, it is much more common for students to want to return after they finish their degrees (37.5 percent). For others, however, studying in the United States is just a springboard to a longer stay: 30.0 percent want to stay at least a few years after finishing their degrees, and 11.7 percent want to stay permanently.

Similar patterns emerge when students are asked more specifically for their plans after graduation in the United States. Almost a third (29.2 percent) want to stay in the United States to work, and another 19.2 percent hope to continue their education at another university in the United States. By contrast, 21.7 percent want to return to their home countries to work, with an additional 12.5 percent planning to continue their education in their home country. While for most students the decision is between their home country and the United States, for 6.6 percent the future might be in a third country for study or work. It is important to remember that international students stated their intentions in these responses; whether or not they actually stay or return cannot be assessed by this study.

The decision what to do after graduation is in many ways even more complex than the original decision to come to the United States to study, as international students are now familiar with two countries and education systems. They can compare them with one another, and more broadly consider the advantages and disadvantages of returning home or staying in the United States (Table 3.2).

In regards to factors that encourage international students to stay in the United States, the most popular choices are broadly connected to economic issues as well as quality of life. The most popular choices were the "better quality of life [noneconomic factors] in the United States compared to the home country," a "more diverse society in the United States," and "better job prospects in the United States," all marked by about 40 percent of the respondents. A "higher salary" and the "higher economic standard of living," two economic factors, were considered important by about a third of the respondents. Beyond quality of life and economic standard of living as well as professional factors, more freedom was also an important factor for many students, especially those from Asia,

Table 3.2 Factors Considered Regarding a Possible Return Migration

	Number	*Percentage*
Factors Encouraging Staying in the United States		
Better quality of life (noneconomic factors)	52	41.9
More diverse society than in my home country	49	39.5
Better job prospects in my home country	48	38.7
More academic freedom than in my home country	47	37.9
Higher salary compared to my home country	44	35.5
Higher standard of living than in my home country	43	34.7
More political freedom/stability	37	29.8
Family ties/opportunities for children in the United States	11	8.9
Factors Discouraging Staying in the United States		
Not really feeling at home	59	47.6
Difficulty in getting a visa	43	34.7
Feeling lonely or isolated	34	27.4
Different cultural priorities (e.g. work-life balance)	33	26.6
Prejudice or discrimination encountered in the US	27	21.8
Feeling alienated from United States culture	26	21.0
Different understandings of friendship in the United States	24	19.4
Poor quality of life (e.g. few friends, materialism, etc.)	23	18.5
Factors Encouraging a Return to the Home Country		
Family and friendship ties in my home country	102	82.3
Feeling more comfortable in my home country	63	50.8
Family obligations in my home country	57	46.0
Better quality of life in my home country (noneconomic factors)	27	21.8
Better job prospects in my home country	19	15.3
Higher salary in my home country	17	13.7
Factors Discouraging a Return to the Home Country		
Difficulty in finding a job	51	41.1
Poorer standard of living in my home country	43	34.7
Poorer quality of life in my home country	42	33.9
Economic situation in my home country	38	30.6
Political situation in my home country	31	25.0
Conflict or lack of political freedom in my home country	30	24.2
Restrictive cultural practices (e.g. status of women)	18	14.5
Concern whether US degree will be accepted	12	9.7

Africa, and the Middle East, with 37.9 percent marking "more academic freedom" and 29.8 percent "more political freedom" as factors they considered. For a relatively small proportion of students, family ties in the United States were an important motivator to stay.

While generally speaking economic or professional factors were particularly important in encouraging international students to stay in the United States, it is mostly personal factors that discourage them from doing so. Almost half (47.6 percent) of international students report "not really feeling at home" as a significant factor discouraging them from staying. This factor was particularly important for students from world regions that are culturally quite different from the

United States (Africa, Asia, and the Middle East). About a quarter of respondents each marked "feeling lonely or isolated" and "different cultural priorities [e.g. family vs. career] in the US" For about a fifth of the students "feeling alienated from US culture" and different "understandings of friendship" as well as "poorer quality of life" were significant factors. Which factors most discouraged students from staying in the United States varied by world region. To cite just two examples, Europeans were particularly likely to struggle with different understandings of friendships, while for Latin Americans different priorities in life were an important factor.

In summary, for many the main factors speaking against staying in the United States are linked to them not feeling comfortable in the country, in large part due to cultural differences. However, two other factors stand out as not falling under this broad heading. The second most popular answer choice was "difficulty in getting a visa," with 34.7 percent of the students expressing concern. Interestingly, this concern was most pronounced among Europeans, who probably face the least difficulty with obtaining a visa. This confirms that one of the biggest obstacles to keeping international students in the country is actual or perceived difficulty connected to immigration status. A second factor that was marked by one fifth (21.8 percent) of respondents also warrants attention: "prejudice or discrimination encountered in the United States," reported mostly by students from Asia and Africa.

Beyond providing us with information about which factors discourage international students from staying in the United States, these results also provide the basis for a call for action. If the United States wants to continue to keep international students in the country as workers, visa and green card procedures must be simplified and streamlined, as has been demanded multiple times since 2001. However, action also has to be taken at the universities themselves. While it is difficult to fight prejudice and discrimination, it is necessary that universities review their policies and programs to see whether there is anything else they can do to address such issues. Furthermore, universities should also seriously consider the fact that a substantial proportion of international students do not feel comfortable. Once again, there is no easy recipe to "fix the problem," but cultural awareness programs and other programming aimed at increasing intercultural understanding, offering mentoring and counseling, and other interventions supporting international students can go a long way in cushioning the effects of cultural shock and feeling out of place.

While economic factors encouraged many international students to stay in the United States for a longer period, the most important factors encouraging students to return home are friends and family (Table 3.2). Over four-fifths (82.3 percent) of respondents marked "family and friendship ties" as an important factor in favor of returning home. For almost half of the students this goes beyond wanting to be with family as they are motivated by "family obligations" to return home, a factor that was more frequently mentioned by men than by women. Cultural factors also act as a pull to return home, with half of student respondents marking "feeling more comfortable at home" as a reason to return. For at least some students, the expected "quality of life" at home is higher. Surprisingly this factor was not just marked by Europeans, but also a strong consideration for African students. Some also consider "better job prospects" and "higher salaries" as attractions. Again, in addition to Europeans, these answers were particularly frequent among African students.

Whether or not job prospects, salaries, standard of living, and quality of life are higher or lower in the home country than in the United States is obviously dependent on the specific home country, explaining why these factors were listed less frequently than the family-related and cultural factors encouraging a return home. Because of the differences among countries of origin, the same factors listed by some as encouraging a return home were listed by others as factors discouraging a return to the home country. For example, 41.1 percent of the students were concerned about "difficulty in finding a job" and about a third believed that their "standard of living would be poorer in my home country" and expected the "quality of life" to be less desirable. Interestingly, these factors were reported at higher rates by Latin American students than those from other world regions.

A second set of factors discouraging a return home refers to the economic and political situation in the home country, which obviously also varies significantly among home countries. About a third of student respondents were concerned about the "economic situation," and a quarter about the "political situation" and "conflict or lack of political freedom." Some respondents were also discouraged by "restrictive cultural practices" in the home country.

When students consider whether or not to stay in the United States or return home after graduation they think through a large number of factors spanning the broad realms of economic and political issues, quality of life, culture, family and friends, and others. Which factor or group of factors is ultimately most important depends on the individual and his or her family situation (e.g. being married to an American might tip the balance in favor of staying in the United States rather than returning home to be with family there). However, students from countries that struggle economically and/or politically have to deal with the additional complication of finding their personal choices constrained by the conditions in the country.

Migration to Third Countries

As described above, almost half of the international students surveyed had considered a country other than the United States as their destination country for studying abroad. After graduation, students once again face the choice of potentially going to a country other than their home country or the United States. When asked about their plans for the future, only a relatively small percentage (6.6 percent) indicated that they planned to go to a third country to work or continue their studies. Nevertheless, in an open response box, students provided a list of other countries that they would consider going to. A very small number of students were open to just about any place, with one student writing:

"Anywhere. I don't really care about which country will be better, but what I can do there." For most respondents, possible destination countries were the same as those many had initially considered for studying abroad, with Canada (26.3 percent), the UK (21.0 percent), Germany (21.0 percent), and Australia (17.5 percent) topping the list.

In their comments, some students provided brief explanations. Several students commented that Canada was their top choice mainly because it was easier to get a work permit, green card, and citizenship than in the United States. Some students, however, saw rather specific advantages of the country they considered. For example, one student wrote: "Germany: higher salary, higher living quality, better insurance." For other students, geographic proximity was an important factor. For instance, one student said: "Somewhere in the Middle East because I can be closer to my home country." Finally, some respondents thought primarily about quality of life issues. For example, one chose "Costa Rica, Mexico, Brazil—tropical countries with friendly people and good job opportunities" and another "Canada or Australia: beautiful environment, diverse culture, and people are nice."

To date, little is known about students who migrate to a third country after graduation. In my sample, only a small percentage of the students pondered going to another country, yet external circumstances such as the availability of jobs or difficulties with getting a visa to stay in the United States may mean that ultimately more students have to consider this possibility.

Concluding Thoughts

This study examined international students' migration decisions at two key points in their academic careers: their initial decision to seek a degree in the United States as well as their thoughts about returning home or staying in the United States after their graduation. For most students, factors such as wanting to gain international experiences, perfecting their English skills, or experiencing another culture are important motivators for going abroad. These expectations can be met by multiple locations; consequently a significant proportion of international students considered other, predominantly English-speaking, countries as possible destinations. For many, the reputation and quality of a US education was important, explaining why many eventually chose to come to the United States. While many students did not have a preference for a particular place within the United States, some wanted to come to a particular state, a particular city, or a particular university, which can partly be explained by information they obtained through social networks. This aspect clearly warrants more research, as little is known about what information prospective international students have available and how strong the influence of their social networks is on the destination choice.

The decision what to do after graduation is even more complex, as international students now possess much more knowledge about the host country and can compare it to their home country. For many, the decision involves considering a large number of different factors. Which factors are ultimately the most important depends on the personal situation of a student, perceived job prospects, and the general conditions in the home country. Clearly, more work involving students from a wide variety of countries is necessary to further unravel how external circumstances (in addition to the personal situation) influence future plans. In particular, it is important to distinguish among students who have engaged in horizontal migration (migration between two countries with a similar level of development) and those who migrated vertically. For the latter, there is not only potentially a larger difference in general conditions between the two countries, but also more cultural difference, which shaped their experiences as international students and is likely to continue to affect their future lives.

Gaining a better understanding of how international students make migration decisions is important for several different reasons. First, making migration decisions is difficult, complex, and often agonizing, so prospective migrants need the best information possible to help them every step of the way. Second, while they are getting their degrees, it is important to offer support services that help students feel comfortable in the United States. Beyond helping the students during their stay, this may have an influence on their future migration decisions as well as the recruitment of additional international students through their social networks. Third, beyond the benefits to the students themselves, having a better understanding of which factors are critical to students' migration decisions can also help the United States stay competitive in the race for global talent.

Conceptually, this study clearly demonstrates the need for approaching the migration of international students and other highly skilled people holistically. This work draws on and contributes to various bodies of literature, as the migration and experiences of individuals cannot be divorced from the larger contexts in which they are embedded. Furthermore, a complex issue such as a migration decision cannot be boiled down to just a few factors or considerations. Only by studying students from different backgrounds and different contexts of reception in the host country as well as a wide range of factors can we begin to reveal the full spectrum of motivations, opportunities, and constraints that shape their migration decisions.

This study shows that studies of the international migration of the highly skilled simultaneously need to become more broad and more specific. Many studies to date have focused on students from particular countries or world regions. All these contribute important pieces to the puzzle of explaining student migrations, yet a broader understanding can only be reached when we can separate the factors that matter for all migrants from those that are specific to particular countries or regions through studies with a comparative approach. At the same time, studies need to become more specific, to move beyond the level of the country to explaining how skilled migrants choose their destinations at the scale of the region, state, city, or institution/employer, what information they have available when they make their decision, and how their decisions are influenced by their social and professional networks.

Note

1. The Patriot Act was signed into law by President George W. Bush after the terrorist attacks of September 11, 2001. The official name of the act (USA PATRIOT) stands for "Uniting and Strengthening America by Providing Appropriate Tools Required to Intercept and Obstruct Terrorism."

References

Alberts, H., and H. Hazen. 2005. 'There are always two voices …' International students' intentions to stay in the United States or return to their home countries. *International Migration* 43 (3): 131–154.

Beech, S. 2014. Why place matters: Imaginative geography and international student mobility. *Area* 46 (2): 170–177.

Bevis, T. B., and C. J. Lucas. 2007. *International students in American colleges and universities. A history.* New York: Palgrave Macmillan.

Borjas, G. 2002. Rethinking foreign students: A question of the national interest. *National Review* 54 (11). Available at: www.hks.harvard.edu/fs/gborjas/publications/popular/NR061702.htm (last accessed March 2, 2016).

Brooks, R., and J. Waters. 2011. *Student mobilities, migration, and the internationalization of higher education.* London: Palgrave Macmillan.

Butcher, A. 2004. Departures and arrivals: International students returning to the countries of origin. *Asian and Pacific Migration Journal* 13 (3): 275–303.

Childress, L. 2009. Internationalization for higher education institutions. *Journal of Studies in International Education* 13 (3): 289–309.

Eland, A., and K. Thomas. 2013. Succeeding abroad: International students in the United States. In *International students and scholars in the United States: Coming from abroad*, eds. H. C. Alberts and H. D. Hazen, 145–162. New York: Palgrave Macmillan.

Finn, M. 2011. Stay rates of foreign doctorate recipients from U.S. universities, 2007. Oak Ridge Institute for Science and Education. Available at: https://orise.orau.gov/files/sep/stay-rates-foreign-doctorate-recipients-2007.pdf (last accessed March 2, 2016).

Florida, R. 2005. *The flight of the creative class: The new global competition for talent.* New York: HarperCollins.

Gaillard, J., and A. M. Gaillard. 1997. The international mobility of brains: Exodus or circulation. *Science, Technology & Society* 2 (2): 195–228.

Geddie, K. 2013. The transnational ties that bind: Relationship considerations for graduating international science and engineering research students. *Population, Space and Place* 19: 196–208.

Hazen, H., and H. Alberts. 2006. Visitors or immigrants? International students in the United States. *Population, Space and Place* 12: 201–216.

———. 2013. 'Too many things pull me back and forth'. Return intentions and transnationalism among international students. In *International students and scholars in the United States: Coming from abroad*, eds. H. C. Alberts and H. D. Hazen, 65–87. New York: Palgrave Macmillan.

King, R., and P. Raghuram. 2013. International student migration: Mapping the field and new research agendas. *Population, Space and Place* 19: 127–137.

King, R., A. Findlay, J. Ahrens, and A. Geddes. 2013. British students in the United States: Motivations, experiences, and career aspirations. In *International students and scholars in the United States: Coming from abroad*, eds. H. C. Alberts and H. D. Hazen, 25–45. New York: Palgrave Macmillan.

Lee, J. 2007. Neo-racism toward international students. A critical need for change. *About Campus*, January/February. Available at: http://onlinelibrary.wiley.com/doi/10.1002/abc.194/pdf (last accessed March 2, 2016).

Lu, Y., L. Zong, and B. Schissel. 2009. To stay or return: Migration intentions of students from People's Republic of China in Saskatchewan, Canada. *International Migration & Integration* 10: 283–310.

Mosneaga, A., and L. Winther. 2013. Emerging talents? International students before and after their career start in Denmark. *Population, Space and Place* 19: 181–195.

NAFSA. 2003. In America's interest: Welcoming international students." Report of the Strategic Task Force on International Student Access. Available at: www.nafsa.org/uploadedFiles/NAFSA_Home/Resource_Library_Assets/Public_Policy/in_america_s_interest.pdf (last accessed March 2, 2016)

Perkins, R., and E. Neumeyer. 2014. Geographies of educational mobilities: Exploring the uneven flows of international students. *The Geographical Journal* 180 (3): 246–259.

Raghuram, P. 2012. Theorising the spaces of student migration. *Population, Space and Place* 19: 138–154.

Rizvi, F. 2004. Debating globalization and education after September 11. *Comparative Education* 40 (2): 157–171.

Soon, J.-J. 2012. "Home is where the heart is? Factors determining international students' destination country upon completion of studies abroad. *Journal of Ethnic and Migration Studies* 38 (1): 147–162.

Sümer S., S. Poyrazl, and K. Grahame. 2008. Predictors of depression and anxiety among international students. *Journal of Counseling & Development* 86: 429–436.

Van Mol, C., and C. Timmerman. 2013. Should I stay or should I go? An analysis of the determinants of intra-European student mobility. *Population, Space and Place* 19: 127–137.

Wadhwa, V. 2012. *The immigrant exodus: Why America is losing the global race to capture entrepreneurial talent*. Philadelphia, PA: Wharton Digital Press.

4 European Mobile Students, (Trans)National Social Networks, and (Inter)National Career Perspectives

Christof Van Mol

Introduction

Over the last decades, the economic value of international students is increasingly recognized. Today, international students are considered important human capital for remaining competitive among global knowledge economies, which is reflected, for example, in the fact that many countries intend to attract the best and brightest students in order to incorporate them into their domestic labor market after graduation (Tremblay 2005; Kuptsch 2006; Lange 2013; Van Mol 2014b). Apart from their potential value for national economies, international students also often represent a lucrative source of funding for higher education institutions, as foreign students often pay high tuition fees compared to domestic students (Findlay 2011). Given this value of students for both national economies and higher education institutions, an increasing marketization of international higher education can be observed. Most recently, this trend is exemplified by the growing number of branch campuses, at which students can gain a degree from another country without actually moving residence (see Chapter 7 for a discussion of branch campuses in South Africa). Such exportation of higher education towards other countries, for example, generated approximately £496 million for the British economy in 2012–2013 (Mellors-Bourne et al. 2014).

In contrast to other world regions, however, the situation in Europe is different. Because of the establishment of the right to freedom of movement within the Schengen area, European students who move to another European country for study enjoy the same rights as domestic students. Therefore, they do not pay higher tuition fees and do not represent such a lucrative funding source for higher education systems compared to students from outside the European Union. Furthermore, in contrast to other world regions, credit mobility, whereby students move abroad for a delineated period of time (usually a semester or a full academic year) in the framework of their degree, is more common than degree mobility in Europe (Brooks and Waters 2011). This prevalence of credit mobility can be attributed to a large extent to the establishment of the Erasmus program (European Community Action Scheme for the Mobility of University Students) in 1987. Between 1987 and 2013, more than 3 million students spent an exchange period abroad within the framework of this program (European Commission 2014a).

One of the main rationales of the program is in line with the trend described above—namely, ensuring economic competitiveness of the European Union among global knowledge economies (Van Mol 2014b). It is expected that European students participating in the program will be more prone to become mobile workers within the European labor market after graduation (Van Mol 2014a, 2014b). This is particularly important as intra-European labor mobility remains rather low (Castro-Martín and Cortina 2015), and the European Commission tries to stimulate such mobility to enhance a more integrated and efficient economy (Recchi 2015).

The assumption that former exchange students would be more prone to move in their future careers is in line with the traditional migration literature suggesting that once moved, migrants are likely to move again (Bailey 1989, 1993; Massey and Espinosa 1997; Massey and Zenteno 1999; Deléchat 2001). Whereas students who participate in student exchange programs also show greater willingness for later geographical mobility compared to those who did not go abroad (King and Ruiz-Gelices 2003; Harzing 2004; Cammelli, Ghiselli, and Mignoli 2008; Fabian and Minks 2008; Rosenmund, Geiderer, and Kickingereder 2012; Van Mol 2014a, 2014b), few studies investigated the ways exchange experiences influence returnees' behavior and aspirations after their return (Gu and Schweisfurth 2015). Therefore, in this chapter I investigate possible mechanisms explaining why some former Erasmus students are more prone for remigration than others. Drawing on the literature on repeat migration, I particularly focus on how individual human and social capital acquired abroad influences students' propensity to move again in the future. My analysis is based on a large-scale online survey I conducted in 2011 with 2,298 former European exchange students in Austria, Belgium, Denmark, Finland, Italy, the Netherlands, Norway, Portugal, Spain, Sweden, and the United Kingdom. The findings illustrate that student mobility can be considered a precursor to international skilled migration. Compared to non-participating students, exchange students have higher aspirations to move again in their future careers. Based on migration theory, it should be expected that students' remigration intentions are explained by the human and social capital they accumulated abroad. Contrary to these expectations, however, the findings illustrate how particularly personal characteristics and competences in terms of acquired human capital play a key role in explaining migration aspirations, when controlling for confounding factors. Considering social capital, the findings strongly suggest that instead of the newly formed international social networks, the local friendship network in the home country is more constitutive in forming students' spatial aspirations. Furthermore, maintenance of contact with the majority of international friends made abroad shows to be more important than merely the formation of an international social network. In sum, students' mobility experience is linked to specific places of origin and destination as well as national and international spatial relationships, stretching the boundaries of spaces wherein they used to move. Nevertheless, the analysis suggests that students' future migration aspirations are mainly grounded within local spaces and places instead of in the transnational arena.

The chapter is structured as follows. First, I give a contextual overview of intra-European exchanges. Second, I provide the theoretical background underpinning this chapter. Thereafter, I present the methodology and in the following section, I present the results. In a final section, I discuss the results and conclude.

Setting the Context: European Student Mobility in Numbers

Although intra-European student mobility has historical antecedents such as the *Grand Tour* during the Renaissance (e.g. Brilli 1995) or the exchange programs of the *Deutscher Akadmischer Austauch Dienst* (DAAD) and the British Council (Gürüz 2011), it is only from the mid 1980s onwards that student mobility became a key issue of internationalization policies of European universities, particularly with the introduction of the Erasmus program in 1987 (Van Mol 2014b). The program experienced a significant growth in outgoing student numbers. Whereas in 1987, only 3,244 students from 11 European countries participated, in 2013 the third millionth student participated in the program. Furthermore, in the academic year 2012–2013, the number of participating countries was 33 (28 EU member states, Iceland, Liechtenstein, former Yugoslav Republic of Macedonia, Norway, and Turkey), and it covered about 90 percent of European universities. The budget allocated to the program can also be considered impressive: between 2007 and 2013 alone, €3.7 billion has been allocated to the Erasmus program, and the average monthly grant students received in 2012–2013 was €272 (European Commission 2014a). The grant varies per country of origin and destination, but can be combined with any additional national mobility and/or study grants. These numbers illustrate the growth of the program as well as the importance attached to it at a political level. Today, student mobility is considered a central element of the Europe 2020 strategy for growth and jobs, in the form of one of the seven flagship programs aiming to enhance the competitiveness of Europe (European Commission 2010b). Within this strategy, the flagship initiative "Youth on the Move" aims to facilitate the entry of young people into the European labor market after graduation. Student mobility is considered a key element within this program, providing member states a much needed, highly educated and mobile workforce (Van Mol 2014a, 2014b). After all, it is expected that those who move will be more prone to consider work abroad later on in their careers as well (European Commission 2010a).

Nevertheless, the Erasmus program is also confronted with many stereotypes. Critics argued that students would spend a long holiday abroad on costs of the European Commission, placing their academic interests largely in a secondary place while being abroad. Furthermore, it is often suggested that students would mainly head towards Southern Europe, motivated by factors such as the favorable climate and the relaxed culture. Indeed, if we consider the ten most popular institutions receiving Erasmus students in 2012–2013 (European Commission 2014a), this comprises six Spanish, two Italian, and one Slovenian institution. Also, at the aggregate country level, this trend seems to be confirmed: the most popular destination country is Spain, which receives approximately 40,000 students annually.

Nevertheless, Spain is not followed by other Southern European countries but by Germany, France, and the United Kingdom. Furthermore, at the city level, the most popular destinations are major European capitals and secondary cities like Madrid and Paris, followed by Barcelona, Lisbon, Valencia, Istanbul, Berlin, Prague, Vienna, and London (Van Mol and Ekamper 2016).

In sum, the mobility of European students has been lavishly funded by the European Commission, partly because of its anticipated economic outcomes. Nevertheless, whether the experience abroad makes those students more prone to move abroad again or whether they already have a priori a migrant personality (Boneva and Frieze, 2001) remains an open question.

Theoretical Considerations

Student Mobility and Highly Skilled Migration

When considering definitions of highly skilled migration, international students often do not fit. Lowell and Findlay (2001, 7), for example, defined it as "the movement of 'tertiary' educated persons, primarily those with at least four years of education after primary and secondary school (12 years)." Clearly, international students at the bachelor and master level do not hold their degree yet, and are consequently not covered by this definition. As such, rather than considering international students as a subcategory of international skilled migration, they form a distinct category of international migration (King 2002). In this chapter, I argue that even though they are different forms of mobility, student mobility and highly skilled migration show remarkable similarities. As Raghuram (2013) argued, the boundaries between international students and highly skilled migrants are increasingly blurring, due to often overlapping and shifting migrant categories through which individuals move. Furthermore, international students share many characteristics with highly skilled migrants. After all, highly skilled migrants are often mobile several times for obtaining specific skills needed by markets and clients (Beaverstock 1996). Mobile students regularly follow similar patterns: many of those who move during their studies already have prior international experience (e.g. Van Mol and Timmerman 2014). Furthermore, highly skilled migrants frequently have limited choices in terms of destination country or the duration of their stay abroad (Föbker, Temme, and Wiegandt 2014). The available options are generally highly dependent upon the structure and corporate policies of the company they are employed at (Föbker, Temme, and Wiegandt 2014). Similarly, participants in the Erasmus program are offered a limited range of potential destinations, as the destination offer depends on formal exchange agreements between higher education institutions. The duration of their stay abroad is commonly already established within these agreements as well. Finally, migration of the highly skilled is often not limited to a single movement to a single place, but regularly forms part of a chain of subsequent movements (Kõu et al. 2015). International student migration/mobility might only constitute a single fragment of students' mobile lives as well, and should therefore be studied in connection to mobility intentions in their future career (Findlay et al. 2012). As such, it is worthwhile to investigate whether future migration aspirations are indeed forged by participating in international exchange programs, as well as the mechanisms behind it.

Human and Social Capital Gains Abroad

In this chapter, I build on theories of repeat migration. In contrast to studies of migration and return migration, research into repeat migration and circular migration remains rather scarce (Constant and Zimmermann 2011, 2012). In traditional migration studies, "migration" points to the movement of an individual to another country. "Return migration" generally refers to the return of individuals to their home country. "Repeat migration" then points to regular movement of individuals between their country of origin and multiple other destinations. Finally, "circular migration" refers to movements whereby an individual migrates from country A to country B, returns to A, and remigrates to country B. Although these forms are not identical, they can be considered to be related (Constant and Zimmermann 2011).

Return migration is generally connected with a successful or failed migratory project (Gmelch 1980). In line with rational choice theory, migrants who accumulate enough financial capital abroad would return home (success), and migrants who are unable to fulfill their economic ambitions abroad would do the same (failure; Cassarino 2004). Depending on such outcomes, former migrants might consider new moves. Particularly when the migration experience was negative, the odds of moving again may drastically decrease (DaVanzo and Morrison 1981; Van Mol 2014b). As exchange students *have* to return to their home country to finish their degree at their home institution when their exchange period finishes, their return decision is not related to the eventual success or failure of their stay abroad. Nevertheless, the mechanism for considering repeat migration might work similarly. According to this line of reasoning, it can be expected that when the exchange experience was positive, the likelihood of moving abroad in the future will be higher (*hypothesis 1*).

However, it can be expected that repeat migration is not only related to eventual success or failure of a previous migratory experience. Throughout their stay abroad, migrants acquire "migration-specific capital" (Massey and Espinosa 1997) or "mobility capital" (Murphy-Lejeune 2002). In this chapter, I focus on the role of human and social capital an individual acquires abroad in the development of repeat-migration aspirations. Although there might be a discrepancy between migration aspirations and actual migratory behavior, it has been argued that aspirations are a good proxy for future mobility when data on migration behavior is not available (e.g. Cairns 2014; Cairns and Smyth 2011). Apart from human and social capital, there are undoubtedly other forms of capital that play a role, such as economic capital. Nevertheless, as exchange students rarely gain economic capital abroad (for an exception, however, see Van Mol and Timmerman 2014), I deliberately limit the analysis to human and social capital. This focus is also informed by empirical evidence showing that accumulation of these two forms of capitals are central elements for making migration self-perpetuating (Massey and Zenteno 1999).

When moving abroad, migrants accumulate individual human capital in terms of, for example, knowledge of a new language, different lifestyles and strategies to adapt in diverse cultural settings. Because of this process of human capital accumulation, the costs and risks of moving again might diminish, whereas the potential gains increase (in terms of, for example, finding employment or housing; Massey and Zenteno 1999). So repeat migration can be expected to be influenced by the knowledge that individuals acquire through mobility/migration, which can be termed as an increase in location-specific capital and a reduction of information costs (DaVanzo 1981). Whereas location-specific capital refers to the specific place where a migrant stayed, this form of capital is often transferable to other locations in terms of, for example, increased language proficiency, intercultural competences or tacit knowledge on how to cope with new contexts. Each move thus provides an individual with additional moving experience, which makes subsequent moves easier (DaVanzo and Morrison 1981; Constant and Zimmermann 2012). This leads to the hypothesis that the more an exchange student gains in terms of human capital, the more likely it is she/he will have aspirations to move again in the future (*hypothesis 2*).

Apart from individual human capital, migrants generally also broaden their social capital through their stay abroad. Social capital is defined by Bourdieu (1986, 249) as "the aggregate of the actual and potential resources which are linked to the possession of a durable network of more or less institutionalized relationships of mutual acquaintance or recognition." Later, Lin (2000, 786) conceptualized it as the "quantity and/or quality of resources an actor can access or use through; and its location in a social network." A key characteristic of social capital is that it is convertible into other forms of capital (Coleman 1988). Generally, it is expected that social capital leads to instrumental returns such as better wages or better jobs (Lin 2000), which can help to improve or maintain individuals' position within society (Bourdieu 1986). Nevertheless, the value of the different resources within individuals' social capital, and consequently the returns an individual might expect, is dependent upon the strength of the tie between two individuals (Granovetter 1973; Coleman 1988; Burt 1992). Furthermore, whereas some authors (e.g. Coleman 1988) suggest that strong ties (e.g. family and friends) are most relevant considering the benefits of social capital, others (e.g. Granovetter 1973) argue exactly the opposite—namely, that weak ties (for example, between colleagues) are more important. It should be noted, however, that the relevance of strong and weak ties is highly dependent upon the context studied. Individuals might draw on different contacts when searching for a job compared to, for example, gaining access to housing or finding informal child care. In this chapter, I argue that Erasmus students accumulate transnational social capital, which links them with a variety of social networks spanning several European countries. Such social capital might be helpful to lower the costs and risks of migration and enhance the benefits of another stay abroad

(Massey and Zenteno 1999). As this social capital might be dispersed over Europe as their fellow students also had to return to their countries of origin, the range of potentially attractive destinations for future jobs—because of the presence of friends—might be much broader among Erasmus students compared to traditional migrants. It can hence be expected that these mobile students have a more complete set of information on specific destinations through their social contacts as well as prior experience of living abroad, making it more likely to move again in the future. Although these friends might not necessarily provide direct links to jobs, they can provide specific information on the destination lowering the migration and settlement costs. This leads to the assumption that it is especially transnational social capital acquired abroad (in contrast to contacts established with fellow co-nationals abroad) which leads to increased repeat migration aspirations. After all, the establishment of new social relationships in the place of destination is translated into a spatial stretch across international borders upon students' return. As such, the acquired international social capital might transform the space wherein students move from a more local to a more international scale as well as give them access to specific information on potential destinations, lowering the migration costs. Consequently, I expect that repeat migration aspirations are positively correlated with (1) a larger share of international friends abroad (*hypothesis 3a*), (2) a larger share of host country nationals in the friendship network abroad (*hypothesis 3b*), and (3) the maintenance of active contact with the network established while being abroad (*hypothesis 3c*).

In this chapter, I thus explore whether aspirations for repeat migration can be explained by the accumulation of human and social capital abroad. Whereas it has been demonstrated that social networks are important for the initial decision to study abroad (Cairns and Smyth 2011; Beech 2014; Van Mol and Timmerman 2014; Frändberg 2015), to my knowledge, the role of the newly established networks in new migratory decisions as well as the accumulation of human capital on repeat migration of formerly mobile students remains largely unexplored. By seeking to investigate whether traditional migration theories on repeat migration can also be applied to a specific group of intra-European movers, I thus aim to advance our understanding of students' transnational practices and networks.

Methods and Data

Data

The presented results are based on an online survey I conducted among higher education students in Austria, Belgium, Denmark, Finland, Italy, the Netherlands, Norway, Portugal, Spain, Sweden, and the United Kingdom between April and June 2011. The survey was conducted in the framework of a study into international student mobility funded by the Research Foundation – Flanders, which aimed to advance current understandings of the determinants of international student mobility, the social networks of Erasmus students, as well as the outcomes of student mobility in terms of European identity formation and future migratory behavior (for an overview of the main results, see Van Mol 2014b). The invitation to participate in the questionnaire, which was built in LimeSurvey, was sent out to all students of the participating faculties by the dean's office, as students show to be more motivated for participation when an invitation originates from their institution (Durrant and Dorius 2007). The response rates lie between 10 and 20 percent for all studied countries, which is not uncommon for web surveys (Fricker 2008), particularly among higher education students as they are frequently surveyed (Sax, Gilmartin, and Bryant 2003). To assess whether this rather low response rate potentially biases the presented results, I applied "time of response analysis" (Porter and Whitcomb 2005) for investigating the response quality. More specifically, I analyzed differences in the distribution of survey responses between early responders and students who answered after (several) reminders by cross-tabulation. Statistical significance was estimated by chi-squared tests. No significant differences could be detected, allowing to safely proceed with the analysis. We restricted our sample to respondents aged maximum 30 years old for reasons of comparability, and filtered students who went on exchange outside Europe out, as the overall aim of the study was to analyze intra-European student mobility. These cases could potentially bias the analyses, particularly in regard to the question of European identity, which was central to the overall project. The final sample contains 2,298 formerly mobile students. An overview of the distribution across the case-countries can be consulted in Table 4.1. Respondents could answer the questionnaire in three languages: Dutch, English, and Spanish.

Variables

Dependent Variable

The dependent variable in our analysis is former exchange students' aspirations to move abroad again. These aspirations were measured by two statements—namely, (1) "I can imagine to live abroad for a year or more after graduation," and (2) "I would like to work in a foreign country after graduation." Students could rate these statements on a 7-point Likert scale, ranging from 1 (strongly disagree) to 7 (strongly agree). In this chapter, I use the combined (restricted) median score on both statements.

Independent Variables: Human Capital and Social Networks

As the main interest of this chapter is the relation between acquired social and human capital and migration aspirations, various indicators are used to capture both concepts. First, acquired human capital is measured by a (restrictive) sum scale of seven statements that asked how worthwhile their exchange period was. These seven statements were "Enhancement of my academic and professional knowledge," "Relevance to my general career prospects," "Relevance to my potential for developing an international career," "Foreign language proficiency,"

Table 4.1 Descriptive Statistics

	Mean	*s*	*n*	*Min.*	*Max.*
Migration aspirations	5.88	1.35	2,119	1	7
Acquired human capital	3.30	0.46	2,190	1.29	4
Co-national contacts during exchange	3.21	1.41	2,274	1	5
Host country contacts during exchange	3.40	1.18	2,274	1	5
International contacts during exchange	4.04	1.20	2,273	1	5
Satisfaction with exchange	4.55	0.66	2,231	1	5
Foreign friends in home country	0.81	0.69	2,298	0	4
Foreign travels	2.65	1.56	2,298	0	5
Years since Erasmus	1.12	1.68	2,289	0	10
Age	24.36	2.39	2,298	20	30

	%	*n*	*Min.*	*Max.*
Contact with Exchange Contacts		2,272	0	3
No	3.7	85		
With a minority	32.2	731		
With half of them	16.0	363		
With the majority	48.1	1,093		
Participation Home Country Friends in Exchange		2,298	0	3
None	12.4	284		
A minority	53.2	1,223		
Half of them	22.1	509		
The majority	12.3	282		
Parents Lived Abroad		2,285	0	1
None of them	68.5	1,566		
At least one of them	31.5	719		
Gap Year Abroad		2,287	0	1
No	83.6	1,911		
Yes	16.4	376		
Gender		2,298	0	1
Male	33.7	774		
Female	66.3	1,524		
Parents Higher Education Degree		2,298	0	1
None of them	43.9	1,009		
At least one of them	56.1	1,289		
Study Field		2,207	1	6
Language studies	18.9	418		
Humanities	5.2	115		
Social Sciences	34.7	766		
Medical Sciences	5.5	121		
Science and Technology	19.7	435		
Business Studies and Economics	15.9	352		
Country of Origin		2,298	1	11
Austria	330	14.4		
Belgium	222	9.7		
Denmark	168	7.3		
Finland	139	6.0		
Italy	224	9.7		
The Netherlands	132	5.7		
Norway	162	7.0		
Portugal	287	12.5		
Spain	220	9.6		
Sweden	205	8.9		
United Kingdom	209	9.1		

"Knowledge and understanding of another country/culture," "Maturity and personal development," and "New ways of thinking about my home country." Students could rate these items on a 4-point Likert scale, ranging from 1 (not worthwhile at all) to 4 (totally worthwhile).

Second, a varied set of indicators is used for measuring social network characteristics. Three different variables indicate the composition of students' network during their exchange. These three variables indicate the level of interaction with (1) co-national; (2) other international; and (3) host-country students. Students were asked to rate their interaction during their exchange period with these three groups on a 5-point Likert scale, ranging from 1 (not at all) to 5 (very much). Apart from specific interaction patterns abroad, it can also be expected that the degree of contact after their return home has an influence on students' migration aspirations. Therefore, I included a measure on their current contact with their exchange friendship network. This variable is based on the question "Are you still in contact with the friends you made abroad?" and ranges from 0 (none) to 3 (the majority).

Third, as it has been reported that when migrants are unhappy about the outcome of their mobility experience the probability of going abroad decreases (DaVanzo and Morrison 1981), I include a measure on their subjective satisfaction with the exchange period. Satisfaction was measured by the question "All things considered, how satisfied are you with your exchange period abroad?" Students could rate this question on a 5-point Likert scale, ranging from 1 (very dissatisfied) to 5 (very satisfied).

Control Variables

In order to disentangle the specific influence of transnational human and social capital acquired during the exchange experience, three groups of control variables are included. First, I included several variables measuring the "internationality" of students' social network in the home country. This is important, as prior mobility experiences of friends, family and the student him/herself shows to influence mobility decisions (e.g. Cairns and Smyth 2011; Beech 2014; Frändberg 2015; Van Mol 2015). A first variable indicates how many friends of the respondent participated in similar exchange programs, ranging from 0 (none) to 3 (the majority). A second variable indicates how many foreign friends are included in the friendship network of the respondent in the home country, ranging from 0 (none) to 4 (all of them). A third variable indicates whether at least one parent of the respondent lived abroad for studying and/or work (0 = no, 1 = yes).

Second, I included two variables indicating the degree of internationality a student already had before his/her studies. A first variable indicates whether the respondent spent some time abroad during a gap year between high school and university (0 = no, 1 = yes). A second variable indicates how often a student engaged in independent traveling on his or her own or with friends. This variable was measured by the question "How often have you traveled to a foreign country on your own or with friends?" I recoded this variable to 5 categories, ranging from 0 (none) to 5 (more than 20 times).

Third, I included several basic control variables. A first variable indicates the time between the Erasmus exchange and the time of the survey in years, as it can be expected that over time, the propensity to migrate again may diminish (DaVanzo and Morrison 1981). Furthermore, I included control variables on gender (0 = male, 1 = female), age (in years) and socioeconomic background. Socioeconomic background is measured by parental education (0 = neither of them completed higher education, 1 = at least one of them has a higher education degree), as most of the respondents had not yet obtained their higher education degree. In addition, I included a control variable on students' major, as it can be expected that some study fields are more international than others (e.g. business studies vs. law). Finally, the specific labor market situation in students' country of origin might also influence their migration aspirations (see, for example, Van Mol 2014a). Therefore, a control variable on the country of origin was included in the models.

Analytic Strategy

For the analysis, I conduct a stepwise OLS regression analysis on students' aspirations to remigrate. Given the skewed nature of our dependent variable, with many students indicating the highest score on the scale, violating the assumption of normality, the analysis is based on robust estimations. More specifically, I applied bootstrapping to the regression estimations. The bootstrap method is regularly used to estimate the population distribution by using a number of resamples from the original sample. The method provides estimates of the standard error, confidence intervals and distributions if the normality assumption does not hold. Although the method is relatively easy to implement today, it is still computationally intensive (Hammarstedt and Shukur 2006, 299). The number of bootstrap samples used in this chapter is 1,000, given the relatively large starting sample size. At stage one, I added acquired human capital. In stage 2, the characteristics of the social network abroad are added. At stage three, the model is broadened with a variable indicating students' satisfaction with their exchange period. In the final model, the different control variables are introduced. Previous to conducting the regression analysis, I examined interrelationships between variables through bivariate correlations. Only weak correlations exist. Thereafter, I tested for multicollinearity. Acceptable Tolerance values (ranging from .523 to 1.000) and low Variance Inflation Factor values (ranging from 1.000 to 2.146) indicate no multicollinearity.

Results

Descriptive Statistics

An overview of descriptive statistics is presented in Table 4.1. As can be noticed, migration aspirations are quite high among formerly mobile students, with a mean score of 5.88. Furthermore, most students affirm having accumulated a considerable amount of individual human capital during their exchange. Considering the interaction patterns of exchange students, it can be observed that overall, students mainly interacted with other international friends during their exchange, followed by contacts with host country nationals. Interaction with co-nationals abroad is lowest. In addition, the vast majority of students appear to be satisfied with the exchange experience, which is reflected in a mean score of 4.55. Lastly, it can be noticed that most students were still in contact with the majority of their exchange contacts at the moment of surveying.

When considering the control variables, it can be noticed that students reported to have few foreign friends in the home country. Nevertheless, the vast majority (87.6 percent) has friends in their country of origin who participated in an international exchange, and most of them traveled more than five times to other countries. Furthermore, about a third of the surveyed students have at least one parent who lived abroad for study and/or work. Less than one in five students, however, spent a gap year abroad during high school and university. All in all, these descriptive findings might point to the existence of a "mobility culture" among formerly mobile students. Such culture might influence their future migration aspirations as well, so it is of paramount importance to control for these factors in the analysis.

The variables characterizing personal characteristics show that the exchange experience was relatively recent for most of the respondents, with an average of 1.12 years ago. Furthermore, it can be observed that female students are overrepresented in the sample, constituting 66.3 percent of the respondents. However, this is consistent with an overall overrepresentation of female students among the Erasmus population. Official statistics of the European Commission (2014b) show that 61 percent of Erasmus students are women. A similar pattern can also be found in the United States, where female students are also more likely to study abroad (Salisbury, Paulsen, and Pascarella 2010), and this also applies to male-dominated disciplines such as Physics and Mathematics (Redden 2008). Although explaining this pattern falls outside the scope of this chapter, it should be noted that the unequal gender balance represents one of the major gaps in research on international student mobility and migration (Salisbury, Paulsen, and Pascarella 2010; King and Raghuram 2013; Van Mol 2014b). The mean age of 24.36 is also slightly higher than the median age of 22 in the full population (European Commission 2014b). This, nevertheless, can be attributed to the fact that our sample includes former Erasmus students, who are logically older compared to those who are currently on Erasmus. In addition, it does not appear that students from higher socioeconomic classes are more represented in the sample. Finally, it can be noticed that students from the Social Sciences are overrepresented in our sample. Nevertheless, this is also consistent with the overall Erasmus population. Statistics from the European Commission (2014a) reveal that most Erasmus students (41 percent) study Social Sciences, Business and Law, followed by Humanities and Arts (21.9 percent), Engineering, Manufacturing and Construction (15.6 percent), Science, Mathematics and Computing (7.6 percent), and lastly Health and Welfare (6 percent). Overall, our sample thus appears to represent the overall Erasmus population quite well.

As a final step in the descriptive analysis, it is worthwhile to examine whether international differences can be detected regarding students' migratory aspirations. After all, it is not unthinkable that in countries that were severely hit by the economic crisis and with high levels of youth unemployment, such as the southern European countries, migration aspirations might be higher. As indicated earlier, the overall mean score for migration aspiration was 5.88. Three countries significantly differ from this general score—namely, the Netherlands (5.58), Spain (6.29), and the United Kingdom (5.66). Students from Spain thus have significantly more migratory aspirations compared to their counterparts from other European countries, whereas students from the Netherlands and the United Kingdom report lower aspirations. A possible explanation for these differences might derive from macro-level statistics. Statistics from Eurostat and the Labor Force Survey indicating the average number of months for the education-to-work transition in 2009 as well as the level of youth unemployment among tertiary education graduates aged 20–29 in 2011 show that Spain has the highest level of unemployment of higher education graduates of the case-countries (23.4 percent), making migration a plausible option for coping with this situation. The Netherlands and the United Kingdom, in contrast, have the smoothest education-to-work transition of the countries under study, with an average of three months between graduation and first employment, compared to an average of five months for the EU-27, and seven months in Spain. Furthermore, the Netherlands has the lowest share of youth unemployment among tertiary educated young adults in the age range of 20 to 29 years old—namely, 3.4 percent. As these three countries most probably affect the models presented in the subsequent section, I will control for country of origin in a final model.

Regression Analysis

A stepwise OLS regression analysis is presented in Table 4.2. Model I includes the human capital that students accumulated abroad, and reveals a highly significant correlation between accumulated human capital and remigration aspirations. As such, hypothesis 2, which postulated a positive correlation between these two variables, is confirmed. In Model II, the social network characteristics are introduced. The correlation between human capital and remigration aspirations persists. Furthermore, interaction with co-national students abroad is negatively related to migration aspirations. No correlation, however, could be detected for socializing with the host population and student's migratory aspirations, contradicting hypothesis 3b. Nevertheless, there is a significant relationship between the amount of international friends in the social network abroad and remigration aspirations, confirming hypothesis 3a. Furthermore, hypothesis 3c is also confirmed: maintaining contact with the international social network shows to be also related to higher migration aspirations. Interestingly, whether there is still contact with a small or large share of these friends does not appear to make a difference in this model. These correlations persist when introducing satisfaction with the international exchange experience in Model III. This model confirms

Table 4.2 Regression Analysis

	Model I *Human Capital*	*Model II* *Social Capital*	*Model III* *Satisfaction*	*Model IV* *Controls*	*Model V* *Final Model*
Constant	4.635 (.226)***	4.025 (.303)***	3.220 (.353)***	3.617 (.566)***	4.084 (.005)***
Human capital accumulation	.376 (.069)***	.323 (.069)***	.218 (.072)**	.221 (.072)**	.195 (.073)**
Social capital on exchange					
Home country friends abroad		−.046 (.022)*	−.042 (.022)*	−.035 (.022)	−.042 (.022)
Host country friends abroad		.045 (.026)	.021 (.026)	.008 (.026)	.009 (.026)
International friends abroad		.068 (.027)*	.053 (.027)*	.041 (.027)	.041 (.027)
Contact with international social network (ref: none)					
With a minority		.499 (.193)**	.388 (.197)*	.332 (.196)	.336 (.192)
With half of them		.568 (.202)**	.426 (.206)*	.308 (.204)	.315 (.201)
With the majority		.527 (.191)**	.443 (.196)*	.361 (.199)	.388 (.196)*
Satisfaction with exchange			.303 (.054)***	.298 (.055)***	.300 (.055)***
Control Variables					
Social network at home					
Friends on exchange (ref: none)					
A minority				.193 (.110)	.188 (.109)
Half of them				.270 (.121)*	.240 (.121)*
The majority				.284 (.132)*	.252 (.133)*
Foreign friends				.067 (.049)	.057 (.050)
Parents lived abroad				.121 (.067)	.124 (.067)
Previous international experiences					
Gap year abroad				.202 (.076)**	.248 (.081)**
Foreign travels				.041 (.023)	.041 (.023)
Individual characteristics					
Year of birth				−.027 (.017)	−.040 (.017)*
Gender				.036 (.070)	.021 (.069)
Years since exchange				−.024 (.025)	−.024 (.025)
Parental higher education				.036 (.063)	.038 (.064)

(Continued)

Table 4.2 Continued

	Model I *Human Capital*	*Model II* *Social Capital*	*Model III* *Satisfaction*	*Model IV* *Controls*	*Model V* *Final Model*
Study field (ref: Business Studies)				−.098 (.104)	−.069 (.114)
Language Studies				.004 (.136)	.053 (.142)
Humanities				.001 (.088)	.042 (.092)
Social Sciences				−.057 (.152)	−.117 (.158)
Medical Sciences				−.125 (.113)	−.119 (.121)
Science and Technology					
Country of origin (ref: Portugal)					−.031 (.127)
Austria					−.183 (.139)
Belgium					−.174 (.161)
Denmark					−.150 (.168)
Finland					−.034 (.140)
Italy					−.379 (.143)**
The Netherlands					−.007 (.157)
Norway					.293 (.138)*
Spain					.014 (.147)
Sweden					−.357 (.169)*
United Kingdom					
R^2	.017	.031	.049	.071	.087
ΔR^2	.017***	.014***	.018***	.022***	.016***

Note: Reported values are bootstrapped coefficients based on 1,000 bootstrap samples, with standard errors between parentheses.
$* p \leq .05$; $** p \leq .01$, $*** p \leq .001$

hypothesis 1—namely, that a positive experience abroad has the potential to lead to new migration moves in the future.

In Model IV, the control variables are added. Interestingly, the specific interaction patterns of students become non-significant, as well as the maintenance of contact with the international social network. This model clearly shows that particularly a positive exchange experience and human capital accumulation abroad heighten migration aspirations. Interestingly, this model reveals that the social network at home—particularly the share of friends who also went on exchange—is significantly correlated with remigration aspirations, as well as previous international experiences in terms of spending a gap year abroad. As argued in the previous section, however, migration aspirations might also be related to the current economic conditions for young adults who enter the labor market. Therefore, in the final model (Model V), I control for country of origin of the students. Portugal is chosen as the reference category given its intermediate position considering migration aspirations (they are the closest to the average). In this final model, human capital accumulation, extensive contact with the international social network and satisfaction with the exchange period abroad are still correlated with remigration aspirations of former exchange students, providing strong empirical evidence for the influence of these factors on repeat migration patterns.

Discussion and Conclusion

In this chapter, I focused on a specific group of international migrants—higher education students—who are often expected to become highly skilled migrants in their future careers. I particularly investigated which forms of capital gained abroad might inform repeat migration aspirations. For the analysis, I build on previous studies on repeat migration, which suggested that social and individual human capital are crucial elements in explaining remigration decisions.

Four major conclusions can be made based on the findings. First, moving abroad indeed shows to be related to a greater likelihood of moving again in the future. All respondents showed relatively high levels of remigration aspirations, and the models revealed that previous international experiences in terms of spending a gap year abroad between high school and university are also related to an increased aspiration of moving again. Second, the results provide strong empirical evidence for the link between accumulated human capital and future migration aspirations. The more skills and competences they acquire abroad, the greater the likelihood of moving again in the future. Third, the relationship between acquired social capital and remigration aspirations is more ambiguous. Whereas the first models showed a correlation between the composition of the social network abroad and remigration intentions, this correlation disappeared when introducing the control variables. The findings therefore suggest that it is not the specific composition of the social network abroad that is related to higher migratory aspirations, but rather keeping in touch with a large share of the network established abroad. Fourth, a positive mobility experience is related to greater remigration aspirations. Negative experiences, in contrast, might curb mobility aspirations.

In sum, in this chapter, I showed that two forms of capital can explain part of the transition that former international students might make towards the status of highly skilled migrant. Individual human capital consists of specific competences an individual acquires throughout his or her mobility trajectory, giving him/her direct experience with moving. As such, and in line with traditional migration theories, each additional move will give more experience, increasing the likelihood of a new migratory move. The results suggest this form of capital is most constitutive in the development of remigration intentions. Social capital also plays a role in students' aspirations to become highly skilled migrants. Newly made contacts abroad, when maintained after the return home, might provide individuals with the necessary networks through which information on potential destinations can be gained. Furthermore, as the social networks of former exchange students might span several European countries, it is likely that they use these networks as well once they move again, as they might offer practical help in, for example, searching employment and/or housing. Hence, it seems that the transformation of the spaces wherein students move throughout their exchange and upon their return, from the local/national to the international level, heighten migratory aspirations. Upon their return, students' networks are no longer situated in one particular place, but they connect a myriad of places in Europe and across the globe, enlarging the information sources on specific destinations and employment opportunities.

Finally, some limitations of the presented analysis should be mentioned. First, this study is limited to students who spent a delineated period of time abroad in the framework of an exchange program. It remains questionable whether the uncovered mechanisms also hold true for degree mobile students. As education-to-work transitions are increasingly being facilitated for international students in destination countries, it is likely that many immediately use the accumulated human capital for incorporation in the host country's labor market. Future research might shed light on this issue. Second, the analysis is based on cross-sectional data, and included only migration aspirations of students. As such, no causal interpretations can be made, and it remains a question whether these students will effectively become highly skilled migrants in the future. Although migration intentions are considered a good predictor of migration behavior (e.g. van Dalen and Henkens 2012), migration aspirations do not necessarily feed into real migration behavior (Epstein and Gang 2006). More longitudinal studies, following international students for several years after graduation, might be helpful for explaining why some formerly mobile students move again, whereas others do not. Along similar lines, qualitative research might be very informative in explaining and nuancing repeat migration decisions of formerly mobile students.

In conclusion, I showed that it is likely that European mobile students become highly skilled migrants in the future as well. The specific influence of the exchange period on this probability can be explained by two different forms of capital students gain abroad—namely, human and social capital. Upon their return, students evaluate the usefulness of their experience abroad, and combined with the maintenance of contact with an international friendship network, these two forms of capital partly explain repeat migration aspirations.

Acknowledgments

This chapter is based on the individual research project "The influence of European student mobility on European identity and subsequent migration intentions," funded by the Research Foundation – Flanders (Aspirant FWO, grant number 1136712N).

References

Bailey, A. J. 1989. Getting on your bike: What difference does a migration history make? *Tijdschrift voor Economische en Sociale Geografie* 80 (5): 312–317.

Bailey, A. J. 1993. Migration history, migration behavior and selectivity. *The Annals of Regional Science* 27 (4): 315–326.

Beaverstock, J. V. 1996. Revisiting high-waged labour market demand in the global cities: British professional and managerial workers in New York City. *International Journal of Urban and Regional Research* 20 (3): 422–445.

Beech, S. E. 2014. Why place matters: Imaginative geography and international student mobility. *Area* 46 (2): 170–177.

Boneva, B. S., and I. H. Frieze. 2001. Toward a concept of a migrant personality. *Journal of Social Issues* 57 (3): 477–491.

Bourdieu, P. 1986. The forms of capital. In *Handbook of Theory and Research for the Sociology of Education,* ed. J. G. Richardson, 241–258. New York: Greenwood.

Brilli, A. 1995. *Quando viaggiare era un'arte: Il romanzo del Grand Tour.* Bologna: il Mulino.

Brooks, R., and J. Waters. 2011. *Student mobilities, migration and the internationalization of higher education.* Basingstoke: Palgrave Macmillan.

Burt, R. S. 1992. *Structural holes: The social structure of competition.* Cambridge, MA: Harvard University Press.

Cairns, D. 2014. "I wouldn't stay here": Economic crisis and youth mobility in Ireland. *International Migration* 52 (3): 236–249.

Cairns, D., and J. Smyth. 2011. I wouldn't mind moving actually: Exploring student mobility in Northern Ireland. *International Migration* 49 (2): 135–161.

Cammelli, A., S. Ghiselli, and G. P. Mignoli. 2008. Study experience abroad: Italian graduate characteristics and employment outcomes. In *Students, staff and academic mobility in higher education,* eds. M. Byram and F. Dervin, 217–236. Newcastle: Cambridge Scholars Publishing.

Cassarino, J-P. 2004. Theorising return migration: The conceptual approach to return migrants revisited. *International Journal on Multicultural Societies* 6 (2): 253–279.

Castro-Martín, T., and C. Cortina. 2015. Demographic issues of intra-European migration: destinations, family and settlement. *European Journal of Population/Revue européenne de Démographie* 31 (2): 109–125.

Coleman, J. S. 1988. Social capital in the creation of human capital. *American Journal of Sociology* 94: S95–S120.

Constant, A. F., and K. F. Zimmermann. 2011. Circular and repeat migration: Counts of exits and years away from the host country. *Population Research and Policy Review* 30 (4): 495–515.

Constant, A. F., and K. F. Zimmermann. 2012. The dynamics of repeat migration: A Markov chain analysis. *International Migration Review* 46 (2): 362–388.

DaVanzo, J. S. 1981. Repeat migration, information costs, and location-specific capital. *Population and Environment* 4 (1): 45–73.

DaVanzo, J. S., and P. A. Morrison. 1981. Return and other sequences of migration in the United States. *Demography* 18 (1): 85–101.

Deléchat, C. 2001. International migration dynamics: The role of experience and social networks. *Labour* 15 (3): 457–486.

Durrant, M. B., and C. R. Dorius. 2007. Study abroad survey instruments: A comparison of survey types and experiences. *Journal of Studies in International Education* 11 (1): 33–53.

Epstein, G. S., and I. N. Gang. 2006. The influence of others on migration plans. *Review of Development Economics* 10 (4): 652–665.

European Commission. 2010a. *Geographical and labour market mobility: Special Eurobarometer 337.* Brussels: European Commission.

European Commission. 2010b. *Youth on the move. An initiative to unleash the potential of young people to achieve smart, sustainable and inclusive growth in the European Union.* Luxembourg: Publications Office of the European Union.

European Commission. 2014a. *Erasmus – Facts, figures & trends. The European Union support for student and staff exchanges and university cooperation in 2012–13.* Luxembourg: Publications Office of the European Union.

European Commission. 2014b. *The portrait of the typical Erasmus student.* Available at: http://ec.europa.eu/education/tools/statistics_en.htm (last accessed November 10, 2015).

Fabian, G., and K-H. Minks. 2008. Muss i denn zum Städtele hinaus? Erwerbsmobilität von Hochschulabsolventen. *HIS Magazin* 3: 4–5.

Findlay, A. M. 2011. An assessment of supply and demand-side theorizations of international student mobility. *International Migration* 49 (2): 162–190.

Findlay, A. M., R. King, F. M. Smith, A. Geddes, and R. Skeldon. 2012. World class? An investigation of globalisation, difference and international student mobility. *Transactions of the Institute of British Geographers* 37 (1): 118–131.

Föbker, S., D. Temme, and C. C. Wiegandt. 2014. A warm welcome to highly skilled migrants: how can municipal administrations play their part? *Tijdschrift voor Economische en Sociale Geografie* 105 (5): 542–557.

Frändberg, L. 2015. Acceleration or avoidance? The role of temporary moves abroad in the transition to adulthood. *Population, Space and Place* 21 (6): 553–567.

Fricker, R. D. 2008. Sampling methods for web and e-mail surveys. In *The SAGE handbook of online research methods*, eds. N. Fielding, R. M. Lee, and G. Blank, 195–216. Los Angeles, London, New Delhi & Singapore: SAGE.

Gmelch, G. 1980. Return migration. *Annual Review of Anthropology* 9 (1): 135–159.

Granovetter, M. S. 1973. The strength of weak ties. *American Journal of Sociology* 78 (6): 1360–1380.

Gu, Q., and M. Schweisfurth. 2015. Transnational connections, competences and identities: experiences of Chinese international students after their return "home." *British Educational Research Journal* 41 (6), 947–970.

Gürüz, K. 2011. *Higher education and international student mobility in the global knowledge economy.* Albany, NY: State University of New York Press.

Hammarstedt, M., and G. Shukur. 2006. Immigrants' relative earnings in Sweden—A cohort analysis. *Labour* 20 (2): 285–323.

Harzing, A-W. 2004. Ideal jobs and international student mobility in the enlarged European Union. *European Management Journal* 22 (6): 693–703.

King, R. 2002. Towards a new map of European migration. *International Journal of Population Geography* 8 (2): 89–106.

King, R., and P. Raghuram. 2013. International student migration: Mapping the field and new research agendas. *Population, Space and Place* 19 (2): 127–137.

King, R., and E. Ruiz-Gelices. 2003. International student migration and the European "Year Abroad": Effects on European identity and subsequent migration behaviour. *International Journal of Population Geography* 9 (3): 229–252.

Kõu, A., L. van Wissen, J. van Dijk, and A. J. Bailey. 2015. A life course approach to high-skilled migration: Lived experiences of Indians in the Netherlands. *Journal of Ethnic and Migration Studies* 41 (10): 1644–1663.

Kuptsch, C. 2006. Students and talent flow. The case of Europe: From castle to harbour? In *Competing for global talent,* eds. Kuptsch, C., and E. F. Pang, 33–61. Geneva: International Institute for Labour Studies.

Lange, T. 2013. Return migration of foreign students and non-resident tuition fees. *Journal of Population Economics* 26 (2): 703–718.

Lin, N. 2000. Inequality in social capital. *Contemporary Sociology* 29 (6): 785–795.

Lowell, L. B., and A. M. Findlay. 2001. *Migration of highly skilled persons from developing countries: Impact and policy responses: Synthesis report.* Geneva: International Labour Office.

Massey, D. S., and K. E. Espinosa. 1997. What's driving Mexico–U.S. Migration? A theoretical, empirical, and policy analysis. *American Journal of Sociology* 102 (4): 939–999.

Massey, D. S., and R. M. Zenteno. 1999. The dynamics of mass migration. *Proceedings of the National Academy of Sciences of the United States of America* 96 (9): 5328–5335.

Mellors-Bourne, R., J. Fielden, N. Kemp, et al. 2014. The value of transnational education to the UK. *Bis Research Paper* 194: 1–147.

Murphy-Lejeune, E. 2002. *Student mobility and narrative in Europe. The new strangers.* London and New York: Routledge.

Porter, S., and M. Whitcomb. 2005. Non-response in student surveys: The role of demographics, engagement and personality. *Research in Higher Education* 46 (2): 127–152.

Raghuram, P. 2013. Theorising the spaces of student migration. *Population, Space and Place* 19 (2): 138–154.

Recchi, E. 2015. *Mobile Europe. The theory and practice of free movement in the EU.* Basingstoke: Palgrave Macmillan.

Redden, E. 2008. Women abroad and men at home. *Inside Higher Ed.* www.insidehighered.com/news/2008/12/04/genderabroad (last accessed 22 December 2015).

Rosenmund, M., D. Geiderer, and Kickingereder. 2012. Eine Studie zu Berichten Österreichischer Erasmus-Studierender. In *Mit Erasmus durch Europa. Österreichische Studierende berichten üben ihren Auslandsaufenthalt. Eine Studie*, eds. Gesslbauer, E., G. Volz, and M. Burtscher, 25–115. Innsbruck, Vienna and Bozen: StudienVerlag.

Salisbury, M. H., M. B. Paulsen, and E. T. Pascarella. 2010. To see the world or stay at home: Applying an integrated student choice model to explore the gender gap in the intent to study abroad. *Research in Higher Education* 51 (7): 615–40.

Sax, L. J., S. K. Gilmartin, and A. N. Bryant. 2003. Assessing response rates and nonresponse bias in web and paper surveys. *Research in Higher Education* 44 (4): 409–432.

Tremblay, K. 2005. Academic mobility and immigration. *Journal of Studies in International Education* 9 (3): 196–228.

van Dalen, H. P., and K. Henkens. 2012. Explaining emigration intentions and behaviour in the Netherlands, 2005–10. *Population Studies* 67 (2): 225–241.

Van Mol, C. 2014a. Erasmus student mobility as a gateway to the international labour market? In *Globalisierung, Bildung und grenzüberschreitende Mobilität,* eds. J. S. Gerhards, S. Hans, and S. Carlson, 296–314. Wiesbaden: Springer VS.

Van Mol, C. 2014b. *Intra-European student mobility in international higher education circuits: Europe on the move.* Basingstoke: Palgrave Macmillan.

Van Mol, C. 2015. Why do students move? An analysis of mobility determinants among Italian students. In *The new politics of global academic mobility and migration,* eds. F. Dervin, and R. Machart, 19–40. Frankfurt am Main: Peter Lang.

Van Mol, C., and P. Ekamper. 2016. Destination cities of European exchange students. *Danish Journal of Geography* 116 (1), 85–91.

Van Mol, C., and C. Timmerman. 2014. Should I stay or should I go? An analysis of the determinants of intra-European student mobility. *Population, Space and Place* 20 (5): 465–479.

5 Mental Health and the Student-migrant Experience

Sources of Stress for Norwegian Quota Scheme Students

Scott Basford

Introduction

Concomitant with the precipitous global rise in international student migration (ISM) is a growing, if still limited, scholastic commitment to understanding its ramifications (Findlay 2011; King and Raghuram 2013). Extant research indicates student migrant flows are increasing both as a result of demand for international students from receiving countries and students' desire to study abroad. With respect to the former, international students are particularly sought after by universities struggling to supplement declining state funding (Hazen and Alberts 2013). Relatedly, after graduation, they tend to be an attractive pool of skilled, acculturated labor for domestic businesses in need of a skilled workforce (Ziguras and Law 2006). At the same time, the pursuit of personal fulfillment and the perceived quality of a Western education incentivize many students from economically advanced and developing countries alike to look abroad to meet their academic needs (Hazen and Alberts 2006; Brooks and Waters 2010).

This chapter examines the sources of emotional distress experienced by international students in the host society. It does so by relating the perspectives of international students in Norway studying under a Norwegian state-funded scholarship program called the Quota Scheme. This initiative provides 1,100 scholarships annually to bring students from developing countries to Norway for *only* the duration of their studies (Trondstad et al. 2012). Funded by the Ministry of Foreign Affairs and conceptualized as a form of development assistance, the purpose of the Quota Scheme is twofold. First, it is intended to provide education to students in fields of critical need but limited supply in their countries of origin. Second, the scheme is designed to advance the internationalization of higher education in Norway by strengthening international cooperation among Norwegian universities and increasing the number of international students at Norwegian institutions (SIU 2005). Upon receiving their degrees, students are expected to return to their countries of origin and reside there for a period of at least ten years (Brekke 2006). If students renege on their initial agreement and remain in Norway, pursue opportunities in a third country, or leave their home countries before the ten-year period has expired, they are required to repay the cost of their scholarships, although this requirement is often difficult to enforce (Brekke 2006).

In order to be selected for Quota Scheme scholarships, students must be citizens of countries on the Organization for Economic Cooperation and Development's (OECD) Development Assistance Committee (DAC) list. DAC countries are uniformly poorer and are typically culturally distant from Norway. In this chapter I show that the litany of cultural differences experienced by Quota Scheme students coupled with the typical pressures of migration and college life contribute to a high susceptibility for stress among students in the program as they adjust to life in their new, temporary home.

This chapter rethinks scholarship on ISM by focusing on heretofore overlooked influences on the mental health of international students that occur as a result of their dual roles as students *and* migrants. It does so in three primary ways. First, ISM research is primarily limited to countries of the Anglosphere, such as the United States, the United Kingdom, Australia, and Canada. While this research is instructive, the cultural context of receiving countries plays a significant role in both the academic and nonacademic experiences of international students. Here, I broaden the existing narrative on student experiences by studying Norway, an emerging destination for international students outside of the English-speaking world (see Brekke 2006; Tronstad, Bore, and Djuve 2012; van Mol 2013; Wiers-Jenssen 2013 for other studies of ISM in Norway). Second, research on the mental health outcomes of international students is most often methodologically quantitative and focused on self-financed students in vocation-oriented programs (Robotham and Julian 2006; Robotham 2008). In this chapter, I qualitatively engage with the experiences of non-self-financed international students across a variety of academic disciplines to show how the unique constraints of a state-regulated scholarship program can shape mental health outcomes for international students. Third, the students in this project represent a more diverse group whose perspectives are often neglected in existing literature. In addition to populating a variety of academic programs, the students in this project originate from world regions less frequently the focus of ISM investigation, such as Sub-Saharan Africa and Latin America (Smith 1999; Appadurai 2000; Maringe and Carter 2007). By collecting the perspectives of heretofore overlooked groups, the narratives presented here represent a fuller picture of the student-migrant experience.

Importantly, I identify four primary categorical sources of emotional distress experienced by international students: acculturation, finances, distance from home and family, and bureaucracy. Each of these stressors has an integral connection to place and space. Plainly, the tumult of international student migration places all cross-cultural sojourners at risk of undergoing emotional stress. Geography, however, mediates the degree to which international students are likely to encounter mental health difficulties. Students from countries at a greater cultural, socioeconomic, and geographic distance from the host country face more significant challenges in adapting to life in their new home. Given the large separation between the cultures of most Quota Scheme students and Norway, the risk of emotional distress is likely more significant for these students than those who originate from nearby countries within the European Union/European Economic Area (EU/EEA).

This chapter is organized into four sections. What follows is a brief overview of existing literature on mental health and students of higher education. In the second section, I describe my methodology, followed by a discussion of my findings in the third section. I conclude by relating interview data to existing literature to propose procedures that institutions can implement to improve the mental health of international students.

Student-migrant Experiences of Stress

College students—whether studying abroad or domestically—are at high risk of experiencing emotional distress. Major sources of stress common to most college students include: increased workloads, strict time constraints, financial difficulties, forming new social bonds, meeting personal, parental, and institutional demands for academic progress, and determining future career paths (Thomas and Althen 1989; Ross, Niebling, and Heckart 1999; Robotham and Julian 2006).

Research on the mental health of international students is growing; Zhou et al. (2008, 63) go so far as to suggest that "student sojourners are probably the best-researched group of cross-cultural travellers, as they tend to be easily accessed as research participants." Much of the existing literature suggests the acculturative pressures unique to international students—as a result of their migrant status—makes them particularly vulnerable to encountering emotional difficulties (Redmond and Bunyi 1993). However, international students' susceptibility to stress is influenced by their cultural backgrounds (Yeh and Inose 2003; Misra and Castillo 2004). To this end, Hechanova-Alampay et al. (2002) found that cultural distance, in addition to self-confidence and social support, was predictive of emotional adjustment for international students.

One of the most commonly invoked theories to explain the acculturative stress endured by international students (and migrants of all types) is "culture shock" (see Robertson et al. 2000; Chapdelaine and Alexitch 2004; Zhou et al. 2008 for examples related to student mental health). Culture shock in this context can be defined as "a series of mental health changes that might be a consequence of migration experiences, including negative life events, lack of social support networks and the impact of value differences" (Zhou et al. 2008, 64). The concept implies stress induced by lack of familiarity with the new cultural framework in the host society, wherein this adversity is negotiated and ameliorated through experience. While culture shock varies according to the relative distance between the cultural background of the migrant and the community into which she relocates (Yeh and Inose 2003), Redmond and Bunyi (1993, 247) found that "stress is apparently experienced regardless of how familiar or communicatively competent a sojourner might be."

The culture shock framework also has relevance in educational contexts. According to Hofstede (1986) there are four circumstances that are most likely to produce intercultural misunderstandings in cross-cultural learning situations: social positions of teacher and student; relevance of curriculum; profiles of cognitive abilities; and expected patterns of student–teacher and student–student interaction. Thomas and Althen (1989, 214) specifically suggest that international students from non-Western countries may struggle with "objective-type (as opposed to essay) examinations; the need to do assignments and take examinations throughout each semester, rather than just at the end of the term, and the need to cover a large amount of material and then analyze and synthesize the information," as this type of academic structure is often absent in their countries of origin. Relatedly, Yeh and Inose (2003) found that international students from Europe suffered less acculturative stress in the United States than did students from Asia, Latin America, and Africa, again emphasizing the role that geography plays as a mediator of stress for foreign students.

In addition to problems connected to cultural misunderstandings, Mori (2000) identifies language barriers as the most pressing source of emotional and academic difficulty encountered by foreign college students. Inability to communicate fluently in the domestic tongue generates a host of negative consequences (Poyrazli et al. 2004). First, it impedes the creation of new social networks, which are doubly important for international students as their friends and families are typically left behind in their countries of origin (Lee, Koeske, and Sales 2004). Second, it has strong potential to impede educational success, as students lacking fluency in the language of instruction are likely to struggle to comprehend lectures and course materials. Third, for international students who work as graduate teaching assistants, it diminishes their ability to effectively convey knowledge to students under their guidance, hampering the experience of undergraduate students and contributing to faculty dissatisfaction with their performance (Plakans 1997; Trice 2003).

As students and migrants both, international students encounter challenges that may render them particularly susceptible to suffering emotional distress. Importantly, each of the predominant sources of stress outlined above is embedded within the process of navigating and negotiating place and space. The distinct acculturative demands faced by international students—particularly those from more culturally distant countries—places them at greater risk of sustaining emotional distress. This chapter shows that in addition to acculturative pressures, international students are also subject to stress resultant from noncultural aspects of migration including state-imposed bureaucratic constraints, adjusting to a foreign educational context, and financial concerns.

Methods

Robotham and Julian (2006) identified two major trends in literature on post-secondary student stress. First, it tends to be methodologically quantitative. Second, it often directs attention to students in vocation-oriented degree programs. Arguing in favor of more qualitative assessments of stress in the lives of college students, they postulate that "it is by no means clear that stress is a concept which is amenable to measurement," and they argue that the relatively narrow focus on particular disciplines may be misrepresentative of college students as a whole (Robotham and Julian 2006, 114). I set out in this chapter to address both lacunae by asking the following question: what are the primary sources of emotional distress experienced by Norwegian Quota Scheme students?

The narratives presented in the following section are culled from a series of sixteen semi-structured interviews: fourteen with international students enrolled at two Norwegian universities who are recipients of a Quota Scheme grant and two with faculty members who teach Quota Scheme students. Each interview was conducted in English from May to June 2013 as part of a broader project concerning the role of institutional stakeholders in the student migrant experience. The majority of the interviews were conducted in person, six students were interviewed by Skype, and one faculty member was interviewed by telephone. Each interview lasted between forty-five minutes and one hour.

Students were asked questions concerning their educational, professional, and personal ambitions and experiences in Norway. Faculty members were asked broader questions about the internationalization of higher education in Norway and their experiences teaching Quota Scheme students. Of the fourteen students interviewed for this project, seven were male and seven female. Five migrated from Sub-Saharan Africa, three from Eastern Europe, two from Latin America, two from South Asia, and one each from Southeast and East Asia. Each student had resided in Norway between one and three years. The students ranged in age from 22 to 37, six of whom were over 30. The largest number of students—five—were pursuing degrees in international health. This was followed by two students each in business administration, education, engineering, and physics. Finally, one student each was studying international development, architecture, and economics. Study participants were recruited in three ways. First, flyers were posted throughout Oslo to announce the research project and dates of availability for meetings. Second, university staff distributed an e-mail to all currently active Quota Scheme students at two large Norwegian universities, encouraging them to participate in interviews. Third, snowball sampling was used to increase the likelihood of participation (Bradshaw and Stratford 2010). In this chapter, informants are identified by pseudonyms to ensure their confidentiality. All personally identifiable information has been removed.

This study does not aim to be representative of all international students or Quota Scheme students in Norway. Nevertheless, the data presented is illustrative of the stress events experienced by students from developing countries who are pursuing a tertiary education in Norway. In the following section, I use data gathered from interviews to discuss the mental health experiences of foreign students.

Mental Health and ISM: The Case of Quota Scheme Students in Norway

Students interviewed for this project described four primary triggers of emotional distress: acculturation, finances, distance from home and family, and bureaucracy. Below, I use interview excerpts to contextualize how each type of emotional distress was experienced by Quota Scheme students.

Acculturation

As both students and migrants, international students must simultaneously navigate multiple demanding, life-altering experiences. While acculturative stress is influenced by the relative distance between the cultures of the sending and receiving countries, Quota Scheme students typically originate from countries with vastly different cultural norms than what is present Norway. Therefore, acculturative stress was particularly pronounced among the students interviewed for this chapter. Existing research identifies linguistic, academic, and interpersonal challenges as among the most pressing sources of acculturative stress for foreign students (Mallinckrodt and Leong 1992; Leong and Chou 1996; Mori 2000). The majority of interview participants mentioned these dilemmas, as discussed below.

Language barriers present perhaps the most immediate challenge to acculturation (Mori 2000). All coursework approved for Quota Scheme students (except in a limited number of degree programs) is intended to be taught in English. To that end, students who receive scholarships are required to demonstrate English proficiency. They are not, however, required to speak Norwegian. Students can elect to take Norwegian language lessons, but since Quota Scheme students generally begin their degree programs intending to return home, few choose to do so. Nevertheless, being unable to communicate in Norwegian presents a significant social handicap for international students. Consider this exchange with Katungi, an African male student:

> Scott Basford (SB): What is the most difficult aspect of living in Norway?
>
> Katungi: Other than the cost-of-living, it is the language barrier. I feel isolated from the culture and my classmates … they speak a language I cannot understand. In two years here I have found only one Norwegian friend. [Staff of the Office of International Education] say they have classes, but I do not have time to study both my degree and Norwegian. I feel very isolated.
>
> (Personal interview, June 3, 2013)

Linguistic barriers are common for international students in forming interpersonal relationships with domestic students (Yeh and Inose 2003). While it is likely that Katungi's isolation is a result of more than just an inability to converse in Norwegian, it nevertheless contributes to his struggle to feel connected to his Norwegian-speaking classmates.

Cultural differences also made it difficult for some students to access academic resources at the university. Consider this except from an interview with Quon, a male student from an East Asian country:

> I would say that one of my personal favorite things about [studying in] Norway is [the] variety of resources available for students to succeed. The facilities are advanced and staff is happy to offer help with your studies. But it is at first difficult to understand what help is available, especially for

> students in Quota, since we may hesitate to burden others with [our] troubles, and it is not really publicized well by the faculty.
>
> (Personal interview, Quon, June 1, 2013)

Similarly, Emilija, a female student from Eastern Europe, initially experienced Norwegians as rude and unwelcoming, due to cultural differences in how universities manage foreign students. In her country of origin international students are extended additional help and attention without needing to request it. While the same support is provided in Norway, students must take initiative in accessing it. This caused Emilija to feel disrespected until she learned to ask for what she needed. This type of experience may be common for international students from countries with different cultural mores, making it particularly important for university staff to welcome foreign students and encourage them to contact staff when they need assistance (Eland and Thomas 2013).

Similar to Emilija's initial experience, respondents often told stories of alienation. Sanja, an Eastern European female student, thoughtfully put it as such:

> SB: How do you feel about living in Norway?
>
> Sanja: Well, it seems to me that the people I'm surrounded with are just too into their own needs; I feel I am experiencing alienation. I don't know; it [may] be my own sense of being far away from everything familiar and close and friends and family … I have been talking to other internationals and most of us have that as a first thing [we describe about our experiences]. It could be our own fault that we expect from locals to behave and accept us the same way people from our culture would.
>
> (Personal interview, June 3, 2013)

The differences in Sanja's social experiences in her native country and Norway have led her to believe that Norwegians are preoccupied with themselves and uninterested in socializing with new people, making her feel lonely and isolated. In their study of international students in Australia, Sawir et al. (2008) found that two-thirds of students suffered from problems of loneliness or alienation. They describe international students as particularly susceptible to a type of loneliness they refer to as "cultural loneliness," which they define as "the absence of the preferred cultural and/or linguistic environment" (Sawir et al. 2008, 171). This may explain why, although they may eventually develop new social networks abroad, some international students still suffer from feelings of isolation.

Bashirah, a Ghanaian female student, did eventually develop a social network (largely comprised of other international students), but she nevertheless expressed dissatisfaction and feelings of alienation as a result of the relatively individualistic Norwegian culture:

> SB: What is the most difficult aspect of living in Norway?
>
> Bashirah: It is very closed. If they could be more open they could learn more about different cultures. Instead people here are not friendly. They do not

> socialize well with people who are not like them. When I came here I thought it would be easier to make friends, but I was shown to be wrong.
>
> (Personal interview, June 3, 2013)

Basirah, similar to Sanja, described Norwegians as internally focused. Her experiences led her to believe that locals were reluctant to socialize with those they perceive as outsiders. Although she initially sought to develop a social network comprised of Norwegians and internationals, the difficulty she had forming connections with Norwegians eventually led her to seek friendships exclusively with other international students. Another African student called upon the term "culture shock" to describe his surprise at the insularity of strangers in Norway:

> In [my country] eight of ten people on the street would help you if you asked for it. In Norway, two of ten people will do the same. Some people are so reserved here, and it was quite a culture shock to experience this.
>
> (Personal interview, June 3, 2013)

One of the defining cultural characteristics of a country is the degree to which it emphasizes individualism or collectivism (Hofstede et al. 2010). Norway, as most Western countries, is regarded by Hofstede et al. (2010) as an individualistic country, characterized by loose ties between individuals. This contrasts with collectivist societies where group loyalty is emphasized. Many Quota Scheme students, including those quoted above, originate from so-called collectivist societies. Often the social difficulties encountered by these students are in part a result of their difficulty navigating the relatively self-focused Norwegian society. In this context, the feelings of alienation identified by eleven of the sixteen students interviewed for this project are perhaps to be expected.

Indeed, difficulty relating to native students is not uncommon as a source of unhappiness for international students (Yeh and Inose 2003; Sawir et al. 2008; Zhou et al. 2008; Sherry, Thomas, and Chui 2010). This dissatisfaction has even been found to have deleterious ramifications on student academic success, as feelings of isolation sometimes make it more difficult for students to prosper academically (Dobson, Campbell, and Dobson 1987). With respect to these findings, it is important that international students are made aware of the potential cultural differences between their countries of destination and origin in order to stem feelings of distress and resultant complications.

Finances

Financial burdens are widespread among all college students (Ginter and Glauser 1997), but they are particularly acute for non-self-financed and international students, who may have more financial, regulatory, and academic hurdles to navigate. The apprehensions of foreign students are often made worse by the relative difficulty they experience obtaining employment due to immigration regulations and language barriers (Cadieux and Wehrly 1986; Thomas and Althen 1989; Essandoh 1995). The most prevalent financial concern of students in this project was the condition that they must repay the full amount of their scholarship if they decide to remain in Norway or seek employment in a third country. Consider the aspirations of Ankit, a male South Asian student:

> For different reasons I may want to move to [the] US. My field of study is academia. It can easily happen that I find some position elsewhere. If my personal situation allows me to move, why shouldn't [the Quota Scheme] allow me to move?
>
> If this is tailored to develop the countries, my country should have an obligation to employ me. If it does not have work for me, then why should I not move? So say I get a job in a third country that is of [an economic] standard in-between Norway and [my home country], and at the same time [I] don't have appropriate job opportunities in either country, how will I afford to repay my loan, and why do I have to be limited in that case?
>
> (Personal interview, May 30, 2013)

Ankit highlights one of the inherent weaknesses of the Quota Scheme: there is often a lack of suitable jobs for graduating students in their countries of origin. Faced with this dilemma, students often must make a difficult decision. One option is to fulfill the terms of their original agreement and return home, where in many cases suitable employment prospects are limited. The other option is to remain in Norway or seek employment in a third country and repay the scholarship.

Ankit was not the only student to relate a tension between the financial constraints of the return condition and personal fulfillment:

> SB: Do you want to go back … when you're done?
>
> Katungi: Yeah, of course, but at first I would like to work and get some experience, but not under Quota with the loans.
>
> SB: So are you going to go back home even though you would rather stay here?
>
> Katungi: I am going to go back home. Yes. I would like to stay here at least at first after finishing, and maybe after that I would like to go back home. Maybe after one or two years, but I cannot.
>
> (Personal interview, May 30, 2013)

For Katungi, studying international health, employability in his country of origin was not a distressing concern. Still, after living in Norway for three years and acclimating to its culture, he did not want to return immediately. However, his job prospects in Norway were not strong enough to negate the financial penalty he would incur for failing to repatriate. The circumstances of students like Ankit and Katungi make apparent that field of study and consequent job prospects strongly affect whether Quota Scheme students ultimately uphold the program's return obligation. Further, they exemplify a rift between the priorities of the state and students: often what is ultimately in the best interests of graduating Quota Scheme students does not align with the goals of the state.

Many Quota Scheme students also struggle to afford the high cost of living in Norway. The comments quoted below, from an African female student named Rhoda, were echoed by the majority of respondents:

> SB: How could the Quota Scheme be improved?
>
> Rhoda: I think they should change the amount of money [offered to students]; they should raise it. It is far too difficult to live in such an expensive country with so little money … everything is so expensive, but if people happen to have a good job it's okay … with Quota it is not enough money to survive easily. I appreciate the opportunity provided, but the salary is perverse compared to the expenses.
>
> (Personal interview, June 3, 2013)

Upon being offered acceptance in her program with Quota Scheme funding, Rhoda assumed living expenses would be among the least of her concerns. She described being unprepared to adjust to the high cost of everyday items in Norway relative to prices in her home country. Although college education in Norway is essentially free, adapting to the high cost of living is often a concern for international students. As a result, self-financed international students are required to deposit sufficient funds in a Norwegian bank account to demonstrate they can subsist for at least one year in the country (Brekke 2006). Quota Scheme students, however, are exempt from this requirement, which may make them more vulnerable. One of the professors interviewed for this project explained the financial situation of Quota Scheme students as follows:

> The [monthly] stipend is very meager. It's about nine thousand kroner [1,010 USD—according to the exchange rate on January 4, 2015] so it's quite hard for them to survive. In the beginning they think that this is an awful lot of money because it's maybe a year's salary back home, but then they experience Norwegian prices. So, there is not a [Quota Scheme-wide], structured program to assist them with [how to prepare an appropriate budget].
>
> (Personal interview, June 3, 2013)

Quota Scheme students receive funding from the Norwegian State Educational Loan Fund (NSELF) on largely the same terms as domestic students (SIU 2005) with far less understanding of how to subsist on that income. While his university provides an orientation program to help international students adjust to life in Norway, the professor has found these to have minimal impact on his student's spending habits. As a result, he has designed an innovative program in an attempt to mitigate the problem:

> We appoint, early in the semester, a kind of internal government where they have a minister of supplies, for example, who is then telling them where they can find cheap food.
>
> (Personal interview, June 3, 2013)

The department's program helps students stretch their incomes and provides an important source of intercultural communication for students who otherwise may struggle to build social connections. This type of group that brings together domestic and international students to bridge intercultural gaps in understanding was explicitly called for by foreign students at the University of Toledo in the United States (Sherry, Thomas, and Chui 2010). There the authors noted a desire for "a more formalized process of social interaction with American students" (Sherry, Thomas, and Chui 2010, 37). The program in the Department of International Health represents just that, as a controlled yet relaxed process of intercultural communication that international students themselves recognize as important in ameliorating financial and social difficulties adjusting to the local culture and therefore reducing stress.

Distance from Home and Family

Away from childhood friends and family for the first time, even domestic college students often struggle initially to habituate to life on their own (Fisher 1994). This adjustment may be even more challenging for international students, for whom it is often more difficult to build new interpersonal relationships and who are typically further removed from familiar cultural mores and social support networks (Nwadiani and Ofoegbu 2001; Akgun and Ciarrochi 2003). Adversity resultant from living so far away from loved ones was an oft-professed emotional difficulty of the students interviewed for this project.

Jimena, a Latin American female student, told the most poignant case of struggling to adapt to the distance from home and family, which caused her to develop a debilitating depression midway through her first year in Norway. In her examination of common stressors of international students in the United States, Mori states, "lack of familiarity with their surroundings can lead to a period of homesickness, during which they suffer from painful feelings of isolation and loneliness" (2000, 139). Unaware of support available in Norway and struggling too much from her depression to speak up, Jimena did not begin treatment until she returned to her home country over summer break, months later. She described her situation as follows:

> I did not recognize how difficult moving ten-thousand kilometers away from my friends and family would be, to a climate completely different from what I am familiar with, where people do not communicate in the language I speak in my mind, where the culture is so standoffish and friends are difficult to come by. I felt overwhelmed and lost, and I am lucky I was able to maintain just enough focus to not flunk out and lose my scholarship. Fortunately,

> I made it through that first summer and began treatment when I returned home, and ultimately I decided to return with a healthier mindset the following semester.
>
> (Personal interview, June 3, 2013)

The depression that Jimena experienced is unfortunately common among international students who lack sufficiently strong social support networks (Mori 2000; Wei et al. 2007) and again highlights the importance of ensuring that international students are aware of the services available to them (Eland and Thomas 2013).

For some older students, familial responsibilities left behind contributed to feelings of guilt and sorrow. Consider the following excerpt from Nassuna, a female African student:

> I enjoy Norway, but I must go home because I need to go to my family. I like the work culture here and other things, the work system here…even if I had the option working anywhere in the world, for now I would choose Norway, but because I have a family to take care of I must go home…If I had the option I would bring my family to Norway, but I cannot and they need me. I feel guilty for leaving them.
>
> (Personal interview, June 3, 2013)

Nassuna has a spouse, child, and adult parents in her home country for whose care she feels responsible. While international students are allowed to bring spouses and children with them to Norway, they must be approved by the Norwegian Directorate for Immigration (UDI). This process is time-consuming and expensive, and housing is not guaranteed. In addition, financial support is not provided to spouses and families of Quota Scheme students who choose to migrate as a family unit. Given these difficulties, students with families typically choose to migrate alone—a significant source of stress for such students interviewed for this project.

One student from South Asia recalled his regret for missing the birth of his child while he was attending university in Norway:

> My biggest sorrow—really, my only sorrow—has been missing the birth of my son back in [my home country]. There is no way for me to bring my family here with me, and I [did not] have the time or money to fly home to be with my wife as she gave birth. I will never be able to get this moment back, but at least I can be home soon to reunite with my family.
>
> (Personal interview, June 3, 2013)

It is evident that separation from family is one of the most emotionally taxing aspects of the international student experience. A number of studies note the significant source of stress represented by leaving parents and siblings behind (Robotham 2008; Sawir et al. 2008; Sherry, Thomas, and Chui 2010). Rarely, however, does ISM research consider the circumstances of students with spouses and children of their own left in their countries-of-origin (see Sawir et al. 2008 for an exception). All four respondents for this project who left spouses and children in their home countries experienced significant emotional pain in doing so. Future research should devote more attention to international students who have families of their own to better understand their needs and experiences.

Bureaucracy

Lastly, many students encountered bureaucratic difficulties in Norway, ranging from mildly discomforting to potently traumatic. Emilija, a female Eastern European student, gave a jarring account of being arrested, sent to a refugee camp, and temporarily deported based on a clerical error that police officers stubbornly refused to admit to:

> [The] police asked at [the] airport why I am visiting Norway. [My] residence permit was denied accidentally, but they did not tell me. [The] police would not let me in. I was deported, even though it was a mistake. UDI [the Norwegian Directorate of Immigration] admitted they made a mistake but not until days later. [This all occurred] despite much evidence that UDI was wrong. [A university staff member] called, my advisor called, my boyfriend came to the airport, I produced a *Lånekassen* [Norwegian State Educational Loan Fund] document … yet the police still deported me, after taking me to a refugee camp for a night. [The] police didn't even want to consider my evidence, [and they] did not fully inform me about my access to public lawyers. [They] were unprofessional and inflexible and treated my case without any sensitivity.
>
> (Personal interview, June 3, 2013)

Upon returning from a trip to her home country, Emilija was denied entry to Norway. After being forced to spend a night in a refugee camp, she was deported back to her country, unable to return to Norway for nearly a week, until UDI acknowledged the error. This experience understandably left Emilija shaken and distrustful of Norwegian public institutions, as she voiced lingering resentment that she did not receive an apology from the police. UDI has come under public criticism in Norway for being emotionally detached and overly bureaucratic (Eggebø 2013). In addition to the strict scholarship regulations Quota Scheme students must adhere to, the rigidity of UDI is another potential source of stress for Quota Scheme students.

Other students suffered less troublesome but nevertheless onerous conflicts with Norwegian institutions. Given the relatively low stipend allotted to each Quota Scheme student with respect to the high cost of living in Norway, many students expressed a desire to work part-time. While the Quota Scheme does not prohibit this, two students said they were denied work permits when their universities refused to grant them permission to work. For students from outside of the EU/EEA (which includes all Quota Scheme students except those from Croatia,

Bulgaria, and Poland), applications for work permits must be accompanied by two letters, one from a prospective employer documenting a job offer and another from the university declaring that the proposed employment will not interfere with the student's studies. As explained by Quon, an East Asian male student:

> In Norway you must have permission from [the] university to receive [a work] permit. I found a job opportunity and … [felt] confident I could manage the work and school balance, but [my university] would not agree … to allow me [to take] this job. It is frustrating because the [additional] income [from employment] would relieve much stress.
>
> (Personal interview, June 3, 2013)

Although Quon felt he had maintained satisfactory progress toward his degree, the university disagreed with that assessment and denied his permit's renewal. In contrast to the great majority of Quota Scheme students, international students from EU/EEA countries are granted work permits automatically upon receiving their first-time residence permits and need neither proof of employment nor institutional approval to work. The differing regulatory constraints applied to international students based on geographic origin impose a clear economic disadvantage on students from outside of the EU/EEA.

Conclusion

In this chapter I have explored the types of emotional distress experienced by Norwegian Quota Scheme students. The narratives discussed above illustrate how the negotiation of place and space, through cultural norms, financial concerns, separation from family, and institutional bureaucracy can negatively affect the mental health of international students. Yet, international students are resilient. Eventually, most habituate to Norwegian cultural norms and their incidence of acculturative emotional distress becomes less pronounced. Throughout the acclimation process, students interviewed for this project described finding support from other international students as they together struggled to adapt to life in Norway. The resultant bonds they formed served as a significant buffer to the emotional distress they otherwise encountered.

Still, there is more that can be done to help mitigate the stress experienced by international students. Building on existing research and the narratives of students relayed in this chapter, I recommend the following geography-focused measures be taken by university administrators to alleviate the stress felt by international students—whether in Norway or elsewhere. First, if universities are concerned with the health and well-being of their international students, it is important to provide comprehensive orientations to prepare foreign students for the financial, emotional, academic, and cultural stressors they are likely to encounter (Sherry, Thomas, and Chui 2010). Faculty and students interviewed for this project noted that, while some cultural orientation was provided to international students, it failed to adequately inform them of challenges they may encounter and prepare them to surmount them. For example, students were often either not aware of mental health and academic resources at their disposal or unfamiliar with how to access such services. Nor did orientations prepare students for daily life in Norway, such as surviving on a scant budget or how to psychologically *and* physically adjust to the long, dark Norwegian winters. Second, schools should create programs that pair domestic students with international students to help bridge cross-cultural communicative divides and foster intellectual collaboration among students (Yeh and Inose 2003; Sherry, Thomas, and Chui 2010). In the absence of strong university-implemented cultural orientation programs, the faculty of the Department of International Health established an innovative program that promoted cross-cultural communication among its students. This program built interpersonal relationships between domestic students and students from different international backgrounds, taught international students how to survive on a shoestring budget, and facilitated knowledge sharing in the classroom. Third, faculty and staff should engage in cross-cultural training to better understand the needs of international students in their care. While the literature tends to focus on cross-cultural training for students, the needs of international students would be better met if university administrators worked to more holistically understand the positionality of their students. At present, the overwhelming burden is placed upon students to adapt to the new cultural context in which they live and study.

As flows of international student migrants proliferate, it is increasingly important to understand the perspectives of a broader variety of foreign students (van Mol 2013). This chapter has endeavored to address this need by including the narratives of a diverse range of international students typically omitted in the ISM literature. By incorporating the perspectives of non-self-financed students studying in a wide breadth of academic disciplines, of diffuse geographic origins, and encompassing a broad spectrum of ages, I have identified heretofore overlooked challenges confronted by these students. While predominant understandings of ISM and mental health stress the primacy of acculturation in driving emotional outcomes, this chapter also identifies three other primary sources of emotional duress for international students: financial concerns, distance from home and family, and bureaucracy. These stressors manifest in a variety of ways, including but not limited to the following. First, it shows how students from poorer countries and/or studying disciplines with limited job prospects may experience greater financial burdens. Second, it relates how vulnerable international students can be to feelings of stress, guilt, and depression as a result of separation from family and friends. Third, the findings in this chapter highlight the ways in which students studying abroad under scholarship are subject to additional regulatory demands from which other students—including self-financed international students—are exempt. Those state and institution-based obligations create additional pressures for non-self-financed international students. Future research might provide further evidence how university faculty and staff can provide more effective emotional health services for international students while expanding research on international students of non-traditional backgrounds.

References

Akgun, S., and J. Ciarrochi. 2003. Learned resourcefulness moderates the relationship between academic stress and academic performance. *Educational Psychology* 23 (3): 287–294.

Appadurai, A. 2000. Grassroots globalization and the research imagination. *Public Culture* 12 (1): 1–19.

Bradshaw, M., and E. Stratford. 2010. Qualitative research design and rigour. In *Qualitative Research Methods in Human Geography*, ed. I. Hay, 69–80. Don Mills, Ontario: Oxford University Press.

Brekke, J. 2006. International students and immigration to Norway. Oslo: Institute for Social Research.

Brooks, R., and J. Waters. 2010. Social networks and educational mobility: The experiences of UK students. *Globalisation, Societies and Education* 8 (1): 143–157.

Cadieux, R. A. J., and B. Wehrly. 1986. Advising and counseling the international student. *New Directions for Student Services* 36 (1): 51–63.

Chapdelaine, R. F., and L. R. Alexitch. 2004. Social skills difficulty: Model of culture shock for international graduate students. *Journal of College Student Development* 45 (2): 167–184.

Dobson, J.E., N.J. Campbell, and R. Dobson. 1987. Relationships among loneliness, perceptions of school, and grade point averages of high school juniors. *The School Counselor* 35 (2): 143–148.

Eggebø, H. 2013. 'With a heavy heart': Ethics, emotions, and rationality in Norwegian immigration administration. *Sociology* 47 (2): 301–317.

Eland, A., and Thomas, K. 2013. Succeeding abroad: International students in the United States. In *International students and scholars in the United States: Coming from abroad*, eds. H. C. Alberts, and H. D. Hazen, 145–162. New York: Palgrave Macmillan.

Essandoh, P. K. 1995. Counseling issues with African college students in U.S. colleges and universities. *The Counseling Psychologist* 23 (2): 348–360.

Findlay, A. 2011. An assessment of supply and demand-side theorizations of international student mobility. *International Migration* 49 (2): 162–190.

Fisher, S. 1994. Stress in academic life: The mental assembly line. Buckingham: Open University Press.

Ginter, E. J., and A. Glauser. 1997. A developmental life skills model: A comprehensive approach for students. Presentation made at the 22nd Annual University System of Georgia's Learning Support/Developmental Studies Conference, Augusta, Georgia.

Hazen, H. D., and H. C. Alberts. 2006. Visitors or immigrants? International students in the United States. *Population, Space and Place* 12 (3): 201–216.

———. 2013. Introduction. In *International students and scholars in the United States: Coming from abroad*, eds. H. C. Alberts, and H. D. Hazen, 1–22. New York: Palgrave Macmillan.

Hechanova-Alampay, R., T.A. Beehr, N.D. Christiansen, and R.K. van Horn. 2002. Adjustment and strain among domestic and international student sojourners. *School Psychology International* 23 (4): 458–474.

Hofstede, G. 1986. Cultural differences in learning and teaching. *International Journal of Intercultural* Relations 10 (3): 301–320.

Hofstede, G., G. J. Hofstede, and M. Minkov. 2010. *Cultures and organizations: Software of the mind*. New York: McGraw-Hill.

King, R., and P. Raghuram. 2013. International student migration: Mapping the field and new research agendas. *Population, Space and Place* 19 (2): 127–137.

Lee, J. S., G. F. Koeske, and E. Sales. 2004. Social support buffering of acculturative stress: A study of mental health symptoms among Korean international students. *International Journal of Intercultural Relations* 28 (1): 399–414.

Leong, F. T. L., and E. L. Chou. 1996. Counseling international students. In *Counseling across cultures*, eds. P. B. Pedersen, J. G. Draguns, W. J. Lonner, and J. E. Trimble, 210–242. Thousand Oaks, CA: Sage.

Mallinckrodt, B., and F. T. L. Leong. 1992. International graduate students, stress, and social support. *Journal of College Student Development* 33 (1): 71–78.

Maringe, F., and S. Carter. 2007. International students' motivations for studying in UK HE: Insights into the choice and decision making of African students. *International Journal of Educational Management* 21 (6): 459–475.

Misra, R., and L. G. Castillo. 2004. Academic stress among college students: Comparison of American and international students. *International Journal of Stress Management* 11 (2): 132–148.

Mori, S. 2000. Addressing the mental health concerns of international students. *Journal of Counseling and Development* 78 (2): 137–144.

Nwadiani, M., and F. Ofoegbu. 2001. Perceived levels of academic stress among first timers in Nigerian universities. *College Student Journal* 35 (1): 2–15.

Plakans, B. S. 1997. Undergraduates' experiences with and attitudes toward international teaching assistants. *TESOL Quarterly* 31 (1): 95–119.

Poyrazli, S., P. R. Kavanaugh, A. Baker, and N. Al-Timini. 2004. Social support and demographic correlates of acculturative stress in international students. *Journal of College Counseling* 7 (1): 73–82.

Redmond, M. V., and J. M. Bunyi. 1993. The relationship of intercultural communication competence with stress and the handling of stress as reported by international students. *International Journal of Intercultural Relations* 17 (2): 235–254.

Robertson, M., M. Line, S. Jones, and S. Thomas. 2000. International students, learning environments and perceptions: A case study using the Delphi technique. *Higher Education Research and Development* 19 (1): 89–102.

Robotham, D. 2008. Stress among higher education students: Towards a research agenda. *Higher Education* 56 (6): 735–746.

Robotham, D., and C. Julian. 2006. Stress and the higher education student: A critical review of the literature. *Journal of Further and Higher Education* 30 (2): 107–117.

Ross, S.E., B. C. Niebling, and T. M. Heckert. 1999. Sources of stress among college students. *College Student Journal* 33 (2): 312–316.

Sawir, E., S. Marginson, A. Deumert, C. Nyland, and G. Ramia. 2008. Loneliness and international students: An Australian study. *Journal of Studies in International Education* 12 (2): 148–180.

Sherry, M., P. Thomas, and W. H. Chui. 2010. International students: A vulnerable student population. *Higher Education* 60 (1): 33–46.

SIU. 2005. The quota scheme: Academic partnerships for development across borders. Center for International Cooperation in Education: Bergen, Norway. Available at: http://siu.no/eng/Publications/Publication-database/(view)/391 (last accessed February 14, 2016).

Smith, L. T. 1999. *Decolonising methodologies: Research and indigenous peoples*. London: Zed Books.

Thomas, K., and G. Althen. 1989. Counseling foreign students. In *Counseling across cultures*, eds. P. B. Pedersen, J. G. Draguns, W. J. Lonner, and J. E. Trimble, 205–241. Honolulu: University of Hawaii Press.

Trice, A.G. 2003. Faculty perceptions of graduate international students: The benefits and challenges. *Journal of Studies in International Education* 7 (4): 379–403.

Tronstad, K.R., L. Bore, and A. B. Djuve. 2012. Immigration of international students to the EU/EEA: Report to the European Migration Network from the Norwegian contact point, August 2012. Brussels: European Migration Network.

van Mol, C. 2013. Intra-European student mobility and European identity: A successful marriage? *Population, Space and Place* 19 (2): 209–222.

Wei, M., P. P. Heppner, M. J. Mallen, T. Y. Ku, K. Y. H. Liao, and T. F. Wu. 2007. Acculturative stress, perfectionism, years in the United States, and depression among Chinese international students. *Journal of Counseling Psychology* 54 (4): 385–394.

Wiers-Jenssen, J. 2013. *Utenlandske studenter i Norge* (International Students in Norway). Working Paper 12/2013, Oslo: Nordic Institute for Studies in Innovation, Research and Education.

Yeh, C. J., and M. Inose. 2003. International students' reported English fluency, social support satisfaction, and social connectedness as predictors of acculturative stress. *Counselling Psychology Quarterly* 16 (1): 15–28.

Zhou, Y., D. Jindal-Snape, K. Topping, and J. Todman. 2008. Theoretical models of culture shock and adaptation in international students in higher education. *Studies in Higher Education* 33 (1): 63–75.

Ziguras, C, and S. F. Law. 2006. Recruiting international students as skilled migrants: The global "skills race" as viewed from Australia and Malaysia. *Globalisation, Societies and Education* 4 (1): 59–76.

6 Chinese Student Migrants in Transition

A Pathway from International Students to Skilled Migrants

Wan Yu

Introduction

Contemporary economic globalization has resulted in two different yet closely related phenomena in international migration: the accelerated internationalization of the higher education sector, and the global competition for highly skilled professionals. In the past two decades, studying abroad for an academic degree has become a popular pathway for students in developing countries to accumulate human capital for better employment opportunities in the global job market. Nowadays, more international students choose to stay in the receiving countries and join their labor force upon graduation (Lowell and Findlay 2002; National Academies 2005). Thus, international students, especially those who seek post-graduate degrees, are often considered as important human capital sources in popular migrant-receiving countries (Wadhwa et al. 2009). Yet, barriers and obstacles exist when international students enter the receiving countries' job market and transition to highly skilled migrant labors, which discourage them from staying and stimulate their return migration. The increasing return migration of skilled migrants has gained policymakers' attention, as mirrored in President Obama's Inaugural Address in January 2013 on the need for immigration reform: "Our journey is not complete until … bright young students and engineers are enlisted in our workforce rather than expelled from our country" (Obama 2013).

Migrants usually experience a transition period as they move from international students to skilled migrants. In many migrant-receiving countries such as Australia and New Zealand, with policy facilitations such a transition period can be in the form of "two-step" migration or "education-migration nexus" (Hawthorne 2010; Robertson and Runganaikaloo 2013). The transition period of international students is a critical and important juncture of their lives, yet is often overlooked in previous scholarly work (few exceptions are Hawthorne 2010; Geddie 2013; Robertson and Runganaikaloo 2013). It is because students not only directly face the decision of whether to return or to stay within a limited time of legal stay in the receiving countries but also constantly negotiate their transition to the next immigration status—skilled migrants. During this specific time period, migrants construct their individual characteristics that are specifically tied to the social and cultural contexts, usually in the form of social networks and cultural assimilation, to the receiving countries. As a consequence, they are largely influenced by institutional and structural forces, such as immigration policy changes in the receiving countries, economic cycles and restructuring, and economic opportunities in their home countries (Wadhwa et al. 2009; Hawthorne 2010). These become important factors in shaping skilled migrants' mobility and location choices during the transition period (Yeoh and Eng 2008; Geddie 2013).

Previous literature on human capital theory states that skilled migrants' human capital, measured by one's educational attainment and professional skills, largely facilitate their mobility across nation-state boundaries to become footloose global talent (Ewers 2007; Aure 2013). Yet, some studies argue that highly skilled migrants are far from being footloose, but instead a pattern of "middling transnationals" whose movements are largely under institutional constraints (Ho 2011; Parutis 2014). Much relevant work has focused on the institutional forces from the policy level or migrant group level, with little attention to how structural forces manifest at the individual level and shape skilled migrants' career experience post-graduation and further influence their return migrations (exceptions see Robertson and Runganaikaloo 2013; Nohl and Schittenhelm 2014). In fact, some scholars argue that the economic value, or price, of human capital is greatly embedded in the social and cultural contexts of a specific country and plays a key role in skilled migrants' decision-making process (Bankston 2004; Shan 2013; Kõu and Bailey 2014). Bourdieu (1986) defines such socially and culturally constructed individual characteristics as social capital and cultural capital. Specifically, *social capital* refers to "the aggregate of the actual or potential resources which are linked to possession of a durable network of more or less institutionalized relationships" (248), and *cultural capital* refers to "the level or qualification of individuals' cultural competence" (246). The concepts of social capital and cultural capital explain the differences between skilled migrants' professions and their diverse economic outcomes under different societal contexts. By analyzing the change in migrants' social and cultural capital when they transition from international students to skilled migrants, as well as its impact on migrants' career experiences and migration decision-making, this chapter connects the theoretical discussions on the migration movements of international students and their social and cultural capitals in both migrant home and receiving countries. It also addresses the following research questions:

1. Do skilled migrants accumulate their social capital and cultural capital differently during the transition period (from full-time F1 students to OPT holders to first-term H-1B visa holders)? If so, what are the underlying structural and contextual forces that shape their social and cultural capitals?
2. How do migrants' changing social and cultural capitals geographically shape their migration decision-making process and location choices during the transition period?

Using Chinese graduate students in the United States as a case study, this chapter studies the experiences of international students in the transition period. It specifically examines how social and cultural capitals impact the economic outcomes of international students' human capital during the transition period, as well as how student migrants develop strategies to cope with such situations during this specific time period and build future return plans accordingly. It uses migrants in the United States as a case study because the United States has long been viewed as a popular migrant-receiving country and hosts a large population of skilled migrants in its labor force (State et al. 2014). It is also because China is one of the top sending countries of both international students and highly skilled workers to the United States (DHS 2013). In the meantime, China is also witnessing an unprecedented return migration of highly skilled workers from overseas due to the development of China's knowledge economy and recent governmental incentives to attract skilled migrants (Wang and Miao 2013). In the year 2012, for all skilled migrants who returned to China, the United States was the second top sending country for the skilled returnees, after only the United Kingdom (one major reason is due to the United Kingdom's rigid immigration policies; Wang and Miao 2013). The experiences of Chinese student migrants in the United States can be shared with many skilled migrant sending countries, as well as with many developed countries with skilled labor force shortage. The findings of this chapter can shed light on the current discussions on international students' career trajectories and migration movements, as well as the international competition for global talent. It aims to provide policy recommendations to major stakeholders in international migration, including those in migrant sending countries, receiving countries, and migrants themselves.

International Student Migrants

Contemporary international student migrants are predominantly considered as "desired" among many migrant-receiving countries. For policymakers, international students are often politically invisible due to their limited length of legal stay on student visas, and their high human capital level and tuition contribution that don't require much public assistance (Findlay 2011; King and Raghuram 2013, 127). When international students graduate, they often choose to stay in the receiving country as skilled workers, or return to their home countries. Contemporary highly skilled migrant workers draw much larger scholarly and policy attention because of their direct involvement in the labor force and contribution to the tax revenue of the countries they work in (Welch and Zhen 2008; Aure 2013). Many developed countries have recognized the impact of skilled immigration on the development of their knowledge economy and competitiveness in the globalizing world, and incorporated human capital as an important basis for their immigration policies (examples are Australia, Canada, and the United Kingdom). When international students graduate, their career experiences often times are affected by institutional constraints, and social and cultural barriers regardless of their human capital levels or the country they reside in. On one hand, in migrant-receiving countries, institutional forces such as a glass-ceiling in the workplace, "brain abuse" due to migrants' foreign credentials, "brain waste" due to migrants landing in less desirable positions in order to secure their legal status, and country-specific immigration policies all hinder student migrants from fully utilizing their human capital in the labor force (Bauder 2003; Banerjee 2006; Becker 2009). On the other hand, when skilled migrants return home, their return migrations are not always a satisfactory experience. Their lack of social networks and mismatch with the home country's job market in their professions might hinder their contribution to the development of their home countries (Waters 2006). Student migrants' career experiences after graduation are highly connected to their migration movements, which are also linked to the human capital accumulation of the country they settle (Lu et al. 2002; Waters 2006). The "brain gain" concept describes the situation in which receiving countries are able to retain skilled migrants in their labor force, and "brain drain" describes sending countries' human capital loss due to the emigration of skilled migrants (Rosen and Zweig 2005).

Social and Cultural Capitals and Career Experiences of Skilled Migrants

Scholarly attention to contemporary migrant workers' career experiences in the global job market overwhelmingly focuses on their human capital deficiency, their foreign credentials, or their language proficiency, and simultaneously distinguishes skilled migrants' career experiences from the ones of other classes of migrants based on their human capital level (Reitz 2001). Yet, migrants with higher educational degrees also encounter strong social and cultural capital deficiencies that are closely related to specific societal contexts (Duncan and Waldorf 2010). Such social and cultural capitals are especially important in shaping their career experiences during the transition period from international students to skilled labor migrants. In receiving countries, international students' social and cultural capitals are commonly reflected in their lack of *social and professional networks, legal status, ethnic and racial [in]equality,* and *cultural barriers,* which often hinder their opportunities to obtain the desired jobs matching their professional skills and education (She and Wotherspoon 2013). With different cultural backgrounds and knowledge about US higher educational system, international students, many labeled as "newcomers," lack access to social and professional networks, such as alumni associations, professional networks, and ties to professional job information in the market (Putnam 2007; Ryan et al. 2008). This lack of membership in professional networks reflects a relatively lower social capital than their native-born counterparts. International students usually lack the understanding of the receiving country's job market upon graduation. Hence, they are often prone to work at lower-paid jobs than their domestic counterparts with the same educational attainment level, accepting "reservation wage" in order to secure their legal status and future permanent residency (Constant et al. 2010). In addition, ethnic and racial (in)equality is also significant in visible minority migrants' career experiences, usually in the form of "statistical discrimination" (the larger the population size of an ethnic group in a particular industry, the higher chances that applicants from the same ethnic group could obtain employment), "structure-agency duality" (blocked access to some labor sectors leads to migrant concentrations in other industries or sectors that can provide them the best career opportunities such as higher wages or more job opportunities), and institutional racism especially in the hiring practices of the private sector of skilled immigrants (Gatchair 2013; Sarre, Phillips and Skillington 1989). Cultural barriers also impede skilled migrants in finding better job opportunities in receiving countries (Bauder and Cameron 2002). This is largely due to their non-native-speaker background, their limited shared cultural practices, or their lack of cultural assimilation in the workplace (Shan 2013; Vygotsky 1980)—i.e. their lack of "the ability to follow the rules" and "the skills to 'play by the rules'" (Bauder 2005, 83). With an increasing share of populations from Asian and Middle East countries, contemporary international students usually acquire the habitus of "being foreign" (distant from the mainstream culture), which distinguishes them from the mainstream culture in many Western countries (Bauder 2005; Bourdieu 1986; IIE 2014). In sum, despite the educational attainments and professional skills that international students obtained, there are still structural and contextual forces hindering them from obtaining desired jobs after graduation in the receiving countries' contexts.

When student migrants return home after graduation, their Western university degrees can often be viewed as *symbolic capital* (Waters 2006), due to the relative scarcity of such overseas educational experiences in these societies. This enhanced economic value from skilled migrants' overseas education varies in different societal and cultural contexts (usually larger among many Asian countries that emphasize higher education), so it can be viewed as a type of "bonus" social and cultural capitals that offer skilled returnees privileges to restricted professional networks, elite group memberships, and even "boundaryless careers" (Waters 2006). Such "bonus" social and cultural capitals from overseas education also vary by the institutions that migrants attended, with "world-class university" degrees offering migrants highest symbolic value whereas state universities providing migrants less advantages in their home country's job market (Findlay et al. 2012). It could also become stronger if the migrant home country is experiencing an economic transition or a booming economy (Williams and Baláž 2004). Yet, skilled returnees' career experiences are not always a fairytale story—some returnees consider their migrations as an unsatisfactory movement and eventually remigrate to previous receiving countries or a third country (Wang and Miao 2013). Yet, international students' long absence from their home countries during their overseas studies can also result in a lack of social connections with their home society, which might harm their social capital in the job market (Bian et al. 2001). Vanhonacker et al. (2005) argues that, compared to skilled migrants' human capital, returning students' social capital plays a more vital role in their career development when they return home.

Spatialized Knowledge Migration and Capital Transferability of Skilled Migrants

The flows of international student migration can be deeply intertwined with place and space at different scales. At the global level, Kuptsch and Pang (2006) argue that the globalization of higher education and flows of international student migrants reinforce and strengthen the global hierarchy of class. Moreover, they demonstrate that the migration movements of global talent can only benefit some regions, often the developed countries, while disempowering others at the same time. Such uneven geographic distribution of human capital and knowledge echoes with the prominent scholarly discussion on the "zero sum" situation of global competition for talent, in which some countries' brain gain indicates others' brain drain (Wadhwa et al. 2009).

At the nation-state level, skilled migrants' movements reflect a dynamic decision-making process for accumulating and transferring their human, social, and cultural capitals across nation-state boundaries. Chiswick (2008) reveals that for skilled migrants, their ability to speak the dominant language of the receiving country is critical to their labor market success and has been viewed as an indicator of their skill transferability. Their non-transferable skills due to language barriers can result in their declined intention to migrate (de Coulon and Piracha 2003). In addition, the traditional assimilation model suggests that immigrants usually face occupational downgrading upon arrival because only part of their skills can be transferred from their home countries to the receiving country's job market, and if they extend their stay, they gradually acquire the "[receiving country] specific" labor market experience, which can be viewed as a form of social and cultural capital (Dustmann and Weiss 2007). Akresh (2008) specifies that as a U-shaped pattern, revealing that in the United States migrants take downgraded US jobs first and subsequently climb up the occupational ladder. The depth (downgraded level) and width (duration of initial career stage) of the U-shape can be highly associated with skilled migrants' social capital transferability from their home countries to the receiving countries. Last but not least, certain occupations may be in great demand in one country while they face a saturated job market in another, which reflects a diverse transferability of cultural capital of skilled migrants (Lo and Li 2014). Some occupations (e.g. science, technology, engineering and math (STEM) fields professions) may be highly transferable while others (e.g. social sciences and humanities) are country-specific and require profound knowledge of the societal context. Aure (2013) further specifies that skilled migrants are more likely to enter well-established industries that are strongly attached to the globalizing economy and less likely to enter small businesses because the latter prefer employees with comprehension of the specific local contexts and often exclude immigrants. The various human, social, and cultural capital transferabilities across nation-state boundaries reflect a spatialized knowledge migration.

At the local level, institutions of higher education that host student migrants sometimes act as "knowledge brokers" that attract and admit students from different regions, augment migrants' human capital, and market them to various labor markets (Raghuram 2013). World-class universities can become "IQ magnets" that attract mobile students at the global level, accommodate them to contribute to the local economy, and eventually facilitate their skill transferability in the global labor market (Dustmann and Weiss 2007). Moreover, global cities or large metropolitan areas represent a "sufficient depth of employment opportunities," which become a strong attraction to skilled migrants (Geddie 2013 203). Skilled migrants' knowledge exchange, their transnational connections, and cross-border professional networks also contribute to human capital accumulation at the local level, mirrored in many "smart cities" discussions on how to attract globally mobilized elites (Shen 2009). Such uneven local and institutional contexts can also shape current international students' location choices for their studies and career development post-graduation (Findlay 2011).

Case Study: Transition Period of Chinese Students in the United States

This chapter takes the experiences of contemporary Chinese graduate students during the transition period in the United States as a case study. The transition period is a specific time period for international students to become skilled migrant workers, and it drastically varies by immigration policies in the receiving countries. This chapter thus separates this period into three stages based on migrant legal statuses in the United States, because legal status is a key factor defining migrants' length of legal stay and rights to work, as well as influencing migrants' decision-making for return. The first stage of the transition period starts with international students approaching graduation. At this stage, international students hold full-time student visas (F1 visas), which prevent them from working off campus when school is in session. The curricular practical training (CPT) program offers students opportunities to pursue internships during their studies.

When international students finish their programs of study, they can choose to transition to the Optional Practical Training (OPT) program, which offers them a twelve-month legal stay in the United States for each degree they obtain or a seventeen-month extension if their degrees are in STEM fields. The OPT program specifies that students who leave the United States without an official employment contract from a qualified US employer are not guaranteed reentry. Within the OPT period, students need to find qualified employers in their related fields of study who are willing to pay fees to sponsor them to become skilled migrants as H-1B visa holders. The US government issues 85,000 H-1B work visas in private industries each year, much outnumbered by the ever-increasing annual applications for H-1B visas (124,000 in 2013; 172,000 in 2014; 232,000 in 2015), which is largely due to the development of IT industries. This situation resulted in the annual H-1B visa lottery policy by the United States Citizenship and Immigration Services (USCIS) to randomly select qualified skilled migrants. Skilled migrants who work for non-profit institutions in the higher education sector are exempted from the annual quota and the lottery.

By successfully securing an H-1B visa sponsor or winning the H-1B lottery, OPT students are able to become part of the skilled foreign-born labor force and reach the last stage of the transition period, the first-term H-1B visa period. Each H-1B visa term lasts for three years, and skilled migrants can extend their H-1B visas for up to two terms. Thus, H-1B visa holders have six years to find a satisfying position to file for Legal Permanent Residency (LPR). The first-term H-1B visa period is the last stage of the transition period for skilled migrants in the United States because many migrants start to apply for LPR in the second term of the H-1B program.

Data

This chapter focuses on Chinese student migrants at the graduate level, because many Chinese undergraduate students in the United States choose to continue their graduate studies instead of entering the job market when approaching graduation, and also because postgraduate students are commonly considered highly skilled migrants after graduation. The sample population in this study consists of nineteen Chinese graduate students at different stages of the transition period in four tier-one US public universities (two from the east coast, one in the southwest region, and one on the west coast): Chinese students who were approaching graduation (full-time F1 students in the last year of their program of study); Chinese students who graduated from US universities and were in their OPT period; and skilled Chinese migrants who were in the first-term (first three years) H-1B visa program and hadn't applied for LPR when interviews were conducted. Because this chapter focuses on a particular migrant origin country (China), and on a particular migration stage (the transition period of skilled migrants in the United States), it is difficult to conduct random sampling because of the difficulty to obtain public data on this migrant group. Thus, all interviewees in this study were selected by snowball sampling. The author recruited initial research subjects by posting the recruitment letter on multiple Chinese overseas Internet forums and Chinese social media sites, as well as via email lists of Chinese Student and Scholar Associations in the sample universities. Through existing interviewees' recommendations, the author recruited the next potential interviewees while trying to balance participants by gender, field of study, and stage of transition period. Cross-sectional data of interviewees were collected and are listed in Table 6.1.

The identities of all participants in this study have been kept anonymous. Interviews were audio-recorded with participants' consent and were conducted in the language (English or Chinese) that interviewees preferred. Because all interviewees are international graduate students from China who either held a full-time F1 visa, or during their OPT period, or recently obtained H-1B visas, English was still a foreign language for them. All interviewees chose to use their first language, Mandarin Chinese, in their interviews. Interview tapes were

Table 6.1 Basic Demographic Data of Interviewees

	Total	*Gender*		*Major*				
		Male	*Female*	*Business/ Management*	*Engineering*	*Social Sciences*	*Science*	*Arts/ Humanities*
Full-time F1 students	7	3	4	1	2	1	2	1
F1 students during OPT period	6	3	3	2	2	0	2	0
Early stage H-1B visa holders	6	4	2	0	3	1	1	1

transcribed by the author herself due to her proficiency in Mandarin Chinese and translated to English with double translation by a hired translator to test validity. Interview topics incorporated migration background, overseas studying experiences in the United States, the social and cultural factors that shaped their job market experiences in the United States and China, the social and cultural factors that influenced their career plans, and their future return plans and location choices.

Capital Accumulation During the Transition Period in the United States

Before examining the social and cultural capitals of skilled migrants during the transition period, it is noteworthy that Chinese students mainly develop their human capital during their programs of study. When migrants transition to OPT holders, human capital accumulation at this stage is no longer a priority for them in most majors. One exception is students in accounting, whose temporary priority sometimes includes obtaining the certified public accountant (CPA) distinction after graduation, which is a US-specific profession and skill according to Dustmann and Weiss (2010). As one OPT holder mentioned, "We are already on the battlefield … there is no time to sharpen our blades (learning new techniques) now [during the OPT period]" (3FE11). After skilled migrants obtain their H-1B visa, their fear of long-term job insecurity stimulates their desire to accumulate their human capital again, in order to "always be competitive in the job market," according to one H-1B visa holder (4ME4). Such human capital accumulation in the first-term H-1B period is different from the full-time F1 student stage (e.g. knowledge and skill accumulation from school), but instead involves learning specific job-related techniques as well as management and leadership skills.

Social Capital Accumulation During the Transition Period

When first entering the US job market, Chinese migrants face a strong lack of social capital due to their limited social networks in the US, their unstable legal statuses, and their declining transnational connections due to prohibited international travels. Facing such lack of social capital in the US-specific context, Chinese students adopt multiple strategies such as establishing co-ethnic networks, securing legal statuses, and actively extending transnational networks and seeking occupational niches in the US job market.

Social Networks

Accessing professional memberships through the internship opportunities of the CPT program, many international students start to establish their social networks in the workplace and extend their professional networks through alumni connections, which altogether improve migrants' social capital in the job market. As one full-time F1 interviewee mentioned, "[Internship experience] is even more important for international students … It is the biggest chance for us to build professional networks [in the job market]" (4FB2). Transitioning to the time-sensitive OPT stage, migrants actively reach out to all potential social networks, including alumni associations and co-ethnic networks in both the United States and China. As one art major mentioned, "There is no need to be shy and no time to be shy … You only have so many resources in your hands" (4FB9). Specifically, for migrants in STEM fields, their large co-ethnic population in the industry can provide advantages in the job market in terms of co-ethnic ties among skilled Chinese migrants and opportunities for occupational niches. As one OPT holder in a science major mentioned, "Most Chinese [migrants] are willing to help you within their capability … You can always ask for help through our [university] Wechat forum[1] and our social gatherings. Most of the time, we just discuss work … If someone's company is hiring, we circulate the news … Once you are in the loop, when opportunity comes around, they will think of you for the position" (4ME16).

Legal Status

From the interview data, thirteen out of nineteen migrants related their lack of social capital directly to their legal status. Such lack of social capital is greatly due to migrants' immigration status and distinguishes their career experiences from their domestic counterparts. In response to lacking such type of social capital, many interviewees mentioned the option of seeking positions that require a relatively lower human capital level, or positions with "reservation wage" (Constant et al. 2010). Such devaluation of migrants' human capital or migrants' "overeducation" for the position (Chiswick and Miller 2009) were more commonly shared among interviewees from arts/humanities, social sciences, and business/management majors. One possible reason is that these fields require professional skills that are tied more closely to specific US social contexts, which makes their capital transferability relatively low across nation-state boundaries. As one F1 interviewee in a business major at this stage mentioned, "A lot of my previous colleagues are in positions they are overqualified for, but what else you can do … ?" (3FE5).

Transnational Connections

At the full-time F1 stage, Chinese students have frequent transnational activities during school breaks and holidays. Most interviewees mentioned that they traveled back home during school breaks at least once a year during their studies. Yet, their transnational travels at this stage are mainly confined to family visits and personal trips, instead of business and professional knowledge exchanges. Through such transnational travels, Chinese students "perceive understandings about both countries" yet their transnational ties and connections are "rarely built before graduation" (4ME16). At the OPT stage, due to their limited transnational activities, many interviewees mentioned that their strategies for building their transnational social capital were primarily based on reaching out to their former alumni networks in China, such as their former classmates and former advisors, as well as through previous individual professional connections such as former internship experiences in China. Such transnational networks are not limited to interviewees who planned to return but provide boundaryless capital that offers them opportunities for occupational niches in the US job market as well, such as bilingual positions in transnational corporations and transnational businesses opportunities for self-employment. As one OPT holder in a business major mentioned, "You can't abandon your previous mentors, classmates, or friends in China. They are your social resources … We have been in the United States for too long, and China is changing every day. They are your 'eyes and ears' if you would like to find a job in China or start your own transnational businesses in the US … " (4MS12).

Cultural Capital Accumulation During the Transition Period

The empirical results show that interviewees at all stages of the transition period shared a common career concern regarding their "inadequate" (3ME14) cultural capital compared to their native-born counterparts. When approaching graduation, most full-time F1 interviewees at this stage expressed their worries about their lack of ability to share cultural practices with their potential employers or colleagues and about "being foreign" in the workplace. Despite such awareness of their lack of cultural capital, few interviewees considered cultural capital accumulation a career priority before graduation but instead included it in their long-term career development plans. As one F1 student interviewee mentioned, "Their [the employers'] biggest concern is whether you can communicate with them well or not … If you already have an internship experience on your resume, you don't need to worry a lot about your accent or "being a foreigner" [when applying for jobs] in big companies" (3FH7).

During the OPT period, migrants become more aware of their lack of cultural capital in the job market. However, their cultural capital is accumulated at a slow pace, mainly in the form of learning the "underlying cultural rules in interviews" (3FE5) and workplace culture. As one interviewee mentioned, "The priority [now] is not your English … Your accent takes a long time to go away, and there is not enough time for you to pick up American culture either. [At this stage], find a trusted employer first and foremost" (4FS8).

Cultural capital deficiency appears more critical among interviewees in the first-term H-1B stage. Their accumulation of cultural capital such as their ability to play by the rules and their mastery of the "soft skills" becomes priority in their career development when they plan to seek promotions in the workplace. As an H-1B stage interviewee in a STEM field mentioned, "No one wants to be a technician forever, but if I want to move upward, I need to be not an outsider [culturally] … Being good at your work is not enough … You have to learn the workplace culture" (4MS19). Specifically, they accumulate cultural capital by learning the American lifestyle and cultural practices, improving their language skills, and increasing their cultural assimilation level. In addition, some migrants, particularly migrants in high-tech industries, also adopt strategies to relocate and switch jobs to eventually move to a more diverse and "ethnically friendly" workplace, where their lack of language proficiency and cultural background has little impact on their career development. As one H-1B visa holder mentioned,

> One of the reasons that I only applied for jobs in big companies is because they are [ethnically] diverse. In XXX [a top high-tech company in Silicon Valley], your colleagues could be Chinese, Indian, and East European. You don't feel you are different from others … During the last FIFA soccer world cup, pretty much all of our company TVs were playing soccer games on the weekdays, and people talked about the games and watched games together all the time. It is culture similarity: You are part of the family … But in some small companies, things are different. You have to know American football to blend in. Soccer is never an icebreaker.
>
> (3ME14)

In sum, the empirical results of this study reveal an interesting reality of international students during the transition period: although international students possess a high level of human capital when starting their transition periods, their career experiences are still largely shaped by their social and cultural capitals at each stage of the transition period. In response to the institutional barriers in the job market of the United States, student migrants develop their social and cultural capitals differently at each stage. International students gradually develop their social and cultural capital before graduation at a relatively slow pace. When they transition to the OPT period, their social capital accumulation accelerates due to their temporary priority to extend their social network in order to secure legal status. After migrants transition to the first-term H-1B stage, their cultural capital accumulation increases along with their assimilation to the work culture and the acquisition of workplace communication and leadership skills.

How Social Capital and Cultural Capital Shape Return Migration and Location Choices

Based on the findings above, it is evident that compared to migrants' well-established human capital when they start their transition periods, their social and cultural capitals start from being inadequate compared to their native-born counterparts and are gradually accumulated at the latter stages- the OPT stage and first-term H-1B stage. The capital accumulations at different stages greatly affect migrants' decision-making for return migration as well as their location choices at the local level.

When international students approach graduation, their high level of human capital and lack of social and cultural capitals in the United States altogether make their capital highly transferable, which provides immediate returns upon graduation with little cost. Thus, before graduation, students' return intentions are the highest throughout the transition period due to their high capital transferability and their worries about the lack of social and cultural capitals in the US job market. Yet, more students also choose to temporary stay in the United States, because of the available OPT program upon graduation. Many students intend to take advantage of the OPT period with a pragmatic return plan seeking best job opportunities regardless of location preferences in their home country or in the receiving country.

When transitioning to the OPT period, migrants face a lack of social capital and cultural capital in the US job market while they are in a "clock-ticking" grace period for a legal stay in the United States. At this stage, migrants actively build their social capital by extending their existing social connections, building co-ethnic networks, and strengthening transnational ties in order to obtain more information and access to job opportunities, as well as gradually improve their cultural capital. Meanwhile, they also keep their options open for job positions in China, and compare their social and cultural capitals in both countries in order to maximize the economic return to their human capital. In contemporary China, US postgraduate degrees represent a bonus social capital that enables skilled returnees to access exclusive social networks based on their overseas educational degree (Wang and Miao 2013). Moreover, returnees' bilingual and bicultural experiences can also create a bonus cultural capital exclusively related to their US educational experiences (Waters 2006). At this stage, migrants' social and cultural capital is gradually accumulated with part of them highly transferable across nation-state boundaries. Thus, migrants' capital transferability becomes relatively lower than in the F1 stage, yet still partially transferable, which makes China a strong attraction for migrants at this stage. As one OPT holder in engineering mentioned, "I used to reject the return migration option throughout my studies [in the United States], but now … return is an option to me … Working in the United States doesn't mean you are a winner any more. There are opportunities in China too, especially for overseas students … incentive plans, settlement package, you name it …" (4ME16). At the local level, migrants' location choices are highly tied to their job locations, as one business major interviewee mentioned, "do not be picky on the location of the first job" (4MB18). It is also worth mentioning that relationship concerns play an important role in the mobility of migrants during the OPT period. Four OPT holders mentioned that they moved or plan to move to live with their partners after graduation and seek job opportunities closer to their partners' locations. Yet, little gender difference is observed regarding the partnering concerns.

During the H-1B period, skilled migrants are able to travel more frequently between China and the United States and obtain more job market information from both countries. Their transnational network becomes stronger, which makes their social capital more mobile and transferable. Thus, at this stage, migrants' return migration plans become more detailed and sophisticated. Moreover, in addition to considering their bonus social and cultural capitals in China's job market if they return, first-term H-1B visa holders also believe their years absent from Chinese society can put them in a disadvantaged situation in the form of lacking social networks in the workplace and cultural capital in Chinese society. The longer migrants stay and work in the United States and are absent from Chinese society, the higher cultural capital they have in the US context, like Akresh's (2008) U-shape pattern, while they lack social and cultural capital in Chinese society. Consequently, the longer migrants stay in the United States, the lower capital transferability and the larger cost for return migration they have. Thus, at the last stage of the transition period, migrants compare their growing social and cultural capitals in the United States with the possible bonus or lack of social and cultural capitals in China if they return. As one early-stage H-1B visa holder in social sciences mentioned:

> I never imagined that someday I would turn down a job offer in China just because I was afraid I wouldn't fit in … At the onsite interview, I felt like I was a social dumb: having no idea how to speak politically correct in Chinese, not being able to say 'pretty words' to my bosses or my colleagues … It is even after someone pointed out to me that I knew I need to stand up and pour tea when the boss comes around … All these years of learning American culture doesn't give me any edge for working in China. If I went back, I would need to start over learning the Chinese workplace culture again … Right now, the United States feels more like home to me.
>
> (3FSS15)

At the location level, first-term H-1B visa holders have strong location preferences for better career opportunities, partnering concerns, as well as "metropolitan life like [they] used to have in China" (4ME4). Thus, at different stages of the transition period, student migrants accumulate their human, social, and cultural capitals differently as a response to their career experiences at each stage. The different accumulation of human, social, and cultural capitals creates different capital transferability at each stage and eventually shapes migrants' decision-making for return and location choices during the transition period.

Concluding Remarks and Discussion

In the past two decades, economic globalization and the increasing international market of higher education have enabled unprecedented international migration for higher education from developing to developed countries, and generated a reverse and growing migration flow of highly skilled professionals. For international students and early-stage skilled migrants, their migration movements can be considered a calculated strategy to achieve the best economic return on their human capital instead of a family strategy. Despite abundant literature on both migrant groups, little scholarly attention has been given to the transition period between these two migrant groups, especially their social and cultural advantages and constraints in the job market. Yet, the transition period for skilled migrants is critically important because migrants' decision-making for return and their location choices at the local level are greatly shaped by the structural and contextual forces in both sending and receiving countries. Its implication not only is helpful for migrants themselves, but also to policymakers who would like to retain such a skilled labor force.

From nineteen in-depth interviews with Chinese migrants at different stages of the transition period, this chapter has explored how migrants' social and cultural capitals influence their career experiences at different stages of the transition period; how migrants develop their human, social, and cultural capital differently in response to their career experiences and eventually shape their migration movements. It reveals that international students develop their human, social, and cultural capital differently at each stage of the transition period as a result of institutional obstacles that they face at different stages. Moreover, migrants' social and cultural capitals have great impact on their career experiences under different societal contexts, and consequently influence their migration movements and location choices. Migrants compare their social and cultural capitals in both the United States and China during the transition period in order to find the best societal context to maximize the economic outcome of their human capital.

The findings of this chapter bridge the gap between the literature on student migrants and highly skilled migrants. By combining the concepts of social cultural capitals with capital transferability, it also provides a different theoretical perspective from traditional neoclassical economics theories on understanding global skilled migration (De Coulon and Piracha 2005). Its empirical results also provide suggestions for immigration policymakers to better understand the realities of this potential skilled foreign-born labor force. The US Citizenship and Immigration Services (USCIS) recently came up with a new proposal on extending skilled migrants' H-1B visa length beyond six years, in order to facilitate skilled migrants' immigration process to the United States (USCIS 2015). Yet, this chapter reveals that the first and foremost institutional obstacle that keeps skilled international students from staying in the United States after graduation is the low H-1B visa quota and the resulting lottery system which determine migrants' fate by their luck, not their professional skills. USCIS's new proposal on extending the legal status for those who already won the lottery may not address all major issues among skilled migrants. Moreover, on the international level, this chapter provides interesting examples to understand how growing international education accelerates the migration movements between newly emerged economies and popular immigrant-receiving countries in both directions. It also sheds light on the existing discussion of international competition for global talent and human capital accumulation.

Note

1. One of the largest social media forums in China, similar to Twitter and Snapchat.

References

Akresh, I. R. 2008. Occupational trajectories of legal US immigrants: Downgrading and recovery. *Population and Development Review* 34 (3): 435–456.

Aure, M. 2013. Highly skilled dependent migrants entering the labour market: Gender and place in skill transfer. *Geoforum* 45: 275–284.

Banerjee, P. 2006. Indian information technology workers in the United States: The H-1B visa, flexible production, and the racialization of labor. *Critical Sociology* 32 (2–3): 425–445.

Bankston, C. L. 2004. Social capital, cultural values, immigration, and academic achievement: The host country context and contradictory consequences. *Sociology of Education* 77 (2): 176–179.

Bauder, H. 2005. Habitus, rules of the labour market and employment strategies of immigrants in Vancouver, Canada. *Social & Cultural Geography* 6 (1): 81–97.

Bauder, H., and E. Cameron. 2002. *Cultural barriers to labour market integration: Immigrants from South Asia and the Former Yugoslavia*. Research on Immigration and Integration in the Metropolis, Working Paper Series No. 02–03. Vancouver: Vancouver Metropolis Centre.

Becker, G. S. 2009. *Human capital: A theoretical and empirical analysis, with special reference to education*. Chicago: University of Chicago Press.

Bian, Y., X. Shu, and J. R. Logan. 2001. Communist party membership and regime dynamics in China. *Social Forces* 79 (3): 805–841.

Bourdieu, P. 1986. The forms of capital. In *Handbook of theory and research for the sociology of education*, ed. J. Richardson, 241–258. New York: Greenwood Press.

Chiswick, B. R. 2008. The economics of language: An introduction and overview. Available at: http://ssrn.com/abstract=1155862 (last accessed March 1, 2016).

Chiswick, Barry R. and Paul W. Miller. 2009. The International Transferability of Immigrants' Human Capital. *Economics of Education Review* 28 (2): 162–169.

Constant, A. F., A. Krause, U. Rinne, and K. F. Zimmermann. 2010. *Reservation wages of first and second generation migrants*. Berlin: DIW Berlin Discussion Paper No. 5396. Berlin: German Institute for Economic Research.

De Coulon, A., and M. Piracha. 2005. Self-selection and the performance of return migrants: The source country perspective. *Journal of Population Economics* 18 (4): 779–807.

Department of Homeland Security. 2013. *Yearbook of Immigration Statistics, 1996–2013*. Last accessed January 10, 2016. Available at: www.dhs.gov/files/statistics/publications/yearbook.shtm

Duncan, N. and B. S. Waldorf. 2010. High skilled immigrant recruitment and the global economic crisis: The effects of immigration policies. Department of Agricultural Economics, Purdue University. Working Paper: 10–11.

Dustmann, C., and Y. Weiss. 2007. Return migration: Theory and empirical evidence from the UK. *British Journal of Industrial Relations* 45 (2): 236–256.

Ewers, M. C. 2007. Migrants, markets and multinationals: Competition among world cities for the highly skilled. *Geojournal* 68 (2–3): 119–130.

Findlay, A. M. 2011. An assessment of supply and demand-side theorizations of international student mobility. *International Migration* 49 (2): 162–190.

Findlay, A. M., R. King, F. M. Smith, A. Geddes, and R. Skeldon. 2012. World class? An investigation of globalisation, difference and international student mobility. *Transactions of the Institute of British Geographers* 37 (1): 118–131.

Gatchair, S. 2013. Race/ethnicity and education effects on employment in high technology industries and occupations in the US, 1992–2002. *The Review of Black Political Economy* 40 (4): 357–370.

Geddie, K. 2013. The transnational ties that bind: Relationship considerations for graduating international science and engineering research students. *Population, Space and Place* 19 (2): 196–208.

Hawthorne, L. 2010. How valuable is "two-step migration"? Labor market outcomes for international student migrants to Australia. *Asian and Pacific Migration Journal* 19 (1): 5–36.

Ho, E. L-E. 2011. Migration trajectories of 'highly skilled' middling transnationals: Singaporean transmigrants in London. *Population, Space and Place* 17 (1): 116–129.

Institute of International Education (IIE). 2011–2015. *Open doors: Report on international educational exchange*. Washington, DC: Institute of International Education.

King, R., and P. Raghuram. 2013. International student migration: Mapping the field and new research agendas. *Population, Space and Place* 19 (2): 127–137.

Kuptsch, C. and E. F. Pang. 2006. *Competing for global talent*. Paris: International Labor Organization.

Lo, L., and W. Li. 2015. Financing immigrant small businesses in Canada and the United States. In *The housing and economic experiences of immigrants in U.S. and Canadian Cities*, ed. W. Li and C. Teixeira, 328–354. Toronto: University of Toronto Press.

Lowell, B. L. and A. Findlay. 2002. Migration of highly skilled persons from developing countries: Impact and policy responses. International Migration Papers 44: 25.

Lu, Y., L. Zong, and B. Schissel. 2009. To stay or return: Migration intentions of Students from People's Republic of China in Saskatchewan, Canada. *Journal of International Migration and Integration/Revue De l'Integration et De La Migration Internationale* 10 (3): 283–310.

National Academies, The. 2005. *Policy implications of international graduate students and postdoctoral scholars in the United States*. Washington, DC: The National Academies Press..

Nohl, A.-M., K. Schittenhelm, O. Schmidtke, and A. Weiss. 2014. Work in transition: Cultural capital and highly skilled migrants' passages into the labour Market. Toronto: University of Toronto Press.

Obama, B. 2013. Inauguration address, Washington, DC, January 21, 2013. The White House. Available at: www.whitehouse.gov/the-press-office/2013/01/21/inaugural-address-president-barack-obama (last accessed March 1, 2016).

Parutis, V. 2014. "Economic Migrants" Or "middling transnationals"? East European migrants' experiences of work in the UK. *International Migration* 52 (1): 36–55.

Putnam, R. D. 2007. E pluribus unum: Diversity and community in the twenty-first century. The 2006 Johan Skytte Prize Lecture. *Scandinavian Political Studies* 30 (2): 137–174.

Raghuram, P. 2013. Theorising the spaces of student migration. *Population, Space and Place* 19 (2): 138–154.

Reitz, J. G. 2001. Immigrant skill utilization in the Canadian Labour Market: Implications of human capital research. *Journal of International Migration and Integration/Revue de l'Integration et de la Migration Internationale* 2 (3): 347–378.

Robertson, S., and A. Runganaikaloo. 2013. Lives in limbo: Migration experiences in Australia's education–migration nexus. *Ethnicities* 14 (2), 208–226.

Rosen, S., and D. Zweig. 2005. Transnational capital: Valuing academic returnees in a globalizing China, 1978–2003. In *Bridging minds across the Pacific: US–China educational exchanges*, ed. C. Li. 111–132. Lanham, MD: Lexington Books.

Ryan, L., R. Sales, M. Tilki, and B. Siara. 2008. Social networks, social support and social capital: The experiences of recent Polish migrants in London. *Sociology* 42 (4): 672–690.

Sarre, P., D. Phillips, and R. Skellington. 1989. *Ethnic minority housing: Explanations and policies.* Avebury: Aldershot.

Shan, H. 2013. Skill as a relational construct: Hiring practices from the standpoint of Chinese immigrant engineers in Canada. *Work, Employment & Society* 27 (6), 915–931.

She, Q., and T. Wotherspoon. 2013. International student mobility and highly skilled migration: A comparative study of Canada, the United States, and the United Kingdom. *Springerplus* 2 (1): 1–14.

Shen, W. 2009. *Chinese student circular migration and global city formation: A relational case study of Shanghai and Paris.* Ph.D. dissertation. Loughborough University.

State, B., M. Rodriguez, D. Helbing, and E. Zagheni. 2014. Migration of professionals to the U.S. *Social Informatics* 531–543.

U.S. Citizenship and Immigration Services. 2015. USCIS seeks comments on proposed rule affecting certain employment-based immigrant and nonimmigrant visa programs. Available at: www.uscis.gov/news/uscis-seeks- comments-proposed-rule-affecting-certain-employment-based-immigrant-and- nonimmigrant-visa-programs (last accessed January 10, 2016).

Vanhonacker, W., D. Zweig, and S. F. Chung. 2005. *Transnational or social capital? Returnee versus local entrepreneurs.* Working Paper No.7 Hong Kong: Center on China's Transnational Relations.

Vygotsky, L. S. 1980. *Mind in society: The development of higher psychological processes.* Cambridge, MA: Harvard University Press.

Wadhwa, V., A. Saxenian, R. B. Freeman, and G. Gereffi. 2009. *America's loss is the world's gain: America's new immigrant entrepreneurs, Part 4.* Kansas City: The Kaufman Foundation.

Wang, H., and Miao, L. eds. 2013. *The blue book of global talent: Annual report on the development of Chinese returnees.* Vol. 31. Beijing: Mechanical and Industrial Press.

Waters, J. L. 2006. Geographies of cultural capital: Education, international migration and family strategies between Hong Kong and Canada. *Transactions of the Institute of British Geographers* 31 (2): 179–192.

Welch, A. R., and Z. Zhen. 2008. Higher education and global talent flows: Brain drain, overseas Chinese intellectuals, and diasporic knowledge networks. *Higher Education Policy* 21 (4): 519–537.

Williams, A. M., and V. Baláž. 2004. From private to public sphere, the commodification of the au pair experience? Returned migrants from Slovakia to the UK. *Environment and Planning A* 36 (10): 1813–1833.

Yeoh, B. S. A. and L. A. Eng. 2008. Guest editors' introduction: Talent migration in and out of Asia: Challenges for policies and places." *Asian Population Studies* 4 (3): 235–245.

7 Internationalization, Localization, and the Eduscape of Higher Education in the Global South

The Case of South Africa

Ashley Gunter and Parvati Raghuram

In a world of ever-increasing border control, international skilled migration is one of the few forms of mobility that is seen as acceptable in public discourses and in immigration policies globally.[1] Skilled migrants are an exception to the tendency towards increasing border control; they are often welcomed as they are seen as drivers of the global economy (Shachar 2006) of education systems (Robertson 2013), as talented and creative (Solimano 2008; Yeoh and Huang 2013), and as cosmopolitan subjects (Andersson 2013). Hence, they are politically, culturally, socially, and economically seen as more "acceptable" than most other groups. Skilled migrants are seen as being part of the global and in fact, of fashioning the global, through their businesses. However, this global imperative comes up against strong local factors as education is part of welfare policy and hence, subject to national ambitions and legacies. In this chapter we outline how place-based national higher education (HE) policies become noticeable with the introduction of international institutions, students, and staff in the local context. This takes place within the history of HE and it is argued that such a longitudinal perspective is necessary for understanding HE as an evolving and dynamic site where internationalism and localism meet. Using the example of South Africa, we explore how the national history of HE policies as they evolved through the apartheid period and after the dismantling of apartheid has meant that the nature and engagement with internationalization has become skewed.

South Africa is the most important destination country for international student migrants within sub-Saharan Africa. It is also a key regional hub for transnational education and for distance teaching. The sub-Saharan region has one of the highest mobility ratios of students in the world, with 4.9 percent of students moving to study abroad in 2014, while the world average is 2 percent. Most of the staff and student mobility in Africa is regional. Hence, South Africa as a major provider of international education is a key regional player. However, South Africa also has a very particular history of education with both internal divisions in the provision of higher education as a result of apartheid and the isolation from most countries as a consequence of these policies. This has brought a uniquely South African flavor to the culture and dynamics of the internationalization of HE with, for instance, limited presence of global satellite campuses. This eduscape is the context in which transnational education is fashioned in this part of the Global South.

Through the example of a branch campus we argue that the complexities of South African higher education inflect and shape what international skilled mobility means. Furthermore, we add a little studied aspect—race—to the wider literature on international skilled migration by highlighting how the place-based history of race has affected the development of knowledge workers and skill migrants in the South African HE system. In the South African context, the obsession with race by the apartheid government created an environment where higher education was provided in the local context of segregation. However, the regionally acclaimed education system in the country has attached skilled migrants and students into the HE sector, both during and post the apartheid period.

This chapter begins with a brief overview of the global and the local, and how they are intertwined in existing discussions around skilled migration. The following section situates the analysis of the local in South Africa and in doing so it attempts to redress the overarching emphasis in much of the existing literature of the Global North as the site of skills accrual. This section lays out the politics of knowledge production in South Africa and particularly the role of race in the history of knowledge production in a broader global context. The final section moves on to explore the future prospects for the internationalization of HE in South Africa and how the deep historical legacies of South African politics are shaping the landscape in which this internationalization is enacted. The introduction of branch campuses attracts skilled migrants from across the region; however, the perception that a branch campus is somehow a replication of the main campus offering is misguided as there is a strong regional element to the internationalization of HE in South Africa. Moreover, the historical production of the "local" has influenced how South Africa engages with this aspect of global higher education.

The Global Imperative in International Skilled Migration

International skilled migration is precisely that—international in its scope and ambition. As Raghuram (2013; also see Knorr-Cetina 2007) has argued, global connections are the epistementality of knowledge production today. The systems and structures of HE in the global context have created standardizations and norms that are replicated across the globe. International ranking systems only serve to reinforce the homogeneous reproduction of knowledge. For a skill to be recognized as "skill" it must have the ability to circulate. Very localized skills that only have a local remit rarely become recognized as skill; they often lose value. Skills must therefore be recognized and validated as such within global skills recognition regimes through accreditation, through rankings, and through branding (Williams and Baláž 2008; Kofman and Raghuram 2013). A suite of accreditation organizations has flourished in this context (see, for instance, *National Academic Recognition Information Centre* (NARIC) in the UK; and International English Language Testing System, a global English language testing organization). Skills also acquire global status through rankings and branding (Findlay 2011). They play their part by facilitating student migration in the highly competitive international student market. Moreover, indices such as the *Academic Ranking of World Universities* (also known as *Shanghai ranking),* the *QS World University Rankings* and *Times Higher Education World University Rankings* help to shape the destinations of the "brightest and best." These ranking systems are also competing among each other for influence in shaping the nature of global study. Raghuram (2013) therefore suggests that instead of simply thinking about the circulation of skills we must also recognize that skills require mobility. For instance, people move around visiting institutions in order to rank them; data is collated from across the globe to set up forms of accreditation; private companies meet up with government organizations in order to set standards and test the parity of the exams held by IELTS in its multiple locations; advertising organizations move images and prospectuses around globally to ensure that the brand of the university retains a global reach. Moreover, universities also set skills in motion—identifying and wooing the stars who may push up research rankings, attracting students whose exit velocity from institutions will improve their profile and will attract alumni funding and so on. The world of skills is therefore inextricably caught up in the world of mobility so that focusing on migrants alone is simply inadequate (see also Madge, Raghuram, and Noxolo 2015).

However, neither the mobility required by skills nor the mobility of skills are frictionless (Yeoh and Huang 2013). They come up repeatedly against place-based issues. One such issue is the relationships that are historically embedded in the creation of skills and the routes and rites of mobility that are long established. Using the case of medical migrants Raghuram (2009) points out how the trajectories of mobility that are viewed in migration such as brain drain are often shaped by colonial histories and the entanglements arising from the co-development of medicine as a form of knowledge and practice across distant places. Here knowledge is seen as an outcome of spatial relations and of historical habitus, not simply a product acquired in individual sites. Migration plays a *constitutive* role in the production and circulation of medical skills. It is the basis through which the power of both medical knowledge and of the arbiters of medical knowledge, such as the Royal College of Surgeons and the Royal College of Physicians, are established and maintained.

While Raghuram (2009) focuses on the entanglements of different locales in the production of skills, a much larger literature focuses on the singularity and distinctiveness of particular places as sites for the concentration of skills. For instance, the vast literature on global cities (Sassen 2000; Beaverstock 2005) locates the city as the primary destination for global elites (Findlay et al. 1996; Favell 2008). Even global firms have local social practices about how to do business that migrants must learn in order to benefit economically (Beaverstock and Boardwell 2000). The global economy is thus ultimately modulated and altered through place. The universality of cosmopolitan identities too have been questioned (Latham and Conradson 2005; Ho 2011; Meir 2014) as the dominance of

Western ways of comportment and of middle and upper class values in defining the cosmopolitanism associated with skills is explored.

Place is important for students too. It is not just the economic opportunities that particular cities offer that attracts student migrants, but the cultural and social life are often equally significant (Insch and Sun 2013; Lesjak et al. 2015). In the race to attract international students an analysis of what attracts students has therefore been paramount. There has also been some attention paid to the places that students leave behind, although much of this literature focuses on the lack of opportunities that drive migration or the impact of out-migration on sending areas (Crush and Campbell 2005; Ratha et al. 2011; Solimano 2008; Qin 2015). Most of this analysis of place is embedded in push–pull theories and the inherent comparison involved in this theorization has its limitations (see Raghuram 2013 for an extended discussion of the relationship between space and place, and student migration theory). In all these discussions place is seen as a location produced outside and beyond the histories of such mobility. Rather, place is simply a destination to which immigrants move and emigrants leave.

However, the large geographical literature on place would argue that places are composed of multiple relations; they are sites of density where history is produced but in relation to other places. For Massey (1991), this notion of place enables us to move beyond reactionary notions of place that seek rootedness, essentialized notions of history and identity, and a site for romanticized escapism from the present. In these reactionary notions a fixed place is opposed to the flows inherent to space and spatial relations. Instead, Massey (1991) suggests that place should be seen as arising from "a particular constellation of social relations, meeting and weaving together at a particular locus" (28). Furthermore, Noxolo et al. (2008) argue that places should also be seen as produced through moments of disjuncture and difference. These moments are as constitutive of place as those of connection.

Within the context of HE, these understandings of the importance of place require us to go beyond the flat ahistoricity of most analyses of place in contemporary studies of HE. It requires recognition of how those local HE practices are constituted through social relations, both through moments of connection such as those produced through the histories of the development of educational practice but also through moments of disconnection. They go well beyond place as envisaged in push–pull theories (but see Collins 2010). Moreover, the wider literature on student mobility and skilled migration has rarely looked at race and its histories as a key component of the politics of location (but see, for instance, Ho 2011). In the rest of this chapter we point to a very particular way in which the local HE is one site through which a set of connections and disconnections globally are played out. Place then becomes the site at which these relations are accreted, but also through which new connections may be forged. The chapter thus explores the finer textures of HE in place, how they are constituted historically and how they shape national policies today. These textures, we would argue, are often missed in contemporary studies of skilled mobility.

Colonialism, Apartheid, and Post-Apartheid: South African HE as a Site of Connection and Disconnections

In South Africa, internationalization has manifested itself in complex ways in shaping higher education. This section explores how this internationalization and HE are intrinsically linked. It also looks at how, despite the creation of a race-based higher education system, the relatively well-funded South African universities, particularly the historically black only institutions saw regional migration of staff and students.

The first institutions of HE in South Africa were the result of the immigration of highly skilled migrants into the country who were looking to both replicate the educational systems they had come from, as well as link the new institutions to imperial colonizers. This is not just true for South Africa; many of the current regional HE hubs such as Canada, Malaysia, and Hong Kong also had strong colonial links to the imperial HE network which proved to be foundational to the role they play in international skilled mobility today (Marginson and Rhoades 2002). For this reason, the historical context of an HE system is an important, albeit often invisible, contributing factor to current student and academic migration.

Recent controversies in higher education in South Africa have highlighted the deep colonial roots of the sector (O'Connell 2015). The British colonial figure, Cecil John Rhodes, played a significant role in setting up two of the country's most prestigious institutions, the University of Cape Town (UCT) and Rhodes University. In a recent demonstration at UCT, a statue of Rhodes in the main concourse of the university was defaced, vandalized, and after a short sit-in by students, removed by the university management. The student leaders that led this protest action, called "#rhodesmustfall" demanded the transformation of the institution from a Eurocentric Western model of education to an Afrocentric, indigenized form of education (Pather 2015). This call for transformation has been echoed across campuses in South Africa and has led to much debate in the HE sector. The root of this drive for change is in the contested and complex make-up of education in South Africa.

During the colonial period, the first provider of HE in the country was the South African College founded in Cape Town in 1829. The college was primarily used as an exam center for the universities of Oxford and Cambridge, where students could take a limited number of courses and sit exams for the institutions. These centers were thus used to extend the global hegemony of these quintessentially British institutions and of sedimenting colonial power. Moreover, the reproduction of colonial power precisely depended on stretching out across space and re-embedding in distant places (Raghuram 2013). In 1873, the first university was opened in South Africa, the University of the Cape of Good Hope (later to become the University of South Africa) and in 1918, the University of Cape Town was established with endowments given on land donated by Rhodes. Shortly afterwards in 1921, the University of the Witwatersrand opened in Johannesburg and in 1930 the Transvaal University College (TUKS) founded in 1902 was renamed the University of Pretoria. Significant to note is that in 1931, The

University of Pretoria became the first non-English medium[2] university in South Africa, with Afrikaans becoming the language of instruction. This signifies the establishment of two of the three tiers of universities that was to develop under the apartheid system and still plagues the current HE environment. The two languages of instruction limited international migration of both staff and students to the HE sector in South Africa, particularly to the Afrikaans institutions.

The third tier was inaugurated with the establishment of a Church-based university—Stellenbosch—in the early 1900s. It adopted race-based admissions criteria and black African students were not permitted to attend the university. Further entrenching this race-based HE sector was the development of the South African Native College in 1916 (later to become the University of Fort Hare). This institution provided Western university education to Black Africans and very quickly developed a reputation as a center for the African elite—a number of political leaders and liberators studied there, including Nelson Mandela and Oliver Tambo, both leaders of the South African liberation struggle. Moreover, a number of other African leaders, Robert Mugabe, Kenneth Kaunda, Julius Nyerere, Seretse Khama, and Yusuf Lule, who all became presidents of their respective countries, also studied at Fort Hare. These traditionally black universities drew in students from across the sub-Saharan region, and were arguably the first truly African universities in South Africa (Sehoole 2006). Hence, rather perversely, Afrikaans universities with their selective policies aimed at elite education became localized and had a largely South African student and staff base while some of the less privileged and intentionally deprived Black African universities became centers for international education. This is summarized neatly by Nelson Mandela: "For young black South Africans like myself, it was Fort Hare University, Oxford and Cambridge, Harvard and Yale, all rolled into one." Importantly, despite the prestige that many African leaders placed on Fort Hare University, what is also clear is that the race-based HE system had become entrenched in the country. At the same time, it is the black universities that set in motion flows of students from across Africa and particularly from sub-Saharan Africa that still underpin international mobility today.

Restructuring, Merging, and Post-Apartheid Universities

Post the 1994 democratic transition in South Africa, there was recognition that there needed to be a recasting of the institutional landscape of the country. The structure of the sector had not only entrenched racial segregation but also institutional inequality that would be almost impossible to rectify in a short period of time. After deliberation, the government embarked on a series of institutional mergers to consolidate the sector (Jansen 2004). In 1994, South Africa had twenty-one universities and fifteen technikons and of these thirty-six HE institutions about half only allowed "black" students and the other half only "white" students under the apartheid system. Seven of the institutions offered Afrikaans as the medium of instruction and the remainder English. While the post-apartheid period saw a rapid change of the racial make-up of the student body of many previously "white" institution bodies, there was massive inequality between the racial make-up of staff, the quality and output of research, and the funding of the different universities. The 1997 Education White Paper 3 sought to overcome these disparities with an increase in funding to historically black "homeland" institutions. It was hoped that this would lead to an increase in the viability of these institutions and help increase the number of black African academics. At the same time, the massification of HE had begun in the country and the homeland universities were seen as having the best capacity to absorb the influx of new students (Mabizela 2006). This massification was accompanied by an influx of foreign African students and to a lesser extent staff. Equally, the massification of HE in South Africa was coupled with the Southern African Development Community (SADC) protocol on higher education, where students from across the regional block were charged the same student fees as the locals in any given country. This has facilitated the movement of students from across the region to the massified South African system. These immigrants were now able to attend the highly acclaimed South African institutions. The unintended consequence of the deracialization of the HE landscape was an increase in regional migration into South Africa's Universities (Mabizela 2000).

Despite the initial optimism, little changed at the homeland universities; instead, a number of key staff moved to work in the better resourced environments of the previously "white" institutions; motivated foreign students also moved to the previous white institutions with many of the students that previously chose Fort Hare University now opting for the better funded and more prestigious Rhodes University. This prompted the formation of the National Commission on Higher Education (NCHE) in 1999 to develop a strategy for the development of HE in the country. While there were initial thoughts that the NCHE would shut some institutions, they rather recommended the merger of institutions and that:

> The number of public higher education institutions in South Africa could and should be reduced. However, reducing the number of institutions does not imply that some institutions would be closed and discontinue offering higher education programmes.
>
> (Department of Education 2001: 87)

Thus, the number of HE institutions was reduced from thirty-six to twenty-one universities and universities of technology through mergers and incorporations. The new institutions were under pressure to establish themselves as credible and recognizable universities and used internationalization as a key tool for this. As such, newly merged institutions such as the University of Johannesburg went on an international recruitment drive for both foreign staff and students (HEQC 2012). Institutions in the major cities attracted an increasing flow of foreign students, particularly into postgraduate programs.

Figure 7.1 shows the location of these new institutions around the country. What is apparent from this map is that, in some instances, such as the University

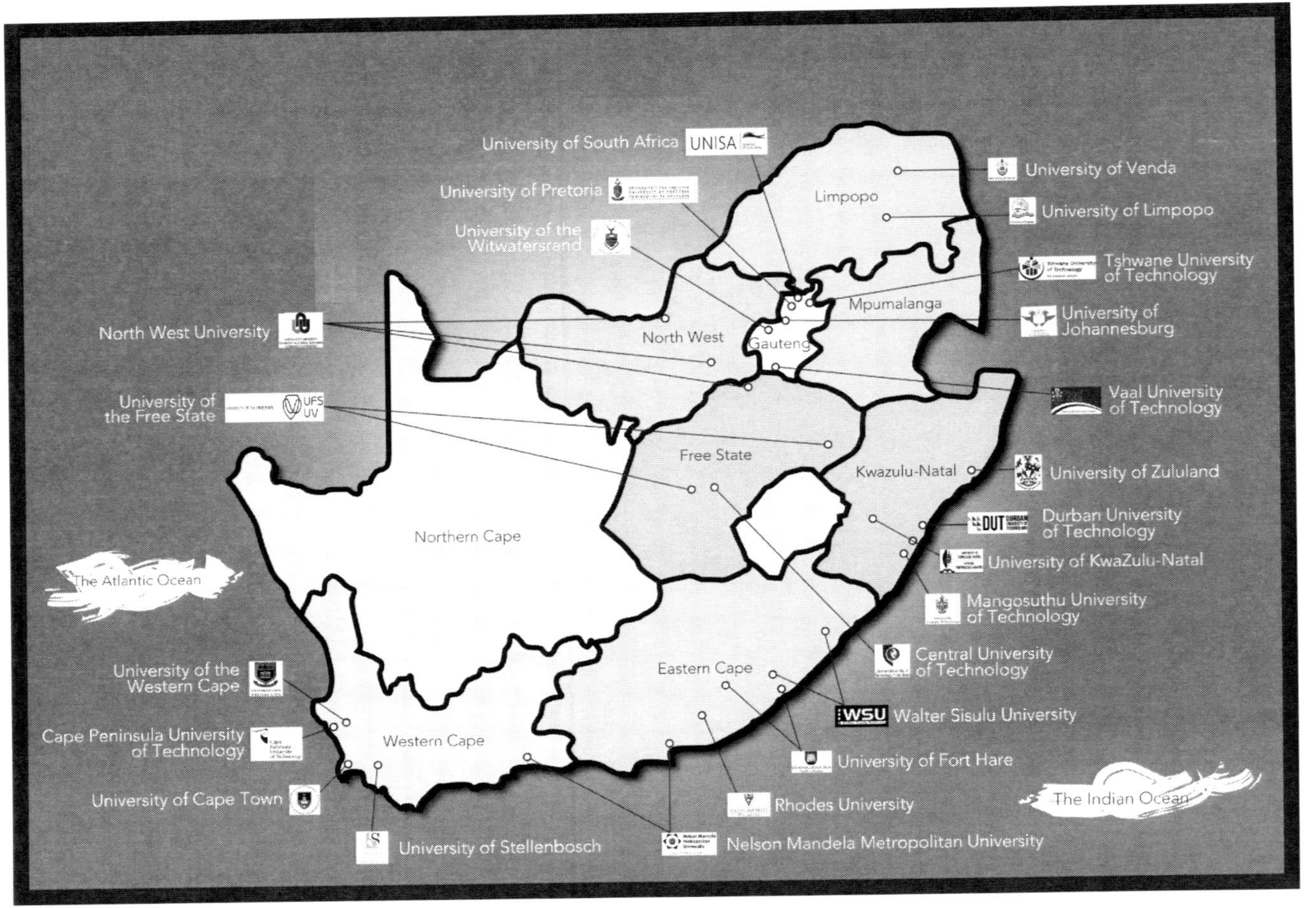

Figure 7.1 The Location of Universities around South Africa

of the North West, the distance between campuses makes the mergers feel ill advised. Yet there was a political drive to merge and realign the higher education landscape in the post-apartheid period (Asmal 2002; Sehoole 2005).

The rationale behind the mergers was that historically disadvantaged institutions could benefit from the financial endowments, institutional capacity, and experienced staff available in the previously white institutions (Harman and Harman 2003). The NCHE also suggested that new institutional cultures would develop and help overcome the lingering prejudice of apartheid found in HE (even up until 2010, the University of the Free State had racially segregated student residences). However, many historically black universities did not support the mergers and felt it was an attack on the autonomy of these institutions. Equally, these institutions lost access to the pool of foreign students from sub-Saharan Africa who chose to attend the better funded institutions created through the mergers (Wyngaard and Kapp 2004). Yet the most cited rationale for the mergers was that the Department of Education (DoE) had to be proactive in two key aims, global competitiveness and national development (Hay et al. 2001).

These dual aims are indicative of the pressures on HE in the Global South, the need to both provide training for the developmental agenda as well as compete within the global HE sector for students, funding, and outputs (Ntshoe, 2004; Kanwar et al. 2010; Alcorn et al. 2015). It is within this context that South Africa is dealing with the global complexities of offering higher education. The global demand of HE has made the country a regional hub within South Africa as a provider of quality education (Kwaramba 2012; Cloete et al. 2015). However, this education is contextualized in a historical legacy that is firmly based in Eurocentric colonial and later apartheid roots (Waghid 2002).

Branch Campuses and Private Higher Education in South Africa

With the opening up of the South African economy post-1994, many industries were interested in the new market that emerged out of the Western-imposed sanctions. One of the most viable markets seemed to be HE. The massification of education in the country and the high unemployment rate had created a huge demand for higher education that the international market was willing to tap (Wangenge-Ouma 2012). This coincided with an increase and expansion of branch campuses and international campuses led by universities in Australia and Britain (Wilkins, Stephens Balakrishanan, and Huisman 2012). There was a particular demand for business qualifications that the public universities could not fill, and a number of private institutions and international campuses started offering the MBA degree to cater to this need (Levy 2002; Nieuwenhuizen and Swanepoel 2015).

These international campuses, however, were not only competing with public institutions, but by 1998, there were 108,700 students studying at private institutions of which 15,000 were enrolled in degree programs (DHET 2004). This is because there is a massive gap in the South African HE model. There is an obvious need for degree programs, particularly in technical and professional programs but they are, however, not offered at the historically black institutions. Thus, it was not only the historically "white" universities that posed a threat to the institutions but equally the provision of private HE that drew students away from black universities (Mabizela 2006).

The prestige of attending a branded international institution not only attracted foreign students, but equally regional migrants who chose the international campus over the South African one. Evidence from private HE institutions points to two key areas of study— Business and Education—with Gauteng, the Western Cape and KwaZulu Natal being the main centers of private education. In the 1990s, it was clear that a new and growing force within the HE sector was emerging and that the private institution both locally formed and international branch campuses could pose a serious risk to many public institutions in South Africa (Kruss 2002). For this reason, in 2000, the DoE placed a moratorium on any joint ventures between public and private instructions, and embarked on a process of accreditation of qualifications of these institutions (Mabizela, Subotzky, and Thaver 2000). There was much criticism of this clampdown on private HE, with many academics in the sector recognizing that private institutions could help to take some burden off public institutions, as was noted by the Vice-Chancellor of the University of Pretoria at the time:

> You know, if you go into the Commonwealth, there is a very strong move which says it is no longer 'publish or perish,' it is 'partnership or perish.' Unfortunately, our friend Minister Asmal is saying 'You can't have it in education.' I think that is incredibly short-sighted and completely contrary to the major South African government moves regarding public–private partnerships.
>
> (Marcus 2001: 26)

The globalization of HE through the extension of branch campuses is an international phenomenon; many regional educational hubs are embracing this strategy as a mechanism to develop their international offerings and links to highly ranked and prestigious institutions. Branch campuses bring with them an internationalization of education and many countries have encouraged the introduction of these institutions to encourage the migration of students and skilled staff to work and study in these often Anglo-American campuses. Singapore, Hong Kong, Kuwait, and the United Arab Emirates have all attracted a large number of international campuses and utilize these as a symbol of their rising status in the international HE arena (Wilkins, Stephens Balakrishnan, and Huisman 2012). In South Africa, the privately owned international campus is seen as a threat by the Department of Higher Education. Of the original six campuses that opened in South Africa in the 1990s, only three remain.

This was due to the different type of investments that international campuses were willing to make within the country. The lack of commitment to investment in physical infrastructure and their limited willingness to embed themselves in the host country's HE landscape are common criticisms of branch campuses (Coleman 2003; Wood et al. 2005). However, Monash University made a significant commitment to South Africa through the development of its branch campus "Monash South Africa." The campus was developed at a time of international expansion by this Australian institution. Monash University at the time wanted to have a campus on each continent to enhance its internationalization and was willing to invest heavily in infrastructure, staff development, and research initiatives. This led to an investment of over $100 million over a ten-year period and significant institutional management was seconded to oversee the establishment of the campus (Malsen 2011).

However, with the changing legislative landscape, the Monash South African campus was not given university status in South Africa. Further, it was not afforded the right to apply for funding from the National Research Council as it was considered a foreign institution (CHE 2007). Yet despite this, and an on-going deficit, Monash University continues to provide financial and academic support to the campus.[3] This strategy was vastly different from De Montfort, a British Institution that established a branch campus in South Africa in 1994. De Montfort delivered programs in rented premises using local lecturing staff. These strategies raise serious questions about the reasoning of why public institutions in the Global North would choose to develop branch campuses in the Global South. The institutions with branch campuses put the decision down to enhancing their academic reach and brand to communities that would not have the ability to travel or study at the main campus. Or equally, a financial decision, where the branch campus income would be used to supplement teaching and learning at the main campus. The institutions, while significantly cheaper than the main campuses, are invariably more expensive than the local counterparts. Educational standards are very often not equivalent to the main campus and educational offerings, and facilities are far below what would be expected by a main campus student (Nhlapo 2004).

Monash University's rationale for the South African branch campus was that this was an attempt by the university to engage with South Africa and Africa both socially through community engagement and politically by educating the future leaders of the continent. With Monash having sold a major stake in the institution, it seems that South Africa will be losing another international branch campus, again bringing in to question the motive for the establishment of these campuses.

It is within this context that our project is situated.[4] Our project involved a survey of staff at the three branch campuses in South Africa that was conducted in June and July of 2014. Eighty-six full-time academic staff members were employed at these institutions at that time. Using a simple random sampling technique, a sample of sixty-two staff were asked to complete a questionnaire, a total of fifty (58 percent of the total) of these staff members responded and a structured questionnaire was administered. The questionnaire asked both closed and open-ended questions with the answers captured and analyzed to provide insight into the behaviours and perceptions on working at an international branch campus. A total of 30 percent of staff were employed as junior lecturers, 44 percent as lecturer, 22 percent as senior lecturer. The responses suggest that there are very few professorial staff (just 2 percent in our survey) at these universities. A total of 88 percent of the staff were employed on full-time contracts and 72 percent on permanent ones, indicating a commitment to permanency by the campuses, while 22 percent of the staff interviewed were in the Social Sciences and 56 percent in management, reflecting the key disciplinary thrusts of these campuses; 12 percent were teaching IT and 10 percent were involved in other programmes. A total of 56 percent of staff were employed in undergraduate teaching, 32 percent in Honours and 12 percent at the Masters level; 58 percent of staff interviewed were women. As we saw earlier in the South African context, the issue of race is central: 52 percent of our respondents classified themselves as African; 38 percent as white with almost equal numbers of the rest identifying as Indians and coloureds. The staff at these universities was overwhelmingly young, with 38 percent aged between 20 and 30, and 60 percent between 30 and 40, showing a lack of senior staff in this sector. We only interviewed one staff member outside these two age cohorts and he was over 60. It suggests that these universities lack a middle grade of staff who can become future leaders in the HE sector.

Branch Campuses as a Route to Internationalization?

There is now a large literature on branch campuses and their role in transnational education (TNE; Waters and Leung 2013a, b; Sidhu and Christie 2014). Waters and Leung (2013a, b) make clear that rather than providing an opportunity to escalate from the local to the global arena and to get ahead in the talent game, in the case of British universities in Hong Kong, TNE is a site for the reproduction of disadvantage. Highly ranked local universities offer a much better route to globally recognized education. British universities' TNE offerings, on the other hand, are often seen as substandard. How far do branch campuses offer an avenue for internationalization in the South African context? This is particularly important in the South African context as the country is often seen as a gateway to broader internationalization by students in other parts of Africa (Mpinganjira 2009) as well as the rest of the world (Lee and Sehoole 2015). There has been little research on international students thus far in South Africa, but it appears that the outcomes for students are varied (Bundy 2005; Kishun 2007; Lee and Sehoole 2015). What is known is that although branch campuses attract large enrolments, they offer a very limited curriculum and have inadequate infrastructure (Altbach 2015). Figure 7.2 shows the origin of foreign students at South African branch campuses; there is a particular Southern African bias with no students reported from outside of Africa.

However, very little is known about the role of academics in the internationalization process of TNE initiatives and the extent to which they participate in these processes. In this section we therefore explore the extent to which internationalization was a process in which mobile academics in South African branch campuses engaged. As the experience of education is likely to be inflected

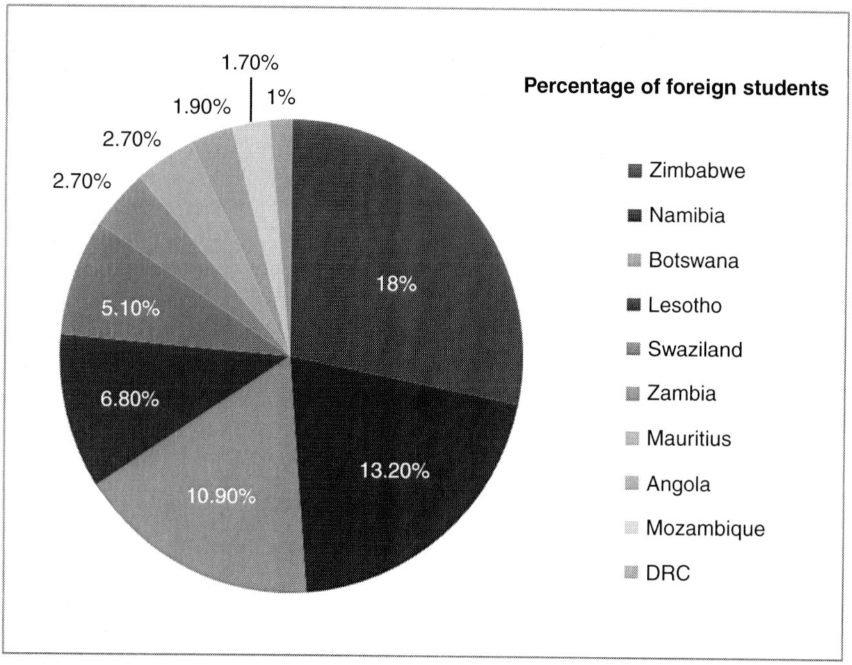

Figure 7.2 The Origin of Foreign Students in South Africa

Source: IEASA, 2014

through the experiences and dispositions of staff, the nature and extent of international engagement of staff in one branch campus in South Africa was explored.

National and regional academics dominate the educational teaching staff in South African branch campuses: 42 percent of branch campus staff were born in South Africa with a further 36 percent in the Southern African Development Community (SADC). A total of 78 percent of staff at these Global North institutions were therefore born locally. This local nature of the staff was further confirmed by the finding that 86 percent of staff at the branch campuses had obtained their first degree in South Africa (36 percent at the same campus in which they were teaching). Only 8 percent had obtained their degrees from outside Africa, with 2 percent obtaining their first degree abroad and 6 percent obtaining the "highest qualification" from outside the continent. There is, therefore, a very localized, internalized process of academic reproduction in what is certainly the most global of structures within South African HE. A branch campus, which recruits locally, will re-create the global homogeneity of the HE curriculum with a local nuance. This becomes the definition of the eduscape—a global homogeneous system that is still embedded in local particularities.

Yet locally trained and educated staff may still have international exposure and experience that would manifest in the internationalization of teaching and research of branch campuses. In many branch campuses across the world, main campus staff teach at the international campuses (Altbach 2013), but this was not so in South Africa. As stated earlier, most staff belonged within the SADC region and had trained there. In fact, being a student at the university was given as the most common reason for staff joining the university. This could be put down to the skills shortage in South Africa, specifically in higher education, making it difficult to attract academics from other institutions (Ensor 2003).

For a number of the others, the opportunity to work with their previous supervisors, the draw of an international brand, good salaries, and the opportunity to be near home were important. While most research has focused on the causes for mobility, we were also concerned to explore forms of academic engagement and how TNE staff participated in the world of mobile knowledges. In South Africa, of the survey participants, 22 percent of academics at branch campuses had worked on international projects (either teaching or research); of these, 7 percent had worked on projects with academics on the main campus. A total of 78 percent had no regular contact with international partners and only 14 percent had participated in international writing collaborations. A total of 22 percent of staff had travelled to a conference, while the remaining staff members had little or no exposure to these sorts of events and had not explored the opportunities for academic exchange. This could possibly be due to junior staff not having the impetus or knowing how to apply for funding. The picture with regard to the main campus was, however, slightly different. All staff had visited the main campus at least once and most (over 90 percent) had also been to other branch campuses of the university by which they were employed. A total of 82 percent had visited the main campus once while the rest had been twice. Yet despite these numerous visits, very few formal projects have materialized between academics of different campuses of the same institution.

Hence, it appears that there is little engagement between South African academics and their main campus contemporaries as 80 percent of staff had only ever visited the main campus once and only 14 percent of respondents had ever co-authored a paper with an international partner. Thus, although global education is in demand in South Africa and branch campuses are the main route to acquiring this, the quality and standards of the offerings are not necessarily very high. Rather, it appears that these institutions do not offer the "real thing" but rather only meet a consumer-driven demand for a "branded" education.

Furthermore, although branch campuses often claim to offer a replication of the HE experience of the main campus—in the form of space (campuses), knowledge and structures—there also needs to be some sort of replication or engagement among the staff and offerings to students in the local campus. This model requires a degree of consistency in curriculum, content, and ability of lecturing staff. It is clear from our research that while there is some form of engagement in some branch campuses, the local context of HE in South Africa limits the ability to have similar academic staff. For instance, only 9 percent of academic staff in Monash South Africa has doctoral degrees (the South Africa average is 37 percent, although this varies greatly with the University of Cape Town with

67 percent and the University of Johannesburg with 33 percent) questioning the extent to which global education or international research is actually delivered in branch campuses. It also points to the need to question the notion of "global education" as a concept and to whether the Global South should be looking to replicate the HE structures of the Global North given the local conditions and histories of the emergence of HE in individual countries. This needs to be done with a broader African context as a significant number of African students are educated at the South African institutions.

However, 24 percent of academics surveyed at branch campuses specifically spoke of their need and desire to link to international content. This desire could stem from a need to have greater prestige of working in a globally ranked institution, or even simply an institution from the Global North. The prestige of working for an "international" campus can play a large part in the decision to overlook some of the shortcomings of the branch campus, such as poor facilities and fewer course offerings (Wilkins, Stephens Balakrishnan, and Huisman 2012). Given the limited contact and capability for achieving true internationalization, it appears that a broader mind-set of globalized education is all that staff can instill in their curriculum. Another way of partaking of the global is through curriculum. The curriculum often has an anglophone bias, with textbooks, academic theory, and prescribed journal readings predominantly coming from authors and institutions from the Global North. This creates an assumption by students that institutions from the Global North, particularly if they are ranked, offer a better quality of education (Jöns and Hoyler 2013). So while there might be much value in the migration of foreign students studying in a new location, there is far less value in the migration of a branch campus "brand" providing an inferior replication of a Global North degree in the Global South. It is, however, difficult to directly compare the quality of one degree qualification to another; the fact that only 12 percent of academics joined the branch campus because of its link to its "international" brand and that 18 percent of academics took the "internationalization" into context when setting their curriculum shows that the attempt to replicate the degree from the main campus is either not a priority or is being actively scuppered by local academic staff. Thus, although there is a desire to be part of the global education processes, branch campuses are clearly not seen as the primary route to this internationalization.

The potential disinterest of "internationalization" of curriculum in HE in South Africa could be linked to the alternative priorities for further education in the Global South. Institutions in South Africa have huge social demands placed on them, from solving practical problems and providing research for social issues to delivering vocational and professional training to an underprivileged and, in many cases, poorly educated youth cohort. The added demand of being globally relevant might be too much. This could be a space that branch campuses fill. However, the branch campuses also have a local pressure—that is, to reproduce a global educational product for a mobile regional elite who will look to immigrate with transferable skills and knowledge from an internationally branded institution.

The Future Eduscape of Higher Education in South Africa

This chapter has outlined the fundamental shift that has taken place in HE in South Africa both during the apartheid period and post the 1994 democratic transition, transforming an insular HE system to one that attracts international staff and students. The rationale for change in the HE landscape in South Africa was to develop internationally competitive instruction that addresses the national development agenda. The mergers and incorporations of public institutions were meant to address a racist legacy while strengthening institutional capacity. While some may argue that this has indeed occurred, the clampdown on private educational providers and branch campuses demonstrates that the DoE perceives international campuses and transnational education as a threat to HE. This is despite the demand by international and local students to be educated to function in a global system where skilled immigrants are in demand. Branch campuses in South Africa are not seen as adequately addressing the particularities of the complex histories of HE in South Africa and the current demands that arise from these histories, limiting the internationalization of the offerings. Thus, South Africa as a regional immigration hub for students and staff is not necessarily reproducing a global model of education, but rather an edu-scape that is local in nature despite the pressures of the global system.

Yet this still leaves the question of capacity and the failure of the university system to deliver. The University of South Africa (UNISA) is a mega distance university, where all course content is offered via correspondence, and consistently "mops up" the excess students who cannot enroll in traditional universities. Typically, these students were full-time employees or others unable to attend contact institutions. For instance, Nelson Mandela obtained his law degree from UNISA while incarcerated on Robin Island. However, due to the huge demand for HE places by students, UNISA has more than doubled in size since the end of apartheid, from 150,000 students to a massive 400,000 in 2014. This huge increase is due to the inability for contact universities to cope with the growing demand by students for an education as contact universities, such as the University of Johannesburg, typically receiving 100,000 applicants for 10,000 places (Savides et al. 2015). This demonstrates the need for an expansion in HE to fill the gap that public intuitions are currently unable to fulfill.

At the moment, UNISA is undertaking this role. However, the rise of massive open online courses (MOOCs) and open university resources might simply mean that institutions such as UNISA will become the dominant type of institution. Moreover, the demand for HE globally has meant that UNISA has students in 173 countries and typically 50,000 of its students are not from Southern Africa. This transition to the online open environment is a further shift in the globalization of HE in South Africa, with UNISA becoming a provider of international education. At present, UNISA has a campus in Ethiopia and exam centers across most major cities in Africa. Students are able to write exams in major centers across the world, creating a disjoin between space and the provision of education. Online education provides a unique disconnection between place and the educational offerings. Students are able to obtain an internationally branded qualification without having the opportunity to develop a sense of place from where that qualification is developed. This is the ultimate "global" experience where branding is more important than location and the internationalization of the institution is based on where the student is based rather than where the student comes from.

Conclusions

Much of the literature on academic mobility of students and staff has focused on movements from the Global South to the North; there is much less literature on the issues of internationalization within south–south mobility contexts. This chapter addresses this gap by looking at higher education in the context of transnational education programs in South Africa and the experiences of academic staff within it.

The huge demand for HE in South Africa both from local and regional students has resulted in a significant demand for branch campuses in countries with inadequate local provision of education. This has been limited in South Africa due to prescriptive legislation placed on external institutions. However, there is huge unmet demand for HE in South Africa with, typically, all universities being oversubscribed by 50 percent, due to the high unemployment rate coupled with a skills shortage. Expansion is anticipated to be strong due to demand for access to mass and elite (or even just foreign) institutions. However, the call locally is to expand and promote local institutions, not to import foreign campuses. The state is also still seeking to adjust and manage the legacies of a very unequal education system, and that remains the priority in shaping higher education provision. As a result, the local HE conditions are not favourable for branch campuses as is apparent from the gradual winding down of these campuses across South Africa. Moreover, foreign brands are not well recognized in the country—for example, Monash University was virtually unknown before it opened in Johannesburg.

With the demand for HE in South Africa, the space to produce/reproduce knowledge workers is influenced by the local legislative and environmental restrictions that limit the amount of global perspective that the local staff and students have. Thus, despite the global movement of campuses, staff, and students, there is still a limitation on the amount of truly global interaction that will take place. This might leave staff and students disillusioned with the branch campuses. However, due to the prestige of working/studying at a "world class" or even just "global North" institution, knowledge workers overlook the negative aspects of the place and focus on the positives. This, however, raises interesting questions about the rationale behind why these institutions initially set up campuses in South Africa.

The process of transplanting a branch campus in a complex HE environment demonstrates that migration takes place at multiple levels. Migration of knowledge, led by branch campuses, is altering the need for individuals to physically relocate. Students and staff could potentially be seen to be benefiting from in-situ globalization. However, it is often projected that instead of migration branch campuses offer a degree of replication—with the replication of place, knowledge, teaching staff, content playing a central role in this eduscape. This chapter shows the extent to which this actually occurs is unclear. Replication is not really occurring within the South African context and therefore does not offer an alternative to skilled migration. Rather, migration of skilled people and globalization of HE through TNEs and particularly branch campuses have complex interconnections that need further exploration.

Notes

1. Regionally, the picture is, however, very different. Some regions such as Europe have loosened entry requirements and even encouraged intraregional mobility, but in doing so they have merely expanded the frontiers of the fortress, not dismantled it.
2. English-medium education system is one that uses English as the primary medium of instruction.
3. This support seems to be waning as Monash University sold 50 percent of Monash South Africa to the Laureate Group of Universities in 2014 with a move to sell another 30 percent in the future.
4. This chapter sets up the complex local context behind internationalization rather than exploring the findings from the empirical study in detail. For a fuller analysis of the empirical findings, see Gunter and Raghuram (2015).

References

Altbach, P. G. 2013. *The international imperative in higher education.* Rotterdam: Springer Science.

———. 2015. Why branch campuses may be unsustainable. *International Higher Education*, 58: 2–3.

Andersson, M. 2013. Cosmopolitan practices in social contexts: Swedish skilled migrants in the Netherlands. *Crossings: Journal of Migration and Culture* 4 (2): 155–173.

Asmal, K. 2002. Private higher education in South Africa: Access and development: Debating process. *Perspectives in education: A contested good? Understanding private higher education in South Africa: Special issue* 4 (20): 125–128.

Beaverstock, J. V. 2005. Transnational elites in the city: British highly-skilled intercompany transferees in New York City's financial district. *Journal of Ethnic and Migration Studies* 31: 245–268.

Beaverstock, J. V., and J. T. Boardwell. 2000. Negotiating globalisation, transnational corporations and global city financial centres in transient migration studies. *Applied Geography* 20: 277–304.

Bundy, C. 2005. Global patterns, local options? Some implications for South Africa of international changes in higher education. *Perspectives in education: Postmodern (narrative) career counselling and education: Special issue* 2 (2): 85–99.

CHE, (2007) *Audit report on Monash South Africa, Higher Education Quality Committee*, HEQC: Pretoria.

Cloete, N., C. Sheppard, and T. Bailey. 2015. South Africa as a PhD hub in Africa?. *Knowledge Production and Contradictory Functions in African Higher Education*, 75 (forthcoming).

Coleman, D. (2003) Quality assurance in transnational education. *Journal of Studies in International Education*, 7 (4), 354–378.

Collins, F. L. 2010. Negotiating un/familiar embodiments: Investigating the corporeal dimensions of South Korean international student mobilities in Auckland, New Zealand. *Population, Space and Place*, 16 (1): 51–62.

Crush, J., and E. Campbell. 2005. *States of vulnerability: The brain drain of future talent to South Africa*. Pretoria: IDASA Publishers.

DHET. 2004. 10 years of higher education and training in South Africa, Department of Higher Education and Training: Pretoria.

Du Plessis, T. 2006. From monolingual to bilingual higher education: The repositioning of historically Afrikaans-medium universities in South Africa. *Language Policy* 5 (1): 87–113.

Ensor, P. 2003. The National Qualifications Framework and higher education in South Africa: Some epistemological issues. *Journal of Education and Work* 16 (3): 325–346.

Favell, A. 2008. *Eurostars and Eurocities: Free movement and mobility in an integrating Europe*. Malden, MA, Oxford and Carleton, Victoria: Blackwell.

Findlay, A. M. 2011. An assessment of supply and demand-side theorizations of international student mobility. *International Migration* 49 (2): 162–190.

Findlay, A. M., F. L. N. Li., A. J. Jowett, and R. Skeldon. 1996. Skilled international migration and the global city: A study of expatriates in Hong Kong. *Transactions of the Institute of British Geographers* 21: 49–61.

Gunter, A., and P. Raghuram. 2015. International study at branch campuses in the Global South: Linking student, staff and institutional mobility. *Globalisation, Societies and Education.* Special issue on cross-border education and careers in glocal knowledge economies.

Harman, G., and Harman, K. 2003. Institutional mergers in higher education: Lessons from international experience. *Tertiary Education and Management*, 9 (1), 29–44.

Hay, D., and M. Fourie. 2002. Preparing the way for mergers in South African higher and further education institutions: An investigation into staff perceptions. *Higher Education* 44 (1): 115–131.

Hay, H. R., M. Fourie, and J. F. Hay. 2001. Are institutional combinations, mergers or amalgamation the answer? An investigation into staff perceptions. *South African Journal of Higher Education*, 15 (1), 100–116.

HEQC, 2012. *Audit report on the University of Johannesburg*. Pretoria: Council on Higher Education.

Ho, E. L. E. 2011. Identity politics and cultural asymmetries: Singaporean transmigrants "fashioning" cosmopolitanism. *Journal of Ethnic and Migration Studies* 37 (5): 729–746.

IEASA, 2014. *Twenty years of the internationalisation of South African higher education*. Johannesburg: International Education Association of South Africa.

Insch, A., and B. Sun. 2013. University students' needs and satisfaction with their host city. *Journal of Place Management and Development* 6 (3): 178–191.

Jansen, J. 2003. Mergers in South African higher education: Theorising change in transitional contexts. *Politikon: South African Journal of Political Studies* 30 (1): 27–50.

———. 2004. Changes and continuities in South Africa's higher education system, 1994 to 2004. *Changing class: Education and social change in post-apartheid South Africa*, 293–314.

Jöns, H., and M. Hoyler. 2013. Global geographies of higher education: The perspective of world university rankings. *Geoforum*, 46, 45–59.

Kishun, R. 2007. The internationalisation of higher education in South Africa: Progress and challenges. *Journal of Studies in International Education* 11 (3–4): 455–469.

Kinser, K., and D. C. Levy. 2007. For-profit higher education: US tendencies, international echoes. In *International handbook of higher education*, eds. J. J. Forest and P. G. Altbach, 107–119. The Netherlands: Springer.

Knorr-Cetina, K. 2007. Culture in global knowledge societies: Knowledge cultures and epistemic cultures. *Interdisciplinary Science Reviews* 32 (4): 361–375.

Kofman, E. and P. Raghuram, P. 2013. Knowledge, gender and changing mobility regimes: Women migrants in Europe. In *Mobilities, knowledge and social justice*, ed. S. Ilcan. McGill-Queen's University Press, Montreal.

Kruss, G. 2002. More, better, different? Understanding private higher education in South Africa. *Perspectives in Education* Special issue 4 (20): 15–28.

Kwaramba, M. 2012. Internationalisation of higher education in Southern Africa with South Africa as a major exporter. *Journal of International Education and Leadership Volume*, 2 (1): 102–125.

Latham, A., and D. Conradson. 2005. Friendship, networks and transnationality in a world city: Antipodean transmigrants in London. *Journal of Ethnic and Migration Studies* 31: 287–305.

Lee, J., and C. Sehoole. 2015. Regional, continental, and global mobility to an emerging economy: The case of South Africa. *Higher Education* 1–17.

Leibowitz, B. 2004. Becoming academically literate in South Africa: Lessons from student accounts for policymakers and educators. *Language and Education* 18 (1): 35–52.

Lesjak, M., E. Juvan, E. Ineson, M. Yap, and E. Axelsson. 2015. Erasmus student motivation: Why and where to go?. *Higher Education*.

Levy, D. 2002. Commercial private higher education: South Africa as a stark example: The private higher education landscape: Developing conceptual and empirical analysis. *Perspectives in Education: A contested good? Understanding private higher education in South Africa: Special Issue* 4 (20): 29–46.

Mabizela, M. 2000. *Towards a typology of structural patterns of private–public higher education in South Africa: A contextual analysis*. Thesis. Cape Town: Faculty of Education, University of the Western Cape.

———. 2006. Recounting the state of private higher education in South Africa. In *Growth and Expansion of Private Higher Education in Africa*, ed. N. Varghese. Paris: Institution for Educational Planning.

Mabizela, M., G. Subotzky, and B. Thaver. 2000. *The emergence of private higher education in South Africa: Key issues and challenges*. University of the Western Cape: Education Policy Unit.

Madge, C., P. Raghuram, and P. Noxolo. 2015. Conceptualizing international education: From international student to international study. *Progress in Human Geography* 39 (6): 681–701.

Malsen, G. 2011. Monash switches to public purpose. *University World News*, 376. Available at: www.universityworldnews.com/article.php?story=20111111214507863 (accessed July 22, 2015).

Marginson, S., and G. Rhoades. 2002. Beyond national states, markets, and systems of higher education: A glocal agency heuristic. *Higher Education* 43 (3): 281–309.

Massey, D. 1991 A global sense of place. *Marxism Today*. June 24–29.

Meier, L. 2014. *Migrant professionals in the city: Local encounters, identities and inequalities*. Routledge: London.

Mpinganjira, M. 2009. Comparative analysis of factors influencing the decision to study abroad. *African Journal of Business Management* 3: 358–365.

Nhlapo, T. 2004. Two institutions closed after MBA ruling, IOL News. Available at: www.iol.co.za/news/south-africa/two-institutions-closed-after-mba-ruling-1.216064#.VbI2WfmqpBc (accessed July 20, 2015).

Nieuwenhuizen, C., and E. Swanepoel. 2015. Comparison of the entrepreneurial intent of master's business students in developing countries: South Africa and Poland. *Acta Commercii*, 15 (1), 10–22.

Nkomo, M., and C. Sehoole. 2007. Rural-based universities in South Africa: Albatrosses or potential nodes for sustainable development? *International Journal of Sustainability in Higher Education* 8 (2): 234–246.

Noxolo, P., P. Raghuram, and C. Madge. 2008. 'Geography is pregnant' and 'Geography's milk is flowing': Metaphors for a postcolonial discipline?. *Environment and Planning D: Society and Space*, 26 (1), 146–168.

O'Connell, S. 2015. A search for the human in the shadow of Rhodes. *Ufahamu: A Journal of African Studies*, 38 (3), 1–4.

Pather, C. 2015. # RhodesMustFall: No room for ignorance or arrogance. *South African Journal of Science*, 111 (5–6), 1–2.

Qin, F. 2015. Global talent, local careers: circular migration of top Indian engineers and professionals. *Research Policy* 44 (2): 405–420.

Raghuram, P. 2009. Which migration, what development? Unsettling the edifice of migration and development. *Population, Space and Place*, 15 (2), 103–117.

Raghuram, P. 2013. Theorising the spaces of student migration. *Population, Space and Place*, 19 (2), 138–154.

Ratha, D., S. Mohapatra., C. Ozden., S. Plaza., W. Shaw, and A. Shimeles. 2011. *Leveraging migration for Africa: Remittances, skills, and investments*. Washington, DC: World Bank.

Robertson, S. 2013. *Transnational student-migrants and the state: The education-migration nexus*. London: Palgrave.

Sassen, S. 2000. The global city: Strategic site/new frontier. *American studies*, 41 (2/3), 79–95.

Savides, M., T. Pillay, and S. Eggington. 2015. Only 1 in 8 students will find a place at university, *Times Live*. Available at: www.timeslive.co.za/local/2015/02/02/only-1-in-8-students-will-find-a-place-at-university (accessed July 19, 2015).

Sehoole, C. 2006. Internationalisation of higher education in South Africa: A historical review. *Perspectives in education: Internationalisation of higher education: Global challenges, regional impacts and national responses:* Special issue 4 (24): 19–33.

Shachar, A. 2006. The race for talent: Highly skilled migrants and competitive immigration regimes. *New York University Law Review* 81: 148–206.

Sidhu, R., and P. Christie. 2014. Making space for an international branch campus: Monash University Malaysia. *Asia Pacific Viewpoint* 55 (2): 182–195.

Solimano, A. 2008. *The international mobility of talent: Types, causes, and development impact*. Oxford: Oxford University Press.

Waghid, Y. 2002. Knowledge production and higher education transformation in South Africa: Towards reflexivity in university teaching, research and community service. *Higher Education*, 43 (4), 457–488.

Wangenge-Ouma, G. 2012. Tuition fees and the challenge of making higher education a popular commodity in South Africa. *Higher Education*, 64 (6), 831–844.

Waters, J., and M. Leung. 2013a. Young people and the reproduction of disadvantage through transnational higher education in Hong Kong. *Sociological Research Online* 17 (3): 65–79.

———. 2013b. Immobile transnationalisms? Young people and their *in situ* experiences of 'international' education in Hong Kong. *Urban Studies* 50 (3): 606–620.

Williams, A., and V. Baláž. 2008. *International migration and knowledge*. London: Routledge.

Wilkins, S., M. Stephens Balakrishnan, and J. Huisman. 2012. Student satisfaction and student perceptions of quality at international branch campuses in the United Arab Emirates. *Journal of Higher Education Policy and Management* 34 (5): 543–556.

Wood, B. J., S. M. Tapsall, and G. N. Soutar. 2005. Borderless education: Some implications for management. *International Journal of educational management*, 19 (5): 428–436.

Wyngaard, A., and C. Kapp. 2004. Rethinking and reimagining mergers in further and higher education: A human perspective: Perspectives on higher education. *South African Journal of Higher Education*, 18 (1): 185–199.

Yeoh, B., and S. Huang. 2013. *The cultural politics of talent migration in East Asia*. London: Routledge.

Part II

Transforming Cities, Transforming Lives

8 "London is a Much More Interesting Place than Paris"

Place-comparison and the Moral Geographies of Highly Skilled Migrants

Jon Mulholland and Louise Ryan

Introduction

Drawing on data from a study of the French highly skilled in London, this chapter explores the nature and dynamics of a migrant population's "sense of place" in a global city. Specifically, it examines some of the ways in which highly skilled migrants construct their own moral geographies through the recursive relationship that forms between the affective qualities of their cities of dwelling, their own status-related perceptions, and their day-to-day space-making practices. We assert that the moral geographies associated with the formulation of highly skilled migrants' sense of place must be understood as an outcome of this complex dynamic, but also produced through the deployment of what we would refer to as a "grounded comparative epistemology of place," in this case through the juxtapositioning of the qualities of London and Paris. By a "grounded comparative epistemology of place" we suggest a process whereby senses of place are actively constructed through a complex play of lived experiences, imaginings, and the affective qualities of a place, but importantly via evaluative comparative practices where particular, "significant other places," are selected to furnish evaluations of current places of dwelling.

First, drawing on the work of Braudel (1977), and specifically the idea of the "soft tissue of urbanism," along with the notion of "affective urbanism" (Thrift 2004; Conradson and Latham 2007), we show how London is granted a particular affective and atmospheric quality deriving from the open and civil nature of its public sociality, and in contrast to Paris.

Second, we show how our participants draw on a rendering of London as a definitively libertarian space, largely as an expression of its attributed ("Anglo-Saxon") neoliberal and cosmopolitan character, and value the capital as more "livable" than Paris on this basis. We also explore the gendered dimensions of such moral geographies.

Third, we examine our participants' attributions of the quality of "buzz" to London, a quality central to the civic planning and branding aspirations of many global cities (Peck 2005), and a quality seen to be a necessary condition for attracting and retaining place-sensitive highly skilled migrants. We show that despite assertions as to the character of London as both buzzing and stressful, it was nevertheless considered both more buzzing, yet less stressful than Paris, suggesting that other qualities of place in London may serve to offset the intensity of life in the capital.

Fourth, we explore our participants' accounts of London as a place of largely unprecedented cultural encounter, both in terms of the high cultural amenities of museums, galleries, theatres, and so on, but also in terms of the popular-cultural characteristics of its "playscapes" (Chatterton and Hollands 2002). In particular, we show how the spatial composition of the pub, and its "traditional" mode of occupation and usage is signified by our participants as a key ingredient in framing London's affective qualities, and its capacity to enable both buzz and a democratically inclusive public sociality.

Finally, we examine the importance to our participants of London's green spaces as "high quality sanctuaries" (Kjølsrød 2013), offsetting the buzz and stress of urban life. We show how historically bequeathed social goods, in all their material configurations, may inadvertently render specific global cities as particularly attractive to highly skilled migrants, and suited to the expectations of the most contemporaneous desires of affluent city dwellers.

We conclude by arguing that we need to pay fuller attention to the place-centric dimensions of the mobility, dwelling, and settlement practices of highly skilled migrants, and in particular to the dynamics that shape the moral geographies associated with such migrants' senses of place, and the role played by "significant other" places in framing a sense of place through practices of comparison.

Literature Review

Flows of international migration have become increasingly complex and diverse, witnessing an ever-larger middling mass of highly skilled migrants (PIONEUR 2013). The study of such highly skilled migration has moved importantly away from a reductionist neoclassical model that diminishes the migrant to a mere rational economic actor (Wang 2013). In this move, migrants become understandable in all their actually existing complexity, where motivations, experiences, relations, processes, and practices come into view as the outcome of critically important interplays between the economic and noneconomic dimensions of the migrant subject and his/her mobility contexts (Ryan and Mulholland 2013; Wang 2013). In this way, the *human* dimension of highly skilled migration has become an emergent area of enquiry (Favell et al. 2006; van Riemsdijk 2014). Within this frame, important advancements have been made in understanding the internal heterogeneities that characterize this migrant constituency and the accordant multidimensional nature of their motivations and desires (PIONEUR 2013; Ryan and Mulholland 2013; Wang 2013), the influential contextual-relational forces that act on their choices, practices and experiences (Ryan and Mulholland 2013), and of the imperfections, compromises and frictions associated with such flows and settlements (Favell, Feldblum, and Smith 2006; Butcher 2009; Tseng 2011).

Central to this shift towards understanding the human dimension of highly skilled migration has been a necessary concern to appreciate the importance of the noneconomic dimensions of migrant motivations and practices, and in specific relation to the nonoccupational dimensions of the places where they dwell (Meier 2015). A space, and place-centric understanding of highly skilled migrants' mobility motivations, experiences, contexts and practices, and the nature and dynamics of the particularities of their dwelling in those spaces/places becomes central to our understanding (van Riemsdijk 2014).

However, the nature of space and place, and of their relations to the social goods and people who occupy them, has become an increasingly complex matter in the context of respatializations associated with processes of globalization and transnationalism (Scholte 2005). But against the excesses of globalization and transnationalist doctrines, that invited us to relinquish traditional spatial ontologies in the interests of understanding a new world of placelessness, flows, nodes, and networks, we are witnessing a revival of interest in exploring the manner in which space continues to be "placed," and in ways of critical import for understanding the heterogeneous nature of highly skilled migration and settlement experiences, practices, and effects (Butcher 2009; Tseng 2011).

Even in a context where the new economic forces of globalization carry powerful drivers of homogenization (Sennet 2005), important differences of place prevail, and even where globalization can be said to have had its greatest impact (Meier 2015). Such differences are in part an outcome of the scalar dimensions of cities (Scott 2006; Glick-Schiller and Cağlar 2011). They also speak to the fact that cities embody still-defining historical trajectories and meanings, and related forms of path dependency (Kazepov 2005). As "open systems," cities nevertheless remain "nested" in broader social, economic, and institutional contexts that also bear witness to the ongoing influence of the national contexts in which those cities are located (Kazepov 2005), despite the relative autonomy that global cities have increasingly come to enjoy vis-à-vis their national homes (Bagnasco and Le Galès 2000). Places continue to offer dissimilar experiences and opportunity structures (Smith 2005), and in ways that even those with the most abundant human capital cannot but fail to experience. London and Paris here serve as pertinent cases in point. Ranked by the Globalization and World Cities Study Group and Network as "Alpha Cities," recent data from the A. T. Kearney's Global Cities Index (GCI) and Global Cities Outlook (GCO), locate London and Paris in 2015 in second and third places respectively on the GCI, and second and nineteenth on the GCO. As a result, incorporating criteria including business activity, innovation, political engagement, cultural experience, and personal well-being, both cities are ranked among just 16 "global elite" cities in the world. But beyond such apparent like-situatedness lie important points of difference, "objectively" illuminated in the metrics of the GCI and GCO, but also "subjectively" in the individual and collective experiences and imaginings of those who have a reason to compare the cities.

Migrant motivations, desires, experiences, relations, and practices remain resolutely informed by place, and by the actual and imagined qualities of particular places. Migrants' place-centric evaluative practices are informed by a multitude of biographical variables; intimate-relational circumstances; life-course positions; and more collectively formulated senses of place, as these emerge from the attributional practices of places themselves (through city branding, for instance) and of collective others (for instance, other nations or cities; Vanolo 2008; van Riemsdijk 2014). Both in terms of branding and civic planning, cities have become increasingly active as agents seeking to attract highly skilled migrants, or the "creative classes" as Florida has defined them, by putting into place the right "people climate" (Florida 2002). Though deeply contested, Florida's (2002) contribution has had the effect of focusing policy, planning, and academic attention on the place-centric orientations of highly skilled migrants, and the qualities of place deemed by such migrants as meeting the necessary and sufficient conditions of a "livable" place (McCann 2008).

We argue that spaces and places provide far more than a mere context for the lives lived within them (Glick-Schiller and Çağlar 2011), but rather frame place-related practices, and are in turn themselves actively produced by the space-making practices of diverse subjects (Glick-Schiller and Çağlar 2011). We can think of such practices as *spacing* (Löw 2008), as processes involving important mechanisms of "synthesizing", where otherwise discrete social goods and people are brought together variably into a coherent singular entity in and through the spatial imaginaries and practices of social subjects (Löw 2008). In turn, such imaginaries (of spaces as they are and "should" be) are formed, not in splendid isolation, but typically within a context of interpretive communities of like-situated subjects (McCann 2008; van Riemsdijk 2014).

However, spacing is more than "merely" an outcome of the attributional practices of the perceiving subject, and the status-dependent pre-structured significations that such practices might express, it is also informed by the character and qualities of places themselves. In this regard, we are also interested in understanding the affective qualities, and related atmospheres, associated with particular urban metropolises. Affect has been defined by Thrift (2004) as "the property of the active outcome of an encounter" (62). Conradson and Latham (2007) define affect in terms of an "embodied appraisal of external stimuli. It is about the involuntary delivery of a somatic verdict on present circumstances" (236). To speak of the affective dimensions of a city is to talk of its "atmosphere." Atmosphere can be defined as "the external effect, instantiated in perception, of social goods and human beings in their situated spatial ordering" (Löw 2008, 44). Of course, there can be no singular, or even necessarily a dominant, affective register to any city, as the affective order/s of a place necessarily expresses the particularities of its multiple ecologies (Anderson and Holden 2008).

As such, we would assert that places, in all their affective and atmospheric character are never experienced as a singularity. In fact, diverse subject positions (gender, class, ethnicity, age, relationship status) serve to frame how a place's affective and atmospheric qualities are perceived through the pre-structuring effects that the life experiences and "cultural vocabularies" associated with such diversities have (Löw 2008; Conradson and Latham 2007). Amin and Thrift's (2007) work points to the ways in which sense of place may inherently carry normative dimensions, where practices of judgment come to construct moral geographies that serve to normatively position, rank, and rate cities in terms of their "worth." This may manifest itself in terms of binaries of slow city/fast city, dull city/happening city, etc. We would propose also that such evaluative practices draw on repertoires of evaluation that may have a national origin (Lamont and Thévenet 2000). While challenging any tendency towards nationally framed cultural essentialisms, Lamont and Thévenet (2000) have nevertheless pointed to the differential availabilities and usages of particular culturally infused "repertoires of evaluation," from one nation to another, where such repertoires serve as resources for collective appraisals of the nature and worth of things, including places. We would also assert that such evaluative practices express formative biographical dimensions (Wang 2013; van Riemsdijk 2014).

The French in London

Census data suggest a significant growth in French migration to the UK. For example, while there were officially 38,000 French people living in the UK in 2001, by 2011 this figure had risen to 129,804 (Office of National Statistics). This suggests further growth since Eurostat (2009) estimated a figure of 114,000 French nationals resident in the UK. Data from the Department of Work and Pensions (DWP 2012) on new national insurance numbers issued to adult overseas nationals in the UK indicates that between 2006/7 and 2009/10, over 80,000 newly arrived French nationals were allocated national insurance numbers. During 2008–2009, only the Poles, Indians, and Slovakians were arriving in the UK in larger numbers. Reflecting a broader pattern, London is the primary destination for the French (DWP 2012). However, these figures are dramatically short of other recent, though unverifiable, estimates. The number of French nationals in the UK has been suggested to be as high as 400,000, based on the French Consulate's estimate (*The Economist* February 24, 2011[1]). Evidence also points to the fact that the French are the most highly qualified European migrants in the UK (72 percent having a university education compared to 46.2 percent of Spanish and 21.3 percent of Germans; see Braun and Glöckner-Rist 2012).

This chapter draws upon data derived from an eighteen-month, Economic and Social Research Council-funded, qualitative study focusing on the life and work experiences of the highly skilled French in London's financial and business sectors, and their families (with interviews taking place between 2011 and 2013). The project adopted a qualitative methodology concerned with illuminating the thick biography of migrant's lived experiences, and the meaningful nature of such mobility experiences for those concerned. The study was based on semi-structured, one-off interviews and one focus group. A total of thirty-seven people participated in the study: sixteen men and twenty-one women, with the bulk aged between 35 and 44. The majority had arrived in the UK in the 2000s, though some had been here for considerably longer. Twenty-three were married, five co-habiting and nine single. Twenty-five were parents. Participants were contacted via a snowballing technique, with purposive sampling used, where appropriate, to secure data from a range of key demographic variables (gender, age, relationship status).

The term "highly skilled" covers a diverse group, but the OECD and European Commission/ Eurostat framework defines them as those who have *either* successfully completed a tertiary education and/or are employed in occupational roles normally requiring tertiary qualifications (such as undergraduate and postgraduate degrees). The majority of our participants satisfy this definition on both counts; twenty-nine were qualified to degree level or above, and sixteen had pursued subsequent education and training in the UK. Though a range of French higher educational institutions were represented among the educational backgrounds of our participants, over 50 percent had attended highly selective, elite academic institutions (*les Grandes Ecoles*). Twenty were currently employed in senior positions in, or allied to, the financial sector; three worked in the field of finance law; four were employed in business-related higher education, while the remainder of those in work were occupied in a range of highly skilled professional positions. Only a small minority of participants who were employed in the business and finance fields at the point of interview had substantive third country working experience prior to migrating to London.

Sense of Place as Moral Geography: Comparing London and Paris

London as a Place to Live and Work

We have referred elsewhere to the multidimensional nature of French highly skilled migrants' significations, evaluations, and experiences of London as a place to live and work, across a range of dimensions. Specifically, we have accounted for the ways in which our participants understand London in multiscalar terms: as a mosaic of localities; as a national capital; and as a global city, bearing the hallmarks of a nationally framed (Anglo-Saxon) neoliberal character that equips it well for its global role (Mulholland and Ryan 2015). We have also explored some of the frictions associated with work and life in London, especially in respect of the challenges of establishing deeper and more meaningful relations with (especially native) others in the city (Ryan and Mulholland 2014), and the dissonances that may come from intercultural experiences in the workplace (Mulholland and Ryan 2014). We have discussed the ways in which the geographical proximity of London to France, even in an age of globalized transportation opportunities and ICT, has enabled important processes of embedding in the capital, precisely because of the manner in which proximity allows for a maintaining of substantive ties with family and "home" (Ryan and Mulholland 2014; Ryan, Klekowski and Mulholland 2015). Here we focus on some key dimensions of our participants' evaluation of the livability of London, specifically on the moral geographies they construct through the practice of comparing London to Paris.

The 'Soft Tissue of Urbanism': The Openness and Civility of London's Public Sociability

Rae (2008), drawing on the ideas of Braudel (1977), emphasizes the somewhat intangible yet important "soft tissue" of urbanism; an "accumulated legacy of habits and expectations for conduct in daily life" (29). For Braudel, urbanism may be marked by the routinized expression of thousands of acts that "flower and reach fruition without anyone's having made a decision, acts of which we are not even fully aware" (cited in Rae 2008). We would suggest that the "soft tissue of urbanism" can be understood as one component of the affective qualities of a place (Conradson and Latham 2007). We propose that, however difficult to operationalize, public sociality is one important dimension of such soft tissue, and informs the affective and atmospheric (Stewart 2011) character of a place. While complex and at times contradictory, our data offered illuminating, though perhaps unexpected, accounts of London as a place valued for particular qualities of public sociality, and in direct juxtaposition to Paris.

Paris was without exception portrayed as unfriendly and tough. Paris was, for some, juxtaposed to the rest of France as particularly unfriendly, reflecting an influential tradition of bifurcated Paris-provincial relations. However, there was also clear evidence that such Parisian unfriendliness, as a feature of public sociality, was seen as a manifestation of a broader French trait. According to Agnès, "I think in France relationships between individuals are much tougher … brutal, more direct … In Paris … people … can't smile. It's bad to be seen actually to be someone who looks happy and cheerful. You have to … be strong."

Adèle, a proud French provincialist, in response to a request for clarification on whether she saw London as friendlier than Paris, insisted, "yes, absolutely. It's changing in London but definitely, 100 percent. And oh boy, I hate Paris."

Luc points to the relative (to London) lack of openness to public communication in Paris: "I personally find that you make a lot easier contacts in London than in Paris I would say, and I'm always amazed because people are more open in terms of conversation" [in London]. In direct contrast, London was valued for everything that Paris was not—namely, its openness and friendliness. Martine reflects: "People are more helpful … they take time to explain … at the beginning they were really friendly … and I think people are more friendly in the street, they smile more and everything is a bit more serious in Paris." In addition to the importance attached to London's playscapes as venues for making friendly contact in London (discussed below), we have discussed elsewhere the relationship-facilitating "openness" (relative to Paris) attributed by our participants to London's work and residential spaces. Perceived national qualities of meritocracy, flexibility, and cosmopolitanism were commonly presented as also facilitating the making of contacts (Mulholland and Ryan 2015; Ryan and Mulholland 2014).

Thierry suggested that the openness and friendliness of London was an outcome of the fact that "there are no barriers between people … I think it's due to the way you live." Offering some substantiation of the "way English people live" in the UK, Elizabeth proposes an explanation grounded in an account of the particular role played by family in England: "there's much less a centre of family in England, people do go out … they live more outside their house." It was not, however, that "the English" were seen as placing less importance on family, as the privatized and bounded English family was presented by our participants as constituting an obstacle to forming close relationships with the English. Rather, it was that a cosmopolitan ethic of openness to the "other" was seen as a pervasive social good oiling the wheels of public sociality. Again suggesting a defining quality of Englishness as an explanation for the character of the urban sociality evident in London, Charles argues that "The English love to be in groups … They live like on a campus … They never sit in a couple two by two, they all sit fifty by fifty."

Not all of our participants were, however, convinced that such contact-facilitating openness was attributable to a national trait as such. While Renée appears to concur on London's friendly openness, she does question the extent to which this can be attributed to the English: "it's more friendly as well … I was really surprised because actually in London I haven't met a lot of English people. I don't know where you are".

The sense of London as a place marked by a virtuous form of public sociality was reflected in our participants' accounts of the capital as a place inheriting a tradition of rule-abiding public civility. For Bertrand, "the UK is seen as a place where the rule of law is respected." Some of our participants drew a direct comparison with Paris; For Luc, "what I like about London is that you have rules and people keep these rules, whereas in Paris it's more in between always." For Luc, this appears to be a manifestation of a broader national legacy: "It's really different, with many rules in England … that you still have, which I think are good things, which probably we have lost in France." For Charles, commenting on the governance of urban space, particularly in respect of traffic, "the English like to tell you the law in their country as if they were all a police officer." In this sense our participants appear to be giving voice to the ways in which even global cities may be perceived as embodying path-dependent historically informed qualities of place (Kazepov 2005), even in respect of their cultural character in a context of globalizing change. It may also suggest something of the *desire* (Wang 2013) of highly skilled migrants to dwell in places that, while defined by their neoliberal quality of energized competitiveness, are still able to embody particular qualities of public sociality.

Here we are offered, through accounts of London's apparently friction-free modalities of public sociality, a virtuous rendering of London's tolerant and inclusive openness. In this sense, the particularities of London would appear to offer the kind of environment so foundational to the requirements of Florida's creative classes (Florida 2002), an environment "rich in possibilities and opportunities for interaction" (Vanolo 2008, 372).

However, we would suggest that such necessarily selective perceptions of London's atmospheric and affective qualities express spacing practices inevitably framed by the status of our participants as affluent white Western European subjects, relatively free of the pathologizing attentions of xenophobic anti-immigrant sentiment. In our participants' juxtapositioning of London and Paris, we would also suggest that our data show how highly skilled migrants may actively draw on a grounded comparative epistemology of place through employing their own partially "pre-scripted" and nationally framed constructs of other places (here Paris) in spacing their city of dwelling. Such comparative epistemologies take on important evaluative-normative forms and functions, serving the purpose of mapping moral geographies. These data also appear suggestive of McCann's (2008) claim that spatial imaginaries typically emerge in the context of interpretive communities, facilitated in our empirical case by the striking patterns of co-national sociality exhibited by sections of the French population in London.

Civility with Liberty: Gendering Moral Geographies

The libertarian nature of London was an influential feature of our participants' sense of place, and seemed closely connected to their accounts of the capital's public civility. Explicitly linking rule-abiding civility with freedom, Omer reflects, "every time I go through the tunnel, every time I arrive here, I feel free, just protected, just really free … you feel that it's really organized, you feel secure. You feel free but secure."

For Irène, freedom is a ubiquitous feature of London: "the sense of freedom is everywhere, from how you look, from what you say, from how you live … ." According to Bernadette, London is defined in terms of its freedom, where the freedom to present oneself entirely as one wishes without judgment from others appears to derive from a certain quality of tolerant disinterestedness: "the fact that you are free and people don't care about you … you can do whatever you want and you can have pink hair, just going out of your house with slippers—nobody cares." Reflecting a libertarian, neoliberal, reading of London as a place marked by precisely the forms of openness and tolerance apparently demanded by the creative class (Peck 2005) our participants drew substantial contrasts with Paris.

While freedom was an important motif across our cohort's account of London as a place, and applied to multiple contexts, it appeared particularly significant, and valued, by our female participants. Here, liberty appeared linked specifically to women's freedom from the normative judgment of others. Unlike Paris, where a woman's presence in the public sphere was seen to be governed by a set of evaluative criteria concerned with how women "look," London was defined as a place where a woman could enjoy autonomy. Margaux contemplates: "I have a feeling it's anonymity almost in London, not being observed … not being controlled, because women on the whole … within the European environment, there is much more control." Valentine draws a stark contrast between the gender order of Paris and London: "I think here you can walk on the streets and be inexistent, whereas in Paris … they stare at you, they malign the way you dress, the way you behave." Irène asserts, through a juxtapositioning with France, the relative absence of a gendered normative regime in London, "in France there is a huge emphasis on how you look, how you dress and how slim or how big you are." Interestingly, while extolling the virtue of such liberation from the gendered regimes of control associated with women's public presentations of self in Paris, our female participants commonly took significant pride in, and attached importance to, what they deemed to be their own, nationally characteristic, good taste in clothes.

We have asserted that the particular and variable subject positions occupied by highly skilled migrants may frame how a place is experienced and perceived (Löw 2011), and in turn informs the space-making practices of those subjects. Research suggests that women's embodied experiences of patriarchal oppression may inform their mobility and settlement practices in the pursuit of self-empowerment and liberation (Wang 2013). Our data suggest that even in the context of a relatively privileged migrant population moving between two like-situated and geographically proximate global cities, two city-places may facilitate quite divergent, gendered moral geographies.

The Affect of Buzz

Conradson and Latham's (2007) seminal work on New Zealand Overseas Experience migrants in London pointed to the sheer intensity and energizing vitality of the lived experience associated with life in London, to its buzz. We would argue, with Conradson and Latham (2007), that this sense of buzz can be read as an affective outcome of the city's material and immaterial characters. On one level, it is not surprising that a sense of London's buzz may become a feature of the perceptual and attributional practices of such diverse migrant constituencies, as instilling a sense of buzz in a city has become a central point of reference for the ambitions of global cities' civic planners and branders alike (Vanolo 2008).

Our data, despite being drawn from a more diverse demographic than that of Conradson and Latham (2007), pointed to a sense of place stamped by the quality of buzz, even if the subject positions of many of our participants made it difficult for them to substantively engage with this quality of the city. The prevalence of data pertaining to the character of London as a buzzing place was particularly striking given that we did not ask a question relating directly to this. Valentine reflects: "up to the … economic downturn … it was just an amazing place to be. You could feel a buzz, an energy in London that you don't feel in Paris or … Milan." Claudine describes London as "a very fast city … it has a very intensive rhythm … It's a very vibrant city … getting your adrenalin working."

Buzz may, of course, be experienced as a defining affective feature of a place, yet still be quite differentially valorized. As with Conradson and Latham's (2007) and Favell's (2006) studies, our participants did make reference to the stress-inducing character of a life lived in a buzzing place. Charles unsurprisingly juxtaposes London and "non-Paris France" (from where a significant proportion of our participants came): "there are many people who come from non-Paris French places and they come to London and they find it very stressful, a lot of commuting and traffic jams and congestions, and car parking is very difficult … Obviously it's very noisy and very polluted." There was also a recognition that such intensity may be more suited to some than others. Claudine points to the life-course dimensions of this: "I don't think I could retire here because I couldn't retire in a place where everything is going too fast, I think it drives me mad." Exhibiting some reflexivity on the class-based determinants of effective inclusion in the capital, Chantal declares: "if you have the means, the financial means, it's a lovely city. I wouldn't venture if you don't have the financial means."

Chantal's testimony epitomizes the near universal consensus among our participants that London was a particularly expensive place to live (even compared to Paris), though a consideration of the implication of this for those without the economic means to participate was remarkably limited across the data. It is characteristic of contemporary "new economic" urban developments that the "dark side of the dialectic" (Gouldner, cited in Scott 2006), embodied in the human casualities of increasingly socially bifurcated cities and lives, becomes not only concealed but neglected (Peck 2005).

However, though London was characterized by our participants as a buzzing place, over and above Paris, London was never described as more stressful than Paris—in fact, quite the reverse. According to Luc, "I've been living roughly in the same kind of areas in Paris and in London. I've found life better organized in a way because what I like about London is that you have rules and people keep these rules … I found living in Paris more stressful than it used to be."

As with all other participants who expressed a view on this, London was valued for its successful, and life-enhancing, balance of rule-abiding behavior and freedom. Luc appears to be suggesting that some aspects of what Rae (2008) has referred to as the "soft tissue" of urbanism, may serve to offset some of the stress-inducing features of an "all-consuming" place, offering in turn a preferable quotient of livability.

From High Culture to Popular Playscapes

Virtually without exception, our participants made reference to London as a place of apparently unprecedented cultural opportunity, as Claudine explains: "I think there's loads of culture, all the museums, all the shows, the theatres. It's a very vibrant city. In London there is much more availability of culture, there is more going on. In Paris it obviously has got a lot … but I would say there is more in London in terms of culture."

Our participants' clear valorization of London's "high" culture appeared to run in tandem with an appreciation of the capital's cosmopolitan popular cultural diversity as a place-enriching feature of the city. London was prized not just for the fact of its cultural effervescence, but for the accessibility and affordability of its cultural provision. Here the data corresponded closely to the central position granted to cultural amenity within the creative city discourses that have come to frame much contemporary urban development (Peck 2005). Given the status of our participants' identities as migrants rich in cultural capital, it should come as no surprise that they may synthesize (Löw 2008) a sense of place out of their usages of London's high cultural amenities. However, the fact that all of those participants who expressed a view on the relative merits of London and Paris as cultural spaces here articulated a moral geography that ranked London as at least matching or even exceeding Paris in these cultural terms did come as something of a surprise. It appeared to be not only the qualitative character of London's high culture that accounted for this particular moral geography, but also the ethic of accessibility and inclusion framing London's cultural policy and practice.

Alongside the valorization of London's high cultural attributes, our participants made frequent reference to one key dimension of the capital's playscapes, explicitly granting "the pub" a key role in facilitating the city's buzz and open public sociality. Playscapes have become an important focus of scholarly interest, especially as features of the contemporary city (Chatterton and Hollands 2002). A playscape may be defined as "a post-modern space, related to recreation and leisure, involving a large number of cultural meanings and social symbolisms" (Crivello 2011, 709). Playscapes have emerged as key features of consumption-driven renewal and are typically located centrally in the iconography of the contemporary urban metropolis. Urban planners have reflexively understood the central role played by playscapes in communicating key valorized features of a city as a buzzing place, a space of affective encounter. As such, significant investments have been made in developing spaces for consumption-driven pleasure as part of a certain "eventification of place" within the experience economy, where eventification can be understood as "the deliberate organization of a heightened emotional and aesthetic experience" (Jakob 2012, 448).

Our participants were clear that the institution of the pub contributed a particular "atmosphere" to London's public sociality, drawing an important contrast with Paris. Luc attaches particular significance to the facilitative role played by the pub's spatial composition and practice of usage: "people are more open in terms of conversation … In many bars in Paris people are all sitting everywhere. You can see the difference, it's cultural … here, people are standing and talking to each other."

Here, something as apparently banal as the necessity of, and/or orientation toward, standing in the pub environment is seen to facilitate forms of sociality not possible in the French equivalent. Thierry concurs: "people can drink and they are mixing together, whereas in Paris it's much more conventional. You have to stay on the terrace with your friends. You're not really mixing with other sorts of people … here it's on every street corner."

Sylvie claims that the pub also serves as a key location, and framing institution, for the sociality practices of existing friendship groups, in contrast to the more private sociality (for instance invitations to dinner) of the French: "I think of course we [the French] do a lot of dinner parties and maybe less of "let's just have a pint in a pub." The institution of the pub was understood as both embodiment, and facilitator, of what might be described as a levelling, democratic public culture. Notwithstanding the fact that "the dominant audiences for nightlife spaces are mainstream, higher-spending, consumption groups such as young professionals, aspiring 'townies' and students" (Chatterton and Hollands 2002), and our own evidence that our participants often use pubs as extensions of work-related sociality with like-situated others, representations of the pub as an institution of inclusive "mixity" were predominant within the data: "if you go into a pub, you can be next to the CEO of Citibank … here, everybody goes to the pub, right? In Paris, it is a bit different. You have got posh cafés, and you have got like you know the lower side cafés … In England, it is easier to mix up with different types of people" (Cedric).

Despite the reality of London's playscapes as the objects of highly strategic, reflexive, and contemporaneous planning, the "pub" appeared to our participants primarily in the form of an inadvertent attribute bequeathed from the past. "Traditional" features of a place (here the "traditional English pub") may furnish it with a capacity to speak to the most contemporaneous needs of its residents. Adèle seems to be suggesting such: "when you adapt to something, but you don't lose who you are, or what makes you such a great place … you can have your pint outside – it's still a pint, it's still ale."

Such perceptions of the democratic inclusivity of London's playscapes sit uneasily with emerging understandings of their de facto exclusions. Crivello (2011) points to the growing divide between different urban locales produced by the particular quality of playscapes increasingly produced in the image of the buzzing creative global city. Zukin (1991) has illuminated the exclusions associated with participation in such playscapes that derive from extant and substantial socioeconomic inequalities. Though there was little explicit recognition of such in our data, our participants' accounts of apparently unfettered sociality did occasionally appear to know some limit, specifically in respect of its gendering. According to Charles, the French "mix boys and girls quicker in our life than maybe here. You've got fifty girls [in a group] in a pub and fifty boys [in a group] in a pub." Martine appears to agree: "it's different in France and England … the separation of women and men. It seems that here lots of women are going out together."

Furthermore, for those who don't drink, the centrality of the pub to public sociality may also serve to effectively exclude, especially where the pub becomes a space in which business-related interaction takes place. Odile, whose role as a single parent made attending pubs additionally difficult, declares: "I'm a very light drinker … It's very difficult for me … Alcohol is everywhere and not lightly. So socializing, yes, with people in my business environment, I do socialize, but I try to figure out ways of doing so without drinking."

Our data are strongly supportive of the role attributed to playscapes in contemporary urban development as places where those with the necessary social and economic position may enjoy open social environments that enable encounter with interaction and belonging (Peck 2005; Vanolo 2008). Pubs appeared an important feature of London's atmosphere. If atmospheres are the outcome of affective qualities emanating "from the assembling of … human bodies, discursive bodies, nonhuman bodies, and all the other bodies that make up everyday situation" (Anderson and Holden 2008, 3), then the spatial composition of the pub, and its traditional mode of occupation and usage, appeared to contribute something important in this respect. Van Riemsdijk (2014) has argued that highly skilled migrants' adoption of established national pastimes in their place of settlement may constitute place-making practices that in turn create a sense of belonging and attachment. We would suggest that for our participants, partaking of the physical geography and practices of usage of the English pub contributed significantly to their sense of belonging in London.

Offsetting Stress in the Alpha City: London's Parks as "High Quality Sanctuaries"

Our data were replete with references to the virtues of London as a green space, in direct contradistinction to Paris, as a place offering readily available opportunities for Londoners to escape the buzz of the city to the "high quality sanctuaries" (Kjølsrød 2013) of the parks. The value of the parks to our participants' sense of place in London is again suggestive of the importance of a city's heritage in rendering specific global cities as particularly attractive to place-sensitive migrants.[2] This points to the importance of the material configuration of social goods within a city in framing its affective qualities.

Our participants articulated a sense of Paris as a planned city, as a city built to be looked at, and appreciated, for its aesthetic beauty. But it was also presented as a "claustrophobic" city, where its current population density only confounds a legacy of urban planning insufficiently orientated to the needs of its ordinary citizens. Pierre asserts: "you shouldn't underestimate the power of London as a green place. Paris actually is suffocating, absolutely suffocating … because there is no green, you can't do any damn thing about it."

Claudine concurs: "open a map of London and Paris … Paris feels very built up compared to London … London is definitely very green compared to Paris."

Linking the number and size of parks to the demand placed upon their usage by the density of the resident population, Agnès reflects: "in Paris you don't have that many parks, just a few, and very small in comparison with the population, so you don't have the impression of space. In London you have this impression of space."

London's space was also seen to be more accessible: "you can't walk on the grass in France, it's very restricted" (Valentine). The number, size, accessibility and usage of London's parks added significantly to the capital's sense of spaciousnous. For Thiery, "the parks are an important part of London, and it's very good to have those kind of parks where you work, whereas in Paris you don't have that kind of thing."

The parks served a key function in offering a certain offsetting of the "buzz" of the urban experience, enabling people access to some relationship to nature and seasonality without leaving the city. Charles makes reference to the parks as one among many amenities that make London a more complete place, a place able to offer such an array of affective experiences as to make its escape at the weekend simply unnecessary, unlike Paris: "we can have a super nice weekend in town which was not conceivable … in Paris. Every weekend it was like rushing to leave Paris. In London, the weekend is gorgeous … There are so many things …; exhibitions, concerts, a visit, walking, parks, restaurants, shopping …"

The parks of London were prized as social goods facilitating: stress-offsetting commuting, weekend leisure, "time-out" during the working day/week, but also as spaces enabling and even celebrating a certain kind of active and diverse public sociality. For Pierre, "I go to Hyde Park. I go with my kids. We do roller-blading, we do skateboarding … I've been meeting quite a number of people from all over the world over there … it's a great feeling." London's green spaces were imagined as places of free and active public access in some part due to their safety. Pierre points to the absence of such safety in Paris: "you don't take your family in the weekends to the Bois de Boulogne … It's a place where people go for well … drugs, this and that."

We would suggest that across a broad spectrum of subject positionings, including a range of age cohorts, and relationship and parental statuses, green space offers an important offsetting of the affective intensity of a city's buzz, and is experienced as contributing significantly to the livability of the contemporary urban metropolis. It is perhaps no surprise, then, that natural environments have become an important feature of the brand images of many global cities (Vanolo 2008). In line with van Riemsdijk (2014), we would claim that "green space" serves as an important, and under-explored component, of highly skilled migrants' moral geographies and place attachments, and may serve as a key point of differentiation even between the most like-situated alpha cities.

Conclusion

Our chapter has sought to contribute to furthering our understanding of the human face of migration in the context of burgeoning middling mass of international highly skilled mobility. In this regard, it has insisted on the importance of adopting a place-centric perspective, and utilized this to argue that highly skilled migration dances not only to the tune of instrumental economic logic, but also and importantly to the nonoccupational dimensions of migrant desires, for themselves and for the qualities of the places where they dwell. We have suggested that the particularities of highly skilled migrants' place-centrism, and their sense of place, must be understood as an outcome of the interplay between subject-specific, desire-infused and multiple motivations, partly pre-scripted perceptions and imaginings of their places of dwelling, and the affective/atmospheric qualities of those places where they live. We have argued, however, that such places, and in the case of highly skilled migration we are mostly talking here about global cities, must also be understood as actively produced by the spacing practices of those who live there, by the manner in which the social goods and people of a city are synthesized by space and place-making practices. We have employed the notion of moral geography to capture some of the ways in which places of dwelling may be signified in normative and judgmental terms. Importantly, we have asserted that this process does not occur in some place-specific isolation.

Rather, that for our participants' moral geographies, London's sense of place was constructed through the active employment of a comparative epistemology of place, whereby London was juxtaposed with Paris as an epistemological mechanism for "knowing" London. Paris became "significantly other" to London not because our participants were Parisian, because many were not, nor because they had all lived there, as some had not, but rather because their national identity, and their career interest in global city locations for work and life, rendered Paris the principal "other" to framing a sense of place in London.

We explored the nature and functioning of this comparative mechanism, and the ways in which it operates for our participants to enable the production of a particular sense of place in London. Drawing on the work of Braudel (1977), and specifically the idea of the "soft tissue of urbanism," along with the notion of "affective urbanism" (Thrift 2004; Conradson and Latham 2007), we show how London is granted a particular affective and atmospheric quality deriving from the open and civil nature of its public sociality, and in contrast to Paris. Second, we showed how our participants construct London as a definitively libertarian space and value the capital as more livable than Paris on this basis. Third, we examined our participants' attributions of the quality of buzz to London. Fourth, we explored our participants' account of London as a place of largely unprecedented cultural encounter, and in particular, how the spatial composition, and mode of occupation and usage of the pub, is signified by our participants as a key ingredient in framing London's affective quality, and its enabling of both buzz and a democratically inclusive public sociality. Finally, we examined the importance to our participants of London's green spaces as high quality sanctuaries (Kjølsrød 2013), offsetting the buzz and stress of urban life.

Our research offers insights and supports a broader agenda of inquiry into the human face of highly skilled international mobilities. In particular, it proposes a focus on the complex and meaningful ways in which highly skilled migrants "actually live in landscapes of new belonging" (Knowles and Harper 2010, 7). It suggests the value of an exploration of the ways in which such international migrants employ comparative epistemologies of place. Such epistemologies are key to the construction of moral geographies in which a sense of their place of settlement is formed through its comparative relationship to specific, biographically informed, significantly other places. These significantly other places need not even be places where the migrants themselves have lived, or for that matter, places that are known (rather than "imagined"). But they are places made pertinent to the task of comparison by the migratory trajectories of the migrant subjects in question, and are creatively employed by them in constructing an evaluatively rich sense of the places where they settle.

Notes

1. *The Economist*, Paris on Thames, February 24, 2011.
2. London's parks, officially "Royal Parks," were established in the main in the 17th century, and became publically accessible via the Crown Lands Act of 1851.

References

Amin, A., and N. Thrift. 2007. Cultural-economy and cities. *Progress in Human Geography* 31 (2): 143–161.

Anderson, B., and A. Holden. 2008. Affective urbanism and the event of hope. *Space and Culture* 11 (2): 142–159.

A. T. Kearney. The A.T. Kearney Global Cities Index and Global Cities Outlook. Available at: www.atkearney.com/research-studies/global-cities-index/2015 (accessed September 5, 2015).

Bagnasco, A., and P. Le Galès 2000. "Local societies and collective actors?" In *Cities in contemporary Europe*, eds. A. Bagnasco and P. Le Galès. 1–32. Cambridge: Cambridge University Press.

Braudel, F. 1977. *Afterthoughts on material civilization and capitalism*. Baltimore, MD: The Johns Hopkins University Press.

Braun, M., and A. Glockner-Rist. 2011. Patterns of social integration of Western European Migrants. *Journal of International Migration and Integration* 13 (4): 403–422.

Butcher, M. 2009. Ties that bind: The strategic use of transnational relationships in demarcating identity and managing difference. *Journal of Ethnic and Migration Studies* 35 (8): 1353–1371.

Chatterton, P., and R. Hollands. 2002. Theorising urban playscapes: Producing, regulating and consuming youthful nightlife city spaces. *Urban Studies* 39 (1): 95–116.

Conradson, D., and A. Latham. 2007. The affective possibilities of London: Antipodean transnationals and the overseas experience. *Mobilities* 2 (2): 231–254.

Crivello, S. 2011. Spatial dynamics in the urban playscape: Turin by night. *Town Planning Review* 82 (6): 709.

Department of Work and Pensions. 2012. Copy of nino_alloc_summ_tables_aug12. Available at: http://research.dwp.gov.uk/asd/asd1/niall/index.php?page=nino_allocation (accessed May 6, 2015).

Favell, A. 2006. London as Eurocity: French free movers in the economic capital of Europe. In *The human face of global mobility*, eds. M. P. Smith and A. Favell, 247–274. New Brunswick, NJ: Transaction Publishers.

Favell, A., M. Feldblum, and M. P. Smith. 2006. The human face of global mobility: A research agenda. In *The human face of global mobility: International highly skilled migration in Europe, North America and the Asia-Pacific, Comparative urban and community research,* eds. M. P. Smith and A. Favell. New Brunswick, NJ: Transaction Press.

Florida, R. 2002. *The rise of the creative class: And how it's transforming work, leisure, community, and everyday life*. New York: Basic Books.

Glick-Schiller, N., and A. Caglar. 2011. *Locating migration: Rescaling cities and migrants.* Ithaca, NY: Cornell University Press.

Jakob, D. 2012. The eventification of place: Urban development and experience consumption in Berlin and New York City. *European Urban and Regional Studies* 20 (4): 447–459.

Kazepov, Y. 2005. *Cities of Europe: Changing contexts, local arrangements, and the challenge to urban cohesion.* Cambridge: Cambridge University Press.

Kjølsrød, L. 2013. Mediated activism: Contingent democracy in leisure worlds. *Sociology* 47 (6): 1207–1223.

Knowles, C., and D. Harper. 2010. *Hong Kong: Migrant lives, landscapes and journeys.* Chicago: University of Chicago Press.

Lamont, M., and L. Thévenet. 2000. *Rethinking comparative cultural sociology: Repertoires of evaluation in France and the United States*. Cambridge: Cambridge University Press.

Löw, M. 2008. The constitution of space the structuration of spaces through the simultaneity of effect and perception. *European Journal of Social Theory* 11 (1): 25–49.

McCann, E. J. 2008. Livable city/unequal city: The politics of policy-making in a 'creative' boomtown, *Revue Interventions Économiques* [En ligne] 37. Available at: http://interventionseconomiques.revues.org/489 (accessed October 1, 2015).

Meier, L. 2015. Introduction: Local lives, work and social identities of migrant professionals in the city. In *Migrant professionals in the city: Local encounters, identities and inequalities*, ed. L. Meier, 1–20. London: Routledge.

Mulholland, J., and L. Ryan. 2015. 'Londres acceuil': Mediations of identity and place amongst the French highly skilled in London. In *Migration of professionals and the city – Local lives and social identities of skilled migrants,* ed. L. Meier, 157–174. London: Routledge.

———. 2014. Doing the business: Variegation, migration and the cultural dimensions of business praxis – the experiences of the French highly skilled in London. *International Migration* 52 (3): 55–68.

Office of National Statistics. 2013. Population by country of birth and nationality report, August 2013. Available at: http://webarchive.nationalarchives.gov.uk/20160105160709/http://www.ons.gov.uk/ons/rel/migration1/population-by-country-of-birth-and-nationality/2012/population-by-country-of-birth-and-nationality-report.html (accessed May 6, 2015).

Peck, J. 2005. Struggling with the creative class. *International Journal of Urban and Regional Research* 29: 740–770.

PIONEUR. Executive summary. Available at: www.obets.ua.es/pioneur/difusion/PioneurExecutiveSummary.pdf (accessed March 1, 2013).

Rae, D. W. 2008. *City: Urbanism and its end*. New Haven, NJ: Yale University Press.

Ryan, L., and J. Mulholland. 2013. Trading places: French highly skilled migrants negotiating mobility and settlement in London. *Ethnic and Migration Studies* 40 (4): 584–600.

———. 2014. French connections: The networking strategies of French highly skilled migrants in London. *Global Networks* 14 (2): 148–166.

Ryan, L., A. Klekowski von Koppenfels, and J. Mulholland. 2015. "The distance between us:" A comparative examination of the technical, spatial and temporal dimensions of the transnational social relationships of highly skilled migrants. *Global networks* 15 (2): 198–216.

Scholte, J. A. 2005. *Globalization: A critical introduction*. Basingstoke: Palgrave.

Scott, A. J. 2006. Creative cities: Conceptual issues and policy questions. *Journal of Urban Affairs* 28 (1): 1–17.

Sennett, R. 2005. "Capitalism and the City: Globalization, Flexibility and Indifference." In *Cities of Europe: Changing contexts, local arrangements, and the challenge to urban cohesion*, ed. Y. Kazepov, 109–122. Cambridge: Cambridge University Press.

Smith, M. P. 2005. Transnational urbanism revisited. *Journal of Ethnic and Migration Studies* 31 (2): 234–244.

Stewart, K. 2011. Atmospheric attunements. *Environment and Planning* 29: 445–453.

Thrift, N. 2004. Intensities of feeling: Towards a spatial politics of affect. *Geografiska Annaler* 86 (1): 57–78.

Tseng, Y.- F. 2011. Shanghai rush: Skilled migrants in a fantasy city. *Journal of Ethnic and Migration Studies* 37 (5): 765–784.

van Riemsdijk, M. 2014. International migration and local emplacement: Everyday place-making practices of skilled migrants in Oslo, Norway. *Environment and Planning A* 46: 963–979.

Vanolo, A. 2008. The image of the creative city: Some reflections on urban branding in Turin. *Cities* 25, 370–382.

Wang, C. 2013. Place of desire: Skilled migration from mainland China to post-colonial Hong Kong. *Asia Pacific Viewpoint* 54 (3): 388–397.

Zukin, S. 1991. *Landscapes of power: From Detroit to Disney World.* Berkeley, CA: University of California Press.

9 High-skilled Migrants, Place Ties, and Urban Policymaking

Putting Housing on the Agenda

Jörg Plöger

Introduction

"Even the basic stuff wasn't there. There should be some basic things to at least come and survive for one or two days. This was the thing that irritated me at that time. Migrants, we don't have to live here for long" (Naveed, 32). In this opening quote a high-skilled migrant mentions just one of the problems he encountered when trying to find adequate housing for himself and his family in Dortmund, a large post-industrial city in Germany. Similar sentiments were echoed by most of the interviewees in a research project examining the processes of local incorporation of mobile high-skilled middle-class migrants, most of whom did not intend to stay permanently. This was a rather surprising finding, considering that this group is usually regarded as privileged from a socioeconomical perspective and has been targeted by recent government policies to facilitate the entry of high-skilled migrants, and that the city in question has a relatively slack housing market.

Such experiences indicate that current efforts by urban policymakers to attract and retain skilled professionals are insufficient, despite human capital having become a key resource in post-industrial, knowledge-based societies (Brown, Green, and Lauder 2003). While individuals are increasingly selected on the basis of their educational qualifications or skills, companies are striving to attract talented staff to remain innovative. Within the context of a demographic change characterized by an ageing and shrinking population and worries about skills shortages, nation states have started to modify their immigration regulations and are increasingly adopting skills-based policies. At city and regional levels this is mirrored by efforts to secure a qualified human capital base for local economies, a move often criticized as being a mass-marketed urban neoliberal development scheme (Peck 2005 in Ewers 2007, 122). High-skilled migrants constitute an increasingly large component of global migration streams (e.g. Koser and Salt 1997; Mahroum 2001; Iredale 2001), turning them into one of the most characteristic groups of a late capitalism that values levels of education and qualification as quintessential for competitiveness and innovation.

The aim of this chapter is threefold. First, it contributes to the literature on the relationship between increased mobility—and its accompanying notion of uprooting—and place, which through place attachment, belonging, and home supposedly has a stabilizing effect. The overarching research question is how, within an overall context of mobility, migrants relate to places. Second, it argues that housing is an integral factor for the formation of place ties, presumably fulfilling a stabilizing function in a context of uncertainty and mobility. Finally, it discusses whether the current vogue of policies aimed at attracting skilled migrants is purposeful in the light of the presented empirical material, indicating considerable problems in accessing the housing market.

The first section indicates how existing work has explored the relationship between mobility and place, both theoretically and empirically. Starting from the observation that the role of housing has so far been under-acknowledged as part of the process of local incorporation, the next section argues for its inclusion in conceptualizations of place transformations during mobility. This is followed by an overview of the study background and the qualitative research design. The chapter concludes by highlighting the crucial role of housing in the local incorporation of high-skilled migrants, suggesting that policymakers need to adapt their strategies accordingly.

Mobility and Place: Theoretical Considerations and Empirical Findings

Since the 1990s, academics from different disciplines have been concerned with the spatial consequences of globalization, pointing out that space has become increasingly fluid or networked (Hannerz 1996; Castells 2000; Amin 2002). The penetration of global flows, they suggest, results in a detachment of social processes from space and an eventual loss of place. Others are more nuanced in their conceptualization, distancing themselves from any sharp dichotomy between the global and the local (e.g. Robertson's notion of "glocalization"). Massey's (1991) "global sense of place" is an early example highlighting the remarkable persistence of place. Places apparently remain key sites in the social organization of space, constituting sources of identity and meaning (Ong and Nonini 1997), although some authors have noted that social ties are increasingly shifting towards networks (e.g. Wellman 2001). More recently, scholars have postulated that profound social transformations are resulting from an intensification of all-encompassing "mobilities" (Sheller and Urry 2006; Urry 2007).

In response to the globalization literature, the transnational and translocal perspectives on migration emphasize the ongoing significance of place by focusing on the evolution of manifold social ties between places and the spatial extension of communities (Glick-Schiller, Basch, and Blanc Szanton 1992; Brickell and Datta 2011). The maintenance of increasingly complex ties on different spatial scales suggests that migrants hold "multiple allegiances" (Ehrkamp and Leitner 2006, 1593). Collins (2012, 319) ascertains that "migrants socially connect places across distances and establish multiple layers of belonging and identity that often do not have locally specific territorial bases." It remains unclear whether being simultaneously attached to different places actually results in a lower level of local incorporation at, say, the current place of residence.

Some research has illustrated that while both local and national attachments appear less significant for mobile professionals, post-national or cosmopolitan orientations become reinforced. Based on a study about transnational knowledge workers, Colic-Peisker (2010, 469) argues that these are transcending the territorial by being embedded in a "space of professional work." Such extraterritorial (e.g. professional communities) or local (e.g. diasporas) communities are becoming increasingly significant (Colic-Peisker 2010, 469), as well as viable through modern telecommunication technologies (Morley 2001). Ahmed (1999, 338) also recounts that "the desire to make connections given the alienation from home … – leads to the discovery of a 'new community of strangers.'" For these "global nomads," home becomes internalized and detached from place, allowing a new global identity to emerge.

Attaching Mobile People to Place

When reflecting on the impact of mobility on place, authors employ the concepts of place attachment, belonging or home, all of which imply a stabilizing function of place during times of instability. One thing they have in common is the salience of social ties for their emergence (e.g. Nowicka 2007). Mee and Wright (2009) note that individuals engage in belonging through interactions with others, thus carving out a place for themselves in the world.

A sense of belonging develops as an emotional bond with specific "entities" (e.g. communities, places). It often has an implicit spatial connotation because it "connects matter to place" (Mee and Wright 2009, 772). Belonging can occur on different geographical scales, ranging from citizenship of a national homeland to one's own residence or home (e.g. Gilmartin 2008, 1837; Arp Fallov, Jorgensen, and Knudsen 2013). A sense of belonging is frequently expressed as place attachment or "place belongingness" (Antonsich 2010), terms referring to an emotional, affective bond between people and place that develops over time and is subject to change. A sense of belonging, which refers to the individual, is usually accompanied by the "politics of belonging," which take overarching power structures into account (Yuval-Davis 2006; Antonsich 2010). Examples of the politics of belonging include citizenship, border enforcement, and the creation of official hierarchies of migrants, facilitating or complicating the entry of certain migrant groups (Gilmartin 2008, 1844). These may be expressed in boundary-making practices such as discriminatory or excluding social and institutional practices (ibid., 1842). The key factors for access are membership (of a group) and ownership (of a place), which are constantly being contested and negotiated (Yuval-Davis 2006, 204).

The literature on transnational migration also raises important questions about the meaning of home. Moving beyond a narrow understanding, home can imply a place, an idea, a feeling (of being at home), or the practice of home-making. Brah (1996, 1) asks at what point a (new) place of residence becomes a home, and Al-Ali and Koser (2002, 8) examine to what extent home is no longer tied to a specific geographical place or whether it can be conceived as more than one home. As a consequence of mobility, the notion of home may become blurry, or more "idealized" than "realized," as if searching for something that is already lost (Ahmed 1999, 331). Nowicka (2007, 73) stresses its processual character by noting that "home is a space in-becoming and not a fixed, pre-established place." Among the strategies of belonging employed by migrants the process of home-making stands out (Staeheli and Nagel 2006, 1600; Blunt and Dowling 2006): "in leaving home, immigrants must make a new home, and they must negotiate the contradictions of both homes, even as they may feel they belong to neither" (Gilmartin 2008, 1599). Nowicka (2007, 82) adds that "home is neither a place nor an object but a network," and can be manifested in more than one location because its constituting elements—people, objects and relationships—are movable. Nonetheless, in most discourses on mobility, home is either the place where one usually lives (e.g. incorporation), where one's family lives (e.g. emotional bonds, social ties), or one's native country (e.g. determined by feeling at home, belonging) (Ahmed 1999, 338; Nowicka 2007, 77).

Mobile Professionals: Roots and Routes

Increased mobility results in increasingly complex attachments to places. Two lines of work in particular have contributed to acknowledging the stabilizing functions of place within an overall context of mobility and fluidity. The first analyzes attachment to place and notions of belonging for the mobile middle-classes in European cities. In a large-scale study of the residential choices of middle-class households in the Manchester metropolitan area, Savage, Bagnall, and Longhurst (2005, 1) find that "attachment to place remains remarkably obdurate," leading them to question whether identities really are diasporic, mobile, and transient. On the other hand, the authors point to the limits of local attachment, arguing that "people's sense of being at home is related to reflexive processes in which they can satisfactorily account to themselves how they come to live where they do," a process they call "elective belonging," which articulates senses of spatial attachment, social position, and forms of connectivity to other places (ibid., 29). Building on this work, Andreotti, Le Galès, and Moreno Fuentes (2013) analyze the relationship between a rise of "mobilities" and (local) "rootedness" for upper middle-class managers in four European cities. They assume that "increased mobility, along with the capacity to access a range of social spaces and networks, considerably expands the playing field of possibilities in terms of how individuals experience their sense of belonging to, and negotiate their involvement in, a given locality" (ibid., 44). They find that "while mobility clearly constitutes an important aspect of their lives, there are also important elements of continuity." Such continuity stems from what Savage, Bagnall, and Longhurst (2005: 208) call "the relative fixity in local routines," which comprises the proximity to family, the reliance on facilities (e.g. transport, healthcare, schools), and active social lives (Andreotti, Le Galès, and Moreno Fuentes 2013, 42). They conclude that the group is both "mobile and rooted," in line with the dialectic between roots and routes (Blunt and Dowling 2006, 199).

Recent migration studies suggest that even highly mobile groups or mobile elites, often associated with an indifference towards place, cannot be entirely footloose or disembedded and are essentially grounded in places through their everyday practices (e.g. Kreutzer and Roth 2006, 38; Kennedy 2007). Yeoh and Willis (2005, 270–271) counter the assumptions that these are "insufficiently grounded rootless merchant sojourners" by arguing that despite their fluidity and transience their (physical) presence does generate "contact zones." Conradson and Latham (2005, 686) remind us that "while the social relations and networks of people 'on the move' are likely to be different from those who do not move, their daily geographies are, for the most part, rather ordinary." Nowicka (2007) argues that their social capital as well as their cosmopolitan disposition enables highly mobile professionals to quickly adapt to new places. As the core residential units of everyday life, "the collective project called family" (Beck and Beck-Gernsheim 1995, 52) or other committed relationships become "the only social ties not sacrificed to mobility" (Colic-Peisker 2010, 476), with children having a particularly grounding effect (Nowicka 2007, 77; Yeoh and Huang 2011, 684).

Building on the notion of grounding, some studies have upheld the concepts of local incorporation or emplacement in examining the degree of local involvement. In addition to looking at individual practices, such approaches also consider structural factors which may be facilitating or complicating (Walsh 2006; Föbker et al. 2011; van Riemsdijk 2014; Plöger and Becker 2015). Looking at foreign academic staff at three German universities, Föbker et al. (2011) find that the motivation for moving is central for understanding their level of local incorporation. In a study of Turkish immigrants in a German working-class neighborhood, Ehrkamp (2005, 345) sees transnational ties and local engagement as complementary rather than contradictory. She argues that their complex and sometimes conflicting ties enable these migrants to forge local attachments through the active production and transformation of place—for example, through transnational consumption, mass media or establishing communal places like mosques or teahouses (ibid., 345).

For high-skilled migrants, the workplace is an important setting for interaction (van Riemsdijk 2014, 12). Being embedded in a workspace may not, however, necessarily coincide with being embedded during private or leisure time, as Beaverstock (2002) has noted for expatriates in Singapore. In addition, access to existing migrant communities remains relevant as well as, increasingly, web-facilitated groups based on specific interests or backgrounds (Plöger and Becker 2015).

Cities also shape migration decisions and flows. Van Riemsdijk (2014, 1–2) argues that "context matters" for place-making practices because of "the salience of history and locality in geographies of belonging." According to Glick-Schiller and Çaglar (2011), cities provide specific opportunity structures (for an empirical analysis of their ideas, see Jaworsky et al. 2012). Cities that are more inserted globally usually host international companies and renowned higher education institutions. They are thus more likely to receive mobile professionals and are generally characterized by diversity and a cosmopolitan, tolerant vibe. Recent research shows that, in addition to beaten migration paths (Gilmartin 2008), moves are regularly initiated by existing social and institutional ties such as company branches, exchange programs or cultural affinity (Tippel, Becker, and Plöger forthcoming).

It is plausible that mobility results in more complex place affiliations, blurring and dissolving the alleged congruence of persons with one place. The evidence that multiple ties coincide with a low local attachment is nonetheless inconclusive and place-based practices remain significant. Mobile people, it appears, aim for a balance of "stability within movement" (King 2002, 144). Stability may manifest itself through different "anchors," ranging from "ethnic enclaves," workplaces, professional communities, civic engagement to "expat bubbles." In the following, I will argue that the role of housing should also be considered.

Housing and Place-attachment

Housing is generally regarded as satisfying the universal human need for shelter, privacy, and reproduction. In contrast to these stability-providing functions, post-colonial and feminist scholars have pointed out that housing can also be a place of oppression and inequality (e.g. Blunt and Dowling 2006). For the purpose of this contribution, housing is understood as both a social process and an individualized practice. While the social relates to aspects such as access to housing, social distinction, and interaction with neighbors, the individual refers to personal preferences, the lived experience (of dwelling), and the process of home-making.

The literature on place ties within a context of mobility referred to in the previous section, while occasionally mentioning the notion of home, makes little reference to the more specific aspect of housing for high-skilled migrants. Older case studies have, for example, examined the urban incorporation of the Japanese community in Düsseldorf (Zielke 1982) or the effect of skilled international migrants on urban segregation patterns in Vienna (White 1988). More recently, the EU-funded project *Accommodating Creative Knowledge – Competitiveness of European Metropolitan Regions within the Enlarged Union* analyzed the location choices and local incorporation of specific skilled groups, including the topic of housing, albeit not as a core research interest (e.g. Musterd and Murie 2010). Their Munich case study highlighted migrants' preference for inner-city residential areas due to proximity to work, urbanity, existing infrastructures or access to public transport (von Streit et al. 2009, 78). Access to housing was regarded as difficult, frustrating, and time-consuming. The main problems identified by the respondents were a lack of knowledge of the housing market, landlords' preference for German (speaking) tenants, and the lack of furnished apartments (ibid.). Unsurprisingly, other works have highlighted the importance of social networks for finding accommodation (e.g. Poros 2001, 243). Research into the local incorporation of international academic staff in three German cities showed that housing is predominantly found via one's own social network, including colleagues, while support provided by the respective cities or universities only played a minor role (Föbker et al. 2011).

I argue here for the inclusion of the housing aspect in conceptualizations of the functioning of place ties and the process of local incorporation. To begin with and due to its physical dimension, housing constitutes an obvious example for grounding migrants. Even the most mobile groups with temporary stays and strong nonlocal ties will need a stable place to rest, particularly when the new environment is experienced as unfamiliar or overwhelming. Housing thus contributes to carving out personal space in a given locality. One's own residential space may serve as a base from which to eventually explore further (Rose 1995, 99). Housing can be simultaneously a component (or subprocess) and contributing factor (or even precondition) for the evolution of place-based ties. In addition to the agency-orientation of place attachment, housing allows for reinserting the social and political dimensions by addressing the issues of access, exclusion or discrimination.

Study Background

Within an overall rationale of competition for talent, many industrialized countries have responded to a real or projected skills gap by introducing policies that facilitate the recruitment of skilled professionals from abroad (e.g. BBSR 2014). In Germany, broader public and political debates about demographic change resulting in an aging and declining population as well as about how to guarantee economic competitiveness and social security are an additional angle for these policy initiatives. The gradual adjustment of Germany's immigration policy has been driven by this "skills turn," as reflected by the introduction of a *Green Card* for ICT professionals (2000), a new immigration law (2005), and the implementation of the EU *Blue Card* for highly qualified migrants (2012). As a consequence, migration has become more polarized along educational levels. While high-skilled migration faces little public or political opposition, particularly in a climate of relatively robust economic development, low-skilled migrants (and refugees) are far less privileged.

Dortmund (pop. 570,000), located in West Germany's traditional industrial core, the Ruhr, is a city characterized by profound economic restructuring. While its migrant population is still dominated by mostly Southern European *Gastarbeiter* and their families who started arriving in the 1960s, the city has received more diverse migration flows since the 1990s. With 13.3 and 30.1 percent respectively, the overall population shares of those not holding a German passport and those with a migration background[1] are typical for West German cities. The city hosts several medium-sized international companies in such economic sectors as manufacturing, engineering, and ICT, as well as a large technical university and several renowned research institutes, all of which attract a high-skilled workforce. The city's economic development policies aim at providing the local economy with a skilled workforce. As one of the first German cities, Dortmund has implemented a well-known skills monitoring program in 2009 as a response to increasing sensibilities about predicted skills shortages and the need to measure its actual scale locally. Based on an annual survey of 490 local companies, the program provides estimates about the supply and demand for skilled workers in key economic clusters.

As is typical for larger cities in Germany, homeowners occupy a relatively small share of the housing stock in Dortmund (29 percent) compared with renters (71 percent; Stadt Dortmund 2013, 35). Within the rental housing, 13 percent are publicly subsidized units (ibid.). Yet, in contrast with other larger cities, the housing stock in Dortmund is relatively affordable. Dortmund has the lowest average rents per square meter (€6,20) of the ten largest German cities (Wirtschaftswoche 2013).

The empirical research was carried out between October 2012 and January 2013 and comprised qualitative interviews with high-skilled migrants residing in Dortmund. The sample selection was based on three criteria (for more information, see Plöger and Becker 2015): a) *highly-qualified*: possessing at least a bachelor's degree; b) voluntary migration from a *non-EU country*: assuming more elaborate planning of the move due to visa restrictions as well as migrating over greater geographical distances; and c) an intermediate *duration of stay*: i.e. avoiding an over-representation of either transnational or local ties.

The sample comprises twenty-four (thirteen female, eleven male) high-skilled middle-class migrants from sixteen nationalities (see Table 9.1),[2] particularly from larger cities in newly industrializing countries such as China, India, and Pakistan, while industrialized nations constituted a minority (four).

In terms of age, the sample is relatively homogeneous, with all respondents aged between 25 and 39. All but three were either married or in a relationship and half had children. Eleven interviewees had resided in Germany between one and three years, eight over three years and five less than one year. The main motivation for migrating was either work and/or further education such as gaining a Ph.D. In addition, five highly qualified female respondents fall into the category of "trailing spouses" (e.g. Hardill 2004). For more than half of the interviewees (fourteen) the move to Germany constituted their first move abroad. The remainder had a more complex migration biography; they either migrated from other countries or had previous experience with international migration. Two-thirds had either achieved additional degrees at higher education institutions in Germany or were currently doing so, as in the case of several Ph.D. students. The interviews were transcribed and coded after content analysis with the software MaxQDA. For the purpose of this chapter, I mainly draw on the codes "home," "assessment of city," and "housing."

Housing: A Barrier for Developing Place Ties?

After arriving, we can broadly distinguish between a first "phase of arrival" and a second "phase of settling-in." These phases overlap with the housing pathways approach (e.g. Robinson, Reeve and Casey 2007). For this sample, a third "phase of improving" rarely occurred and will not be detailed here. The following presents the main characteristics of phases one and two with regard to housing types, intermediation and assistance in finding housing, duration of stay, housing satisfaction, as well as problems that were encountered.

Table 9.1 Overview and Main Characteristics of Sample

Name	*Gender*	*Country of Origin*	*Duration of Stay (in years)*	*Original Motivation for Migration, Current Activity if Changed*	*Age*	*Family Status*
Chris	m.	Australia	1	Expatriate	38	Married, children
Andrew	m.	New Zealand	2	Expatriate, switched to local contract	34	Single
Youssef	m.	Egypt	<1	Expatriate	31	Single
Diego	m.	Chile	8	Studies, now working as engineer	35	Married, children
Shen	m.	China	1	Ph.D., now post-doc researcher	31	Married, children
Luis	m.	Argentina	6	Ph.D., now post-doc researcher	35	Married, children
Kashif	m.	Pakistan	6	Ph.D., now post-doc researcher	33	Married, children
Faiza	f.	Pakistan	3	Ph.D., now post-doc researcher	39	Married
Wang Li	f.	China	4	Studies, now Ph.D. and research post	28	Relationship
Carol	f.	USA	2	Ph.D. and research post	24	Relationship
Naveed	m.	Pakistan	1	Ph.D.	32	Married, children
Dalia	f.	Egypt	1	Ph.D.	32	Married, children
Arif	m.	Palestine	1.5	Ph.D.	31	Married
Tariq	m.	Iraq	<1	Ph.D.	38	Married, children
Li Min	f.	China	<1	Ph.D.	25	Relationship
Carlos	m.	Guatemala	4	Studies, now Ph.D.	28	Married, children
Li Jing	f	China	4	Studies, now looking for a job	27	Married
Lifen	f	China	1	Studies	24	Relationship
Alina	f	Russia	<1	Studies	31	Divorced, in relationship
Sofia	f.	Peru	4	Family reunion, now working as architect	33	Married, child
Amrita	f.	India	4	Family reunion	37	Married, child
Zahra	f.	Iran	2	Family reunion, looking for a job	30	Married
Geeta	f.	India	<1	Family reunion	26	Married
Chinue	f.	Nigeria	1	Family reunion	30	Separated

Arrival: A Stepping Stone

In the first phase after arrival most interviewees found some form of provisional and temporary accommodation, providing the proverbial roof over their heads but usually lacking further qualities. This was widely perceived as a phase that needs to be overcome, merely constituting a stepping stone in developing some sense of the city. During this period the interviewees searched for more appropriate accommodation and, where applicable, prepared for the subsequent arrival of spouses and/or children. The duration of this phase varied between just a few weeks and up to one year. Most respondents reported having little initial information about their options and the specific features of the local housing market.

Provisional accommodation comprised student halls of residence (n = 6), which were usually facilitated either by the university or by a funding body when arriving on a scholarship.[3] The same number found accommodation through their extended social networks and were able to stay with friends, relatives or colleagues. Only in one case was the respondent able to organize a low-budget apartment on his own via the Internet before arriving. The three expatriates were accommodated in hotels by their company.[4]

In terms of quality, this preliminary accommodation was usually described as low standard, lacking privacy, in unattractive locations, and small size. Sometimes individual needs and expectations were not matched due to the temporary nature of the stay, resulting in an extended phase of transition as illustrated by the following quote:

> In the beginning he [her husband] was thinking to change the apartment, because it's a studio apartment. So he was probably thinking that now you are coming … But I was OK with that because it was just a matter of six months, as we might leave Dortmund. So I decided that I can adjust in a small apartment. It does not matter so much to me. … but the next place, wherever we go, we might look for a bigger apartment because if our parents come [to visit] then it's better for them.
>
> (Geeta, 26)

Problematic Transition to Stability

It was during the transition from the phases of "arrival" to "settling in" when many—sometimes overlapping—problems occurred. Most respondents criticized that the housing supply did not match the specific needs of a mobile and transient group. The supply of furnished apartments was perceived as too limited, overpriced and of low quality:

> I didn't like the fact that it took a long time for us to get an apartment here. A furnished one, I think if we'd not been looking for furnished apartments that would have been easier, and it seems a little strange to me because, to rent an unfurnished apartment is very cheap, but to rent a furnished one is very

> expensive. So for someone to make a little bit of money renting an apartment, what I would do, I'd be renting it with furniture not without it.
>
> (Chris, 38)

In addition, this segment of furnished apartments is regularly occupied by the larger international companies, using it for accommodating their international staff on assignment to Germany. For migrants without company affiliations such as individual movers, university staff or Ph.D. students, this limits housing options.

Several interviewees reported encountering prejudices as well as experiencing explicit or implicit discrimination, mostly from private landlords. They attributed these exclusionary practices to their appearance, origin, religion or insufficient language skills. Dalia, arriving on a Ph.D. scholarship from Egypt, for example, experienced open discrimination based on her religious background during her search for an apartment:

> Well, sometimes there was a problem because we are foreigners. Or maybe more specifically because of my appearance [pointing to her headscarf], or religion, I don't know. Sometimes there was a reaction like, "no, we don't want that." Well, that made everything more complicated.
>
> (Dalia, 32)

An Argentine post-doc researcher realized that private landlords became reluctant to invite him to visit an advertised apartment when they realized they could not communicate with him in German:

> It was very common, at least in the area that we were looking for, when the private people were renting the apartments. Of course, I understand they want to check, you know, who you are, and so it was much more difficult to see the house, especially when you don't speak the language.
>
> (Luis, 35)

This quote highlights the role of language during the process of local incorporation, with the ability to speak German greatly facilitating the search for housing. While many respondents did not speak German well enough, many landlords were also reported to have insufficient English skills. Additionally, information and documents such as rental contracts were not available in English.

> I mean, yeah, the website [for searching flats] has an English option, but it doesn't mean that everything actually comes up. Same with … well, just about everything I have dealt with so far.
>
> (Carol, 24)

Many respondents complained about what they perceived as low housing quality and little value for money. Examples included the age of the housing stock, the renovation backlog, insufficient light and ventilation or small size. As the quote at the beginning of this chapter shows, migrants—particularly from countries of the Global South such as Egypt, Argentina or Pakistan—were sometimes puzzled by the lack of basic installations, even when renting unfurnished apartments. Luis from Argentina complained that the flat he eventually found was completely unfurnished and that he even had to purchase the basic equipment for the kitchen:

> We had to install everything! And this constituted an enormous amount of work and money. Especially at the beginning you don't have any money because if you come from a foreign country, your currency is not very useful here [referring to an unfavorable exchange rate]. … So, the fact of not having a kitchen was more complicated than we thought.
>
> (Luis, 35)

As a consequence of these problems during transition to more stable housing, more time than originally expected went into searching for adequate housing. This time is widely associated with frustration and stress—particularly if planning for the arrival of a spouse and children—as well as higher expenses than calculated, the latter resulting from overpriced transitory accommodation, unanticipated security deposits or eating out due to not having a kitchen yet. The manifold frustration associated with accessing housing was often expressed emotionally during the interviews. In some cases, interviewees even questioned their whole undertaking, as is illustrated by the following quote by an established architect from Iraq who came to Dortmund to pursue a Ph.D.:

> When I came here I searched an apartment on the Internet and asked a private company. Private companies take high prices to find an apartment for you. … Then I searched on the Internet and I find very bad apartments, very old, very expensive and far from the center. I searched for about forty days for an apartment. During this time, I give a lot of money. I am very tired; I even decided to return to Iraq, to cancel everything …. If I can't find an apartment, I can't do anything.
>
> (Tariq, 38)

Finally Approaching Stability

After this initial and quite often burdensome period, the second phase of "settling in" can be characterized by an increase in privacy, improved housing quality, and a sense of actual arrival. For the majority of respondents, local incorporation combined with finally the feeling of having made the right decision only started to develop during this second phase.

Finding longer term accommodation was usually facilitated by an interviewee's own social network including friends, colleagues at work or family members. In several cases interviewees were able to take over apartments from acquaintances or colleagues after they had moved out. The Chinese and Pakistani respondents, in particular, benefited from information passed on by larger respective national communities, including advice on useful websites or convenient neighborhoods. The three Chinese respondents mentioned using specific websites and blogs run by the regional Chinese community when searching for accommodation. The following quote by a Chinese Ph.D. student illustrates how she received assistance through both formal (professor) and informal (local Chinese community) channels before and after arriving in Dortmund:

> A: He [another Chinese acquaintance] did me a lot of favors, about how to choose a house and how to use some software [websites] ….
>
> Q: How did you find your first apartment in Dortmund?
>
> A: My professor helped me to the guest house ….
>
> Q: And now you have moved?
>
> A: Yes, I have moved and, you know, this house, my friends have found this house.
>
> (Li Min, 25)

"Formal channels" were used in a few cases, usually when the migrant had few social contacts at the destination. These included employers, universities, academic bodies or real-estate companies. One real-estate company (Home Company) that specializes in furnished rental apartments was well known and sometimes used, although considered expensive due to monthly fees. Larger local housing companies (e.g. LEG, Dogewo) that are managed more professionally were also an important provider of accommodation, although the housing quality differed considerably between companies, with LEG flats often being more basic and in need of renovation.

Of the respondents, all but one rented their apartment. Apart from the often short stays, the prevalence of renting can be attributed to the structure of urban housing markets in Germany, which are still dominated by rental housing. Two of the expatriates moved from hotels to furnished apartments that their company rented from private landlords. Another two shared an apartment. The first was a Ph.D. student residing in a residence hall who frequently travels to visit her partner in the US or friends elsewhere in Europe. She preferred having a serviced apartment and appreciated proximity to the university. The other, a Ph.D. student and researcher, divided her life between two residential locations, in addition to frequent work-related travel. She commuted between Dortmund where she was pursuing her Ph.D., the city where her boyfriend lived, and Vienna where the lead partner of her project was located. As a result of her high mobility, she was the only respondent unable to identify any place as "home":

> It's funny, because when you travel a lot, I think you start to ask yourself that question, because it's nice to have something to go back to and, I mean, I can't …, because I moved around so much; there is not a city I can call home.
>
> (Carol, 24)

Central areas or those close to workplaces were the preferred residential locations. Access to public transport was appreciated, as only a minority of respondents had access to a car. In contrast to more dynamic metropolitan areas elsewhere, most eventually found accommodation in or close to the area they were looking for.

Although being generally less arduous, the phase of "settling in" was not free of problems for some interviewees. Chinue, a female from Nigeria, mentioned unpleasant experiences with her immediate neighbors who showed "racist attitudes." In the case of Lifen from China, her private landlord had obviously taken advantage of the interviewee's little place-specific knowledge and limited language skills. She reported that she did not receive a rental contract, which is a required legal document in Germany, even after requesting it.

The problems that the group of high-skilled migrants encountered around the issue of housing resulted in policy implications that will be discussed in the final section.

Discussion and Policy Implications

> I guess, at the moment I would say my apartment here in Dortmund is my home. But it could change. If I have to pack up and move somewhere else, then that would probably become home. I can't say that I am really attached to one particular country, one particular place.
>
> (Andrew, 34)

Being at home in a place does not have to be associated with physical residence. It may be a dynamic concept tied to equally mobile aspects of life—for instance, one's social network or work as illustrated by the above quote from one of the interviewees. A move does—now less than ever—imply that mobile people move all relevant spheres of their lives. We can assume that highly mobile and -attached groups contribute to an ongoing transformation of cities and urban societies, thereby challenging several areas of urban policymaking such as civic engagement, the housing market or the integration of newcomers (Dittrich-Wesbuer and Plöger 2013).

Places can provide stability because they function as nodes localizing social ties and specific infrastructures. Developing emotional ties to a place can be expressed as place attachment, a sense of belonging or a feeling of being at home. The role of housing in migrants' experiences of a new place of residence and the development of localized ties has so far been under-acknowledged. In changed and unfamiliar surroundings, being able to retreat to a space of privacy offers the necessary stability in a situation of flux. The findings presented here—although not representative due to the small sample size—suggest that housing has a grounding effect on mobile people and can be considered a critical part of the incorporation process.

Nevertheless, the majority of the interviewed high-skilled migrants in Dortmund reported problems with housing. Access is limited by a lack of information, an insufficient supply for such temporary and mobile migrants, discrimination and/or the low quality of the available stock. While formal support is mostly not useful, most migrants ultimately manage to improve their housing situation. In most cases this is achieved through information and support provided by their own social networks, and in a few cases through their own efforts. Housing problems constitute barriers to straightforward settling in and contradict the general assumption of eased local integration based on higher social status. For many respondents, finding adequate housing is the precondition for being able to bring over the immediate family. Difficulties in managing to find housing result in higher costs as well as a prolonged period of family separation (which may also be attributed to the "red tape" of visa applications). As the interviews illustrate, these problems can result in feelings of frustration and stress for the individuals concerned, constituting a significant barrier to fostering local ties and affiliations, and thus negatively influencing the experience in place. This in turn may result in a low place attachment.

As a result of the growing concern for economic competitiveness, high-skilled migrants are being positioned as an attractive target group of contemporary urban policies. The problems mentioned here undermine current strategies. This is thought-provoking on several accounts. The housing market in Dortmund is relatively slack and affordable, for example, particularly when compared with more globalized and dynamic cities. Furthermore, higher social status is generally associated with seamless incorporation into an urban society. The temporary nature of their stay may, however, work against local incorporation. Even then, a lack of integration is rarely perceived as problematic, revealing the social bias and normativity attached to integration concepts in Germany, which were implemented in most German cities since the 2000s. These concepts aim at social integration, yet were often directed towards disadvantaged social and ethnic groups and associated with responding to perceived negative outcomes such as the alleged emergence of a "parallel society" or "ethnic urban ghettos." The problems encountered relate back to the politics of belonging, suggesting that structural barriers as well as a lacking willingness to interact with migrants contradict recent efforts.

It appears that policies aimed merely at attracting specific groups are not sufficient to guarantee longer term effects. Policymakers need to have more knowledge on high-skilled migrants. Although clearly not a disadvantaged group, they are left largely on their own after arriving. Rather than just attracting human capital, policies need to focus on sustaining stability during the early phase prior to and directly following arrival in order to create comfortable environments and to communicate to the target group that they are welcome. In order to achieve this, coordinated actions by different stakeholders are required (including city administrations, housing companies, employers, higher education institutions, academic organizations, and local migrant communities).

As this research highlights, high-skilled migrants are not necessarily positioned with the "privileged staff of globalization" (Williams et al. 2013). Often, this mobility is driven by middle-class aspirations to secure social status or enhance career options. Cities with a lower global profile or a more narrow set of opportunities such as Dortmund (e.g. Glick-Schiller and Çaglar 2011) appear to function as stopovers for this group, rather than inducing long-term perspectives. Here, specific experiences in place, such as those with regard to housing, interfere with the evolution of more profound ties.

Notes

1. According to the German Federal Statistical Office the label "migration background" comprises foreigners, migrants who have received German citizenship, and persons born in Germany to migrant parents.
2. The names of the respondents have been changed to guarantee their anonymity.
3. Most importantly, the German Academic Exchange Service (DAAD) funds incoming and outgoing students and researchers.
4. It must be noted that several interviewees owned or had otherwise access to housing in their place of origin, which may explain the often-temporary nature of their stay and indicate future return intentions.

References

Ahmed, S. 1999. Home and away: Narratives of migration and estrangement. *International Journal of Cultural Studies* 2 (3): 329–347.

Al-Ali, N., and K. Koser. eds. 2002. *New approaches to migration? Transnational communities and the transformation of home*. London: Routledge.

Amin, A. 2002. The spatialities of globalisation. *Environment and Planning A* 34 (3): 385–399.

Andreotti, A., P. Le Galès, and F. J. Moreno Fuentes. 2013. Transnational mobility and rootedness: The upper middle classes in European cities. *Global Networks* 13 (1): 41–59.

Antonsich, M. 2010. Searching for belonging – an analytical framework. *Geography Compass* 4 (6): 644–659.

Arp Fallov, M., A. Jorgensen, and L. Knudsen. 2013. Mobile forms of belonging. *Mobilities* 8 (4): 467–486.

BBSR – Bundesinstitut für Bau-, Stadt- und Raumforschung. 2014. *Wie können Kommunen für qualifizierte Zuwanderer attraktiv werden?* Online Report No. 10/2014. Bonn: BBSR.

Beaverstock, J. V. 2002. Transnational elites in global cities: British expatriates in Singapore's financial district. *Geoforum* 33 (4): 525–538.

Beck, U., and E. Beck-Gernsheim. 1995. *The normal chaos of love*. Cambridge: Polity Press.

Blunt, A., and R. Dowling. 2006. *Home*. London: Routledge.

Brah, A. 1996. *Cartographies of diaspora: Contesting identities*. London: Routledge.

Brickell, K., and A. Datta. eds 2011. *Translocal geographies: Spaces, places, connections*. Farnham/Burlington: Ashgate.

Brown, P., A. Green, and H. Lauder. 2003. *High skills: Globalization, competitiveness and skill formation*. Oxford: Oxford University Press.

Castells, M. 2000. *The rise of the network society*. 2nd ed. Oxford: Blackwell.

Colic-Peisker, V. 2010. Free floating in the cosmopolis? Exploring the identity-belonging of transnational knowledge workers. *Global Networks* 10 (4): 467–488.

Collins, F. L. 2012. Transnational mobilities and urban spatialities: Notes from the Asia-Pacific. *Progress in Human Geography* 36 (3): 316–335.

Conradson, D., and A. Latham. 2005. Friendship, networks and transnationality in a world city: Antipodean transmigrants in London. *Journal of Ethnic and Migration Studies* 31 (2): 287–305.

Dittrich-Wesbuer, A., and J. Plöger. 2013. Multilokalität und Transnationalität – Neue Herausforderungen für Stadtentwicklung und Stadtpolitik. *Raumforschung und Raumordnung* 71 (3): 195–205.

Ehrkamp, P. 2005. Placing Identities: Transnational practices and local attachment of Turkish immigrants in Germany. *Journal of Ethnic and Migration Studies* 31 (2): 345–364.

Ehrkamp, P., and H. Leitner. 2006. Guest editorial: Rethinking immigration and citizenship: new spaces of migrant transnationalism and belonging. *Environment and Planning* A 38 (9): 1591–1597.

Ewers, M.C. 2007. Migrants, markets and multinationals: Competition among world cities for the highly-skilled. *GeoJournal* 68 (2–3): 119–130.

Föbker, S., J. Nipper, M. Otto, C. Pfaffenbach, D. Temme, G. Thieme, G. Weiss, and C. C. Wiegandt. 2011. Durchgangsstation oder neue Heimat – ein Beitrag zur Eingliederung von ausländischen hochqualifizierten Universitätsbeschäftigten in Aachen, Bonn und Köln. *Berichte zur deutschen Landeskunde* 85 (4): 341–360.

Gilmartin, M. 2008. Migration, identity and belonging. *Geography Compass* 2 (6): 1837–1852.

Glick-Schiller, N., L. Basch, and C. Blanc Szanton. 1992. Towards a transnational perspective on migration: Race, class, ethnicity and nationalism reconsidered. *Annals of the New York Academy of Sciences*. New York: The Johns Hopkins University Press.

Glick-Schiller, N., and A. Çaglar. 2011. Locality and globality: Building a comparative analytical framework in migration and urban studies. In *Locating migration, rescaling cities and migrants*, eds. N. Glick-Schiller and A. Çaglar, 60–84. New York: Cornell University Press.

Hannerz, U. 1996. *Transnational connections: Culture, people, places*. London: Routledge.

Hardill, I. 2004. Transnational living and moving experiences: Intensified mobility and dual-career households. *Population, Space and Place* 10 (5): 375–389.

Iredale, R. R. 2001. The migration of professionals: Theories and typologies. *International Migration* 39 (5): 7–24.

Jaworsky, B. N., P. Levitt, W. Cadge, J. Hejtmanek, and S. Curran. 2012. New perspectives on immigrant contexts of reception: The cultural armature of cities. *Nordic Journal of Migration Research* 2 (1): 78–88.

Kennedy, P. 2007. Global transformations and local "bubble" lives: Taking a reality check on some globalization concepts. *Globalizations* 4 (2): 267–283.

King, R. 2002. Towards a new map of European migration. *International Journal of Population Geography* 8 (2): 89–106.

Koser, K., and J. Salt. 1997. The geography of highly skilled international migration. *International Journal of Population Geography* 3 (4): 285–303.

Kreutzer, F., and S. Roth. 2006. Einleitung zu Transnationale Karrieren: Biographien, Lebensführung und Mobilität. In *Transnationale Karrieren: Biographien, Lebensführung und Mobilität*, eds. F. Kreutzer and S. Roth, 7–31. Wiesbaden: VS Verlag für Sozialwissenschaften.

Mahroum, S. 2001. Europe and the immigration of highly skilled labour. *International Migration* 39 (5): 27–43.

Massey, D. 1991. A global sense of place. *Marxism Today* 38: 24–29.

Mee, K., and S. Wright. 2009. Geographies of belonging: Guest editorial. *Environment and Planning A* 41 (4): 772–779.

Morley, D. 2001. Belongings: Place, space and identity in a mediated world. *European Journal of Cultural Studies* 4 (4): 425–448.

Musterd, S., and A. Murie. 2010. *Making competitive cities*, Chichester: Wiley-Blackwell.

Nowicka, M. 2007. Mobile locations: Construction of home in a group of mobile transnational professionals. *Global Networks* 7 (1): 69–86.

Ong, A., and D. Nonini. eds. 1997. *Ungrounded empires: The cultural politics of modern Chinese transnationalism*. New York: Routledge.

Peck, J. 2005. Struggling with the creative class. *International Journal of Urban and Regional Research* 29 (4): 740–770.

Plöger, J., and A. Becker. 2015. Social networks and local incorporation: Grounding high-skilled migrants in two German cities. *Journal of Ethnic and Migration Studies* 41 (10): 1517–1535.

Poros, M. 2001. The role of migrant networks in linking local labour markets: The case of Asian Indian migration to New York and London. *Global Networks* 1 (3): 243–256.

Robinson, D., K. Reeve, and R. Casey. 2007. *The housing pathways of new immigrants*. York: Joseph Rowntree Foundation.

Rose, G. 1995. Place and identity: A sense of place. In *A place in the world: Places, culture and globalization*, eds. D. Massey and P. Jess, 88–132. Oxford: The Open University.

Savage, M., G. Bagnall, and B. Longhurst. 2005. *Globalization and belonging*. London: Sage.

Sheller, M., and J. Urry. 2006. The new mobilities paradigm. *Environment and Planning A* 38 (2): 207–226.

Stadt Dortmund, Amt für Wohnungswesen. 2013. Wohnungsmarktbericht 2013. Ergebnisse des Wohnungsmarktbeobachtungssystems 2012. Dortmund: Stadt Dortmund.

Staeheli, L., and C. Nagel. 2006. Topographies of home and citizenship: Arab-American activists in the United States. *Environment and Planning A* 38 (9): 1599–1614.

Tippel, C., A. Becker, and J. Plöger. forthcoming. Cities, networks and connections: Location decisions of mobile professionals.

Urry, J. 2007. *Mobilities*. Cambridge: Polity Press.

van Riemsdijk, M. 2014. International migration and local emplacement: Everyday place-making practices of skilled migrants in Oslo, Norway. *Environment and Planning A* 46 (4): 963–979.

Von Streit, A., M. Popp, S. Hafner, G. Heinritz, and M. Miosga. 2009. Munich: An attractive place to live and work? The view of transnational migrants. *ACRE Report*, No. 7.7.

Walsh, K. 2006. 'Dad says I'm tied to a shooting star!' Grounding (research on) British expatriate belonging. *Area* 38 (3): 268-278.

Wellman, B. 2001. The rise of networked individualism. In *Community Networks Online*, ed. L. Kneeble, 17–42. London: Taylor & Francis.

White, P. 1988. Skilled international migrants and urban structure in Western Europe. *Geoforum* 19 (4): 411–422.

Williams, S., H. Bradley, R. Devadason, and M. Erickson. 2013. *Globalization and work*. Bristol: Polity Press.

Wirtschaftswoche. 2013. Städteranking 2013. Das Stärken-Schwächen-Profil. Dortmund.

Yeoh, B., and K. Willis. 2005. Singaporean and British transmigrants in China and the cultural politics of "contact zones." *Journal of Ethnic and Migration Studies* 31 (2): 269–285.

Yeoh, B., and S. Huang. 2011. Introduction: Fluidity and friction in talent migration. *Journal of Ethnic and Migration Studies* 37 (5): 681–690.

Yuval-Davis, N. 2006. Belonging and the politics of belonging. *Patterns of Prejudice* 40 (3): 197–214.

Zielke, E. 1982. Die Japaner in Düsseldorf. Manager-Mobilität-Voraussetzungen und Folgen eines Typs internationaler geographischer Mobilität. *Düsseldorfer Geographische Schriften*, 19.

10 Homogenizing the City

Place Marketing to Attract Skilled Migrants to Stavanger and Kongsberg

Micheline van Riemsdijk

> [We] want to welcome you to a rapidly growing region. Exciting jobs, research units, university facilities and good international schools make this region an attractive hub for competent, international employees.
>
> (Stavanger Chamber of Commerce 2014)

> From the seabed to outer space, we are achieving deeper, longer and higher performance capabilities by building stronger, safer and more advanced solutions. In Kongsberg, you will have every opportunity to play a part in these future-oriented developments.
>
> (Kongsberg Chamber of Commerce 2015)

These two vignettes aim to attract skilled migrants to Stavanger and Kongsberg, two knowledge hubs in Norway's oil and gas industry. They highlight factors that are likely to appeal to skilled migrants, such as knowledge and innovation, exciting employment opportunities, a good research infrastructure, and international schools. These factors are branded as competitive advantages of the two cities, trying to set them apart from other cities that aim to attract similar sources of human capital.

This chapter examines the ways in which cities brand themselves to attract skilled migrants. Bringing together literatures on city branding and international skilled migration, this chapter examines the place-based and spatial strategies of cities to attract highly skilled migrants, and the (invisibility of) racial/ethnic diversity and promotion of gender equality in city publications. The findings are placed within a discussion of diversity in city branding, categorizations of skilled migrants, and place branding of lesser known cities.

This chapter analyzes place-branding efforts in Stavanger and Kongsberg, two Norwegian cities that are known for their petroleum-related industries. Companies in these cities employ a large number of foreign-born engineers and other highly skilled migrants, and compete with other companies and cities to attract the best and brightest workers. Stavanger and Kongsberg differ substantially in population size, migration history, industrial base, and place branding strategies. They share, however, a need for skilled migrants and a desire to elevate their international, or even global, reputation among foreign-born skilled workers. This chapter presents an analysis of English-language relocation guides that are produced by public organizations and private enterprises to inform newcomers about working and living in the city.

The findings in this chapter contribute to a rethinking of literatures on international skilled migration in three ways. First, I argue that city branding initiatives for foreign-born skilled migrants reinforce ideals of the "good" migrant (Findlay et al. 2013) and are used as an integration tool for prospective residents. This chapter applies Findlay et al.'s (2013) conceptualization of the "ideal" migrant worker in terms of "bodily goodness" to a migrant's "cultural fit" with the host society. The "good" migrant adopts and embraces national norms and ways of life, integrating into a "common" Norwegian ideology (Gullestad 2002). The relocation guides explain norms and expectations in the workplace, the workings of the welfare state, Norwegian etiquette, and popular leisure activities. The text and images present an idealized image of Norwegianness, emphasizing family, nature, and outdoor pursuits. These integration tools help newcomers become "good Norwegians."

Second, the chapter problematizes the homogeneous representation of skilled migrants in city branding materials, questioning the absence of persons of color and a narrow representation of other personal characteristics of migrants. The relocation guides for both cities represent a homogeneous white, young population that does not reflect the broad range of racial/ethnic identities of skilled migrants. Gullestad (2002, 2004) has argued that Norwegian national identity is centered on ideals of sameness and equality that emphasize common Norwegian values. This homogenizing rhetoric "renders the representation of secular white identity synonymous with, and constitutive of, national belonging (McIntosh 2014, 3). Thus, immigrants who are marked as different present a challenge to the Norwegian community (Bygnes 2010; van Riemsdijk 2010).

Third, this chapter calls for studies of less iconic destinations in skilled migration scholarship. While global cities lure skilled migrants with a cosmopolitan lifestyle and attractive jobs, lesser known cities have to capitalize on other factors such as a safe and family-friendly environment, leisure activities, and close proximity to work and schools. The creation of place identity and the formation of a sense of belonging operate differently in lesser known destinations, but we know thus far little about these processes in these cities. This chapter aims to contribute to scholarship on place-making from the perspective of city-branding professionals in lesser known cities.

The next section examines historical city-branding initiatives and contemporary efforts of cities to attract skilled migrants. This discussion is followed by a literature review of place-branding strategies and city-branding initiatives in the Nordic countries. The methods section precedes an analysis of relocation guides for Stavanger and Kongsberg, and interviews with persons who are involved in city branding. The conclusion highlights the contributions of this chapter to skilled migration research.

Attracting Skilled Migrants to the City

While cities have marketed themselves for centuries, city-branding efforts have intensified in the past three decades (Kavaratzis and Ashworth 2005; for an overview of the origins of place branding, see Govers and Go 2009). Cities initially used marketing approaches to attract tourists, businesses, and capital. More recently, under the influence of neoliberal market reforms and the related global competition for talent, cities have started to target highly skilled migrants. Cities highlight their unique features in an effort to appeal to these valuable workers.

Global economic restructuring processes and the outsourcing of production have contributed to a decline in manufacturing in urban regions, changing the economic base and international positions of cities. In these post-industrial economies, cities had to focus on innovation and knowledge creation to attract new businesses and skilled workers (Hansen and Niedomysl 2009). As cities are competing for similar sources of capital and labor, the quality of place, lifestyle, amenities, and services such as healthcare, childcare, and education are important attraction factors (Jansson and Power 2006; Silvanto and Ryan 2014). Cities have also undertaken urban revitalization projects to make themselves more attractive, and they highlight these comparative advantages in city-branding campaigns.

Studies of regional economic development used to focus primarily on businesses and investors, as they were regarded as key actors in the competitiveness of city regions. Scholars investigated the factors that attracted businesses and investors to a region, and their contributions to regional economic development (Bergsgard and Vassenden 2011). With the transition from manufacturing to a service economy, knowledge has become an increasingly important factor for urban economic development and innovation. Knowledge is embodied in highly skilled individuals who are recruited to fill labor shortages and contribute to innovation. Some scholars have argued that skilled migrants contribute to urban and regional economic growth (World Economic Forum 2012; Florida 2002a; Glaeser 1999), while others have noted that this causal relationship cannot be established (Peck 2005). Either way, skilled migrants are considered an asset by cities and knowledge-intensive companies.

Skilled migrants constitute a heterogeneous group, with different expectations when they select a destination. These prospective residents look for services and amenities that fit their personality and lifestyle. For example, single skilled migrants likely appreciate a vibrant city with trendy cafés and restaurants, entertainment, and opportunities for creativity and innovation (Collett 2014). Migrants with families are more likely to be concerned about safety, the quality of schools, and healthcare. City branding efforts try to address these divergent expectations and needs.

A city's reputation is a key factor in attracting and retaining skilled migrants. For example, Harvey and Groutsis (2015) have noted that skilled migrants are attracted to Hong Kong's status as a global city and the global reputation of its financial and banking industry. These migrants do not tend to stay long, however, due to high work pressure. The reputation and name recognition of a city also influences the location choice of returning skilled migrants. This is evident in China, where the government created the "Thousand Talent Program" to attract IT specialists, academics, and entrepreneurs back to the country (Wang, Tang, and Li 2014; see also Chapter 14). These returning migrants predominantly settle in Hong Kong, Shanghai, and Beijing, while lesser known cities receive few return migrants (Harvey and Groutsis 2015). The preferences of highly skilled migrants for iconic cities make it difficult for lesser known cities to attract human capital.

Föbker, Temme, and Wiegandt (2014) have examined how Aachen, Bonn, and Cologne designed specialized messages to create a welcoming culture for skilled migrants. For example, the city of Cologne created programs for Chinese television to promote the city to Chinese businesses and workers. The city of Bonn placed large signs in its international quarter to welcome visitors in German, English, and French. The authors note that these signs specifically targeted highly skilled migrants and visitors, as they were not found in other parts of the city. The cities also try to meet the needs of skilled migrants by offering attractive accommodations, cultural and leisure activities, and quality schools (including international schools).

Current and former residents are important actors in city promotion (CityLogo-Eurocities 2013). Returning skilled migrants are likely to share their experiences with coworkers and friends, and may send employees on future assignments if they had a positive experience in the city. These "ambassadors" can be more effective than advertising campaigns, as they have direct contact with potential future skilled migrants, and their delivery is more authentic than branded messages (Föbker, Temme, and Wiegandt 2014). However, cities cannot control the message that is being delivered.

Branding the City

Cities commonly use branding strategies to attract prospective residents, tailoring their message to skilled migrants and other target groups. Kavaratzis and Ashworth (2005) have noted a shift from marketing to branding initiatives to promote cities. City branding borrows concepts from company and product branding, treating places as products to be sold to consumers. The selling of the city represents a "commodification of urban space: the city becomes a product to be sold in competition with other similar products" (Jansson and Power 2006, 14). In this competition to attract consumers to the city, branding campaigns select attributes that are likely to appeal most to a target group. However, there is no conclusive evidence what skilled migrants are looking for in a destination. Silvanto and Ryan (2014) call for a better understanding of the drivers and challenges of international skilled migration to make these branding efforts more effective.

City branding campaigns aim to develop a place identity that distinguishes places from one another. These campaigns try to positively influence the mental images that people create of cities, making associations between places and their meanings (Kavaratzis and Ashworth 2005). Place marketing campaigns select positive attributes that best "sell" a city. These values and a perceived quality of place create the mental image of the consumer. Cities are, however, likely to highlight similar features as they compete for the same workers (Peck 2005). For example, cities tend to emphasize their knowledge base and innovation activities to appeal to skilled migrants, which make it difficult to discern the distinctive features of a place.

This formulaic city branding is also evident in promotional materials for European Capitals of Culture, which are selected annually by the European Commission. Stavanger was elected European of Culture in 2008, together with Liverpool. Aiello and Thurlow (2006) note that promotional materials for European Capitals of Culture depict similar iconic images, such as cityscapes, photographs of children, and images of "high culture." Maps in the brochures place the city in the center of Europe, depicting its centrality within the European Union. All promotional materials contain photographs of fireworks, perhaps to celebrate the selection of the city by the commission. These iconic images are taken from a distance and they are disembodied, privileging material culture over individuals. This uniform representation of European culture does not reflect the cultural diversity of cities.

Similarly, in a study of social inclusion on municipal websites in the UK, Paganoni (2012) found that images often display iconic buildings in a decontextualized way to promote a cosmopolitan identity. The buildings are photographed from unexpected angles in deterritorialized spaces. This representation of city buildings creates a cosmopolitan image that enables the viewer to imagine him- or herself in that place.

Florida (2002a, b) has argued that skilled migrants are attracted to technology, talent, and tolerance. In regard to the third "T," Florida emphasized that diversity and tolerance help attract skilled migrants to cities, who appreciate an environment that is open to new ideas. He argues that diversity in ideas and skills contributes to innovation, which in turn helps attract more high-tech companies and contributes to job creation and economic growth. City branding campaigns, however, do not necessarily highlight diversity to appeal to skilled migrants.

Some cities highlight their racial and ethnic diversity as an asset to attract talent, capital, businesses, and large events (Donald, Kofman, and Kevin 2009). They use, for example, cosmopolitan images to showcase the ethnic and racial diversity of their population (ibid., 2009). Collett (2014) argues that a city should showcase its cultural diversity, reflecting the values and identities of its residents. She notes that "without strong community identification and support, a brand will be worthless" (Collett 2014, 7). However, some cities regard branding as separate from immigration and diversity, and render immigrants invisible in their branding narrative. This is the case in Stavanger and Kongsberg, which will be addressed in more detail in the analysis section.

In city branding, the first step is to create a city narrative or "stories" that are communicated through core messages and images (CityLogo-Eurocities 2013). The next step is brand positioning, which targets a particular product to a specific user group, using stories and communication strategies that are likely to appeal to that group (ibid.). In the case of place branding, attributes of a place are promoted that are likely to appeal to a user group. As many groups exist, "the city becomes a multitude of brands" (Kavaratzis and Ashworth 2005, 512) that "sells" different products to different consumers.

Jansson and Power (2006, 16) distinguish between three categories of urban branding strategies: "1) Branding through signature buildings, events, flagship projects etc; 2) Branding through planning strategies, urban redevelopment, institutional and infrastructural support; 3) Branding through advertising, myths, slogans, logos etc." The first category includes iconic architecture and large cultural, music, and sporting events. Iconic architecture conveys the image of the city and reflects urban vitality (ibid.). The second category encompasses efforts to improve the built environment and urban infrastructure to create new images—for example, after deindustrialization. The third category covers marketing strategies to create a positive image of the city and change the attitudes of consumers toward the city. The use of these categories in city-branding efforts in Stavanger and Kongsberg will be discussed in the analysis section.

Some cities try to rebrand themselves to reduce negative associations with the city. For example, Manchester created a new image after the city had outsourced low-skilled jobs in its deindustrialization phase. The city rebranded itself as the world's first post-industrial city, highlighting the innovative, cosmopolitan, and global aspects of the city (Kennedy 2009). In addition, several former industrial cities in the UK have created urban redevelopment projects to attract large meetings to the city. These projects can help transform the image of a city, replacing negative images with more positive connotations (Bradley, Hall, and Harrison 2002). This rebranding strategy is also evident in Stavanger, which brands itself as an energy city in an effort to reduce negative connotations with the oil industry.

City Marketing in the Nordic States

Nordic cities have developed city-branding campaigns to increase their name recognition and international stature. The most well-known branding campaign is "Stockholm, The Capital of Scandinavia," which was developed by British marketing specialist Julian Stubbs. This slogan was understandably disliked by other Nordic capital cities, which felt a need to compete with Stockholm in name recognition and attracting skilled migrants. The city of Oslo hired Mr. Stubbs to develop a branding campaign for the capital city, and the marketing plan was presented in 2015 (Oslo Business Region 2015a). The campaign won the "place brand of the year" award at the City, Nation and Place Conference in London in November 2015. In her acceptance speech, Marit Høvik Hartmann, Director of Communication and Marketing at Oslo Business Region, noted Oslo's product strengths:

> Oslo is not the biggest city in the world – and that is exactly our asset. We believe "small is the new big", and Oslo is on a mission to become the world's

> favourite compact city. Being on a shortlist together with Great Britain, Liverpool, Eindhoven and Sweden, was a great honor.
>
> (Oslo Business Region 2015b)

Like Oslo, Stavanger and Kongsberg promote their relatively small size to appeal to prospective residents. They emphasize their close proximity to nature and leisure activities, and short distances to work and schools. Thus, these smaller cities try to appeal to skilled migrants with an active lifestyle and short distances within the city.

Nordic cities provide a distinctive context for attracting skilled migrants. Hansen and Niedomysl (2009) and Andersen et al. (2010) have importantly noted that Florida's work on place attractiveness was developed in the United States, which has a different migration context compared to the Nordic states. The United States offers more employment opportunities in more cities, which contributes to increased competition between cities. Andersen et al. (2010) also found that tolerance has little impact on the destination choice of members of the creative class in the Nordic countries. These persons appreciated diversity and tolerance, but these factors had little influence on the destination choice if the migrant was not a member of an ethnic minority group. In general, members of the creative class placed more emphasis on cultural offerings than tolerance. This emphasis on culture is also evident in the relocation guides for Stavanger and Kongsberg that will be discussed in the analysis section.

Methods

The findings in this chapter are based on content and image analysis of relocation guides for Stavanger and Kongsberg, examining how the two cities brand themselves to skilled migrants. The guides used in this study are written in English, targeting a foreign-born population. The relocation guide for Kongsberg is available on the Internet (Kongsberg Chamber of Commerce); the Stavanger guide is only published in hard copy.

The author also conducted semi-structured interviews with five individuals who are involved in city-branding initiatives in Stavanger and Kongsberg to gain in-depth perspectives on the cities' place-branding strategies to attract foreign-born skilled migrants. All interviews were conducted in November and December 2015. The interviews took place in the offices of informants, lasted between forty-five and ninety minutes, and were conducted in Norwegian. The interview guide was amended after each interview to incorporate new information (Dunn 2010). The author transcribed the interviews in Norwegian and translated excerpts into English.

Based on the literature review on city branding, the author created a list of themes, and subthemes, in Excel related to city branding for skilled migrants: talent/knowledge (innovation/creativity, technology); jobs/employment (research, university); family (child care/education for children, international schools, safety, healthcare, leisure activities for families); cosmopolitan lifestyle (cafés and restaurants, "high culture," Capital of Culture); leisure activities (not family-specific); iconic buildings; large events; ambassadors; diversity; regional/national map; transportation. More themes were added as they emerged in the relocation guides: cost of living; housing; national identity; nature; immigrant associations. For each theme, the author added text from the relocation brochures, photograph descriptions, and interview excerpts. She then coded branding efforts for skilled migrants and selected key texts that illustrated how Kongsberg and Stavanger try to attract skilled migrants. The chapter uses pseudonyms to protect the identity of study participants.

Stavanger: Norway's Oil Capital

In the early 1970s, Stavanger transformed from a rather isolated city on Norway's southwest coast into Norway's on-shore center for the petroleum industry (Bergsgard and Vassenden 2011). Stavanger was selected because of its good infrastructure, airport, proximity to the oil fields in the North Sea, and the fervent lobbying activities of local politicians to bring the petroleum industry to the city (Hidle and Normann 2013). Stavanger soon became known as the oil capital of Norway.

Engineering is Stavanger's largest industry, attracting an international population of oil and gas engineers (City of Stavanger 2014). Stavanger is Norway's fourth largest city after Oslo, Bergen, and Trondheim, with a population of 130,000. The larger Stavanger region has almost 320,000 inhabitants (City of Stavanger 2014). Historically, Stavanger's main industries were herring fishing, ship building, and fish canning (for a history of Stavanger's industries, see Oftedal and Iakovleva 2015). Nowadays, Stavanger is a knowledge hub that houses a university, a research park, and various knowledge-based industries (Andersen et al. 2010). The annual Oil Service North Sea (ONS) Conference, held in Stavanger since 1974, augments the reputation of Stavanger as the capital of the Norwegian oil industry (Omholt 2013). The conference attracts over 11,000 attendees, some of whom may become future residents in the city.

Almost 19 percent of Stavanger's population is foreign-born, far above the national average of 12 percent (Directorate of Integration and Diversity 2015a). Most migrants are citizens of European Economic Area (EEA) member states. Poles make up the largest number of migrants in Stavanger (over 3,000), resulting from Poland's membership in the European Union in 2004 and related access to the Norwegian labor market.[1] The second largest migrant group is British (over 1,500), followed by Swedes and Danes. The two largest non-EU groups come from India and Turkey (see Table 10.1). The Norwegian immigration authorities unfortunately do not make the educational attainment of immigrants available, and it is therefore not possible to know which migrants are highly skilled. We do know that many oil- and gas- related companies in Stavanger hire foreign-born engineers and other skilled migrants to fill labor shortages (Lewis 2012).

The Stavanger Chamber of Commerce and its nonprofit relocation agency INN International Network of Norway created a relocation guide for the

Table 10.1 Foreign Nationals in Stavanger and Kongsberg by Country of Origin, 2015

Stavanger		*Kongsberg*	
Country of Origin	*Number of Migrants*	*Country of Origin*	*Number of Migrants*
Poland	3,022	India	249
Great Britain	1,512	Poland	244
Sweden	933	Lithuania	224
Denmark	910	Sweden	211
India	795	Denmark	168
Germany	763	Iraq	131
Turkey	751	Great Britain	127
Lithuania	694	Afghanistan	121
USA	624	Philippines	110
Russia	617	Iran	109

Source: The Directorate of Integration and Diversity (IMDi), 2015.

Stavanger and Haugesund region in collaboration with Rogaland County Council, the tourism organization Greater Stavanger, the national labor union, state employment agencies, and the Norwegian Oil and Gas Association (Stavanger Chamber of Commerce 2014). The hundred-page guide targets international skilled migrants, as the welcome page mentions that Stavanger's high-technology industries make the region "an attractive hub for competent, international employees" (Stavanger Chamber of Commerce 2014, 3). The English-language guide provides practical advice about living and working in the Stavanger and Haugesund region, such as work and residence permits, importing goods to Norway, employment terms and conditions, and tax regulations. It also provides information about education and childcare, healthcare, recreational activities, and transportation to Stavanger.

The guide's front-cover motto "Come for the job, stay for the lifestyle" is reflected in the page allocation, devoting almost five times as many pages to recreational activities (thirty-four pages) compared to work (seven pages). The emphasis on sports and leisure activities reflects the importance of work–life balance in Norwegian society, which has been achieved by far-reaching policies to support dual-career households (Crompton and Lyonette 2006). The guide places a strong emphasis on outdoor activities explaining that:

> The abundance of space and a traditionally close relationship with nature means that the majority of Norwegians take part in some form of outdoor leisure activity. The Stavanger and Haugesund region offers majestic fjords, beaches and an impressive mountain landscape. Here you also find some of the most popular natural tourist attractions in the country such as Kjerag and the Pulpit Rock. Accessibility is the key word, as this region is one of few places where you can experience a snow peaked mountaintop and a walk on the beach within a couple of hours.
>
> (Stavanger Chamber of Commerce 2014, 55)

The guide explains the importance of outdoor activities to the Norwegian way of life: "Using the natural surroundings and indulging in an active outdoor life holds an important place in the Norwegian culture. Biking, hiking, jogging, fishing and skiing are popular activities in the region as well as in the rest of the country" (ibid., 57). The textual emphasis on nature and outdoor activities is reinforced by twenty-four photographs of people engaged in outdoor pursuits such as beach walking, mountain hiking and climbing, kayaking, and camping. The guide instructs skilled migrants how to become a "good Norwegian" by engaging in outdoor pursuits and participating in sports activities with their children, thus contributing to the integration of foreign-born skilled migrants into Norwegian society.

Stavanger's city branding initiative differs in two key aspects from branding images of world cities. First, contrary to what one may expect of a relocation guide for international skilled migrants, the guide allocates only eight pages to city life (compared to thirty-four pages on recreational activities). Four pages are dedicated to "high culture," describing music performances, theater, galleries, and museums; three pages discuss dining and nightlife (reflecting "vibrant city life" Collett (2014)); and one page lists international religious groups. This sparse discussion of city life may seem surprising as a cosmopolitan lifestyle likely attracts young and single skilled migrants to the city. Merete, an informant for this study, explained that most skilled migrants move to Stavanger to pursue employment opportunities. The lifestyle becomes more important in the decision to stay long term (personal interview, Stavanger, November 2015). This insight is reflected in the city's motto "Come for the job, stay for the lifestyle."

Second, the guide contains only fourteen photographs of city life and iconic buildings (compared to twenty-four depicting recreational activities). Photographs show people walking in Old Stavanger, a family of four walking in a pedestrian shopping area, and five women dining in a restaurant. Other photographs show graduating high school students (*russ*) in a parade, children playing in the Geopark, and cityscapes of downtown Haugesund. The brochure also depicts the Norwegian Petroleum Museum, the cultural center, concert hall, and cathedral. Most of these buildings are photographed without persons, allowing the viewer to imagine her/himself in the landscape (Aiello and Thurlow 2006).

Stavanger's multicultural population is largely invisible in the relocation guide. While 30 percent of Stavanger's migrants originated in Asia (including Turkey), 9 percent in Africa, and 5 percent in South and Middle America (Table 10.2), all persons in the photographs but one are white. The only person of color is a young woman featured in an advertisement for the language school Lingu Stavanger (Stavanger Chamber of Commerce 2014). The other photographs reinforce the idea of a homogeneous white Norwegian society, rendering residents that belong to minority groups invisible in the branding effort. This can be detrimental to the success of the place brand, as it does not reflect the values and identities of current and future residents (Collett 2014).

Table 10.2 Foreign Nationals in Stavanger and Kongsberg by Region of Origin, 2015

Region	*Stavanger*		*Kongsberg*	
	Number of Foreign Nationals	*% Foreign Nationals*	*Number of Foreign Nationals*	*% Foreign Nationals*
Asia (incl. Turkey)	6,598	27	1,071	30
EU countries in Eastern Europe	1,845	7	712	20
Western Europe, excluding Nordic countries	4,200	17	486	14
Nordic countries	2,368	10	470	13
Africa	2,386	10	327	9
Eastern Europe, excluding EU	4,982	20	230	6
South and Middle America	1,167	5	187	5
North America and Oceania	987	4	105	3

Source: The Directorate of Integration and Diversity (IMDi), 2015.

Photographs in the tourist guide for the Stavanger region also provide a homogeneous image of Norwegianness. When asked about the pervasiveness of whiteness in the guide, Trude, a study participant in Stavanger, explained that:

> People expect a Nordic appearance. Even though 20 percent of Stavanger's population has a foreign passport, 181 countries are presented. That's the way it is, I say unfortunately, it is best to sell the Nordic appearance.
>
> (Personal interview, Stavanger, November 2015)

The terminology of a "Nordic appearance" equates being "Nordic" with being "white." This representation of Nordic peoples negates the existence of indigenous Sami populations and migrants who have settled in the Nordic countries. According to Gullestad (2004, 193), Norwegians used to define their national identity comparing themselves to Danes, Swedes, and other Europeans. Now that Norway has become a more racially and ethnically diverse country, being white has become more pronounced in Norwegian national identity.

As our conversation about diversity continued, Trude mentioned that the free city map for Stavanger, Sandnes, and Egersund represents racial/ethnic diversity. The front cover features three women with dark hair on a shopping trip, fashionably clad in summer dresses and carrying shopping bag with logos for various shops. Trude explains the absence of diversity in the city guide as follows:

> But if you look at the city map you see only foreigners in the picture. Here are the foreigners on a shopping trip [Trude shows the city map] … But diversity, then we talk most about the way to experience culture. For example, for culture, there is everything from new art, street art, they [the street art wall paintings] are best in Norway, the biggest international artists [participate] in a workshop [in Stavanger once a year].
>
> (Personal interview, Stavanger, November 2015)

In this response, Trude switches the conversation to street art rather than discussing the representation of immigrants in the city. The materialities of shopping and street art are less politically charged symbols of diversity, and easier to present to "the people" that expect a "Nordic appearance." But this judgment depends on "the people" who consume these images, as skilled migrants of color are more likely to feel an attachment to Stavanger if they can recognize themselves in the city's branding materials.

Interestingly, the relocation guide acknowledges that Norway and Oslo have become more culturally diverse, but does not discuss this diversity in Stavanger:

> Modern Norway is globalised and culturally diverse. Oslo is increasingly becoming an exciting multicultural city with inspiration from around the world. This obviously influences the cultural nature of the country. The fundamental values persist, combined with newer global influences. This has contributed to Norway being ranked as "best place to live" by the United Nations for many years in a row.
>
> (Stavanger Chamber of Commerce 2014, 19)

The global influences in Stavanger are reflected in the listing of international faith-based organizations in the relocation guide. The guide fails, however, to mention nonreligious organizations for skilled migrants. Stavanger has a long history of expat organizations in the oil and gas industry, offering activities for workers and their spouses. Stavanger also has various expat organizations that meet regularly in the city, including InterNations. The omission of these international organizations renders a salient aspect of the lives of foreign-born skilled migrants invisible (for a discussion of skilled migrant organizations as agents of local incorporation, see van Riemsdijk 2015).

Kongsberg: Technology City

Kongsberg is known in Norway for its subsea engineering industry, but has little name recognition outside the country. The small city of 25,000 inhabitants is located 87 kilometers southwest of Oslo at the tail end of subsea valley, a region between Oslo and Kongsberg that houses almost 200 companies in subsea engineering. Kongsberg has the highest density of engineers in Norway, measured by number of engineers per square kilometer (Kongsberg Chamber of Commerce 2013, 5).

Kongsberg's foreign-born population constitutes 13.5 percent of the total population (Directorate of Integration and Diversity 2015b). Most foreign-born workers come from India, Poland, Lithuania, Sweden, and Denmark (see Table 10.1). The hiring geographies of FMC Technologies can serve as an illustration of an international workforce. In 2009 the company hired 726 foreign-born employees, of which 365 were non-EEA citizens. Many migrants came from Russia and India (Wernersen 2013).

Kongsberg emphasizes its high-tech industries and skilled workforce. A Google search for "Kongsberg" conducted in October 2015 confirmed the dominance of advanced technology in the city, contrary to a search for Stavanger that yielded mostly tourism-related results. Of the top nine hits for Kongsberg (excluding advertisements and news headlines), eight company websites and one Wikipedia entry for the city of Kongsberg were displayed. This result confirms the centrality of technology-related companies in the city.

The front cover of the relocation guide called "Live in Kongsberg" illustrates working life and leisure activities in Kongsberg, featuring a large photograph of a young woman holding a snowboard, a young man measuring a metal object, a woman holding a child on her shoulders at an outdoor festival, and a female performer with a guitar (Kongsberg Chamber of Commerce 2013). The 32-page English-language guide was created by the Kongsberg Chamber of Commerce. It clearly targets foreign-born skilled migrants, emphasizing the city's technology base and international engineering workforce:

> An important reason for Kongsberg's industrial success is our strong focus on expertise. Highly educated individuals from around the world have chosen to live and work in Kongsberg.
>
> (Kongsberg Chamber of Commerce 2013, 14)

Kongsberg brands itself as "city of technology," which is reinforced in various topics in the relocation guide. A section with the heading "city of technology" shows an aerial photograph of Kongsberg Technology Park, followed by a short description of "the new silver," referring to the transformation of the city from a silver mining town to advanced technology industries in subsea engineering, aviation, automotive, defense, aerospace, energy, and maritime industries.

The relocation guide for Kongsberg includes all three categories of city branding that Jansson and Power (2006) have identified. The guide highlights various large events that are hosted in the city, including the internationally renowned Kongsberg Jazz Festival, and festivals for classical music, skiing, and crime novels (Jansson and Power's first category of city branding: events and flagship projects). The guide allocates four pages to descriptions of a cosmopolitan lifestyle, emphasizing its "unique urban experience" and cultural offerings (the second category of city branding: urban redevelopment and infrastructural support). Kongsberg brands itself as a technology city and the Chamber of Commerce uses a city logo in all its publications (Jansson and Power's third category of city branding). This targeted city branding is necessary to compete with nearby Drammen and Oslo that offer more amenities and an urban lifestyle at respectively a thirty-minute and one-hour drive from Kongsberg.

Kongsberg sells itself as a "small town with a big city feel," marketing its urban life as follows:

> Kongsberg's historic buildings create a striking city centre. The former industrial town has become a unique urban experience – a modern community amidst beautiful scenery. There is no need to travel to neighboring towns to meet your shopping needs. Kongsberg has two modern shopping centres with

> a wide range of shops. You will also find exciting niche boutiques throughout the city. Art galleries and numerous events enhance our engaging and friendly urban environment.
>
> (Kongsberg Chamber of Commerce 2013, 20)

The section is accompanied by photographs of a shopping center, a café, performers at music festivals, and children participating in a LEGO League (ibid. 20–21). These photographs show that Kongsberg offers cultural amenities, public meeting places, and street life, which enhance the attraction of peripheral cities (Andersen et al. 2010). The following two pages showcase glass blowing, a musician, an arts and crafts gallery, a child playing the piano, and a ceramics workshop. Despite this effort to "sell" the city as an attractive urban destination, Kongsberg has low appeal for young and single foreign-born skilled migrants. Kongsberg informant Merete explains:

> Kongsberg is struggling a little with the recruitment of young single [immigrants]. Kongsberg is a family town and has not fully succeeded in creating an exciting nightlife. This is one of Kongsberg's challenges. We have had many discussions about this: Is this what we want? Shall we try to start a discotheque and nightlife? We decided that no, that is such a big change that we can't win. We prefer to think about the advantages we have with broad cultural offerings, with sports and activities or music or concerts or volunteering. And we have to work slowly but surely to build up some urban life on the side, more cafés and such things, we should rather try to integrate and involve those who come in the activities that we offer.
>
> (Personal interview, Kongsberg, December 2015)

Kongsberg's city officials and the hiring managers of companies are aware of the challenges of recruiting foreign-born skilled migrants to the city, especially when they are single. To meet their needs for a meeting space, FMC Technologies and the Kongsberg Group organize a monthly *minglemølla* event ("mingling by the mill" is the name of a music and culture venue in downtown Kongsberg). These English-language events provide an opportunity for foreign-born and Norwegian employees to mingle with colleagues outside work. Such collaborations helps companies to compete in semi-peripheral regions such as Kongsberg (Andersen et al. 2010).

Kongsberg also tries to appeal to families. Vidar Lande, Mayor of Kongsberg, mentions in his welcome column: "For many years, Kongsberg has focused on being a great place to raise a family. In 2013, we were ranked the best local authority in Norway for children and young people" (Kongsberg Chamber of Commerce 2013, 2). The family-friendly environment is reflected in twenty-four images of children engaged in play, sports, silver mining, a farm visit, a LEGO challenge, and participation in an outdoor event. The guide notes Kongsberg's family-friendly neighborhoods with low-speed limits, attractive playgrounds, and close proximity to schools and work, and the kindergartens are safe and within short distance to the forest. It also mentions the good quality of schools and the English-speaking Kongsberg International School. Collett (2015) found that marketing materials for Basel, Switzerland, similarly highlighted safe neighborhoods and good quality schools and public infrastructure to compensate for a lack of vibrant city life.

The Kongsberg guide lists a wide array of leisure activities, including sports clubs, music venues, and volunteer organizations. Most of these organizations receive financial support from Kongsberg's companies, as they recognize the importance of these activities to attract and retain skilled migrants (personal interview, Kongsberg, December 2015). The guide mentions that "Kongsberg is one of the sportiest cities in Norway. Every single weekend, someone from Kongsberg represents Norway in a championship or competition!" (Kongsberg Chamber of Commerce 2013, 19). The importance of involvement in recreational activities and volunteer organizations is reinforced in a section on "Living life to the full" [*sic.*]:

> Kongsberg offers a wealth of recreational opportunities that promote safe and sound local environments. We have clubs and associations for mainstream and special-interest sports, run by people committed to both quality and fun. What is your favorite? Whether it's ice hockey, handball, soccer, cycling, golf, skateboarding, snowboarding, skiing, climbing or most any other sport, you can find it here in Kongsberg.
>
> (Ibid., 24)

The Kongsberg guide also promotes outdoor recreation in text and twenty-four photographs. The guide emphasizes Kongsberg's close proximity to nature, and encourages prospective residents to take a bike ride, go fishing, kayaking or hiking. The emphasis on sports and outdoors activities informs prospective residents about Norwegian life and culture, contributing to their integration into Norwegian society.

The guide informs foreign-born skilled workers about Norwegian norms regarding gender equality in two ways. First, the photographs for the Norwegian Centre of Expertise Systems Engineering and GKN Aerospace Norway feature women in traditionally male occupations. Second, the section on kindergartens informs parents of the Men in kindergarten (MIB) network that "aims to retain male personnel, ensure a good environment for male employees and foster gender equality" (ibid., 9). The recruitment of male employees to Norwegian kindergartens is part of an initiative of the Ministry of Children and Equality to promote gender socialization and true equality between the sexes (Ministry of Children and Equality 2009). Norway's goal to achieve full gender equality is supported by various government policies.

The guide also provides ideal pathways of integration in two vignettes of new residents in the city. These persons developed a sense of belonging in Kongsberg through involvement in local organizations. Christian Schmidt, a German employee for rotating equipment company Dresser Rand, joined the basketball team and met friends at work. Bo Espen, Camilla Lobben, and their two daughters joined a local church. Camilla feels that she belongs in Kongsberg: "I feel we've come home. It's a great feeling" (Kongsberg Chamber of Commerce 2013, 7). The narratives of these newcomers reinforce Norwegian values of active participation in the local community through sports and religious institutions.

The relocation guide for Kongsberg projects a racially homogeneous image of Norwegian society, similar to the Stavanger guide. When the author mentioned the lack of racial/ethnic diversity and representation of migrants in the Kongsberg guide, Solveig, a study participant in Kongsberg, responded that Kongsberg integrates refugees well. She was referring to the current refugee situation in Europe, equating diversity with the reception of refugees. When the author asked about the lack of representation of *skilled* migrants in the relocation guide, Solveig acknowledged that this should be addressed (personal interview, Kongsberg, December 2015). Solveig initially equated immigrants with refugees, and did not consider skilled migrants to fall under this category. Solveig, like the majority population in Norway, likely perceives immigrants (*innvandrere*) as persons of non-Western background who perform low-skilled or unskilled work, and whose values differ from the majority population (Gullestad 2002, 2004). Skilled migrants thus occupy an ambiguous position in the categorization—and perception—of immigrants in Norway.

A more inclusive perspective on skilled migrants is evident on the websites for the Kongsberg International School and Norkirken (literally *Norchurch*). Images of class activities in the international school reflect the ethnic and racial diversity of students of twenty-three nationalities (Kongsberg International School 2013). Norkirken acknowledges that Kongsberg is an international community: "We are an international church with members from over twenty countries. English translation is available in our services, so feel free to come even though you don't speak Norwegian" (Norkirken Kongsberg 2015). The website reflects a cosmopolitan identity, stating that "Kongsberg is blessed with residents and visitors from around the world and we are delighted to be part of a living church, where everyone comes as they are to seek and worship God." The international school and church provide multicultural meeting spaces that help create a sense of belonging for foreign-born skilled migrants in the city.

Conclusion

The findings in this chapter help us rethink theories of international skilled migration in three ways. First, city-branding initiatives can be used as an integration tool for foreign-born skilled workers. The relocation guides provide information about living and working in Norway, and prepare newcomers to become "good" migrants (Findlay et al. 2013) by adapting Norwegian norms and values and ways of life. Symbols of "Norwegianness" (Gullestad 2002, 2004) include a love of nature, participation in outdoor pursuits and sports activities, engagement in volunteer organizations, and spending time with children and other family members. The guides also underline the importance of work–life balance and gender equality in the Norwegian welfare state, emphasizing these values in text and photographs. Thus, the city branding materials do more than merely "selling the city"—they help create "desirable" migrants who internalize "proper" behavior and attitudes.

Second, the findings indicate a need for more sensitivity to racial/ethnic diversity in research on international skilled migration. While scholars have importantly disrupted the notion of a homogeneous male elite skilled migrant in scholarship of gender and skilled migration (Kofman 2000; Raghuram 2000), ordinary, everyday migrants (Smith and Favell 2006) and "middling" skilled migrants (Conradson and Latham 2005), few studies have examined the racial/ethnic diversity of skilled migrants, especially its interactions with place. This lack of attention has also been noted in research of city branding campaigns (Aiello and Thurlow 2006; Paganoni 2012). The invisibility of migrants in the text and/or images in relocation brochures of the two cities in this study can partly be explained by the difficulties of discussing race in Norway. Trude redirected that conversation to culture, while Solveig did not consider skilled migrants "immigrants." These conceptualizations of immigration and race make it difficult to discuss racial/ethnic differences in a society that defines its identity on a homogeneous white notion of the nation (Gullestad 2004). This study suggests that city-branding efforts should include members of underrepresented groups in promotional materials, including foreign-born skilled migrants, to ensure a more equitable representation of the population (Collett 2014; Paganoni 2012).

Third, the findings help us rethink the role of place in attracting and retaining international skilled migrants. While Florida (2002a, b) has emphasized the importance of amenities for place attractiveness, it is evident that that is only one of many aspects that skilled migrants take into consideration when selecting a place to live. The Stavanger slogan "Come for the job, stay for the lifestyle" aptly describes what attracts skilled migrants most—the job. In order to retain skilled migrants long term, cities have to highlight their quality of life for prospective and current residents. This task is more difficult for lesser known, smaller cities that have to compete with more cosmopolitan destinations. The former capitalize on their recreational activities, close proximity to nature, and family-friendly environments. These aspects do not necessarily appeal to young, single migrants who may prefer more urban lifestyles. Local sports organizations, voluntary organizations, religious institutions, and contacts with parents at the children's schools can help create a local sense of belonging. For young, single migrants, however, it is more difficult to feel attached to these smaller cities (for a more in-depth discussion of the place-making practices of skilled migrants, see van Riemsdijk 2014).

This chapter provides three suggestions for future research. First, a comparison of relocation guides for larger, well-known cities would provide a fuller understanding of city- branding efforts for skilled migrants in first-, second-, and third-tier cities. Second, it would be beneficial to study how skilled migrants use relocation guides. Are they actively used to make location decisions, or do they merely provide information after migrants have accepted a job offer? Third, future research could examine how skilled migrants perceive the content of relocation guides, whether they notice the representations of "Norwegianness," and if and how they internalize the norms and values of being a "good" migrant.

In closing, it is important to note that this chapter analyzed city-branding materials that were developed when the oil economy prospered. Cities are constantly changing, and place brands have to be regularly evaluated and redefined as the product and its consumers change (Donald, Kofman, and Kevin 2009). Since June 2015, the value of the Norwegian krone has declined considerably in tandem with a steep decline in the global price for brent crude oil (*The Economist* 2015). Companies in the petroleum industry in Norway have laid off many employees, and cities that depend on this industry are forced to reimagine themselves and their workforce. Stavanger plans to develop health, information, and space technology, building on its engineering expertise (Seglem 2015; personal interviews in Stavanger). Kongsberg intends to use its strengths in systems engineering to develop new health and information technologies. Bente, an informant in Kongsberg, is confident that the city will reinvent itself just as it did after the decline of the silver mining industry:

> Kongsberg has always used the possibilities that we have. From the mining times have we seen possibilities. We have used that knowledge for new possibilities … it wasn't automatic that one should find, make good positions for boats in the large sea in a little city in the countryside. It is industry, a curiosity how we can make so much [that is] unique and good.
>
> (Personal interview, Kongsberg, December 2016)

As subsea technology companies in Kongsberg are laying off foreign-born and domestic engineers, the future of these skilled workers in the city is unclear. These developments may require a reimagining of the future and accompanying rebranding efforts in the cities.

Acknowledgments

The author thanks the study participants for their time and insights, Qingfang Wang and Heike Alberts for feedback on an earlier version of this chapter, and Scott Basford for helpful research assistance. The fieldwork research was funded by the National Science Foundation (award number 1155339) and a travel grant from the Royal Embassy of Norway and the Norwegian Center for Cooperation in Education. This financial support is highly appreciated.

Note

1. Norway is a member of the Schengen Agreement, allowing citizens of EU member states to live and work in Norway.

References

Aiello, G., and C. Thurlow. 2006. Symbolic capitals: Visual discourse and intercultural exchange in the European capital of culture scheme. *Language and Intercultural Communication* 6 (2): 148–162.

Andersen, K. V., M. M. Bugge, H. Kalsø Hansen, A. Isaksen, and M. Raunio. 2010. One size fits all? Applying the creative class thesis onto a Nordic context. *European Planning Studies* 18 (10): 1591–1609.

Bergsgard, N. A., and A. Vassenden. 2011. The legacy of Stavanger as capital of culture in Europe 2008: Watershed or puff of wind? *International Journal of Cultural Policy* 17 (3): 301–320.

Bradley, A., T. Hall, and M. Harrison. 2002. Selling cities: Promoting new images for meetings tourism. *Cities* 19 (1): 61–70.

Bygnes, S. 2010. Making equality diverse? Merged gender equality and anti-discrimination measures in Norway. *NORA – Nordic Journal of Feminist and Gender Research* 18 (2): 88–104.

City of Stavanger. 2014. Intercultural profile. Available at: www.naeringsforeningen.no/ShowFile.ashx?FileInstanceId=9eecba4c-771e-4853-9e5d-234ccbcf01c9 (accessed November 7, 2015).

CityLogo-Eurocities. 2013. Integrating city-brand management: Re-thinking organizational models. Oslo: CityLogo.

Collett, E. 2014. The city brand: Champion of immigrant integration or empty marketing tool? Washington, DC: Migration Policy Institute.

Conradson, D., and A. Latham. 2005. Transnational urbanism: Attending to everyday practices and mobilities. *Journal of Ethnic and Migration Studies* 31 (2): 227–233.

Crompton, R., and C. Lyonette. 2006. Work–life "balance" in Europe. *Acta Sociologica* 49 (4): 379–393.

Directorate of Integration and Diversity (IMDi). 2015a. Faktaark for integreringen i Stavanger kommune [fact sheet for integration in Stavanger municipality]. Available at: www.imdi.no/tall-og-statistikk/steder/K1103/fakta (accessed March 5, 2016).

———. 2015b. Faktaark for integreringen i Kongsberg kommune [fact sheet for integration in Kongsberg municipality]. Available at: www.imdi.no/tall-og-statistikk/steder/K0604/fakta (accessed March 5, 2016).

Donald, S. H., E. Kofman, and C. Kevin. 2009. Introduction: Processes of cosmopolitanism and parochialism. In *Branding cities: Cosmopolitanism, parochialism, and social change*, eds. S. H. Donald, E. Kofman, and C. Kevin, 1–13. New York: Routledge.

Dunn, K. 2010. Interviewing. In *Qualitative research methods in human geography*, ed. I. Hay, 101–138. Toronto: Oxford University Press.

Economist, The 2015. Exchange rates: Pegs under pressure. *The Economist*, 17 October.

Findlay, A., D. McCollum, S. Shubin, E. Apsite, and Z. Krisjane. 2013. The role of recruitment agencies in imagining and producing the "good" migrant. *Social & Cultural Geography*, 14 (2), 145–167.

Florida, R. 2002a. The economic geography of talent. *Annals of the Association of American Geographers* 92 (4): 743–755.

———. 2002b. *The rise of the creative class*. New York: Basic Books.

Föbker, S., D. Temme, and C.-C. Wiegandt. 2014. A warm welcome to highly-skilled migrants: How can municipal administrations play their part? *Tijdschrift voor Economische en Sociale Geografie* 105 (5): 542–557.

Glaeser, E. 1999. The future of urban research: Nonmarket interactions. Washington, DC: Brookings Institution.

Govers, R., and F. Go. 2009. *Place branding: Glocal, virtual and physical identities, constructed, imagined and experienced.* New York: Palgrave Macmillan.

Gullestad, M. 2002. *Det norske sett med nye øyne* [Norwegian culture seen through new eyes]. Oslo: Universitetsforlaget.

———. 2004. Blind slaves of our prejudices: Debating "culture" and "race" in Norway. *Ethnos* 69 (2): 177–203.

Hansen, H. K., and T. Niedomysl. 2009. Migration of the creative class: Evidence from Sweden. *Journal of Economic Geography* 9 (2): 191–206.

Harvey, W. S., and D. Groutsis. 2015. Reputation and talent mobility in the Asia Pacific. *Asia Pacific Journal of Human Resources* 53 (1): 22–40.

Hidle, K., and R. H. Normann. 2013. Who can govern? Comparing network governance leadership in two Norwegian city regions. *European Planning Studies* 21 (2): 115–130.

Jansson, J., and D. Power. 2006. Image of the city: Urban branding as constructed capabilities in Nordic city regions. Uppsala: Department of Social and Economic Geography, Uppsala University.

Kavaratzis, M., and G. J. Ashworth. 2005. City branding: An effective assertion of identity or a transitory marketing trick? *Tijdschrift voor Economische en Sociale Geografie* 96 (5): 506.

Kennedy, P. 2009. Living and making the branded city and its contradictions: Skilled EU migrants in Manchester. In *Branding cities: Cosmopolitanism, parochialism, and social change*, eds. S. Hemelryk Donald, E. Kofman, and C. Kevin, 59–74. New York: Routledge.

Kofman, E. 2000. The invisibility of skilled female migrants and gender relations in studies of skilled migration in Europe. *International Journal of Population Geography* 6 (1): 45–59.

Kongsberg Chamber of Commerce. 2013. Live in Kongsberg [English]. Kongsberg. Available at: https://issuu.com/knf.kongsberg.no/docs/11375_live_in_kongsberg_en6 (accessed December 2, 2015).

Kongsberg Chamber of Commerce. 2015 Technology in Kongsberg. Available at: www.kongsberg.no/en/work/technology/ (accessed November 22, 2015).

Kongsberg International School. 2013. Available at: www.kischool.org (accessed October 23, 2013).

Lewis, H. Ø. 2012. Hodejakt på utenlandske ingeniører (headhunting foreign engineers). *Aftenposten*, September 7. Available at: www.aftenposten.no/jobb/Hodejakt-pa-utenlandske-ingeniorer-6985000.html (accessed March 5, 2016).

McIntosh, L. 2014. Impossible presence: Race, nation and the cultural politics of "being Norwegian." *Ethnic and Racial Studies* 1–15. Doi 10.1080/01419870.2013.868017.

Ministry of Children and Equality. 2009. The good kindergarten is a gender equal kindergarten. Available at: www.regjeringen.no/en/dokumenter/the-good-kindergarten-is-a-gender-equal-/id102062/ (accessed March 20, 2016).

Norkirken Kongsberg. 2015. Velkommen til Norkirken Kongsberg/ Welcome to Norkirken Kongsberg. Available at: www.norkirken.kongsberg.no/ (accessed March 12, 2015).

Oftedal, E., and T. Iakovleva. 2015. Stavanger: From petroleum focus to diversified competence through crisis and consensus. In *The entrepreneurial university: Context and institutional change*, eds. L. Foss and D. V. Gibson, 221–248. Abingdon: Routledge.

Omholt, T. 2013. Developing a collective capacity for place management. *Journal of Place Management and Development* 6 (1): 29–42.

Oslo Business Region. 2015a. The Oslo Region Brand Management Strategy. Oslo: Oslo Business Region.

———. 2015b. Oslo wins "Place Brand of the Year." Available at: www.oslobusinessregion.no/news/oslo-wins-place-brand-of-the-year/ (accessed November 22, 2015).

Paganoni, M. C. 2012. City branding and social inclusion in the glocal city. *Mobilities* 7 (1): 13–31.

Peck, J. 2005. Struggling with the creative class. *International Journal of Urban and Regional Research* 29 (4): 740–770.

Raghuram, P. 2000. Gendering skilled migratory streams: Implications for conceptualising migration. *Asian and Pacific Migration Journal* 9 (4): 429–457.

Seglem, E. S. 2015. Vil lokke Google og Microsoft til Stavanger [Wants to attract Google and Microsoft to Stavanger]. *Aftenbladet* November 27.

Silvanto, S., and J. Ryan. 2014. Relocation branding: A strategic framework for attracting talent from abroad. *Journal of Global Mobility* 2 (1): 102–120.

Smith, M. P., and A. Favell. 2006. *The human face of global mobility: International highly skilled migration in Europe, North America and the Asia-Pacific*. New Brunswick, NJ: Transaction Publishers.

Stavanger Chamber of Commerce. 2014. New in the Stavanger and Haugesund Region. Stavanger: Stavanger Chamber of Commerce.

van Riemsdijk, M. 2010. Variegated privileges of whiteness: Lived experiences of Polish nurses in Norway. *Social and Cultural Geography* 11 (2): 117–137.

——— 2014. International migration and local emplacement: Everyday place-making practices of skilled migrants in Oslo, Norway. *Environment and Planning A* 46: 963–979.

——— 2015. Agents of local incorporation: Skilled migrant organizations in Oslo, Norway. In *Migrant professionals in the city: Local encounters, identities, and inequalities*, ed. L. Meier, 77–97. London: Routledge.

Wang, Q., L. Tang, and H. Li. 2014. Return migration of the highly skilled in higher education institutions: A Chinese university case. *Population, Space and Place* 21 (8): 771–787.

Wernersen, C. 2013. En hard kamp om de beste (a tough struggle over the best workers). January 29. Oslo: NRK. Available at: www.nrk.no/okonomi/norske-bedrifter-trenger-arbeidere-1.10890610 (accessed March 5, 2016).

World Economic Forum. 2012. Talent mobility good practices: Collaboration at the core of driving economic growth. Geneva: World Economic Forum.

11 Expatriate Mobility, Firm Recruitment, and Local Context

Skilled International Migration to the Rapidly Globalizing City of Dubai

Michael C. Ewers and Ryan Dicce

Introduction

On November 27, 2013, the Bureau of International Expositions held a meeting in Paris to determine the location of its quinquennial universal World Fair/Expo in 2020, ultimately awarding the honor to Dubai, United Arab Emirates (UAE). The selection represents the culmination of years of urban growth and economic development, which has positioned the city as an emerging global hub (Pacione 2005). The theme that Dubai has chosen for the Expo is "Connecting Minds, Creating the Future," which is underpinned by three drivers of global development: sustainability, mobility, and opportunity. Mobility and opportunity, in particular, seem very fitting, as the city has become a magnet for international labor migration. Urban development and skilled international migration have gone hand-in-hand in Dubai's evolution from its origins as a trade entrepôt over a century ago, through the oil boom of the 1970s and subsequent building frenzy in the 21st century (Buckley and Hanieh 2014). As such, this chapter studies the determinants of skilled international labor migration to the rapidly globalizing city of Dubai. More specifically, it describes how local specificities characterizing particular cities condition skilled international migration and global talent mobility. This is accomplished through studying how firms in Dubai formulate their hiring and recruitment strategies in response to the city's urbanization. In particular, Dubai's manifestation of the "global city" includes unique business environment characteristics and labor market dynamics that distinguish it from other global cities.

The global city literature has taught us a great deal about the importance of skilled international labor mobility as both a precursor to and an outcome of global city formation (Findlay et al. 1996). For Sassen (2001) this reflects the rise of advanced producer services as the primary economic base with globalization and structural change. In a similar light, Castells (2000) describes how global cities act as nodes and hubs for elite labor flows, embodying the spatial manifestation of the network society. The processes through which skilled workers are mobilized across international borders and incorporated in global city labor markets cannot be explained by artificially distinguishing between global processes and urban outcomes. Multinational firms (MNCs), in particular, provide "an enabling environment for the (re)production of transient professional migration in the world system" (Beaverstock and Boardwell 2000, 299). Beaverstock (2002, 2005) is an important contribution in this regard, describing the role of expatriate workers as vehicles for global knowledge transmission and active participants in reproducing agglomeration economy dynamics in international financial centers.

Yet, this literature has been less successful in accounting for the ways in which skilled labor mobility is differentially conditioned by unique local development contexts characterizing particular cities (Williams, Baláž, and Wallace 2004). As firms formulate labor market strategies in response to particular global cities, they must navigate international borders and national institutional frameworks for regulating investment, wealth redistribution, and immigration, as well as the local cultures of work and ways of doing business, which distinguish regional production systems. Moreover, paths and processes of global city formation are not uniform (Olds and Yeung 2004), and there has been criticism concerning the Western bias of broader global city research, which primarily focuses on the upper echelons of the global city hierarchy, and the failure to account for processes in world cities "beyond the West" (Robinson 2002). In emerging markets we find state regulatory frameworks that diverge from conventional varieties of capitalism and labor market dynamics that do not conform to Western-based understandings of employment, skill formation, and segmentation.

Therefore, this chapter studies the determinants of skilled international migration to Dubai by emphasizing the role of firms as key intermediaries in global human capital markets, linking migration from particular origins to particular global city destinations. It studies how firms act as agents of skilled international mobility through their international hiring and recruitment decisions, and as local labor market actors and mediators of local development outcomes. Thus, the goal is to acknowledge those geographically specific urban growth dynamics and institutional structures characterizing particular global cities as well as the more spatially expansive constellation of networks and social relations in which that city is embedded (Williams, Baláž, and Wallace 2004). This is accomplished through a survey of 103 foreign and local corporations operating in Dubai designed to elicit information on workforce structure, recruiting practices and preferences, and firm characteristics.

Global Cities and Transnational Elite Labor Mobility

Research on "global" or "world cities" has described how global city regions act as nodes and hubs through which transnational elite labor flows operate (Castells 2000; Sassen 2001). Yet, if we accept the premise that regional economies are not containers for spatial phenomena, but rather intersections of multi-scalar spaces and flows, then we must reconceptualize our treatment of labor mobility as both a driver and an outcome of urban and regional economic development (Williams, Baláž, and Wallace 2004). This includes, first, how the scale and distribution of migration flows transforms the spatial constitution of a place, and second, how particular migration flows are incorporated into the division of labor in a place. Thus, we must acknowledge those geographically specific factors characterizing individual cities, as well as a more spatially expansive constellation of networks and social relations in which that city is embedded (Williams 2009). In this regard, work on structuration theory has emphasized the importance of migration networks and channels as key institutions which link individual behaviors and societal structures as spatially stretched social relations which "articulate the individual migrant and the global economy" (Goss and Lindquist 1995, 331). Thus, it focuses on the intermediary processes, which shape—directly and indirectly—the relations between various employment processes and labor market spaces.

The social networks and relationships of international migrants, which channel and connect labor flows between specific places, condition migration practices. Building on Castells and Sassen from a global-local or translocal perspective, others have described the ways in which global cities articulate the transnational organizational and social networks of skilled migration (Smith 2001; Beaverstock 2005). Hannerz (1996) emphasizes the active role that transnational elites play in maintaining the global-urban network, and in shaping the social and cultural organization of global cities. In this sense, Hannerz underpins the nature of global cities as places as well as nodes and hubs. Similarly, Smith's (2001) conceptualization of transnational urbanism describes the ways in which migration networks, which provide social links connecting various urban locales and act as conduits through which migration takes place, are localized within translocal expatriate social spaces (Beaverstock 2005).

Global and local knowledge mobility is necessary for global cities to reproduce the agglomeration economies, which characterize international financial centers (IFCs), according to Beaverstock (2002). This reflects the skill and knowledge demand of global city financial centers and agglomeration economies, which require high levels of knowledge circulation, as well as the importance of shared local context for the transmission of tacit knowledge (Beaverstock 2002). Internal firm labor markets and knowledge networks, which are spatialized in international financial centers, stimulate expatriate mobility. Although expatriation strategies vary significantly across firms, mobilizing and overseeing global knowledge networks remains a key challenge for all of today's multinational firms (Millar and Salt 2008). The geography of international career assignments correlates with subsidiary locations, but changes over time in response to market conditions and firm strategies, reflecting the importance of some key markets or key firm units over others (Tamásy, Stringer, and Le Heron 2008). Moreover, different types of workers and professions have different mobilities, spatialities, and temporalities. Much of the current literature on expatriate labor mobility focuses on supply side dynamics—how firms manage expatriates. Three main factors have been identified to determine firm expatriate labor requirements: 1) the need to fill temporary skill gaps or supplement local skill supplies in host investment locations; 2) the deployment of highly specialized expatriate managers to initiate firm operations in new markets or expand operations in existing markets; and 3) the need for firms to develop a globe-trotting cadre of senior managers and specialists knowledge workers who can travel between subsidiaries and affiliates in multiple countries or regions (Millar and Salt 2007, 2008).

Global Cities and Local Contexts

Despite the rapid growth of the global city literature since the 1980s, significant limitations of this research agenda have been documented. The world city research agenda has been criticized for the narrow view of both the varieties of globalization and the ways in which these varieties form, transform, and maintain the global-urban network, as well as the prioritization of the global scale in exploring the spatial and functional organization of urban areas. Robinson (2002), for instance, claims that by emphasizing the concentration and connectivity of advanced producer service firms as a key proxy, analysis is limited to a narrow set of economic activities and geographic locations. The subsequent rankings of places based on such limited economic activity reproduces power relations and marginalizes cities that do not contain such activity. Moreover, by focusing on the top of the urban hierarchy, defined by Western standards and values, the research has excluded many non-Western globalizing cities and many highly international economic activities (Bassens, Derudder, and Witlox 2010).

Although there have been many contributions to our understanding of what global cities look like and the processes that are an inherent part of them, Olds and Yeung (2004) argue that there is a need to critically analyze how exactly global cities come into being. They argue that, contrary to what the literature tells us, there is not one particular form of a global city but rather a variety of global cities. In the same way, they argue that, contrary to the literature, there is no general combination of processes that lead to the creation of global cities, but that instead there are a number of different dynamic pathways. The term "globalizing cities" help expound desire to "become" and "longing" for global city status (Short 2004). Using such a perspective allows us to see how a large number of cities "act as transmission points for globalization and are the focal point for a whole nexus of globalization/localization relationships" (Short 2004, 45). The more recent literature on mobile cities explores how mobility is politicized within the confines of the city. In effect, the concept of the mobile city discards the notion of urban areas as containers for economic activity or nodes and hubs for global flows, and attempts to move beyond conceptualizing migration as the movement of people between places as these narrow paradigms confine the realm of potential analysis (Oswin and Yeoh 2010). Instead, the mobile cities literature seeks to blend the existing glut of global and world city literature with a more nuanced approach consisting of "mobility, critical migration study, transnationalism, [and] new urbanism" (Oswin and Yeoh 2010, 170).

Several authors have pointed to the need for integrating micro- and macro-level perspectives in examining the nexus of migration and labor market segmentation in global cities (Bach 2007). In particular, there has been a call for more research on the employment practices and preferences of firms as key labor market actors in order to understand the processes through which segmentation dynamics are produced and reproduced (MacKenzie and Forde 2009). Thus, studies of firm employment strategies allow us to examine "micro level processes in a wider analytical framework, which includes the broader regulatory context" (MacKenzie and Forde 2009, 155). Gordon (1995) describes how firm recruitment strategies, employment preferences and hiring practices reflect a broader allocation of particular sets of workers to particular types of jobs in a given labor market. As firms recruit workers internationally, their hiring decisions reflect the characteristic allocative processes of their local labor market. Similarly, Hermelin (2005) describes the role of organization-level recruitment practices in producing ethnically segmented labor markets in Stockholm. These practices do not emerge from thin air, but are generated in the socioeconomic context of the Stockholm region and the broader Swedish labor market. Employers are adapting their recruitment strategies to match a dynamic and evolving employment landscape, reproducing existing labor market structures as well as producing forms of segmentation. This line of research is especially germane to the rapidly globalizing urban areas of the Middle East, and in particular, the Gulf States. Often touting urbanization rates above 70 percent, the Gulf Cooperation Council (GCC) states are among the most urbanized countries in the world (United Nations Habitat 2012). The low content of local skilled labor produces a high demand for international workers. However, the influx of foreign workers has led many of these countries to institute nationalization initiatives, which increase the content of local workers and restrict access for foreign workers. As such, the cities of the GCC provide a potentially rich means of exploring the intersection of transnational firm employment networks and local institutional contexts.

Dubai Migration–Urbanization Context and Research Methods

Dubai's emergence as a global city has been characterized by a massive influx of foreign labor, first as a regional trade hub for the Middle East and South Asia, and subsequently as an outcome of oil production and related construction, and most recently, in response to labor demand associated with the city's unique global spectacle—best exemplified by the construction of buildings such as the Burj Khalifa and the man-made Palm Jumeriah. The rapid development in the emirate has witnessed a population composition shift from 38 percent foreign in the mid-1960s to 60 percent in the 1970s and 83 percent in 1998. Today, the influx of foreign labor has drastically altered the demographic landscape with 96 percent of the population being foreign born (Davidson 2008).

Regional migration literature has primarily examined the impact of highly skilled out-migration (i.e. brain drain) from the resource-poor, labor-abundant sending countries of the Middle East to the resource-rich, labor-importing Gulf or to the West (Choucri 1977; Girgis 2002). Similarly, studies of Gulf labor markets have focused on the large numbers of low-skilled construction and service workers, whose large numbers make their presence a politically delicate issue (Birks, Seccombe, and Sinclair 1986; Looney 1994; Winckler 2005). Highly skilled migrants, however, not only supplement the region's labor force, but also occupy positions of economic sensitivity and dominance as holders of vital skills—including accounting, marketing, and legal skills—which the Gulf economies cannot produce (Myusken and Nour 2006). The local populations of the Gulf States (with the exceptions of Saudi Arabia and Oman) comprise less than 20 percent of each country's total population. This, combined with an incentive scheme favoring public sector employment over private sector occupation, provides a powerful stimulant for forgoing the private sector, thereby limiting the amount of local, skilled labor (Forstenlechner and Rutledge 2010). Indeed, these migrants are the objects of the Gulf States' very open and public strategies for becoming global hubs for talent (Al-Kibsi, Benkert, and Schubert 2007). Yet, at the same time, the UAE and Dubai governments have had to figure out how to leverage the presence of expatriate workers in order to develop local capacities and capabilities. In order to meet this challenge, the UAE has employed strategies to "emiratize" key occupations and sectors, mandating local citizen content (Forstenlechner and Rutledge 2010). This includes quotas mandating a minimum content of local workers as a percentage of the total workforce for entities with more than fifty employees—2 percent for commercial firms, 4 percent for banks, and 5 percent for insurance companies (Jones 2015). In theory, these quotas set hard minimums for local content that must be accomplished; however, in practice, these quotas are loosely enforced, but companies found to be in violation of the mandates have reported issues obtaining visas for foreign workers (Jones 2015).

Data Collection and Analysis

This chapter employs data from the authors' survey of foreign and local firms currently operating in Dubai conducted in 2009. Surveys were conducted with senior human resource (HR) professionals at 103 firms (foreign n = 59; local n = 44). The strategy in selecting this particular group to complete surveys was that individuals in this occupation were most likely to have the necessary information on their firm business and workforce characteristics. The survey itself sought to elicit information concerning each firm's general business operations, workforce characteristics and composition, hiring and recruitment practices, and broader employment strategies. By gathering this information, the ultimate goal of the research was to uncover how firms condition the mobility and incorporation of skilled international workers in Dubai. The web-based survey was sent to 700 firms compiled from a database of human resource mangers in the UAE with 158 firms responding, 103 of which are based in Dubai. The gross response rate for all firms in the UAE is 22.57 percent. Following the collection of the surveys, the data was aggregated to draw out overarching themes and trends. Each response was classified as either "foreign"—meaning the respondent worked at a multinational corporation (MNC)—or "local"—meaning the respondent worked at a local firm—in order to elicit similarities and differences between firm types. Additionally, the firm level data was aggregated by nationality of workers and by profession to determine any trends linking the two factors.

Firm Business and Human Capital Internationalization

This section begins by describing the business and workforce characteristics of surveyed multinational corporations and local enterprises located in Dubai. From the survey, it is evident that many of the surveyed firms are recent arrivals in Dubai with a median year of establishment around 1997. Moreover, approximately half of the firms have arrived between 2000 and 2009. Thus, it is reasonable to assume that many of these firms are products of the development stemming from the second oil boom (1997 through 2008).

While all firms in the sample exhibit varying degrees of internationalization, the foreign firms located in Dubai tend to be more internationalized than their foreign counterparts as measured by percent of foreign ownership, international revenue, and branches. It is important to note that the foreign firms are not simply outposts of their parent company and many of them maintain a significant presence in Dubai. Additionally, both foreign and local firm workforces are highly educated with approximately 60 percent of the total workforce engaged in activities that require a university degree. The internationalization of these firms' business activities and revenue sources is also represented through their workforce characteristics. For example, foreign workers represent a large proportion of the workforces at both foreign and local firms—94 percent and 90 percent respectively. The bias toward foreign workers is further pronounced when sampling knowledge workers with Dubai-based firms reporting that foreign workers constitute an average of 96 percent of their workforce. Due to the high content of foreign workers in local firms, the internationalization of the skilled and unskilled workforce is not solely the domain of MNCs as local firms are also key drivers of international migration.

By looking at these firms' knowledge workforces more closely, we can better understand the role of firms as intermediaries linking global labor migration dynamics with local urban development processes. Figure 11.1 displays the disaggregation of knowledge workers by position and nationality. It is immediately noticeable that the content of local, Emirati workers is comparatively low across all knowledge-intensive occupations. Most significantly for this chapter, the lack of local human capital in emerging sectors presents a powerful source of demand for expatriate knowledge workers. This dearth of local human capital stems from a local preference for public sector positions due to their high wages, favorable working hours, increased job security, and fringe benefits (Randeree 2012). Similarly important, a pervasive belief among locals that work in the private sector is for foreigners prevents many potential local applicants from applying for jobs (Shah 2008). As such, the UAE imports both knowledge and labor from a variety of regions. Skilled and unskilled workers from other Gulf and Middle Eastern countries represent approximately 20 percent of the workforce in Dubai, both in total and across occupations. The high content of these workers—approximately 20 percent of the workforce in both skilled and unskilled occupations—likely reflects the historical linkages and geographic proximity, which facilitate labor mobility. Meanwhile, highly skilled workers from Europe

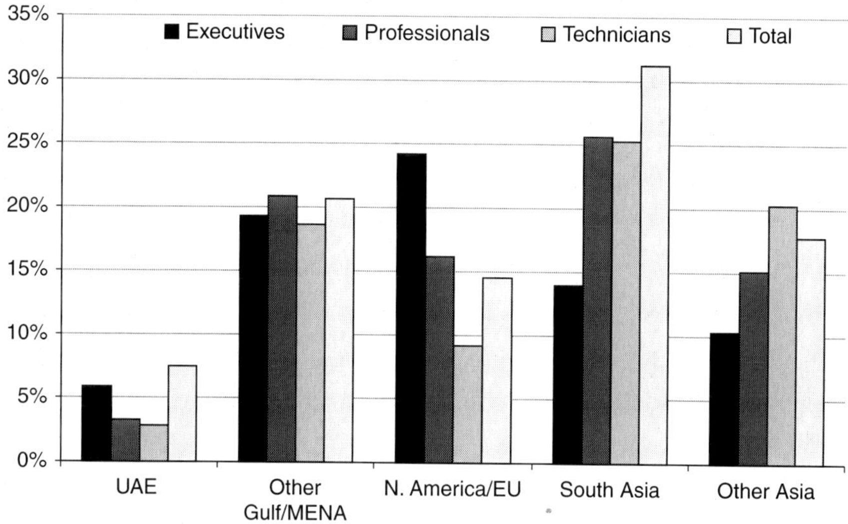

Figure 11.1 Dubai Knowledge Workers by Occupation and Nationality (total firms)

and North America were instrumental to the emirate's spectacular economic growth during the first oil boom. More recently, the increasingly regional and international profile of the city has created a powerful demand for jobs, which acts as a pull function, further stimulating the influx of North American and European firms and workers. These workers represent the highest proportion (nearly 25 percent) of executives and managers, but are less represented in the professional and technical categories as these occupations are sourced from elsewhere—primarily South and Southeast Asia—at a lower cost. As described above, firms utilize expatriation as a tool to manage operations across their international affiliates and subsidiaries. Many of the surveyed firms are North American or European in origin, and thus may use expatriation as an attempt to reproduce the culture of their parent corporation abroad (Faulconbridge 2008). In contrast, South Asian and other Asian workers are much less likely to be found in managerial occupations but possess the highest proportions of workers in professional and technical occupations as they provide the necessary skills at lower wage costs. Presenting firm workforces in this light helps elucidate the matching of workers from certain nationalities with certain occupations, reflecting the migrant division of labor in the UAE (Mohammad and Sidaway 2012).

Firm Recruitment Practices and Preferences

The previous section discussed patterns of workforce internationalization and localization among foreign and local non-oil firms in Dubai. First, the results from the previous section show that, while the business activities and workforces of foreign firms are more internationalized, the workforces of all firms remain dominated by foreign workers, regardless of occupation. Second, workforces of foreign and local firms mirror local labor market dynamics and the institutional context of the city, which differentially eases and restricts access to the city's labor market through nationalization schemes and visa availability. While some firms have more internationalized workforces than others, all firms share similar preferences of nationality and occupation, only some more exaggerated than others.

To better understand how firm preferences and recruitment methods stimulate flows of skilled international labor migration to Dubai, firms were asked about positions for which they almost always search locally (within the Gulf) versus internationally (outside the Gulf).[1] These questions were designed to ascertain which occupations could be filled locally or which occupations required recruitment outside the Gulf region. Considering that many of these firms have workforces that are over 90 percent foreign, it could be reasonably expected that firm responses would have a significant bias towards hiring internationally; however, this is not the case. The survey gathered information on firm strategies for filling vacancies for executive, professional, engineer, IT, sales, and clerical fields. Our results indicate that for the highest level positions (executives, professionals, and engineers), firms tend to search equally for talent, both locally and internationally. Meanwhile, these same firms are much more likely to recruit locally for the remaining service-oriented or lower skill occupations. For example, while companies reported hiring professionals both internationally and locally (approximately 50 percent each), they disproportionately reported hiring individuals locally for clerical work (approximately 65 percent). At first glance, this appears to contradict the finding that firms almost always hired foreign workers, especially with respect to high-skilled labor; however, the subsequent survey findings help to elucidate this apparent discrepancy.

Surveyed firms were questioned about their main methods of recruitment for high-skilled positions. As described above, much of the literature on highly skilled labor migration emphasizes the role of multinational firms in mobilizing skilled international workers through their internal labor markets. Yet, from the firms surveyed here, it is evident that "placement from foreign headquarters" is rarely chosen as the main method of recruitment (only 25 percent of firms selected this option). Instead, the vast majority of recruitment decisions seem to be made through extra-firm networks, including recruitment agencies (70 percent of firms), employee networks (60 percent of firms), and the Internet (55 percent of firms). This contrasts the majority of studies on the role of firms in skilled international labor mobility, which often emphasize MNC employment via direct investment and internal firm labor markets as the key channels of migration (see, for example, Millar and Salt 2008). As such, it reinforces more recent literature describing the role of recruitment agencies, including executive search firms, as key intermediaries connecting global city destinations with skilled workers in sending country labor markets (Beaverstock, Faulconbridge, and Hall 2010). These actors condition knowledge mobility to and incorporation in the Dubai labor market, channeling international workers, connecting the UAE to sending countries, and in reproducing local labor market dynamics.

This point raises a few important questions in light of the survey workforce data presented. Where are foreign knowledge workers coming from, if not from other international firms or foreign branches of their Gulf employer? Moreover, why is it that firms reported recruiting locally for knowledge workers almost as much as internationally, even though the composition of these workers remained largely foreign? Through a combination of the previous discussion on methods of recruitment and survey responses concerning the main sources of new hiring for positions that require at least a university degree, we can better understand contradictions described above. Other international companies provide a significant source of these new hires for both multinational firms and local firms—50 percent and 45 percent respectively. More interestingly, however, the main source of new employees for both types of firms is other companies in the UAE (over 60 percent of multinational firms and 55 percent of local firms). Additionally, neither foreign nor local firms highlighted universities (international or local) as significant sources of hires. As such, the majority of the "local" hiring stems from expatriate knowledge workers who are circulating locally among multiple foreign and local companies. This finding speaks to recent research on the agency of expatriate workers as preference-seeking individuals who are responsible for their mobility and settlement decisions, and as key local development actors who transfer tacit knowledge to local workers through their interactions in global cities (Al-Ariss and Syed 2011; Ho 2011). The shift in the global economy toward a more knowledge-intensive production process has created a less secure working environment. As such, workers overall, regardless of skill level, must be more flexible in changing employer or moving to new locations within firm internal labor markets in order to obtain occupational mobility. Therefore, the most qualified workers perceive spatial mobility as a preferred outcome, as something that permits a rewarding lifestyle and new experiences (Findlay et al. 2009). In a broader sense, these findings relate to the potential significance of secondary spatial and occupational mobility that follows as a result of a primary, international migration decision (see Chapter 4). The resulting patterns of cumulative causation, whereby contemporary migration processes build on previous rounds of migration, are ultimately responsible for the longer term evolution of settlement in a city (Findlay et al. 2009; Storper and Scott 2009).

Despite the emphasis on foreign workers and experience as the key determinants of hiring in the UAE and as a salient feature of Dubai's migrant division of labor, the survey findings presented an alternative interpretation of the employment preferences that ultimately influence migration outcomes. Regardless of firm type, respondents overwhelmingly highlighted the importance of local Gulf work experience as the most important factor when hiring someone for a position requiring a university degree (almost 90 percent of both local and foreign firms). In this way, local Gulf experience represents the importance of local context as well as a barrier to entry (Ewers 2013). Indeed, like the Asian labor markets, it is difficult to gain entry to Gulf labor markets; however, once this barrier is overcome, individuals have more flexibility and are able to move around. Thus, context-specific labor market demands help to determine skilled migration processes but also facilitate local and regional labor market mobility. Another important factor concerns the level of international experience for potential workers. Both foreign and local firms highlighted the importance of this experience as a key requirement when hiring skilled workers (57 percent of foreign firms and 52 percent of local firms). The preference for workers with international experience speaks both to the availability and types of jobs available in the city, as well as its increasingly global nature.

Conclusion

How do the local specificities of particular global cities influence skilled international labor mobility? This chapter attempted to provide one answer to this question by examining how local and foreign firms located in the rapidly globalizing city of Dubai formulate their hiring and recruitment strategies in response to that city's local context. The study made two key findings.

First, the employment practices of the surveyed firms were substantially influenced by place-specific urban developments, local labor market conditions and the city's unique pathway of global city formation. For example, the low levels of local, Emirati human capital in highly skilled jobs serves as a powerful source of demand for skilled international workers; the relative economic success and political stability of Dubai in the context of a faltering Middle East environment, which is highly dependent on the volatile nature of oil prices and reeling from the recent unrest of the so-called Arab Spring, make the city a key regional destination for knowledge workers; the influx of foreign investment which has accompanied the construction frenzy in Dubai has attracted flows of European and North American managers and executives as part of multinational enterprises. We feel that these findings also reinforce the significant, and indeed unique, role that firms play as vehicles for global talent mobility and as tools for migration research.

Second, and contrary to our initial assumptions, the hiring and recruitment practices of these firms showed that migrant workers, both individually and collectively, influenced international migration processes and local employment outcomes far more than the companies themselves. This reflects "middling transnationalism" in which a broader range of workers and occupations participate in global labor market mobility, but also the agency of these workers in making migration and employment decisions (Conradson and Latham 2005). Under current regulations, entry to Gulf labor markets remains heavily restricted. These include both access to visas and the linkage between visas and employment, as well as nationalization schemes mandating a local content of citizens in key industries. Thus, it is difficult for workers to participate in the local labor markets of the region's dynamic economies. Therefore, firms present a means of market entry, acting as conduits for migration through their ability to grant local work visas, which individual workers cannot obtain on their own. Once workers gain sponsorship and entry to the Gulf, secondary mobility within its regional and local labor markets is much easier as workers can seek out better employment options.

Finally, the results presented in this chapter also have implications for future research on skilled international migration to (especially non-Western) global cities. In particular, and echoing the findings of van Riemsdijk (2014), we need to further examine how skilled international workers are incorporated into host societies. While researchers have examined these processes from the perspective of undocumented migrants and guest workers, skilled migrants are also involved in related experiences of integration and belonging as they settle in destination cities.

Note

1. According to Figure 11.1, fewer than 8 eight percent of individuals employed at surveyed firms are nationals. As such, this question sought to examine where individuals hired in Dubai were last employed. In this way, those hired locally could be either a citizen or an expat hired from a different local firm. Similarly, those hired internationally could be a citizen who previously worked abroad or a foreigner who is entering the region for work.

References

Al Ariss, A., and J. Syed. 2011. Capital mobilization of skilled migrants: A relational perspective. *British Journal of Management* 22: 286–304.

Al-Kibsi G., C. Benkert, and J. Schubert. 2007. Getting labor policy to work in the Gulf. *The McKinsey Quarterly Special Edition: Reappraising the Gulf States,* 1–29.

Bach, S. 2007. Going global? The regulation of nurse migration in the UK. *British Journal of Industrial Relations* 45: 383–403.

Bassens, D., B. Derudder, and F. Witlox. 2010. Searching for the Mecca of finance: Islamic financial services and the world city network. *Area* 42: 35–46.

Beaverstock, J. 2005. Transnational elites in the city: British highly-skilled inter-company transferees in New York city's financial district. *Journal of Ethnic and Migration Studies* 31: 245–268.

Beaverstock, J. V. 2002. Transnational elites in global cities: British expatriates in Singapore's financial district. *Geoforum* 33(4): 525–538.

Beaverstock, J. V., and J. T. Boardwell. 2000. Negotiating globalization, transnational corporations and global city financial centres in transient migration studies. *Applied Geography* 20: 277–304.

Beaverstock, J. V., J. R. Faulconbridge, and S. J. E. Hall. 2010. Professionalization, legitimization and the creation of executive search markets in Europe. *Journal of Economic Geography* 10: 825–843.

Birks, J. S., I. J. Seccombe, and C. A. Sinclair. 1986. Migrant workers in the Arab Gulf: The impact of declining oil revenues. *International Migration Review*: 799–814.

Buckley, M., and A. Hanieh. 2014. Diversification by urbanization: Tracing the property-finance Nexus in Dubai and the Gulf. *International Journal of Urban and Regional Research* 38: 155–175.

Castells, M. 2000. *The rise of the network society.* Chichester: Blackwell Publishing.

Choucri, N. 1977. The new migration in the Middle East: A problem for whom? *International Migration Review* 421–443.

Conradson, D., and A. Latham. 2005. Transnational urbanism: Attending to everyday practices and mobilities. *Journal of Ethnic and Migration Studies* 31: 227–233.

Davidson, C. M. 2008. *Dubai: The vulnerability of success.* New York: Columbia University Press.

Ewers, M. C. 2013. From knowledge transfer to learning: The acquisition and assimilation of human capital in the United Arab Emirates and the other Gulf States. *Geoforum* 46: 124–137.

Faulconbridge, J. R. 2008. Negotiating cultures of work in transnational law firms. *Journal of Economic Geography* 8: 497–517.

Findlay, A., C. Mason, D. Houston, D. McCollum, and R. Harrison. 2009. Escalators, elevators and travelators: The occupational mobility of migrants to South-East England. *Journal of Ethnic and Migration Studies* 35: 861–879.

Findlay, A. M., F. L. N. Li, A. J. Jowett, and R. Skeldon. 1996. Skilled international migration and the global city: A study of expatriates in Hong Kong. *Transactions of the Institute of British Geographers* 21: 49–61.

Forstenlechner, I., and E. Rutledge. 2010. Unemployment in the Gulf: Time to update the "social contract." *Middle East Policy* 17: 38–51.

Girgis, M. 2002. Would nationals and Asians replace Arab workers in the GCC? Draft paper submitted to the Fourth Mediterranean Development Forum, Amman, Jordan.

Gordon, I. 1995. Migration in a segmented labour market. *Transactions of the Institute of British Geographers* 20: 139–155.

Goss, J., and B. Lindquist. 1995. Conceptualizing international labor migration: A structuration perspective. *International Migration Review* 29: 317–351.

Hannerz, U. 1996. Transnational connections: Culture, people, places. London: Routledge.

Hermelin, B. 2005. Recruitment procedures in the construction of labour market relations the ethnic divide in Sweden. *Geografiska Annaler: Series B, Human Geography* 87: 225–236.

Ho, E. L. E. 2011. Migration trajectories of 'highly skilled' middling transnationals: Singaporean transmigrants in London. *Population, Space and Place* 17: 116–129.

Jones, N. 2015. Emiratisation: A recap. Available at: www.tamimi.com/en/magazine/law-update/section-11/april-8/emiratisation-a-recap.html (accessed March 2, 2016).

Looney, R. E. 1994. *Manpower policies and development in the Persian gulf region.* Westport, CT: Praeger.

MacKenzie, R., and C. Forde. 2009. The rhetoric of the 'good worker' versus the realities of employers' use and the experiences of migrant workers. *Work, Employment and Society* 23: 142–159.

Millar, J., and J. Salt. 2007. In whose interests? IT migration in an interconnected world economy. *Population, Space and Place* 13: 41–58.

———. 2008. Portfolios of mobility: The movement of expertise in transnational corporations in two sectors—aerospace and extractive industries. *Global Networks* 8: 25–50.

Mohammad, R., and J. D. Sidaway. 2012. Spectacular urbanization amidst variegated geographies of globalization: Learning from Abu Dhabi's trajectory through the lives of South Asian men. *International Journal of Urban and Regional Research* 36: 606–627.

Muysken, J., and S. Nour. 2006. Deficiencies in education and poor prospects for economic growth in the Gulf countries: The case of the UAE. *The Journal of Development Studies* 42: 957–980.

Olds, K., and H. W. C. Yeung. 2004. Pathways to global city formation: A view from the developmental city-state of Singapore. *Review of International Political Economy* 11 (3): 489–521.

Oswin, N., and B. S. A. Yeoh. 2010. Introduction: Mobile city Singapore. *Mobilities* 5: 167–175.

Pacione, M. J. 2005. Dubai. *Cities* 22: 255–265.

Randeree, K. 2012. Workforce nationalization in the Gulf Cooperation Council States. *Center for International and Regional Studies*. Doha: Georgetown University School of Foreign Service in Qatar.

Robinson, J. 2002. Global and world cities: A view from off the map. *International Journal of Urban and Regional Research* 26: 531–554.

Sassen, S. 2001 *The global city: New York, London, Tokyo*. 2nd ed. Princeton, NJ: Princeton University Press.

Shah, N. M. 2008. Recent labor immigration policies in the oil-rich gulf: How effective are they likely to be? *ILO Asian Regional Programme on Governance of Labour Migration*. Available at: http://digitalcommons.ilr.cornell.edu/intl/52 (accessed March 2, 2016).

Short, J. R. 2004. *Global metropolitan: Globalizing cities in a capitalist world*. London: Routledge.

Smith, M. P. 2001. *Transnational urbanism: Locating globalization,* Malden, MA: Blackwell Publishers.

Storper, M., and A. J. Scott. 2009. Rethinking human capital, creativity and urban growth. *Journal of Economic Geography* 9: 147–167.

Tamásy, C., C. Stringer, and R. B. Le Heron. 2008. Knowledge transfer in a globalising world economy: Fonterra's management of its mobile work force. *Geographische Zeitschrift* 96: 140–157.

United Nations Habitat. 2012. *The state of Arab cities: Challenges of urban transitions,* 2nd ed. United Nations Human Settlements Programme (UN-Habitat).

van Riemsdijk, M. 2014. International migration and local emplacement: Everyday place-making practices of skilled migrants in Oslo, Norway. *Environment and Planning A* 46: 973–979.

Williams, A. M. 2009. International migration, uneven regional development and polarization. *European Urban and Regional Studies* 16: 309–322.

Williams, A. M., V. Baláž, and C. Wallace. 2004. International labour mobility and uneven regional development in Europe. *European Urban and Regional Studies* 11: 27–46.

Winckler, O. 2005. *Arab political demography,* Portland, OR: Sussex Academic Press.

Part III

Transnational Lives and Return Migration

12 Exodus, Circulation, and Return

Movements of High-skilled Migrants from India in a Transnational Era

Elizabeth Chacko

International migration, particularly over long distances and to developed countries, was once considered to be unidirectional (Gmelch 1980), and the migrants involved as having "no 'home' to go back to" (Hall 1987, 44). The "myth of return" referenced the idea that immigrants usually stayed on permanently in the receiving country even when their stated intention was to return to the country of origin. Traditionally, return migration was not considered a deliberate and intentional move on the part of successful migrants. However, the movements of migrants and immigrants are now recognized as having multiple directions, including that of return.

Return migration is gaining acknowledgment as a phenomenon that has critical implications for individuals, communities, cities, regions, and countries. The movements of skilled migrants, a subset of the more than 230 million people (UN-OECD 2013) crossing international boundaries annually may be viewed as the migration of persons with specialized training, skill sets, and experience in response to economic, sociocultural, and sometimes, political imperatives. While the predicted movements of the highly skilled are still from less developed to more developed countries (MDCs), often with the expectation of settling in the MDC, these migrants also participate in South–South migration, circular/pendulum migration, and return migration to the origin countries.

In this chapter, I examine the multifaceted nature of the reverse migration of first-generation skilled migrants from India. I argue that the type of moves that these skilled international migrants make, the duration of their stay in receiving countries, and return to the countries or cities of origin can be voluntary or involuntary and is context driven, taking place due to multiple, interlinked reasons. I analyze voluntary and involuntary return within the framework of the life course of the migrants and also examine the roles of space and place in the intention to return, actual return, and experiences of return of skilled migrants to the sending country of India.

This study underscores the idea that migration decisions and experiences for even the highly skilled returnees, who have greater agency than their low-skilled counterparts, are not driven merely by economic reasons, but are anchored in place. Neoclassical migration theory, assimilation theory, disappointment theory, target income, and new economics of labor migration theory all view return migration through an economic lens and explain the return of the highly skilled to the sending country as an outcome of economic imperatives and maximization of utility. This chapter urges a rethinking of theoretical perspectives on skilled migration through its addition and emphasis on place as a critical aspect that influences return intent and practice of the high skilled to their countries of birth.

The desire to stay or leave for high skilled migrants is colored by beliefs, attitudes, and perceptions held about place as well as attachments to it. High-skilled migrants wish to build their lives in places that are meaningful to them due to the presence of opportunities, support systems, and a sense of being "in place." However, as this chapter demonstrates, even the highly skilled who are drawn to countries and locales where they feel they could reach the acme of their personal and professional potential while feeling included and "in place" may be hampered by more mundane aspects of a place such as its immigration policies and laws.

Methods Used

This chapter is based on ongoing research that aims to delve into the sociocultural, economic, and political relationships that immigrants from India have with sending and receiving countries, and how these are manifested in processes and practices of adjustment, identity, and belonging. It draws on narratives of intended return and experiences of actual return provided by India-born skilled migrants who had worked and lived in the United States, the United Kingdom, Australia, Malaysia, and Singapore (all countries with sizable Asian Indian immigrant populations) for periods varying from six months to over two decades.

In this chapter I use data from three separate studies: in 2005–2006 I interviewed fifteen Asian Indian migrants who had lived in the United States, the United Kingdom, and Australia, who had moved back to India and were living in the high-tech cities of Bangalore and Hyderabad; in 2007 I conducted in-depth interviews with ten Indian engineers who were employed on either short- or long-term contracts in the Malaysian city of Cyberjaya, and in 2013 I interviewed twenty high-skilled Indian professionals who were working in Singapore, seven of whom reported that their plan was to return to India. I also refer to the case of a physician returnee whom I had interviewed for a study on medical tourism in Kerala, India. I used semi-structured interviews to understand the migrants' reasons for intended return or return, and the thoughts and feelings that attended their experiences as returnees to the homeland. I supplement data from these interviews with published reports of successful return migrants.

Reverse Migration of High-skilled Migrants: Reasons for Return

Neoclassical migration theory posits that return migration occurs due to a failure to integrate and thrive in the society of the destination country. This interpretation is in line with classical immigrant assimilation theory, according to which immigrants are expected to gradually assimilate into the receiving society and concomitantly decrease their social and economic ties with the sending country (Castles and Miller 2003). Assimilation is viewed as the end goal for immigrants, whose interests lie in being fully integrated and accepted in the receiving society.

Several theories offer economic factors as the primary reasons for return. For example, according to the disappointment theory, individuals return to their countries of origin because of their failure to achieve success in the destination country (Borjas and Bratsberg 1996). The target income theory suggests that economic immigrants emigrate in the hope of accruing a certain amount of wealth and once this target has been met, they return home (Massey et al. 1993; Borjas 1994). Return migration would therefore appear be the logical next step for individual migrants who have gained knowledge and skill sets as well as amassed assets that could be invested in their places of origin when these present new opportunities and offer the highest returns on their human capital (Bauer and Zimmerman 1998).

According to the new economics of labor migration, labor outmigration (especially from developing countries) is not an individual's decision but rather a family or household livelihood strategy to send the most suitable individuals away to earn an income. The money these persons remit to the household is used to improve living conditions, make investments and also reduce risks (Stark 1991). When motives for return are viewed through the lens of the new economics of labor migration as well, migrants are likely to return to their country of origin once their goals of accruing sufficient financial capital to make investments in the sending country have been met.

Educational levels could play a role in intention to return, as Carling and Pettersen (2014) demonstrate in their study of migrants in Norway. They note that people with very low or very high levels of education are the least likely to intend to return but that these intentions are shaped by the migrants' relative degree of attachment to their country of origin and country of residence. While the authors do not explain why migrants with mid-level education are more likely to wish to return, it is possible that several factors including wage compression in Norway, greater parity between income and cost of living in India and Norway for this group and even opportunities in India could play important roles. An economic downturn in the receiving country with consequent loss or diminishing paid employment can act as a push factor, causing migrants to return, while economic opportunities, higher wages, and a better standard of living in the sending country might act as pull factors, luring the diaspora back home.

However, maximizing utility need not be the primary objective for immigrants. Even among immigrants who have achieved economic success, perceived discrimination at work and halting career advancement as well as inequities in wages and upward mobility vis-à-vis the dominant majority can act as incentives to leave (Wong et al. 1998; Tang 2000; Woo 2000). Continued strong emotional and cultural ties can also possibly pave the way for return migration (Siar 2014).

King (2000) conceptualized return migration using temporal descriptors such as occasional return, seasonal return, temporary return, permanent return, and circular return. The reasons he provided for the return of international migrants to their country of origin included a failure to become acculturated and assimilated in the host/destination country, lack of success and the achievement of the desired financial status in the receiving country, as well as desire to be a positive agent of change through innovation and service in the country of birth. Constant and Massey (2002) and Fokkema and de Haas (2011) note that there is no uniformity to the processes of return migration and that competing explanations for return intentions and actual return are complementary in nature, and vary within and between different immigrant groups and across different space and time contexts.

Most of the explanations provided above for return focus on the individual migrant and his/her family, underscoring the importance of agency (the capacity of individuals to freely and independently make choices) in migration across international borders. While the voluntary return migration of skilled professionals is likely to be due to a desire to come back to live and work in their country of birth, the roles played by national migration policies, the needs of both sending and receiving countries and their attributes as places should also be taken into consideration. The influence of structure on reverse migration of the highly skilled may be seen in migration policies that aim to encourage this segment of the diaspora to return. In recent years some country governments have tried to bring back skilled members of their diaporas, especially those with qualifications and experiences that would directly contribute to origin country development in areas varying from healthcare and tertiary education to science and technology.

For example, return migration of skilled professionals is increasingly facilitated by the Chinese government's global talent recruitment programs. China incentivized the return of overseas talent starting in the mid-1990s by providing returnees with financial aid and various privileges. Hoping to draw skilled professionals who could engage in innovative research, the Chinese government initiated programs such as the Hundred Talents (see Chapter 14), the National Science Fund for Distinguished Young Scholars, and the Cheung Kong Scholars Program, easing return via long-term multiple-entry visas, and by offering personal and professional rewards. Furthermore, a National Medium and Long-Term Talent Development Plan was launched in 2010 with the intention of attracting highly skilled expatriates to live and work in China for significant periods of time. The success of these programs may be seen in the statistics: a China Organization and Human Resources Report notes that the number of high-skill returnees increased exponentially from 69,300 in 2008 to some 800,000 in 2013 (Wang, Tang, and Li, 2014; Salvino 2015).

Multilateral organizations often collaborate with country governments to facilitate the return of skilled expatriates. Agencies such as the International Organization for Migration (IOM) have capacity-building programs such as Return of Qualified African Nationals (RQAN) and later, Migration for Development in Africa (MIDA), that are endorsed not just by country governments but by pan-African entities such as the Organization for the African Unity (IOM 2009). Under the RQAN scheme, begun in 1983, IOM facilitated the return migration of over 2,000 skilled professionals to the African countries from which they hailed (Haidara 2013). Individual country governments, such as those of Nigeria, Ghana, and Kenya, all of which have substantial numbers in the diaspora in the MDCs too have put in place policies to encourage professional expatriates to return to live, work, and invest in their native lands. Governments have created special units to oversee and promote diaspora activities and return, allowed those who had become citizens of other countries to adopt dual citizenship and established funds to facilitate diaspora investment and return (Black, Crush, and Peberdy 2006; Wong, 2014). In addition to using economic factors and theories to analyze and understand reverse migration, this study will also investigate the role played by place in the return migration of high-skilled migrants to India.

The Exodus and Return of High-skilled Migrants from India

Among the push factors that drive highly skilled labor from less developed countries (LDCs) including India, to engage in international labor migration are under- and unemployment among highly educated persons, relatively low wages, cronyism, and the lack of promotion opportunities within a system based on meritocracy (Iravani 2011). The promise of a materially superior lifestyle, and better professional and other opportunities for themselves and their children in a globalized world are also factors that drive outmigration.

In 2014, there were approximately five million Indian citizens working outside the home country, and over 800,000 emigration clearances were granted in that year for workers going overseas. More than 90 percent of India's migrant labor is to the Persian Gulf countries and South East Asia as temporary workers who expect to return to India after their contractual obligations have been fulfilled (MOIA 2014). While guest workers to Asian countries comprise largely of unskilled and semi-skilled labor, there is also a significant number of high-skilled workers in this regional flow.

In the 1960s and 1970s, India began losing her highly educated professionals through a process known as "brain drain." Engineers, medical doctors, and scientists left for the United States, Canada, the United Kingdom, Australia, and other MDCs, drawn by the opportunities for professional advancement and a better standard of living in the developed countries. However, in the 1980s the rhetoric of brain drain was replaced by that of the "brain bank"—i.e. a store of human capital abroad that could be drawn upon as needed (Khadria 2008). During the decade of the 1980s and continuing into current times, Indian IT professionals were brought to the United States on short-term contracts to develop software, a practice known as "body shopping."

In the late 1990s, even greater numbers of information technology professionals from Asia (among them thousands of Indian software engineers) were brought to the United States to avert the expected Y2K crisis (van der Veer 2005). But even those who had obtained coveted work visas were on limited-time contracts. In the aftermath of Y2K and the economic recession that followed, many of these technology professionals lost their H-1B (work) contracts and therefore their right to stay in the United States and had to return to India. Luckily, this coincided with the opening of jobs in India, as the country became an important locale for Business Process Outsourcing (BPO) operations (Khadria, 2008). The reverse flow of high skilled migrants to India is relatively small in comparison with the outflow. Only some 25,000 IT professionals returned to India between 2000 and 2004 after working abroad (Nasscom-McKinsey Report 2005), while during 2004 alone some 38,443 persons from India were admitted to the United States on employment-based preferences (US-DHS 2006). In 2013, Indian nationals who entered the USA on employment-based visas numbered 35,720 and accounted for 52 percent of all admissions from India that year (US-DHS 2014).

Particularly after the liberalization of the Indian economy in 2000, the Indian government attempted to promote an ethnic identity among the diaspora by facilitating the solidification of sociocultural and economic ties to the ancestral homeland (MOIA 2015). A Ministry of Overseas Indian Affairs was constituted in 2004 and soon thereafter the Overseas Citizenship of India (OCI) program was instituted. Although India does not permit dual citizenship, persons who were born in India and had once held Indian citizenship could acquire OCI status. Holders of the OCI enjoy many of the benefits of Indian citizenship with the exception of voting rights, the right to stand for political office, and the ability to buy agricultural property. The OCI is for life, and allows holders to enter India at will and the length of their stay in the country is not restricted as it is for other foreign nationals.

In the twenty-first century the notion of returning high-skilled emigrants as constituting "brain gain" and "brain circulation" began to hold greater sway in India. Concomitantly, the advent of globalization and improved transportation systems and communication technologies helped international migration become more transnational in nature. Transnationalism is the phenomenon that allows immigrants to forge and maintain multiple linkages simultaneously that connect them with societies in their countries of origin and settlement (Schiller, Basch, and Blanc 1995). The ties that are engendered through transnationalism include those forged between and among people, institutions, organizations, and networks. Within the transnational framework, movements between country of origin and that of settlement are fluid and continuous rather than terminal and permanent (Ley and Kobayashi 2005).

The return of skilled professionals trained in engineering, science, finance, medicine, accounting and others with advanced and specialized degrees represent a potential resource for the accelerated socioeconomic development of the home country, boosting its economic growth and enhancing its competitiveness in an increasingly globalized world. In a study that involved Asian Indian high-skill immigrants in the United States, the primary reason provided by this group for a hypothetical return to India was for professional advancement and career opportunities (Harvey 2009). In his study of 10,000 Silicon Valley engineers who were members of local Chinese and Indian associations, Dossani (2002) found that younger Asian Indian engineers (aged 26–35 years) at 53 percent were more likely to return than their counterparts over 35 years of age (34 percent). The predominant stated purpose (76 percent) for return was to start their own firm or enterprise. There was also a place component to their return; while many preferred to return to their home states or cities, there was a strong preference for establishing a new firm or joining an established one in Bangalore, acknowledged as India's premier IT city. However, even for these returnees, there was usually a list of experiences and achievements that they hoped to check off during their sojourn abroad. Chief among these items was an advanced academic degree and work experience.

Involuntary and Voluntary Return of High-skilled Migrants to India

Approximately 3.4 million Indian migrants over the age of 15 years lived in the OECD countries during 2010–2011 and of this population, 2.1 million were considered highly educated, evidence of the preponderance of the highly skilled among inflows from India to these countries (UN-OECD 2013). The return of members of this group can be involuntary, necessitated by immigration policies and lack of employment opportunities, or a deliberate and voluntary act, due to reasons that span the personal to the professional. The motivations and experiences of these two sets of returnees will now be examined in greater detail.

Involuntary Return

The primary reasons for the migration of young people from India to developed countries are for tertiary education, employment and the better working conditions, higher incomes and superior lifestyles that these countries offered. Lifestyles are usually understood as being largely shaped by the consumption of certain goods and services as well as shared practices and experiences that provide the foundation for meaning and identity (Featherstone 1987; Chaney 1996). Stebbins (1997) notes that lifestyles encompass related sets of values and attitudes and comprise tangible practices and orientations that form the basis of a common identity. Lifestyle migration is usually considered to be the movement of relatively privileged individuals to places that are meaningful to them and that offer the possibility of a better quality of life.

Often seen as an "anti-modern, escapist, self-realization project" that responds to changing circumstances that are viewed and experienced unfavorably, lifestyle migration is regarded as the search for an imagined good life in a different locale (O'Reilly and Benson 2009, 1). Scholars who have explored the intersections of migration and lifestyle note that regardless of whether the migrants are young people in search of an alternative lifestyle or retirees pursuing a simpler life in a more pleasant climate (O'Reilly and Benson 2009), such movements need not be permanent and can be for the short or long term. Changing immigration policies that curtail the length of stay abroad and escalating or unexpected costs in the country of settlement may necessitate a return to the country of origin.

The migration of students earning advanced degrees abroad can be seen as a precursor of skilled labor migration, as students may view international education as a stepping-stone to short-term or long-term jobs in the receiving country (Ivancheva 2007). Several developed countries, among them the United States, Canada, and Australia, have recently put in place policies to recruit international students studying in the country's educational institutions to stay on as skilled workers after completing their degrees. In 2008, Canada launched the Canadian Experience Class program, a formal policy initiative aimed to attract talented foreign students specializing in fields that are integral to increasingly knowledge-sector driven global and national economies to Canada and retain them as part of the Canadian workforce (Government of Canada 2015). Between 1997 and 2013, 24,106 student visas were granted to Indian nationals to study in the United States, accounting for 8.2 percent of all global student visas.

In the United States, students can stay on after the optional practical training (OPT) only if they can obtain a sponsor and an H-1B (employment) visa. Indian nationals accounted for a sizable number (74,078) and large share (46 percent) of all H-1B visas granted between 1997 and 2003, an indication that a high proportion of students probably transition from F-1 student visas to H-1B work visas (USCIS 2013). However, many others have to return to India if they cannot find sponsors. This essentially forced return can be a problem for students who had hoped to work in the degree-granting country, gaining experience and also earning money to help defray some of the costs of their international education.

Geographers note that place has location as well as meaning (Tuan 1974; Cresswell 2004). Linkages between place and particular meanings and their associated practices and identities lead to the construction of normative places, where persons can be "in place" or "out of place" (Cresswell 2004). The desire to stay on in the MDC is not just based in pragmatism, but also a strong sense of feeling for the high-skilled immigrant that s/he is "in place" in terms of life trajectory and career path in the MDC. Involuntary return, often necessitated by a change in legal status or the lack or loss of a job, shifts the high-skilled migrant from being "in place" to "out of place." While the highly skilled individual who has the legal right to work in an MDC is usually considered a valuable contributor to the economy and development of the nation, those who are "out of place" are seen as expendable.

However, forced return can sometimes be a boon for both the returning trained student and India, the sending country. Wadhwa (2014) highlights the case of Kunal Bahl, who, on graduating from an Ivy League university, wished to start his own enterprise in the United States, but could not do so due to visa issues. Forced to return to India, he started Snapdeal, a company similar to Groupon in the United States, later expanding it to become an online merchandiser selling goods obtained from 50,000 merchants to over 25 million customers. The India-based Bahl is actively investigating US companies that he could acquire. His success demonstrates that even though the United States is characterized as a land of opportunity and Silicon Valley, the place typically associated with start-ups, entrepreneurs can use their technical expertise and knowledge of home country cultures and markets to launch successful start-ups there as well, complicating the notion that new IT-based enterprises necessarily begin in locales in the MDCs.

Even attaining the status of a permanent resident after working for several years on the H-1B visa does not offer protection against involuntary return to the country of origin for Asian Indians. As the US economy began its slump in the early 2000s, many were laid off, and despite their skill sets could not find work in their fields of expertise. Dinesh (age 35) had an MBA from a prestigious American university, obtained the coveted green card that signaled his status as a permanent resident and was working as a financial analyst when he was laid off by his firm. Hoping to find another job, he sent his résumé to multiple employers and used his social and professional networks to identify suitable openings. After six months without work, his savings depleted and anxious not to have to resort to unemployment benefits, Dinesh reluctantly decided to return to India with his wife and toddler son.

Although he obtained a fairly well-paid position in his hometown of Hyderabad, when I interviewed him, Dinesh's aim was to return to the United States, which he did after working for four years in Hyderabad. Dinesh's involuntary return to India was tinted with financial hardship, forfeiture of his status as a successful NRI[1] and possible loss of face as someone who had to depend on the dole to survive. His unanticipated departure from the United States was not the triumphal return often associated with the high skilled who come back to their country of birth with offers of a high-status job or plans to start their own company.

The notion of belonging as it relates to immigrants has been associated with identity in its various forms: as immigrant and socioeconomic, citizenship, nationality, race/ethnicity, attachment, and emotional ties (Bhimji 2008). Identity and belonging, although fluid and changing in relation to spatial conditions and temporal shifts are critical to the ways in which migrants experience place. For Dinesh, identity as a marker of his sense of self intersected differently in personal, familial, social, and work spaces. While he had strong emotional attachments to India, he felt that in terms of work and career, he "belonged" in the United States at this juncture in his life. Dinesh also wished for his son to grow up American and to develop roots in the United States, and the forced return interrupted his plans for his family and his career.

The greatest problems skilled migrants had with unintended return was the lack of choice associated with the movement. While some came back with human and financial capital that could readily be put to use, others wished they could have stayed in the receiving country for at least a few more years so that their legal status there was more secure, and they could be truly transnational and flexible in their interactions with both sending and receiving countries and spaces within them.

Voluntary Return: Intentional Temporary and "Permanent" Return

Temporality of a stay abroad can be an intentional strategy on the part of the skilled migrant. Rather than settling permanently in the receiving country, migrants move back and forth between their source country and receiving country/countries, a movement that has been referred to as circular or pendulum migration. For some skilled migrants, studying and working abroad is a strategic career-building move to obtain credentials from globally recognized institutions of higher education, increase or develop language proficiency, and gain work experience and cultural competency that will help them in the global marketplace and also assist in upward social and economic mobility in their countries of origin.

Subramaniam (aged 29 years), a software engineer working in Cyberjaya, an IT hub on the outskirts of Kuala Lumpur, Malaysia, deliberately opted for circular migration, moving between India and Malaysia on a series of 1–2-year contracts. When asked why he had decided to do contract work, he replied,

> I wanted the experience and the money isn't bad. Malaysia seems familiar. You can get Indian vegetarian food and there are plenty of Indian faces here. Life is similar to India. Chennai (his hometown) is only four hours away, so I can visit my parents quite often. But I would never want to settle here.

Subramaniam's plan was to return to India permanently after he got married as he did not think his current peripatetic lifestyle would be suitable for a happy wedded life. Despite a sizable Indian population in Malaysia and a familiar culture, Subramaniam did not feel at ease with the country's Bhumiputra policy that gave Malays more rights and privileges than other resident ethnic groups. The impossibility of equal treatment and assimilation made him view Malaysia as a place that offered excellent career-building opportunities and good wages, but not a potential home, a place where he felt he could belong.

Subramaniam's intended return can be explained by elements of the new economics of labor migration as well as the target income theory that stress accruing capital to invest in the sending country as well as neoclassical migration theory that posits that return occurs due to a failure to integrate. However, these theories do not consider that some receiving countries are places with policies that may make integration impossible and are therefore less attractive to migrants for permanent settlement or that migrants' attachment to the homeland and people living there may play an important role in their return.

The lure of superior facilities such as state-of-the-art labs, financial and administrative support to conduct cutting-edge research, and a fulfilling and invigorating educational and work environment in MDCs are primary draws for skilled migrants. However, innovative research is not only the preserve of the developed world today. In fact, environments in developing countries such as India, China, and Brazil may be equally or more conducive for some kinds of innovations (Wang and Li-Ying 2014; Woetzel et al. 2015).

Skilled migrants have returned to India, which is sometimes seen as a better place than MDCs to create new products, services, and processes that they have envisaged and wish to develop. *Jugaad* is a Hindi word that means "a frugal fix" or "an ingenious solution," but the concept goes beyond finding low-cost solutions; the term captures the spirit of doing something innovative with limited resources (Radjou, Prabhu and Ahuja 2012). Often born of necessity, the practice of *jugaad* is credited with the creation of affordable and adaptable products, processes and systems in fields as varied as industry, business, medicine, and social services. Several foreign-trained Indian engineers and scientists who find India more open to *jugaad* and experimentation have returned to the sending country to take advantage of its stimulating and more malleable environment.

An Indian neuroscientist couple who had been based in California's Silicon Valley where they worked for established IT companies for over a decade, moved to India to launch an artificial intelligence start-up company. They noted that for them, relocation was a very intentional decision, adding that, "People in India and Asia are leapfrogging generations of technology, and we thought, 'Where better to experiment with this stuff'?" The couple hope to entice top talent from Silicon Valley to join their enterprise, which they plan to expand first to the rest of Asia and ultimately, the world.

Misra (2014) reports that an Asian Indian researcher at an American university returned to India to build an inexpensive and portable device that could be used for medical diagnostic tests. Prohibitively high costs in terms of money and time, bureaucratic red tape, expensive regulatory approvals of new inventions, and the high costs of marketing such as device in the United States guided his decision to build a prototype of the device in India. Tested and found to be as accurate as standard equipment used in medical labs, the device, known as the Swasthya Slate (Health Tablet) has been successfully deployed by the Indian government in a pilot program to improve maternal health. For the returning entrepreneur-engineer, an additional bonus was being able to participate in the development of his country of birth through improvements in preventive healthcare.

Shamshir Ali, a medical doctor who had trained in the United Kingdom and was a Fellow of the Royal College of Surgeons, had worked in Ireland for five years and in Saudi Arabia for ten years before moving back to India to set up a hospital with three partners. He saw potential in a facility that offered state-of-the-art care to local residents as well as to medical tourists from neighboring countries such as the Maldives, Bangladesh, and Sri Lanka. His hospital, located in Kerala in southern India, has rooms for family members accompanying patients from overseas and offers local, Bangladeshi, and Maldivian food. According to Dr. Ali, the availability of trained medical and health personnel, suitable land, and India's push to increase its share of global medical tourism all made return an attractive prospect. Ali is one of the more successful returnees who has seen his hospital grow in reputation, staff, and patients, and says he would never consider returning to either Ireland or Saudi Arabia.

Although the transnational nature of their existence may mean multiple dwellings, homes, and polycenterdness for high-skill immigrants, for some, the ideology of home is intertwined with the geography of place. Several returnees expressed topophilia or "the affective bond between people and place" (Tuan 1974, 4) in relation to the sending country or a geographical locale within it, and for them, home took on the mantle of sacred space (Entrikin 1991).

Through embodied return, these migrants constructed and reinforced culture, identity, and community as place-based ideas. Return had multiple and interlinked meanings for them; home corresponded very strongly to an actual, physical geographic entity of a country, state, or city, while culture and identity were also viewed as being inextricably moored to place. The social and cultural contexts in which they wished to lead their lives not just as individuals, but also as members of natal and extended families as well as communities had a strong influence on their desire to return to a particular place that provided all the desired elements of home: belonging, intimacy, safety, and security. Their emotional ties to India as homeland and home, ideas that were often conflated, were evident in conversations.

For some high-skilled immigrants, career building in the destination country and the needs of immediate and extended family diverged and were difficult to reconcile if they continued to live and work in the receiving country. This discordance, which could stem from concern about older and future generations such as the need to be in close proximity to aging parents living in India or a desire to raise their children in a place where they did not need to prove that they belonged often prompted the decision to return.

Amita (aged 32) said that she realized that she never thought of her apartment in Washington, DC as her real home and that when she talked about "returning home," she invariably meant India, even though her job required her to take multiple international trips every year. The dissonance between where she lived and the place she considered her home was strong enough for Amita to contemplate and then act on returning to Mumbai, the city of her birth and where her parents still lived. An additional factor for Amita was that she was an only child and she felt badly about leaving her parents to fend for themselves.

While most returnees said that they felt at home and comfortable in India's metropolises such as Mumbai, Delhi, Bangalore, Hyderabad, Kolkata, and Chennai, for some, the feeling of belonging was heightened when the city in which they settled on their return was one in which they had lived and/or worked prior to emigration or one in which they were fluent in the local language(s) and social mores. Their return was in search of what Antonsich (2010) calls "place-belongingness"—the feeling of being "at home" in a particular locale.

Several of those interviewed identified periods during their lives they viewed as better or even ideal times to return home. A reason provided for return while still in an early stage of the family life cycle was to ease the adjustment process for children and to ensure that they were firmly anchored in origin country cultures, so that they too would consider it their home. Shoumit, who returned to India after spending several years abroad as a student and a professional, explains that he and his wife thought that if they were to move, return should occur "Before the kids' roots in the UK became too strong and our [the parents] attachment to India became too weak." The couple made the return to India when their sons were 6 and 4 respectively. However, they and other returnee parents also wrestled with the appropriateness of their return, worrying that their "selfish desire to come back home" was at the expense of their children's future opportunities as well-placed and competitive players in the global economy. Those who returned to be closer to aging parents wondered whether their attachment to place in India would be the same once their parents had passed on, one noting that "It is the people who make a place special."

In his Silicon Valley study, Dossani (2002) found that substantial numbers of his respondents expressed a keen interest in returning to their countries of birth or starting a business there. Among the reasons to return, Indians in his sample assigned culture and lifestyle issues the highest priority and also expressed the greatest interest in helping their homeland. Returning migrants I interviewed who chose to stay in India indeed believed that the country offered a more fulfilling way of life, with greater social connectivity, and a stronger and more reliable social support network of friends and family than the Western societies that they had left. Despite some difficulties in adjusting to a work culture radically different from what they were used to in the MDCs, those who decided to make India their home base in general did not regret the move. They maintained that their lifestyle in India was also superior and allowed for better work–life balance.

Many lived in gated communities with amenities such as a gym, swimming pool, landscaped grounds, store, children's play area, and spaces for recreation (Chacko 2007; Chacko and Varghese 2009). These living conditions sheltered them to some extent from the chaos of urban India. Moreover, the return migrants could hire maids, nannies, chauffeurs, and cooks, help that they could not have afforded on even their relatively high incomes in the MDCs. Nevertheless, crowds, pollution, traffic, old and inadequate infrastructure, poor enforcement of rules and regulations, and corruption continue to be a source of distress for those transplanted from the MDCs to India (Chacko 2007; van Riemsdiijk 2013). Additionally, they viewed their permanent resident or MDC citizen status as a safety-net that allowed for greater flexibility and the possibility of return to the MDC if such a move was warranted.

Conclusion

This chapter shows that high-skilled migrants' return to India can be both involuntary and voluntary in nature and that their experiences of return are colored by whether they had agency in determining the move. Those whose return was involuntary were likely to view the move with some regret, and reported that they would have preferred to stay for a longer period of time in the receiving country, and those whose immigration status permitted return usually made their way back if the opportunity presented itself. Among those who decided to come back to India of their own volition, a mix of societal, personal, and career factors dictated the decision to return. Immigrants' experiences and aspirations as individuals, and members of natal and extended families and communities set within wider cultural, life cycle, and structural contexts were often associated with the move. Some desired deeper spatial reconnection with family members and cultures in the material and symbolic homeland, to which they felt they belonged in a manner that was not possible in the country of settlement.

Others felt that the reasons behind their decision to immigrate and settle abroad, such as better career opportunities and lifestyle abroad were no longer as valid as India offered job satisfaction and a more satisfying way of life than the countries they had lived in as immigrants. A sense of not being completely at home in the receiving country or the recognition that India was where they truly belonged was also provided as a reason for return. Many believed that by virtue of their lives straddling MDCs and LDCs and their lived experiences as professionals in both they were truly global and transnational.

Their stage in the family life cycle also played a very important role in the migrants' decision to remain in the destination country or return to the land of their birth. The periods that were considered the best both for the individual migrants and their families was early in the family life cycle, before the children and the first-generation immigrants started putting down roots, and later when the immigrants had acquired good positions but wished to make their mark in their area of expertise in a manner that was not possible in the country of settlement. In the case of the latter, it was possible to return to India on a permanent or semi-permanent basis as the children were of college age and did not require the close supervision of their parents. Although the Indian government did not have policies that encouraged the highly skilled to return, the acquisition of the status of Overseas Citizen of India and the ease of maintaining a transnational existence allowed the returnees to experience what they hoped would be the best of both worlds.

Finally, this study underscores that place as context and the sense of "being in place" are important in high-skilled migrants' intentions of return and actual return. However, the fluidity of place in a globalized world increasingly allows different geographical settings to offer combinations of different ideal attributes so that the highly skilled can feel that they are "in place" in multiple locales and for varied reasons. This implies that for both the highly skilled who return to the sending country of their own volition or those who did not have much choice in their return, the continually evolving nature of place makes it difficult to easily differentiate desirable from less desirable without the benefit of living, working in, and therefore actually experiencing place at a personal level.

Note

1. NRI stands for Non-Resident Indian. The term is used to describe an Indian citizen who resides abroad for at least six months for work, study, or other purposes.

References

Antonsich, M. 2010. Searching for belonging: An analytical framework. *Geography Compass* 4: 644–659.

Bauer, T. K., and K. Zimmermann. 1998. Causes of international migration: A survey. In *Crossing Borders: Regional and urban perspectives on international migration*, ed. P. Gorter, P. Nijkamp, and J. Poot, 95–127. Aldershot: Ashgate.

Bhimji, F. 2008. Cosmopolitan belonging and diaspora: Second-generation British Muslim women travelling to South Asia. *Citizenship Studies* 12: 413–427.

Black, R., J. Crush, and S. Peberdy. 2006. *Migration and Development in Africa: An overview.* African Migration and Development Series No. 1. Cape Town: Idasa Publishing. Available at: www.queensu.ca/samp/sampresources/samppublications/mad/MAD_1.pdf

Borjas, G. J. 1994. The economics of immigration. *Journal of Economic Literature* 32: 1667–1717.

———. and B. Bratsberg. 1996. Who leaves? The out-migration of the foreign-born. *Review of Economics and Statistics* 78: 165–176.

Carling, J., and S. V. Pettersen. 2014. Return migration intentions in the integration–transnationalism matrix. *International Migration* 52: 13–30.

Castles, S., and M. J. Miller. 2003. *The Age of Migration.* Houndmills: Macmillan.

Chacko, E. 2007. From brain drain to brain gain: Reverse migration to Bangalore and Hyderabad, India's globalizing hightech cities. *GeoJournal* 68: 131–140.

Chacko, E., and P. Varghese. 2009. Identity and representations of gated communities in Bangalore, India. *Open House International* 34: 57–64.

Chaney, D. 1996. *Lifestyles.* London: Routledge.

Constant, A., and D. S. Massey. 2002. Return migration by German guestworkers: Neoclassical versus new economic theories. *International Migration* 40: 5–38.

Cresswell, T. 2004. *Place: A short introduction.* Oxford: Blackwell.

Dossani, R. 2002. Chinese and Indian engineers and their networks in Silicon Valley. The Asia/Pacific Research Center (A/PARC), Stanford University. Available at: http://aparc.fsi.stanford.edu/sites/default/files/Dossani_Survey.pdf

Entrikin, N. J. 1991. *The betweenness of place: Towards a geography of modernity.* London: Macmillan.

Featherstone, M. 1987. Lifestyle and consumer culture. *Theory, Culture and Society* 4: 55–70.

Fokkema, C. M., and de Haas, H. 2011. The effects of integration and transnational ties on international return migration intentions. *Demographic Research* 25: 755–782.

Gmelch, G. 1980. Return migration. *Annual Review of Anthropology* 9: 135–159.

Government of Canada. 2015. Get a post-graduation work permit. Available at: www.cic.gc.ca/english/study/work-postgrad.asp (last accessed July 14, 2015).

Haidara, A. 2013. No place like home: Africa's skilled labour returns. *Africa Renewal,* United Nations Department of Public Information, 7 and 26.

Hall, S. 1987. Miminal selves. In *Identity – The real me: Post-modernism and the question of identity*, ed. H. Bhabha. London: ICA Documents 44.

Harvey, W. S. 2009. British and Indian scientists in Boston considering returning to their home countries. *Population, Space and Place* 15: 493–508.

IOM. 2009. *The MIDA Experience and Beyond.* Geneva: International Organization for Migration. Available at: http://publications.iom.int/bookstore/free/MIDA_2009.pdf

Iravani, M. R. 2011. Brain drain problem: A review. *International Journal of Business and Social Science* 2: 284–289.

Ivancheva, M. 2007. Strawberry fields forever? Bulgarian and Romanian student workers in the UK. *Focaal: European Journal of Anthropology* 49: 110–117.

Khadria, B. 2008. India: Skilled migration to developed countries, labour migration to the Gulf. In *Migration and development—Perspectives from the South*, ed. S. Castles and R. D. Wise, 79–113. Geneva: International Organisation for Migration. Available at: www.heindehaas.com/Publications/Castles%20and%20Delgado%20Wise%20-%20ed%20-%202008.pdf (accessed July 14, 2015).

King, R. 2000. Generalizations from the history of return migration. In *Return migration: Journeys of hope or despair?* ed. B. Ghosh, 7–55. Geneva: International Organization for Migration and the United Nations.

Ley, D., and A. Kobayashi. 2005. Back to Hong Kong: Return migration or transnational sojourn? *Global Networks* 5: 111–127.

Massey, D. S., J. Arango, G. Hugo, A. Kouaouci, A. Pellegrino, and J. E. Taylor. 1993. Theories of international migration: A review and appraisal. *Population and Development Review* 19: 431–466.

Ministry of Overseas Indian Affairs (MOIA). 2014. *Annual Report: 2014–2015*. New Delhi: MOIA. Available at: http://moia.gov.in/writereaddata/pdf/Annual_Report_2014-15.pdf (accessed July 15, 2015).

Ministry of Overseas Indian Affairs (MOIA). 2015. *India and its diaspora*. Available at: http://moia.gov.in/accessories.aspx?aid=10 (accessed October 13, 2015).

Misra, U. 2014. Swasthya Slate: Scripting new-age diagnostics. *Forbes India Magazine*, April 16. Available at: http://india.forbes.com/article/work-in-progress/swasthya-slate-scripting-newage-diagnostics/37556/0 (accessed July 19, 2015).

Nasscom-McKinsey Report. 2005. *Extending India's leadership in the global IT and BPO industries*. Available at: www.nasscom.org

O'Reilly, K., and M. Benson. 2009. Lifestyle migration: Escaping to the good life? In *Lifestyle Migration: Expectations, aspirations and experiences,* ed. K. O'Reilly and M Benson, 1–13. Burlington, VT: Ashgate.

Radjou, N., J. Prabhu, and S. Ahuja. 2012. *Jugaad Innovation: Think frugal, be flexible, generate breakthrough growth*. San Francisco, CA: Jossey-Bass.

Salvino, L. 2015. China's talent recruitment programs: The road to a Nobel prize and world hegemony in science? *Research brief: Study of innovation and technology in China*. San Diego, CA: University of California Institute on Global Conflict and Cooperation.

Schiller, N. G., L. Basch, and C. S. Blanc. 1995. From immigration to transmigrant: Theorizing transnational migration. *Anthropological Quarterly* 68: 48–63.

Siar, S. 2014. Highly skilled migrants' strong ties with their home country: Evidence from Filipinos in New Zealand and Australia. *Journal of International Migration and Integration* 15: 655–676.

Stark, O. 1991. *The Migration of Labor.* Cambridge: Blackwell.

Stebbins, R. A. 1997. Lifestyle as a generic concept in ethnographic research. *Quality and Quantity* 31: 347–360.

Tang, J. 2000. *Doing Engineering: The career attainment and mobility of Caucasian, Black, and Asian-American engineers*. London: Rowman & Littlefield.

Tuan, Y. F. 1974. Space and place: Humanistic perspective. *Progress in Geography* 6: 213–252.

UN-OECD 2013. *World Migration in Figures: United Nations Department of Economic and Social Affairs and OECD*. Available at: www.oecd.org/els/mig/World-Migration-in-Figures.pdf (last accessed July 16, 2015).

United States Citizenship and Immigration Services (USCIS) 2013. *7-month extension of post-completion optional practical training (OPT) for F-1 students*. Available at: www.uscis.gov/sites/default/files/files/nativedocuments/OPT_STEM_Extension.pdf (accessed October 6, 2015).

United States, Department of Homeland Security (US-DHS). 2006. *Yearbook of immigration statistics: 2004*. Washington, DC: U.S. Department of Homeland Security, Office of Immigration Statistics.

United States, Department of Homeland Security (US-DHS). 2014. *Yearbook of immigration statistics: 2013*. Washington, DC: U.S. Department of Homeland Security, Office of Immigration Statistics.

Van der Veer, P. 2005. Virtual India: Indian IT labor and the nation-state. In *Sovereign bodies: Citizens, migrants, and states in the postcolonial world*, ed. T. B. Hansen and F. Stepputat. Princeton, NJ: Princeton University Press.

van Riemsdijk, M. 2013. Talent acquisition in the IT industry in Bangalore: A multi-level study. *Tijdschrift voor Economische en Sociale Geografie* 104: 478–490.

Wadhwa, V. 2014. Snapdeal — the flourishing company America passed on — offers a lesson about immigration reform. *The Washington Post* November 7.

Wang, Q., L. Tang, and H. Li. 2014. Return migration of the highly skilled in higher education institutions: A Chinese university case. *Population, Space and Place* 21: 771–787.

Wang, Y., and J. Li-Ying. 2014. How do the BRIC countries play their roles in the global innovation arena? A study based on USPTO patents during 1990–2009. *Scientometrics* 98: 1065–1083.

Woetzel, J., Y. Chen, J. Manyika, E. Roth, J. Seong, and J. Lee. 2015. *The China effect on global innovation*. The McKinsey Global Institute. October.

Wong, M. 2014. Navigating return: The gendered geographies of skilled return migration to Ghana. *Global Networks* 14: 438–457.

Wong, P., C. F. Lai, R. Nagasaki, and T. Lin. 1998. Asian Americans as a model minority: Self-perceptions and perceptions by other racial groups. *Sociological Perspectives* 41: 95–118.

Woo, D. (ed.). 2000. *Glass ceilings and Asian Americans: The new face of workplace barriers*. Walnut Creek, CA: Altamira Press.

13 Immigration Policy Change and the Transnational Shaping of Place

Margaret Walton-Roberts

Introduction

Immigration policy in many OECD nations now places a premium on migrants with specific skills that are seen as vital to national development, innovation, and competitiveness (Saxenian 2006; Hawthorne 2008). Nations are in competition for this talent, often reverting to what Shachar (2006) calls a "citizenship for talent exchange," where those with the needed skills are enticed to settle permanently in select locations through preferential access to citizenship and the rights it entails. The convergence of migration policies that promote greater migrant selectivity and differential access to citizenship rights can be seen in the growing orthodoxy of points-based type immigration systems used by many immigrant receiving states to attract skilled migrants (Duncan 2012). A great deal of the literature on the issue of skilled migration has examined this immigration policy change from the perspective of the policymakers, with less attention focused on how migrant-sending regions respond to changes in immigration policy.

Using the case of India, the world's second most populated country, and Canada, one of the most active immigrant receiving states, this chapter examines the consequences of Canada's increased policy focus on skilled and selective immigration. The chapter contextualizes immigration policy changes in terms of how it interacts with place, in this case through an assessment of regional immigration links between Canada and one of its key source regions for migration, the northern Indian state of Punjab. A focus on understanding policy change in terms of the influence exacted on the ground in sending regions adds to our scholarship on skilled immigration by critically assessing the role of place not as an abstract stage where people are merely read into policy, but a context where policy interacts with places marked by histories of engagement, exchange, and uneven development. These are meta-narratives that must continue to frame our analysis of skilled immigration policy today.

The chapter begins with a brief conceptualization of the critical tradition of the scholarship on the interaction between space and policy in terms of immigration and mobility. Moving to the regional scale I explore how place, rather than abstract space, informs our understanding of migration and policy change by explaining the historical development of a migration culture rooted in the place of Punjab, India. I illustrate the more recent interaction between place and policy over the last decade by assessing the changing composition of migration flows from India to Canada through three lenses: *spatial* change in terms of where migrants come from (gauged in terms of linguistic groups); *social* changes (in terms of visa class); and *temporal* shifts in terms of an increase in temporary visa holders. I conclude by arguing that place is central to understanding current knowledge-based migrant flows, that the rise of skilled migration creates social changes in terms of who has access to the benefits of international mobility, and that the rise of temporary skilled migration categories indicates the literature, including the "citizenship-talent exchange," is subject to review.

Migration Policy and Spatial Difference

Scholars have increasingly highlighted how migrant-receiving states are in competition for skilled migrants (including international students), from software engineers to healthcare professionals to business services professionals (Florida 2005; Shachur 2006; Faist 2008). Management scholars have examined the global sourcing of science and technology personnel by developed nations and linked it to new models of offshoring (Manning, Massini, and Lewin 2008; Saxenian 2006). Research has further highlighted the intersection of skilled migration and competitive immigration policy regimes in terms of new models of citizenship (Shachar 2006), and the gendered and racialized social construction of "skill" (Tyner 1999). This desirable view of skilled migration by Western nations produces a social bifurcation of migration streams, with skilled workers and international students gaining more opportunities for mobility and settlement, while mixed flows comprising asylum seekers and lower skilled economic migrants face more intense surveillance and control—by both states and multiple intermediaries (Ashutosh and Mountz 2011). Unlike skilled migrants—deemed desirable—refugees and asylum seekers are consistently being constructed as undesirable and threatening (Hyndman and Giles 2011). This bifurcation is also spatial, and can be seen in terms of the emergence of a "global mobility divide" marked by the relative closure of visa-free travel opportunities for those from non-OECD nations, while visa-free travel opportunities between OECD member states has increased (Mau et al. 2015). For example, between 1969 and 2010 various changes in visa policies resulted in India losing the opportunity for visa-free travel to approximately twenty nations (Mau et al. 2015, 15).

This global mobility divide also reflects the different value, or "heft" of national passports (Macklin 2007), such that "the primary value of citizenship lies in the mobility rights attached to passports" (Shachar and Bauböck 2014, 1). Citizenship and the mobility rights that accompany it reflect geographies of uneven development, which then frames how people access channels of education in order to become "skilled." Skilled migration is thus another means by which education can reproduce inequality and privilege (Brown and Tannock 2009; Waters 2006). The policy discourses of skilled migration and its sociospatial influence is thus of significant global importance.

Migration policy control over human mobility remains one of the key arenas where the state performs through exclusive sovereign rule, resistant to global governance and multilateral policy initiatives (Torpey 2000; Benhabib 2005; Koser 2010). The degree of control the state attempts to exercise through skilled migration policy reflects selectivity management processes enacted at the scale of the individual. Skilled migration applicants are typically assessed as a bundle of human capital inputs derived from formal education and professional experience. This type of selection process distinguishes individuals based on preferred human capital and demographic criteria that typically represent the most "self-reliant" and "productive" economic citizens possible; the state thus attempts to manage human mobility in order to reduce social "risk" and thereby enhance perceived economic rewards to the state (Walsh 2011). The heightened Canadian policy focus on skilled migration recursively entrenches the instrumentalist individualized nature of immigration discourse and settlement practices. Skilled immigration models seek to reproduce the "flexible citizens" Aihwa Ong (1999) problematizes—those who espouse and advance the neoliberal tendencies of globalization.

For sending regions the development impact of this policy shift represents at best an opportunity to build channels for brain circulation and remittances (Saxenian 2006), or more negatively acts as an instrumental tool of high-value skill extraction that can be squandered after arrival through a process of foreign credential devaluation. Such deskilling also contributes to furthering the global flexiblization of labor (Bauder 2006). Other scholars examine this global knowledge transfer as evidence of an emerging global pattern of effective labor export, and interpret it as a new form of unequal exchange that "delineates the contours of a new international division of labour that implies an asymmetric model based on the reintegration of peripheral nations into the global capitalist system" (Wise and Covarrubia 2012, 131). The global race for skilled immigrants is thus seen to create an imbalance in the development ledger, where receiving states gain the benefit of semi- and fully trained personnel, but carry little of the burden of investment in their creation. Khadria (2009, 4) argues that this should be considered through an adversarial index—an analysis of age, wage, and vintage where receiving nations:

> optimise age-structural changes in population, maximize incomes, and accumulate quality human capital embodying the latest "vintages" of knowledge-through mobility of both types – the 'finished' (established professionals, scientists and researchers), and the 'semi-finished' (post-graduate students).

Migration research has attended to the spatial limits of skill construction both in terms of the devaluation of immigrant credentials (Reitz, Curtis, and Elrick 2014), and in the more fluid domain of immigrant entrepreneurialism (Hiebert 2002). Spatial analysis of skilled migration suggests the significance of the historical patterning of immigration processes and flows. One conceptual approach that does capture this *longue durée* frame of reference is the international migration systems approach (Kritz, Lim, and Zlotnik 1992), which argues that migration patterns are not random, but the product of the interaction of economic, social, and political connections among nations. The systems approach calls for examination of both sending and receiving nations in an effort to build a comprehensive overview of specific migratory frameworks over time that incorporate macro, meso, and, to a lesser extent, micro factors into the overall analysis. This approach has arguably been eclipsed by transnational migration frameworks, which attempt to understand the actions of immigrants who bridge sending and receiving states. However, transnational migration approaches have tended to diminish the meso and macro scale of analysis for more detailed examination of micro social processes (Glick Schiller 2005). Using a transnational migration systems approach in the case of skilled labor mobilization encourages us to explore the interactions between policy and place over time with reference to meso and macro structures, which includes the policy cycle process in the receiving state as well as institutional and societal responses to such policy changes in the main immigrant sending regions.

To explore this intersection in more detail this chapter examines the consequences of Canada's immigration policy change on sites of migrant origin—in this case, Punjab, India. I begin by assessing recent changes in Canadian immigration policy toward greater skill selectivity.

Canadian Skilled Immigration Policy

The Canadian shift toward more selective immigration has been highly evident during the last two decades. Since the Immigration Act of 1976 immigrants to Canada have entered the country as permanent residents through three streams: economic (especially through Federal Skilled Worker (FSW)), family, and refugee class. The Immigration and Refugee Protection Act of 2001 maintained these three categories, but made assessment of FSWs more flexible by removing occupational specifications in place of more general human capital-based assessment criteria (Ray 2005). During the 1990s there was an increased focus on FSWs, but by the 2000s a FSW backlog began to develop. At the same time temporary foreign worker (TFWs) streams increased substantially, resulting in an immigration system geared toward greater skill selection and the use of temporary residence visas. For example, by 2013 Canada registered over 250,000 temporary migrant entries compared to approximately 150,000 permanent migration entries (CIC 2013). This process of skill-based immigrant selection was further operationalized in 2015 with the introduction of a new application management system called Express Entry. This system was introduced to make the selection process act more like a "just in time" application management system, effectively incorporating migrant job market suitability of the temporary migrant system with the human capital selectivity of the FSW points system. Before the Express Entry system was introduced, applicants joined a queue and waited their turn to be processed; under the Express Entry system each applicant effectively competes with others in the pool in order to be selected based on the number of comprehensive scoring points they accrue based on their human capital profile and the labor market demand for their skills. The most desirable applicants in the pool are invited to apply for permanent residence. In order for an applicant to "rise to the top" of the pool they need to have a labor market impact assessment approved job offer, which virtually guarantees selection. "Stale" applicants who have not been invited to apply after a period of twelve months can be removed from the pool.[1]

Several critics of the general move to greater selective and temporary immigration argue that rather than a nation-building process based on incorporating all migrants as permanent citizens, Canada's immigration policy has become a tool for the capture of human capital through competitive permanent and growing forms of temporary migration streams (Fudge and Macphail 2009). Canada's engagement in this type of skill selectivity has been marked by several profound changes to the nature of national immigration policy. These include various restrictions to FSW programs to manage or eradicate backlogs, the expansion of various programs that grant some selection control to the provinces and territories, significant expansion of Temporary Foreign Worker programs (TFWP) that may incorporate greater input from third parties, and new policy routes that allow the conversion of some temporary workers to permanent residents (Alboim 2009; Flynn and Bauder 2014).

Much of the debate that has accompanied these changes in Canada's immigration policy has focused on assessing immigrant incomes, rights, and protections once in Canada (Picot and Sweetman 2012; Reitz 2013)—what Canada's changing immigration policy means for Canada. What is often lost in this debate is the influence of these policy changes on the ground in sending regions—how do potential migrants and institutions in the sending region respond to these policy shifts? This chapter contributes to this debate in the context of Indian immigration to Canada by examining the historical interaction between Canadian policy change and socioeconomic response in India.

Research Methods

This chapter calls upon a range of primary and secondary data sources to examine changes in immigration policy in Canada and immigrant flows from India, principally Punjab in the north of India. The quantitative data used is from Citizenship and Immigration Canada (CIC) and includes records of immigration landings from India. An overview of Canadian immigration data can be found in the annual CIC *facts and figures* reports. More detailed linguistic data was extracted from custom data sets requested through one of the national Metropolis Research Centers.[2] The observations I develop in this chapter also emerge from six key informant interviews conducted with Canadian immigration officials based in India and Canada during the period 2000–2014, as well as interviews with and field observations of potential and return immigrants, and migrant intermediaries in northern India. The data is informed by over ten years of fieldwork conducted during five different research trips to India between 1999 and 2013. While the explicit research agenda for each field trip differed, one overarching research issue during each visit was the assessment of how Canadian immigration policy changes were being experienced in this region of India. The field research was qualitative and inductive in nature. Interviews and focus groups were the main forms of data collection used in India, as well as secondary data collection from local newspapers and government reports. Canadian immigration policy change was assessed through official government press releases and communications, and interviews with Canadian immigration bureaucrats in both Canada and India. The research can be considered part of a larger multi-sited program that explored transnational migration systems and immigration policy formation over the *longue durée*. In this regard the research parallels transnational migration methodologies that aim to escape methodological nationalism, in that they do not take the state as the natural container for examining migration and other social policy issues (Wimmer and Glick Schiller 2002; Amelina and Faist 2012).

The Formation of an International Migration System in Punjab, India

Key to understanding how international migration operates as a system and how transnational practices have formed between Canada and regions of India is the need to understand the *longue durée* of this migration system. Immigration links between Canada and India have traditionally drawn disproportionate numbers of Jat Sikh migrants from the state of Punjab in northwest India (Bhatti 2007). Jats are traditional agriculturalists and a subgroup of the Jat caste. Sikhs comprise one of India's religious groups, and traditionally the Sikh homeland is considered the greater Punjab region (including parts of modern-day Pakistan). Early Sikh settlers arrived in Canada in the late 19th century and set the foundation for subsequent migrations. The historical roots of this migratory system can be partly explained by the rise of Western education, improved transportation, and intensification of agriculture that occurred under British colonialism (Talbot and Thandi 2004).

Beginning in the 19th century three processes contributed to the formation of "a culture of migration" for Jat Sikhs in Punjab: canal colony construction, preferential land grants to Sikh Jats, and the overrepresentation of Sikhs into the colonial military. First, state-led construction of canals in western Punjab during the colonial period resulted in large-scale internal migration and the resettlement of agriculturalists from central Punjab to the western part of the state. This colonial investment in agricultural intensification began in 1886 in west Punjab and included irrigation projects aimed at converting the lands between the main rivers in the region, which resulted in significant internal migration (Tatla 2004, 48). The rising incomes that resulted from the intensification of agricultural productivity allowed agriculturalist families to sponsor the overseas migration of family members (most often young males). The migration of these young men became part of a cycle of income generation needed to both protect land holdings and pay the increasing tax demands made by the colonial state (Washbrook 1981; Kaur

2012). Second, Orientalist colonial authorities understood that the success of state-driven irrigation projects lay in granting land to Jat farmers (among others) who they perceived as "sturdy" and "natural" cultivators (Gilmartin 2004). The third process which contributed to the development of a migration culture or system in the region was the British preference to enlist Sikhs into the army; practicing Sikhs were perceived as a "natural" militia "race" (Fox 1985; Walton-Roberts 2011). These processes of military recruitment and preferential land grants reinforced each other as native cavalry regiments took advantage of colonial land grants (Buck 1906).

Colonial systems of administration and development clearly articulated with the existing economic and caste authority position Jat Sikhs held in Punjab at the time; the land grant system and active recruitment in the colonial military reproduced and consolidated this social hierarchy. International migration (especially as soldiers and policemen) during and after colonial rule is one example of a social resource the Jat landowning classes were able to extract and reproduce due to their privileged position within the British colonial system (Tatla 1995; Ali 1988; Fox 1985).

Enlistment as soldiers in the British Indian army provided opportunities for migration as recruits moved through the empire to London for official spectacles (such as Queen Victoria's Golden Jubilee in 1887 and the Coronation of King George VI in 1902), as well as to the battlefields of World War I. In this regard Sikhs were drawn into international migration networks in service of the needs of empire, the core economy at that time. Their skills were selected for this purpose.

These migratory flows represent an early variation of skilled migration, since Sikh valor and loyalty to the British Empire were seen as a key trait and valuable skill during this time period; thus, Sikh soldiers were transformed into preferential migrants in the late 19th and early 20th centuries (Walton-Roberts 2011). Orientalist colonial perceptions of Sikhs can therefore be interpreted as a form of cultural and human capital that manifests itself in the mobility Sikh migrants initially enjoyed at this time as they moved between colonial outposts in Asia as security guards and policemen. Some of the earliest Indian migrants to arrive in Canada at the turn of the 20th century had arguably been informed of the promising opportunities Canada offered through reports from Sikh troops who had passed through Canada as part of their official functions (Buchignani, Indra, and Srivastava 1985; Sharma 1997; Bhatti 2007). Many Sikh migrants also came indirectly from Hong Kong and Shanghai, where they were employed as security personnel, having secured these positions through their British military connections (Bhatti 2007).

By the turn of the 20th century, early pioneer Indian migrants (including a majority of Sikhs) began to arrive in Canada. As their numbers slowly increased, resistance to Asian immigration in Canada, particularly on the west coast, increased, and racial discrimination and anti-Asian immigrant resistance took firm hold (Anderson 1991). The Canadian state attempted to control Asian immigration during this time through the use of various restrictive policies shaped by the nature of international relations with the specific sending nations. This included various head taxes for Chinese migrants and voluntary exit controls with Japan to control Japanese migration. Canada faced a political problem in its attempts to limit Indian migration. India was formally part of the British Empire, and the illusion of empire was partly sustained by the idea that Indians gained some benefit from British rule, including mobility. Were British authorities to explicitly deny Indians the right to move freely about the empire it would reveal the limits of colonial membership during a time of rising demands for Indian independence. This diplomatic problem was solved through the use of a 1908 Canadian order in council that demanded that migrants could only arrive using a "continuous passage." While the law did not mention specific national groups (thus shielding Britain from the claim that Indians were not being allowed to travel throughout the empire), its use was understood by Canadian immigration officials to apply to those coming from India. Additionally, all Canadian continuous transport services from India to Canada were cancelled at this time (Johnston 2014; Sharma 1997).

The use of such legislative instruments marks a transition toward selectivity based explicitly on national origins, rather than the socially constructed characteristics colonial service generated. Mongia (1999, 554) argues that the continuous passage legislation is an example of control formed along the axes of "nation-race." She argues that

> the emergence of the nation-state as the first state formation to exercise a monopoly over migration indicates not that control over mobility begins *after* the formation of the nation-state but that the very development of the nation-state occurs, in part, to control mobility along the axes of the nation-race.

The early 20th century thus marks a period of relative migration closure for Indians, and indicates an early form of selective migration based on racially inscribed nationality, rather than colonially constructed human/social capital. Nationality in this case was a proxy for a series of racially constructed characteristics deemed desirable or undesirable during this age of racial and racist imaginaries (Anderson 1991).

During the interwar period, Canada further consolidated this nation-race formation by preventing practically all immigration from India (Bhatti 2007). During this period the Sikhs in Canada focused on community building through work and religious faith (Sharma 1997). It was not until 1967 that a new immigration policy that was not based on discriminatory factors of race or nationality was launched. The 1967 white paper established a policy that was:

> adapted to our manpower needs, a policy that will assist Canada's growth by bringing here every year a good number of people able to adapt to our society and qualified to contribute to our economy … it is not discriminatory. It established principles and procedures that can and will operate without regard to race, colour or creed.
>
> (House of Commons debates 1966, cited in Bhatti 2007, 509)

The period of the late 1960s thus saw an immigration system emerge based not on racial preference, but on the three pillars of economic, humanitarian, and family migration. Even though skilled migration was one of the key streams, the dominant pattern of Indian migration that emerged from the 1970s through to the 1990s consolidated around family and chain migration networks, and was increasingly oriented toward the larger metropolitan regions of western and central Canada (Walton-Roberts 2003). This migration process intensified Indo-Canadian sociospatial networks, so that even by the early 2000s Punjabi linguistic groups continued to dominate the share of spousal and family class chain migration that occurred (see Figure 13.1).

Canadian immigration policy at this time supported the migration of those with family networks, since these networks provided support for new migrants to effectively settle and locate employment in the expanding industrial and manufacturing sectors of the Canadian economy. For Sikhs, family-linked migration is strengthened by cultural marriage practices that are caste and religion endogenous, but village exogenous. This process further consolidated the social capital invested in Jat Sikh families with links to Canada (Mooney 2006). Access to international migration opportunities through marriage and immediate family sponsorship thus conferred substantial social status, and thus continued the historical construction of Jat Sikhs as beneficiaries of various globalization processes, beginning with racist colonial preference, and the transnational social capital networks that resulted from an immigration policy orientated to increasing the Canadian labor market through social network migration. A similar process of chain migration has been identified in the UK by Roger Ballard (2002, 203):

> Once the mass-transit system promoted by chain migration was in place, these four communities [Punjabi Sikhs and Muslims, Mirpuris, Sylhetis] gained a near-monopoly of migratory opportunities within the British labour

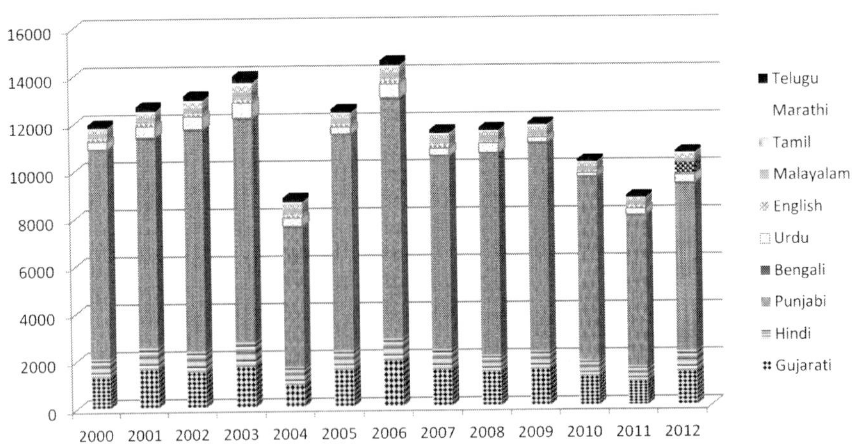

Figure 13.1 Indian Family Class Immigration to Canada by Mother Tongue

market. However much members of other communities rooted elsewhere in the sub-continent might wish to muscle in to these arenas, they were in no position to compete with the operators of these well-established networks.

Today, the Canadian Sikh population has settled in many of the major centers and suburbs of Canada's largest urban regions (Walton-Roberts 2003). By 2001, South Asian Canadians were fairly equally divided between Hindu, Muslim, and Sikh religious adherence, but linguistically English and Punjabi, followed by Tamil, were the most common mother tongues or languages spoken at home (Tran, Kaddatz, and Allard 2005, 23). In 2011, 48 percent of the core working-age immigrant labor force was born in Asia; the largest national group from this region was India (19 percent), followed by the Philippines (18 percent) and China (14 percent). In 2013, the Punjabi mother tongue population in Canada was estimated at 305,400, and 1.4 percent of Canada's population (455,000 people) identified themselves as adherents of the Sikh religion (Statistics Canada 2013).

To conclude this section we can see that the migration system in place between Canada and India during the post-1970s period increased the social capital that Sikh communities possessed. While racist ideologies stemmed the movement of migrants in the interwar years, as economic growth took off in the 1960s the Sikh community benefited from immigration policies that conceived of social networks as valuable components in the settlement of new Canadians. Such immigration flows continued throughout the later half of the 20th century, but application backlogs grew throughout the 1990s and early 2000s. Immigration policy was still selective at this time, but it was selective in terms of social as well as human capital attributes.

How have recent Canadian immigration policy changes informed the nature of migration flows from India? How have new policy dimensions reshaped the selective nature of immigration, and what kind of social responses on the ground in India have paralleled Canadian immigration policy change? I examine this in the next section by considering spatial, social, and temporal changes in India–Canada migration flows.

India–Canada Immigration: Spatial, Social, and Temporal Shifts

Spatial Patterns at Source and Destination

In the last few years Canada has been fine-tuning its immigration policy to capture more skilled workers and students. This policy shift is evident when we look at temporary and permanent immigration flows from India. Part of the policy shift toward more skilled migration also entails a geographical shift in how Canada promotes itself in India by targeting areas beyond the traditional sending regions in northern India. For example, in announcing the opening of new trade offices in Hyderabad and Kolkata in 2008 at a Canada–India Foundation dinner, Canada's then Prime Minister Stephen Harper stated: "These new trade offices will expand Canada's reach in India beyond our traditional focus on the north. India's boom is not just happening in the northern region, and Canada needs to be where all the action is" (Harper 2008). Canada's ability to tap into India's booming commercial development has long been idealized as based in strong "people to people" links. While such connectivity was reproduced through family class chain migration, policy changes meant that immigration flows were more explicitly framed by skills selection criteria. The data clearly indicate that the number of family class migrants from India has declined as other classes of migration, especially skilled and temporary classes (including students), have increased (see Figure 13.2).

Identifying how policy change results in spatial changes in migration flows is complicated by the fact that public data on immigration is available only at the national level. Nevertheless, regional dimensions of skilled immigration flows can be determined by using linguistic data as a proxy for regional origin. This data indicates that in early 2000s Gujarati and Hindi speakers became the leading linguistic groups in the Indian FSW class. This reflects the move away from processing large numbers of family class applicants in place of more skilled workers. However, by 2008 Punjabi speakers were again the leading linguistic group within the Indian FSW class. This suggests that skilled immigration policy changes resulted in a temporary increase in other linguistic (read regional) groups from India as the Canadian government processed applications from the growing technology hubs of southern India and the industrial heart of Gujarat. Nonetheless, by 2008 Punjabi speakers had again regained their dominance in the flow of immigrants to Canada. These fluctuations in linguistic groups in the Indian migration flows suggest that while selection policy processes can temporarily alter the composition of migration flows, the social demand for migration opportunities from Punjab eventually meets the revised demands of Canadian immigration policy.

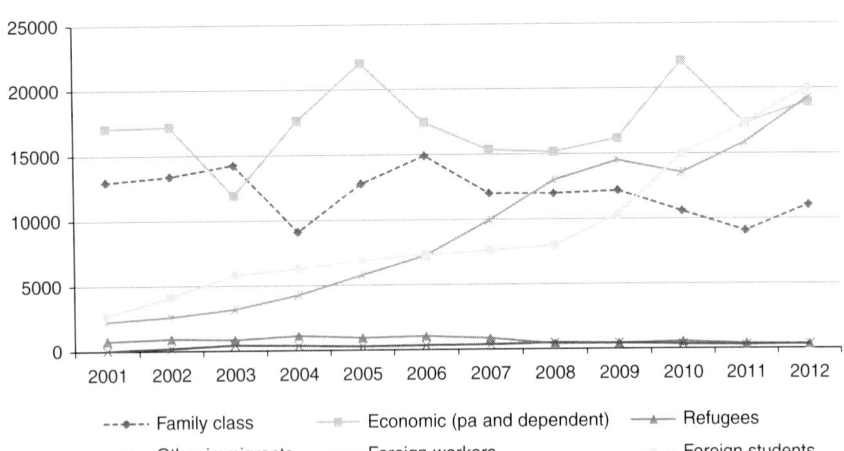

Figure 13.2 Indian Permanent and Temporary Immigration to Canada by Year and Visa Class

Social: Visa Classes

The share of FSW class immigrants as a percent of total immigration to Canada has increased from about 40 percent of total permanent immigrants in the 1990s, to about 66 percent in 2010 (Citizenship and Immigration Canada 2011). This shift in the class of immigrant is clearly evident when we look at India. As Figure 13.2 revealed, skilled and temporary classes of migration have surpassed family class as the leading category of immigrants from India. This transition to economic migration has not necessarily been a smooth and continuous process for Indian applicants. Indian immigration flows increasingly shifted toward the FSW program in the late 1990s and early 2000s as Canada expanded the number and location of visa offices to promote opportunities for skilled migration beyond the traditional northern Indian region. Applications for the FSW program grew, and long processing backlogs built up. By 2008 a significant FSW backlog had developed and the Canadian federal government introduced the Action Plan for Faster Immigration, which changed how FSW applications were processed. All new applications submitted after February 27, 2008 were subject to tightened criteria, which included either having a Canadian job offer, being present in Canada on a valid temporary visa, or meeting one of the thirty-eight specific occupations deemed required. This still left a backlog of pre-February 2008 applications that had to be processed under previous immigration rules; in 2010 the total number of these cases globally stood at 380,000.[3]

In March 2012 under Bill 38, the Jobs, Growth and Long-term Prosperity Act, the federal government announced that it was abandoning all pre-2008 backlogged cases that had not received a decision (about 280,000 cases globally), and would return all CIC-related fees to the applicants. Defined by the government as "stale" cases that slowed down CIC's ability to move to a "just in time" immigration system, the move was presented as a way to make Canadian immigration more responsive to the imperative of finding immigrants with the skills that Canadian employers needed. Applicants in the backlog had their federal fees returned, but this likely represented only a small portion of what they had invested in the application process, since immigration consultant and other professional fees (such as English language testing, medical examination fees, and other related credential assessment fees) can amount to at least C$1,800–2,000, or about one lakh (100,000) rupees.[4]

These changes in processing priority also resulted in increasingly long waits for family class applicants, especially parents and grandparents. India is a site of high demand for family class applicants, and processing times were longer than other overseas offices. While temporary visas are currently issued in three cities across India (Delhi, Chandigarh, and Bengaluru), permanent applicants must be submitted online to a central Canadian office, and then are dealt with through the New Delhi High Commission office. To further reshape the nature of migration from India, in 2011 the federal government placed a moratorium on all parent and grandparent sponsorships, while introducing a "super visa" that would allow for extended visits up to two years by relatives as long as they qualified for the visa and purchased their own health insurance (this was revealed around the same time as the moratorium on family sponsorship was announced; Government of Canada 2013).[5] By late 2012 the Canadian government also introduced new regulations for conditional permanent residence in the case of sponsored spouses/partners in order to prevent marriage fraud (*Canada Gazette* 2012). This set of restrictive policy changes was not in isolation. While the FSW and family class immigration streams became more restrictive, new forms of migration opportunity were emerging that were directed at younger semi-skilled migrants and more targeted to skilled migrants with temporary employment opportunities. These new visa streams provided temporary rather than permanent residence. The "citizenship for talent" or social network migration was being replaced by elongated settlement opportunities that allowed for more gradual integration through approved educational or employment channels. The permanence of early migration streams was being replaced by temporary modes of settlement.

Temporal: New Temporary Visa Regimes

Since the early 2000s Canadian immigration policy has seen the expansion of Temporary Foreign Worker programs (TFWP) and new policy routes that allow the conversion of some temporary workers to permanent residents (Alboim and the Maytree Foundation 2009). This is no longer "citizenship for talent exchange," but the *potential* to convert talent, plus residence, to permanent settlement. Rather than a long-term demographic nation-building exercise based on incorporating all migrants as permanent citizens, these immigration policy changes are seen as facilitating increasingly selective demands from employers (Fudge and Macphail 2009), and subsidizing Canada's educational market (Foreign Affairs and International Trade Canada 2012). This pattern of temporary migration increased during the early 2000s driven by both employer demand and government policy response (Lenard and Straehle 2012). The long-term outcome of these migration streams is variable, since *some* higher skilled workers are given an opportunity to apply for permanent resident status, but some are not.

The number of temporary workers heading to Canada has been increasing, and the responsiveness of major sending countries such as India is telling. Data by National Occupational Category (NOC) suggests that TFW stock figures for Indian TFWs during 2009–2011 increased from 12,363 to 16,299. The highest number of recent Indian TFWs has been in NOC O (management occupations), NOC A (occupations that require university education), followed by NOC B (occupations that usually require college or vocational education or apprenticeship training). In addition to India's use of the higher skill temporary worker channels, student visa opportunities have also dramatically increased (see Figure 13.2).

Educational migration is an area of significant complementarity for India and Canada. Canada has an internationally well-respected post-secondary education sector that the nation is increasingly keen to promote (Foreign Affairs and International Trade Canada 2012). India has identified the need for massive educational expansion in order to reap the benefits of its demographic dividend (Bhatia and Dash 2010). In 2011, the flow of international students to Canada from India was about 24,000, which represents a substantial growth over the previous years (see Figure 13.2). Canadian policy changes in the area of international students now allows for conversion from study to work visa and in some cases to permanent residence (Williams et al. 2015). This changed position toward international students echoes similar policy developments in other OECD nations, where students are increasingly feted as permanent migrants (Faist, 2008; Wadhwa, Bhandari, and Blumenethal 2011; Hawthorne 2008).

Policy innovation in this domain highlights Canada's approach to Indian demand for education and immigration opportunities. In 2009, Canada launched the Student Partners Program (SPP) in India, which partnered with Canadian Community Colleges. Just fewer than 5,000 visas were processed in the first year, increasing to 12,000 in the third year. While the SPP is India wide, in the first year over 60 percent of applications came from Punjab.[6] Before the emergence of the SPP, Canada was seen as seriously lagging in the international student market in India, especially compared to Australia. However, by 2013 India was the second largest source of international students in Canada (after China), representing 31,665 (over 10 percent) of total international students in Canada (CBIE 2014).

This policy transition toward more facilitative student visa processing in India has been well received, but the use of temporary status to promote this migration moves risk from the state to the migrant applicant. International student flows from India necessitate pre-departure planning and investment in the form of English language proficiency training. While there is the promise of long-term settlement, there is always a risk that this can be denied. Express Entry, the new immigration application management process introduced in 2015, has raised some concerns about the ability of international students to convert from temporary to permanent residence status (Williams et al. 2015). This educational visa stream has resulted in a steady and continuous increase in international student applicants, so that today it represents the largest flow of migrants to Canada from India (see Figure 13.2). The migration economy of Punjab has also shifted toward educational migration (Gill and Walton-Roberts forthcoming). The following example illustrates this reorientation of the Punjab's migration culture. In conversations with a consortium of Punjabi college educators visiting Canada, the main interest they expressed was not how to enhance skills training for the needs of India's domestic economic development, but rather how to provide an education in Punjab that could more easily be translated into a Canadian credential.[7]

Along with improvements to international student visa processing, Canada has also been active in improving visitor and business visa processes in the India–Canada corridor. The difficulties that Indian citizens faced in being granted visitor visas were often one of the most contentious issues for Canada–India business associations (Walton-Roberts 2010). Since 2010, the Canadian government claims that "Fast-track processes have been instituted to expedite processing of visas for designated business travellers." The Indian Consul General in Toronto also stated that the visa issue was no longer a problem for India–Canada relations.[8] The Canadian government claims that over 99 percent of applications through the Business Express program are approved, most within two working days, and the maximum validity of the temporary resident visa has increased from five to ten years (subject to passport validity).

Immigration policy change has influenced the nature of Indian migration to Canada. We can see these changes in terms of the regional origin of migrants, moving from the dominance of northern India and the Punjabi language to more diversified migrant streams; greater diversity in the type of visas Indians use to travel to Canada, including more skilled, less family and more temporary work; and study visas that are not automatically made permanent. This creates greater precarity for the migrant, while reducing the "risk" for Canada—only the most self-sufficient applicants will be selected out of the Express Entry pool. Students have also become a key market for Indian migration to Canada, but how far this will convert into permanent residence through the Express Entry process in Canada needs to be assessed in the coming years.

Conclusion

By examining the resilience of spatiality in transnational immigrant networks between Canada and India, this chapter helps to rethink highly skilled immigration processes not in terms of poaching professionals but producing them. Skilled immigrants do not just appear out of thin air in response to policy change; systems are already in place that feed immigrants into transnational migration corridors. These systems reorient themselves to the demands of policy change. Skilled migration policies must be seen as part of a longer historical trajectory where human mobility between sites of uneven development are marked by the demands and desires of the receiving region, but are variably exploited and resisted by the source communities that are invested in the social capital that international migration can bring.

Colonialism integrated the region of Punjab into the global economy, and reinforced the mobility not only of goods and ideas, but also people. Jat Sikhs benefited from colonial migration opportunities due to their sociopolitical position and desirable "militia" qualities, but this process of migration also became necessary in order to maintain their social and economic status in light of colonial taxation demands. Migration emerged as a key dimension of social and spatial mobility during the early 1900s, but soon after this period nationalist race-based immigration exclusions increased in Canada. In the 1960s, Canadian immigration policy became less racially determined, and the Sikh community exercised its social and political capital by reproducing community via family and spousal migration, a system of immigrant settlement the state facilitated through policy design. In the 1990s and 2000s, immigration policy began to emphasize increased skill-based selectivity, while restricting and delaying family class processing. The movement of migrants from Punjab was not reduced for long, however. Temporary and skilled migration opportunities have been embraced in Punjab, as indicated by the continued presence of Punjabi language dominance in skilled migration streams, and the orientation of a migration-education economy in the region. Linguistic diversification has certainly accompanied the policy shift toward greater migrant selectivity and visa diversity, but the effort of the region of Punjab to meet the selectivity of skilled immigration policy change is testament to the argument that policy change alone is not the story. Rather, we need to understand contemporary shifts through the lens of place and policy, joined through sensitivity to the *longue durée*.

Three key issues are worth recounting as we reflect on how the rise of skilled migration policy has been reflected in the pattern of migration from India. Spatially, immigration has diversified as linguistic data reveals; the social class of immigration has also changed toward greater skilled migration and away from family class. More recently, immigration policy has continued the move toward greater selectivity, but through the process of temporary and student migration, which in turn is facilitated by a migration economy in Punjab that has oriented to serve the needs of the Canadian system. Throughout the structural policy shifts Canada has developed, the regional pull of the northern state of Punjab continues to exert its influence on migrant flows between the two countries. The growth in skilled migration from India accompanied linguistic diversity, but eventually Punjabi speakers regained their dominant presence in these flows. The rise of student migration has also been significantly taken up in Punjab.

Contextualizing policy changes in relation to place—to the social and economic processes occurring within sending regions—enhances scholarship on skilled immigration by explicitly recognizing how histories of engagement, exchange, and uneven development have structured human mobility and movement. For example, Canada's recent shift toward more "just in time" methods of skilled migration must continue to be assessed in terms of uneven development (Wise and Covarrubia 2012), transfers of demographic wealth (Khadria 2009), and the influence of meritocracy and social exclusion (Waters 2006). Furthermore, the "citizenship for talent" exchange debate has to be re-evaluated in the Canadian case, since temporary migration offers only the potential (no guarantee) of a pathway to permanent citizenship status. Temporary migration extends the settlement process, increases the costs borne by the migrant, and transfers the majority of socioeconomic risk to the migrant before any commitment to citizenship exchange is offered by the state. Calculating the transnational costs and benefits of new skilled migration policies, what sectors of society they will be borne by, and what ongoing influence such policies will have in sending regions are all key research questions.

Rather than replicate the atomized human capital view of skilled migration, this chapter suggests that migratory processes are embedded in the historical social context of connectivity between places. By placing India and Canada migration flows into their longer historical context, the chapter traced how Canadian immigration has always shaped the selection of the immigrant in accordance with some kind of differentiation process, be it the valiant colonial soldier, the hardy resource worker, the family-connected migrant, the skilled IT worker, or the youthful partly trained student. Policy changes shape the nature of migrant flows from India over time, but throughout these policy transformations sociospatial tendencies that have historically dominated the migratory pathways find a way to retain their influence. Further research must examine the institutions that respond to these policy shifts in places where immigration processes are already embedded into the social fabric. How do the bureaucratic attempts of immigrant-receiving countries to reshape immigration flows adapt to the spatial and temporal resiliency of already existing immigration networks? Understanding how place intersects and interacts with migration policy change is key to mapping the variable nature of this global knowledge transfer system.

Acknowledgments

Funding for this research was provided by Shastri Indo-Canadian Institute, The Asia-Pacific Foundation, the BC Metropolis Centre, Wilfrid Laurier University research office, and Social Sciences and Humanities Research Council. I would like to thank Keegan Williams and Sarah Ingle of the International Migration Research Centre for their assistance in the preparation of this chapter, and the editors of the collection for their valuable insights and comments on earlier drafts.

Notes

1. See the Citizenship and Immigration Canada website for more details: www.cic.gc.ca/english/immigrate/express/express-entry.asp
2. Metropolis Canada was a network of national research centers through which immigration data was made available. The Metropolis research network funding ended in 2014.
3. Speaking notes for The Honorable Jason Kenney, P.C., M.P. Minister of Citizenship, Immigration and Multiculturalism at a news conference to announce changes to the Federal Skilled Worker and Investor Immigration programs in Toronto, Ontario, June 26, 2010. Available at: www.cic.gc.ca/English/department/media/speeches/2010/2010-06-26.asp (accessed June 21, 2011).
4. There were 105,000 cases as of September 2012. A legal case against the process has been heard. The argument rests on discrimination since "A significant majority, 91.9 per cent, of the unprocessed files, which were terminated, originated in visa offices in Asia, the Middle East or Africa." The Federal Court of Canada eventually ruled that the Immigration Minister had the right to make these changes. Available at: http://decisions.fca-caf.gc.ca/fca-caf/decisions/en/item/73144/index.do (accessed October 24, 2015).
5. "Effective November 5, 2011, no new applications to sponsor parents or grandparents are being accepted for processing for up to 24 months. However, parents and grandparents may be eligible to visit Canada for up to two years under the Parent and Grandparent Super Visa." Available at: www.cic.gc.ca/english/immigrate/sponsor/relatives.asp (accessed November 3, 2013).
6. Personal communication June 9, 2011 with CIC New Delhi visa processing officer.
7. Personal meeting with delegation of Punjabi vocational colleges and schools, Ottawa, November 24, 2015.
8. Indian High Commissioner to Canada Preeti Saran comments made at Wilfrid Laurier SBE conference 2011.

References

Alboim, N. 2009. Adjusting the balance: Fixing Canada's economic immigration policies. Maytree, July 2009. Available at: http://maytree.com/policy-papers/adjusting-the-balance-fixing-canadas-economic-immigration-policies.html (accessed March 29, 2012).

Ali, I. 1988. *The Punjab under imperialism, 1885–1947.* Princeton, NJ: Princeton University Press.

Amelina, A., and T. Faist. 2012. De-naturalizing the national in research methodologies: Key concepts of transnational studies in migration. *Ethnic and Racial Studies* 35 (10): 1707–1724.

Anderson, K. J. 1991. *Vancouver's Chinatown: Racial discourse in Canada, 1875–1980.* McGill-Queen's Press-MQUP.

Ashutosh, I., and A. Mountz. 2011. Migration management for the benefit of whom? Interrogating the work of the International Organization for Migration. *Citizenship Studies* 15 (01): 21–38.

Ballard, R. 2002. The South Asian presence in Britain and its transnational connections. In *Culture and economy in the Indian diaspora*, eds. H. Singh and S. Vertovec, 197–222. London: Routledge.

Bauder, H. 2006. *Labor movement: How migration regulates labor markets.* New York: Oxford University Press.

Benhabib, S. 2005. Borders, boundaries, and citizenship. *Political Science and Politics*, 673–677.

Bhatia, K., and M. K. Dash. 2010. National knowledge commission–A step towards India's higher education reforms on India's higher education. *International Research Journal of Finance and Economics*, 53.

Bhatti, E. M. 2007. *East Indian immigration into Canada 1905–1973.* Lahore: Pakistan Study Centre.

Brown, P., and S. Tannock. 2009. Education, meritocracy and the global war for talent. *Journal of Education Policy* 24 (4): 377–392.

Buchignani, N., D. M. Indra, and R. Srivastava. 1985. *Continuous journey: A social history of South Asians in Canada.* McClelland & Stewart.

Buck, C. H. 1906. Canal irrigation in the Punjab. *The Geographical Journal* 27 (1): 60–67.

Canada Gazette 2012. Regulations amending the immigration and refugee protection regulations. November 7. Available at: www.gazette.gc.ca/rp-pr/p2/2012/2012-11-07/html/sor-dors227-eng.html (accessed April 15, 2016).

CBIE 2014. Canada's performance in international education 2014. Available at: www.cbie.ca/about-ie/facts-and-figures (last accessed November 30, 2015).

Citizenship and Immigration Canada (CIC) 2011. Immigration facts and figures. Available at: www.cic.gc.ca/english/resources/statistics/facts2011 (accessed December 3, 2015).

Citizenship and Immigration Canada (CIC) 2013. Immigration facts and figures. Permanent and temporary resident overview. Available at: www.cic.gc.ca/english/resources/statistics/menu-fact.asp (accessed December 3, 2015).

Duncan, N. T. 2012. *Immigration policymaking in the global era: In pursuit of global talent.* New York: Palgrave Macmillan.

Faist, T. 2008. Migrants as transnational development agents: An inquiry into the newest round of the migration–development nexus. *Population, Space and Place* 14, 21–42.

Florida, R. 2005. *The flight of the creative class: The new global competition for talent.* New York: Harper Business.

Flynn, E., and H. Bauder 2014. The private sector, institutions of higher education, and immigrant settlement in Canada. *Journal of International Migration and Integration*, 1–18.

Foreign Affairs and International Trade Canada 2012. International education: A key driver of Canada's future prosperity. Available at: www.international.gc.ca/education/assets/pdfs/ies_report_rapport_sei-eng.pdf (last accessed March 31, 2016).

Fox, R. G. 1985. *Lions of the Punjab: Culture in the making*. Los Angeles, CA: University of California Press.

Fudge, J., and F. MacPhail. 2009. The temporary foreign worker program in Canada: Low-skilled workers as an extreme form of flexible labour. *Comparative Labor Law and Policy Journal* 31, 101–139.

Gill, H., and M. Walton-Roberts (forthcoming). Placing the transnational migrant: Social inclusion and exclusion. In *Urbanization in a global context*, eds. A. Bain and L. Peake. Oxford: Oxford University Press.

Gilmartin, D. 2004. Migration and modernity: The state, the Punjabi village, and the settling of the canal colonies. In *People on the move: Punjabi colonial, and post-colonial migration,* eds. I. Talbot and S. Thandi, 3–20. Oxford: Oxford University Press.

Glick Schiller, N. 2005. Transnational urbanism as a way of life: A research topic not a metaphor. *City and Society* 17 (1): 49–64.

Government of Canada (2013). India–Canada relations fact sheet. Available at: www.canadainternational.gc.ca/india-inde/bilateral_relations_bilaterales/canada_india-inde.aspx?view=d&lang=eng (accessed December 3, 2015).

Harper, S. 2008. Prime Minister urges stronger trade relations with India. Press release, April 18. Available at: www.pm.gc.ca/eng/media.asp?id=2072 (accessed March 21, 2016).

Hawthorne, L. 2008. The growing global demand for students as skilled migrants. Migration Policy Institute. Available at: www.migrationpolicy.org/transatlantic/intlstudents.pdf (accessed March 21, 2016).

Hiebert, D. 2002. The spatial limits to entrepreneurship: Immigrant entrepreneurs in Canada. *Tijdschrift voor Economische en Sociale Geografie* 93 (2): 173–190.

Hyndman, J., and W. Giles 2011. Waiting for what? The feminization of asylum in protracted situations. *Gender, Place and Culture* 18 (3): 361–379.

Johnston, H. J. 2014. *The voyage of the Komagata Maru: The Sikh challenge to Canada's colour bar*. Toronto: UBC Press.

Kaur, H. 2012. Reconstructing the Sikh diaspora. *International Migration*, 50 (1), 129–142.

Khadria, B. 2009. Adversary analysis and the quest for global development: Optimizing the dynamic conflict of interest in transnational migration. *Social Analysis*, 52 (3), 106–122.

Koser, K. 2010. Introduction: International migration and global governance. *Global governance: A review of multilateralism and international organizations*, 16 (3), 301–315.

Kritz, M., L. L. Lim, and H. Zlotnik (eds.). 1992. *International migration systems: A global approach*. Oxford: Clarendon Press.

Lenard, P. T., and C. Straehle (eds.). 2012. *Legislated inequality: Temporary labour migration in Canada*. Montreal: McGill-Queen's Press-MQUP.

Macklin, A. (2007). "Who is the citizen's Other? Considering the heft of citizenship" *Theoretical Inquiries in Law* 8.2, 333–366.

Manning S., S. Massini, and A. Lewin. 2008. "A dynamic perspective on next-generation offshoring: The global sourcing of science and engineering talent." *Academy of Management Perspectives,* 22, 3: 35–54.

Mau, S., F. Gülzau, L. Laube, and N. Zaun. 2015. "The global mobility divide: How visa policies have evolved over time." *Journal of Ethnic and Migration Studies* 41 (8): 1192–1213.

Mongia, R.V. 1999. Race, nationality, mobility: a history of the passport. *Public Culture* 11, 527–556.

Mooney, N. 2006. Aspiration, reunification and gender transformation in Jat Sikh marriages from India to Canada. *Global Networks* 6: 389–403.

Ong, A. (1999) *Flexible citizenship: The cultural logics of transnationality*, Durham, NC: Duke University Press.

Picot, G., and A. Sweetman. 2012. Making it in Canada: Immigration outcomes and policies. *IRPP Study* 29 (1).

Ray, B. 2005. Country profiles. Canada: Policy changes and integration challenges in an increasingly diverse society. Migration Information Source. Available at: www.migrationinformation.org/Profiles/display.cfm?ID=348 (accessed October 22, 2010).

Reitz, J. G. 2013. Closing the gaps between skilled immigration and Canadian labor markets: Emerging policy issues and priorities. In *Wanted and Welcome?,* ed. T. Triadafilopoulos, 147–163. New York: Springer.

Reitz, J. G., J. Curtis, and J. Elrick. 2014. Immigrant skill utilization: Trends and policy issues. *Journal of International Migration and Integration* 15 (1:) 1–26.

Saxenian, A. 2006. *The new Argonauts: Regional advantage in a global economy.* Cambridge, MA: Harvard University Press.

Shachar, A. 2006. The race for talent: Highly skilled migrants and competitive immigration regimes. *New York University Law Review*, 81: 148.

Shachar, A., and R. Bauböck. 2014. Should citizenship be for sale? *Robert Schuman Centre for Advanced Studies Research Paper* 2014/01.

Sharma, K.A. 1997. *The ongoing journey: Indian migration to Canada.* New Delhi: Creative Books.

Statistics Canada. 2013. Immigration and Ethnocultural Diversity in Canada. Available at: www12.statcan.gc.ca/nhs-enm/2011/as-sa/99-010-x/99-010-x2011001-eng.pdf (accessed November 30, 2015).

Talbot, I., and Thandi, S. (eds.). 2004. *People on the move: Punjabi colonial and post-colonial migration.* Oxford University Press: Oxford.

Tatla, D. S. 1995. Sikh free and military migration during the colonial period. *Cambridge Survey of World Migration*, ed. R. Cohen, 69–76. Cambridge: Cambridge University Press.

———. 2004. Rural roots of the Sikh diaspora. In *People on the move: Punjabi colonial, and post-colonial migration,* eds. I. Talbot and S. Thandi, 45–59. Oxford: Oxford University Press.

Torpey, J. 2000. *The invention of the passport: Surveillance, citizenship and the state.* Cambridge, New York: Cambridge University Press.

Tran, K., J. Kaddatz, and P. Allard. 2005. South Asians in Canada: Unity through diversity. Canadian Social Trends Autumn 2005. Available at: www.statcan.gc.ca/pub/11-008-x/2005002/article/8455-eng.pdf (accessed August 20, 2012).

Tyner, J. A. 1999. The global context of gendered labor migration from the Philippines to the United States. *American Behavioral Scientist* 42: 671–689.

Wadhwa, R., R. Bhandari, and P. Blumenthal. 2011. International students and global mobility in higher education: National trends and new directions. *Higher Education,* 1–3.

Walsh, J. 2011. Quantifying citizens: Neoliberal restructuring and immigration selection in Canada and Australia. *Citizenship Studies*, 15 (6–7), 861–879.

Walton-Roberts, M. 2003. Transnational geographies: Indian immigration to Canada. *The Canadian Geographer* 47 (3): 235–250.

———. 2010. The trade and immigration nexus in the India–Canada context. In *Transnational and immigrant entrepreneurship in a globalized world*, eds. B. Carmichael, B. Honig, and I. Drori, 145–180. Toronto: University of Toronto Press.

———. 2011. Relocating the Sikh subject: Sikh veterans and the royal Canadian legion. *Sikh Formations*, 7 (2): 195–210.

Washbrook, D. A. 1981. Law, state and agrarian society in colonial India. *Modern Asian Studies* 15 (03), 649–721.

Waters, J. L. 2006. Emergent geographies of international education and social exclusion. *Antipode* 38 (5), 1046–1068.

Williams, K., G. Williams, A. Arbuckle, M. Walton-Roberts, and J. Hennebry. 2015. International students in Ontario's post-secondary education system 2000–2012. Research Report for Higher Education Quality Council Ontario.

Wimmer, A., N. Glick Schiller. 2002. Methodological nationalism and beyond: Nation-state building, migration and the social sciences. *Global networks* 2 (4): 301–334.

Wise, R. D., M. Covarrubia. 2012. Strategic dimensions of neoliberal globalization: The exporting of labour force and unequal exchange. *Advanced in Applied Sociology* 2 (2): 127–134.

14 Experiences of Returned Chinese Migrants in Higher Education Examined through a Case Study

Qingfang Wang, Li Tang, and Huiping Li

> In 2007, shocking many of his peers, Rao Yi, a biologist, gave up his position as head of a scientific institute at Northwestern University in Illinois to take up a post as dean of the School of Life Sciences at Peking University. In 2008, the Princeton molecular biologist Shi Yigong also chose his homeland over the US after rejecting a $10m research grant from the Howard Hughes Medical Institute and accepting a job as dean of life sciences at Beijing's Tsinghua University.
>
> (*New York Times*, 2010)

Obviously, Rao and Shi are not the only highly educated overseas-trained Chinese who returned to China. In 2012, 272,900 overseas-trained Chinese returned to China, a 50 percent growth from the previous year, which increased the total number of returnees to 1.09 million (Wang and Miao 2013). Such a growth of return migration is closely related to the Chinese government's talent policies in recent years. From the central to the local governments, major programs in China have been aggressively aimed at attracting top-notch overseas ethnic Chinese (Cao 2008). In this process, Chinese universities have embraced these talent recruitment programs so as to increase their global competitiveness. Their participation in the programs will further dictate resource allocation between governments and universities. Therefore, the universities have both institutional motivation and outside pressure to be highly involved and play a major role in implementing these talent programs.

In many other countries, in both the developed and developing world, higher education institutions (HEIs) have also acted as major instruments to attract and retain highly skilled transnational migrants (Dill and van Vought 2010; Robertson 2010). While these government programs have been presented through collective interests and national goals (Xiang 2011), we have known very little about the post-migration experiences of these "targets" themselves, "talent" or "the highly skilled." Still taking China as an example, while the large volume of returnees paints a promising picture, we sometimes heard stories like the following:

> In 2011, Min-Xin Guan, who gave up a tenured professorship in the Department of Human Genetics at Cincinnati Children's Hospital Medical Center,

> signed a four-year contract to work at Zhejiang University as the Dean of College of Life Sciences. He is the recipient of the "Thousand Talents Plan," one of most prestigious national talent recruitment plans. November 2013, he was unexpectedly informed by the university that "the contract was terminated" before his term was due, without being provided valid explanations.
>
> (*ScienceNet* 2013)

> Xuxin Tu, who was born in 1977 and earned a PhD degree in Civil Engineering at Northwestern University in 2007, returned to China and was employed at Zhejiang University in 2009. In the same year right after he submitted his tenure and promotion package, he was found dead by jumping off an eleven-floor building. He left a letter before his death which says that "the reality of domestic academic circles: cruel, unreliable and ruthless."
>
> (*People's Net* 2015)

While nobody should generalize these "accidents" and tragic stories, or further speculate the factors and impacts without investigation, these stories urge us to examine the process of highly skilled migration as multi-layered and in more nuanced ways. Traditional migration theories, such as the "brain drain" and "brain gain" debates, have advanced our knowledge of migration of the highly skilled. However, not only have these theories treated international migration as a "zero-sum" process, but they have also focused more on the "aggregated" impacts at the national or regional level, lacking the nuances of interactions among individual migrants (and their families), their institutional and professional settings, and the national and global networks of knowledge production.

Through a case study in a highly ranked Chinese university in a global city, we seek to understand why these highly skilled migrants decide to return to their home country and what their work experiences are after returning. Through quantitative analyses of individual level data, in-depth interviews, and documentation analyses, we find that these individual return migrants, as transnational bodies of knowledge, have actively utilized their transnational ties to negotiate with higher education institutions and maintain their elite positions. At the same time, their experiences, with both challenges and barriers, have reflected the uneven production of global knowledge and power of academic ranking nation- and worldwide.

Insights from this study will contribute to the understanding of highly skilled migration through a case of return migration, with China as an emerging power that diligently promotes national and regional development through technology and science innovation. It integrates the role of higher education as an industrial sector and HEIs as institutional agents to the framework of high-skilled/talent migration; and, thus, it extends the traditional focus of international migration on macro-level economic change only to include social transformations at the local and institutional level. At the same time, while existing focus in the field of higher education internationalization is mainly at the HEI institutional level and/or international students, this study provides a geographic, multi-scaled, and relational approach to bridge scholarship in transnational labor migration and global knowledge production. Ultimately, results from this study contribute to migration and immigration policies for both immigrant sending and receiving countries, especially with China emerging as a promising higher education market, a competitor, and a collaborator in the global higher education system.

Return Migration in Higher Education and the Chinese Contexts

Return or Not to Return: Academic Contexts

Existing migration studies have offered different perspectives as to why people move, especially to other countries (Lewis 1954; Boyd 1989; Borjas 1990). The reverse migration phenomenon, including return migration, challenges traditional theories of international migration in that it contradicts the assumption that migratory patterns are linear and unidirectional. Rather, movement is continuous, multidirectional, fluid, and temporary (Ley and Kobayashi 2005; Solimano and Avanzini 2010). To make the decision to return or not to return, previous studies have suggested that personal and family factors, feelings of belonging, prospects of career development, new technologies of communication, discriminatory experiences, restrictive immigration policies in host countries, and economic development in the home country have all contributed to the decision-making process (Gmelch 1980; Zweig 1997; Simon and Cao 2009; also see Chapter 15 in this book).

Similar to general labor migration, individual motivation, professional networks, career advancement opportunities, wage differentials, and quality of life factors have all motivated academic migration (Kofman 2007). In addition, life course has played significant roles in the migration decision-making processes of male and female scientists, particularly, partnering and dual science career situations in a family (Ackers 1998, 2005; Williams 2009; Kim 2010).

Furthermore, academic settings determined by professional norms, geographic flexibility, and spatial variation, are very important factors in shaping the migratory flow of academics. Working effectively in academia often implies access to high quality infrastructure, facilities, funding, and human capital, as well as some informal institutional factors such as value systems of scientists, and research autonomy and freedom. These resources are increasingly "clustered" in resource-rich, often highly specialized, centers or institutes (Ackers 2001). For these features, different from many other types of highly skilled migration, academic migration is more often shaped by the intellectual relationships rather than merely directed by pure economic incentives. Therefore, the hierarchical nature of the professional and institutional forces can significantly structure the boundary and direction of academic migration across place (Williams 2009; Cantwell 2011; Tremblay and Hardwick 2014).

"Aggregated" Impacts vs. Individually Accumulated Social Capital

The migration of the highly skilled from less developed to more developed countries has raised concerns of "brain drain" in that movement of skill and talent increasingly benefits the receiving countries at the expense of sending countries (Koser and Salt 1997; Beine, Docquier, and Rapoport 2001). However, this perspective has been challenged by the emerging trends of return migration, remigration, and multiple migrations. A "brain gain" perspective argues that skill outflow could be a potential resource for the source country because migrants returning with cutting-edge knowledge and networks of nationals abroad are considered important transmitters of technology and tacit knowledge (Davenport 2004). Further, researcher argues that both sending and receiving countries could benefit from the circular movement of highly skilled migrants, termed as "brain exchange" or "brain circulation" (Saxenian 2005; Yang and Welch 2010; Jöns 2011).

While these perspectives have provided valuable insights, they have focused on the "aggregated" impacts at the national or regional level. Leung (2013) has criticized that this averaged and aggregated treatment of impacts from migration does not provide a grounded understanding of the lived experiences of academic mobility and the impact of mobility at the individual level. For instance, Waters (2005, 2006) has demonstrated that middle-class families in Hong Kong send their children to Canada for an "overseas education." International schools and overseas schooling then serve to reinforce the boundaries of upper-middle-class privilege and actively create a distinctive group identity, which is subsequently rewarded in the labor market. Similarly, Findlay et al. (2012) argue that study abroad especially in those "world class" universities has served as important social and cultural capital to enter or maintain an elite class status for the student participants in these programs. For academic returnees from overseas to China, however, we still do not know how the Western educational credential is negotiated through practices at both personal and institutional level, and how the process of return migration is reflected through the interactions among individual migrants, academic institutional and professional settings, and national and global networks of knowledge production.

Uneven World Higher Education System and HEIs in China

The global higher education system is asymmetric (Altbach 2004). Academic centers located in Western Europe and North America provide leadership in most aspects of science and scholarship for the world, with the developing countries in a weak position to compete. Researchers have argued that transnational mobile academics are under the imperatives of "academic capitalism," most of which are the extension or transformation of academic centers in the Global North (Kim 2010). Nevertheless, asserting that transnationally mobile academics are entirely dependent upon the world's higher education hierarchy belies the substantial power of institutions in the periphery and academic individuals themselves.

As a major part of a national higher education reform, China has sought to attract highly talented scholars from around the world (Simon and Cao 2009; Xiang 2011). With a variety of government programs, the central government launched a national talent development plan in 2010, *The National Medium- and Long-term Talent Development Plan (2010–2020)*. As the first national comprehensive plan in China's history of national human resources development, it creates a blueprint for a highly skilled national workforce within the next ten years. The tenets of this national policy express China's efforts to combat emerging issues with national development and maintain the Chinese growth locomotive, with a target to transform China into a more innovative and creative country by 2020 (Wang 2010). A dozen high-level talent recruitment plans have been launched by the central government that further generated numerous regional and local-level recruitment programs nationwide.

Key to the Chinese recruitment strategy is Chinese HEIs who have actively embraced these programs. Many universities are striving to become "World-Class Universities" that are featured with highly talented faculty and students, adequate facilities, appropriate funding, and international diversity, among other characteristics (Jöns and Hoyler 2013). Of all the different strategies, a university vying for world-class status always actively recruits highly talented faculty globally and uses the recruitment programs as the most effective way to increase its global research rankings. It is generally accepted that overseas returnees and the transnational collaborations they fostered significantly contributed to the rise of Chinese universities' rankings in the world (Jonkers and Tijssen 2008; Yi 2011). The June 2013 issue of *Nature Publishing Index 2012 Global* reported that China ranked sixth in the world in research paper output, with nine of its institutions in the top 200, an increase from just three the previous year. And, whereas in 2008 there were no Chinese institutions in the top 200 world universities listed in the Academic Ranking of World Universities (ARWU) ranking, by 2013 five Chinese universities—Fudan, Peking, Shanghai Jiao Tong, Tsinghua and Zhejiang—had made it into the top 200.

Altogether, the multidisciplinary literature in the above discussion indicates that the rationales and consequences of transnational academic migration need to be understood in the interactions among individual migrants (and their families), academic institutional and professional settings, national systems of higher education, and global networks of knowledge production. We believe the HEI system and the state's policies on transnational migration do not merely contextualize our study, but also function as constitutive political forces to shape and be reshaped by transnational academic migration between China and the world.

Data and Method

The case study was conducted in an urban university in the eastern region of China (with a pseudonym of "East Region University" or "ERU" hereafter). It has about 22,000 students and 800 full-time faculty members. It is a top-ranked research university specializing in applied social science related disciplines.

According to the latest ranking from a globally recognized indicator, ERU ranks first in 2012 among all the universities in the Greater China Region, which include the Mainland, Hong Kong and Taiwan, ranks seventh place in all of Asia and is rated eighty-seventh worldwide.[1]

Since 2005, ERU has recruited overseas talents through unconventional means including high economic incentives, pioneering tenure-track evaluation systems, and active international academic exchange programs. From 2005 to 2012, ERU recruited 158 doctoral recipients from abroad, 70.1 percent of those from the US and Canada, 22.6 percent from Asia, and 7.3 percent from Europe. Most of these talents are young, with 105 of them (about three- quarters) as newly awarded Ph.Ds or those with work experience of no more than one year. In recent years it has drawn much national and global attention for its rapid growth in research productivity and pioneering practices in adopting a "dual-track" faculty evaluation system. Under this system, faculty members trained in China are in the traditional faculty management system, while those overseas doctoral recipients on the faculty are managed and evaluated by a tenure track system. The tenure track system is very similar to that of the United States. Of the total 800 full-time faculty members at ERU, about 20 percent in the tenure track system are mainly overseas trained.

Our research was conducted at three stages from 2013 to 2014. At Stage One, due to availability and the confidential nature of the data of job applicants, we focused on one college within ERU. This college has five departments, a total of 1,700 students, nearly half of whom are undergraduate students and the others either masters or doctoral students. With one particular field ranked as the strongest nationally, this college has developed multidisciplinary specializations including public finance, economics, political science, public administration, and sociology. The college started recruiting overseas returnees in 2008. When the research was conducted, it had eighty faculty members, twenty-one of whom were in the tenure-track system.

At the first stage, we first collected data for each individual job applicant who applied for the job from 2010 to 2012. Then we retrieved these applicants' CVs by using Google to search the websites of either the respective individuals or their organizations. All full CVs were collected in the period of May–June 2012. Next, we ran a probit regression analysis to examine the personal characteristics associated with the probability of being on the final list of job candidates (the "short list") eligible for further interviewing and those who were given job offers. After this, we conducted fourteen in-depth interviews in late 2012 with the job candidates who received and accepted offers to obtain information about their experiences in the job-searching process.[2] Finally, we talked to the Assistant to the Dean. Both the Dean and the Assistant were the key persons responsible for overseas recruitment.

At stage two from 2013 to 2014, we expanded the interviews with overseas trained faculty members to all the five colleges at ERU that have adopted the "dual-track" faculty evaluation system. Based on the directory of the overseas trained faculty members, we randomly selected and conducted twenty in-depth interviews in these five colleges. Since most returnees are new to the university, there is little variation among the population of returnees in terms of their age and rank at ERU. Each participant was presented with the same set of open-ended questions, which permitted a high degree of flexibility and allowed informants to move their narratives to topics outside the immediate scope of the guide (Dunn, 2000). The interview questions are focused on the following dimensions: why they decide to return to China, their experiences after returning, opportunities and challenges after they return, their interaction with domestically trained faculty members, how they are evaluated, and their future plans.

Further, to understand the experiences of post-migration from a comparative perspective, at stage three, we conducted twenty-seven in-depth interviews with China domestically trained faculty members in these five colleges. We first ranked the population of the domestic faculty by age and professional rank, and then randomly selected the participants from the faculty roster. Again, each participant was presented with the same set of open-ended questions. These questions included their current opportunities and challenges, their interaction with overseas returnees, how they are evaluated, and their future plans. Results for the current chapter mainly came from results at stages one and two. However, insights from stage three are useful to interpret our findings and we frequently referenced our interaction with domestically trained faculty members when necessary.

All the interviews were conducted at the interviewee's office. The interviews with oversees returnees were mainly conducted by the second and third author who themselves are overseas returnees as well. The authors' personal experiences and understanding of the local contexts helped them build trust and rapport easily with the returnee participants. To reduce sensitivity and protect confidentiality, the interviews with China domestically trained faculty were conducted by the first author who is full time working in a US university. Interviews were conducted in Chinese and lasted for 45–120 minutes. Of the total forty-seven interviews at stages two and three, forty-four interviews were audio recorded. For the three nonrecorded interviews, notes were taken during the interviews and expanded notes were prepared right after the interviews. For the recorded interviews, each was transcribed verbatim by the researcher who conducted the interview. The quotations in this article were translated from Chinese to English by the authors. Finally, using the qualitative software package QSR NVivo, we employed the techniques of narrative analysis outlined by Strauss and Corbin (1998) to code each interview transcript (or the expanded note). The next section discusses the major themes that have emerged from the analyses.

Findings and Discussion

Why Return?

Almost all the interviewees confirmed that high salary was one of the most important factors when considering the job offers. Traditional theories on international migration have long argued that pull factors, especially higher wages, better working conditions, and a better quality of life in more developed countries, have drawn people to particular places. For academic returnees, the power of the "pull" factors, such as salaries, working conditions, and the lure of scientific and scholarly centrality, is extremely important as well (Altbach 2005). Researchers have noted that social and cultural capital can be accumulated by attending elite schools (Waters 2009; Hall and Appleyard 2011). In the current case, overseas credentials are valued highly and those who were trained overseas are expected to have a higher potential for research outputs. Naturally, a higher salary and better economic package were believed to be necessary and reasonable, as well as expected, by the job candidates.

Another key element that successfully drew the overseas returnees to the ERU was the institutional environment perceived and reflected through three aspects: a cluster of overseas returnees, proactive recruiting, and a "dual-track" faculty evaluation system. Thirteen out of thirty-four interviewed returnees explicitly stated that a larger number of overseas returnees, in comparison with many other universities, are attractive to them because such a cluster may indicate a "friendly" intellectual environment for returnees. Strong leadership has played a significant role in forming, or having a potential to form, a cluster of research excellence through their proactive recruiting strategies. For example, interviewees indicated that their dean often times was a "star scientist" in his research domain and was recruited from overseas as well. These deans' prestigious position in their field, reputation, a clear vision, and strong leadership are very attractive to these young scholars who have passion for the future and for academic life. As one interviewee commented: "The Dean has drawn a very beautiful career picture for me. He told me that he would build the best (in his field) research team in China at our university. I was very excited about this!" (L5)

Previous studies had identified that institutional factors, such as research culture, politics, *guanxi* (interpersonal relationship and social networking) were among the major barriers for many academics in choosing to work in Chinese universities (Cao 2008). As discussed earlier, ERU has actively recruited overseas talents through unconventional means and adopted two different evaluation systems between overseas returnees and domestically trained faculty. On one hand, such a tenure track system was regarded as symbolic to show the importance attached to overseas talent cultivation plans from the "top-down"; on the other hand, such a system was attractive to most returnees because it provided a favorable environment for them to concentrate on research activities. Most interviewees commented that the "dual-track" evaluation system for returnees was the most valued. Some of them stated that they would not have come to this university if this special evaluation system did not exist. For instance, one interviewee commented that "The University defines 'returnees' clearly through such an evaluation system. I feel knowledge obtained overseas is valued." (T1)

About one third of the interviewees admitted that a personal connection with the current university was important in their application process. In some cases, the candidates knew the job through their former advisors who had connections with the group responsible for recruitment. In other cases, connections with former returnees helped the potential migrants understand the university environment better. Compared to kinship, friendship or other formal and strong social ties, connections generated from the identity of "being returnees" seem natural and "fair" which help the job candidates to "sense" the institutional environments at the university.

More than half of the interviewees indicate that family is a significant factor for them to return. In some cases, their spouses are working in China; in other cases, the university promised to provide positions for both husband and wife. Several interviewees mentioned that they had to come back to take care of parents as the only child in the family. While talking about returning to the home country, the returnees always added something like that, "*and*, the booming economy and globalization of China promise a bright future." Especially for social scientists and social science-related researchers, China provided "the best natural laboratory" for their research endeavors.

Finally, the quality of life and the geographic location of the city are important. A lack of social life and the isolation of university towns in the United States were regarded as push factors, contrasted to the Chinese university in a cosmopolis that is "full of charm and vitality" for a Chinese. Overall, the decision to return is made based on factors at the individual, household, and institutional level, as well as the ever-changing environments in the city and the home country.

The Academic "Elite" and Invisible Wall

Under the "dual-track" evaluation system, most of the overseas returnees were on a "tenure-track" that was similar to those found at most Western universities. Required by this evaluation system, tenure-track faculty members had to publish in highly ranked English journals and were evaluated differently from their domestically trained colleagues. For these criteria, the returnees clearly know their advantages over the domestically trained faculty. The majority of the interviewees believe that they are much more advanced than the domestically trained faculty in "the most fundamental understanding about social sciences," "familiarity with current state of knowledge," "the way of doing research," "competence in methodology," and "the overall training" that go much beyond "only writing in English." Related to their "privileges" in human capital, the overseas returnees actually earned an average annual salary of about three times that of domestically trained faculty members at the same professional rank.[3] Commonly joked by both returnees and domestically trained faculty, the faculty members in the same university are paid at different rates even though they are doing the same job (*Tong Gong Bu Tong Chou*) which fundamentally violates Chinese constitutional labor law.

For such a significant economic disparity between the two groups, first, the majority of the returnees explicitly argued that they would not have returned without such a high salary. Second, many of them believed that the salary reflects their "market value." As someone commented, "They [referring to the domestically trained faculty] may think I'm earning a lot. But the (job) market is fair. You have the choice as well (if you could publish in English and meet those criteria)." Others indeed showed their sympathy (e.g. Tp2-2, Tp2-6):

> They [domestically trained Chinese] are under huge pressure, too. You know, there are so few 'core' journals in Chinese that they can publish. The competition is so cruel! … They may get money through teaching or doing projects (*ke ti*) for others; but, their salary is very low, in addition to their inner feeling of unfairness (in comparison with us).[4]
>
> (Tp2-2)

Clearly, there was no significant trend of collaboration between the returnees and domestically trained faculty members. The returnees' collaborators are predominantly former advisers, other overseas Chinese, or other returnees who were also trained in Western countries. According to the interviewees, it is because "we share similar research interests, care about similar issues, have similar training and common language, and trust each other" (L4). Sporadically, there were one or two cases of collaboration between members from the two groups; however, the role of these domestically trained faculty members was nothing more than providing data sources.

For this situation, the returnees commented that it is very hard to collaborate with domestically trained faculty because the two groups differ by training, interests, and research goals. They particularly noted that research by domestically trained faculty is too focused on immediate goals with eagerness for quick success and instant benefits. Someone said,

> It's still a legend to collaborate on 'pure academic research' between both sides in my field. There is too much difference in the literature and the current state of knowledge … It's almost impossible to have dialogues between us from the academic research perspective.
>
> (Lp2-6)

When talking about the way of doing research among the domestically trained faculty, someone lamented that:

> many times they want to write something by knocking their head (*pai pai nao dai*). … we write based on our accumulation of the current literature in the field; but they always borrow the concepts from the dictionary. Therefore there are huge differences in both theory and methodology between us, [and] I don't have time to train them.
>
> (T6)

Beneath the surface of economic disparity and academic background differences, there is a more subtle social and cultural divide between the two groups.

Occasionally, one or two returnees commented that they "get along well" especially with the younger domestically trained faculty members (L2). However, the majority felt the indifference between the two social groups, and sometimes a significant divide or even conflict. For instance, they commented that:

> I feel like something *unnatural* between some professors and me. Maybe it's only my illusion. I didn't want to do anything consciously; but, I feel that some domestic professors seem to keep a distance from me on purpose.
>
> (L4)

> Those domestic graduates, more or less will hold discrimination on you. They may think that 'since the State already favored you so much, then I shouldn't treat you better in other aspects.' I just have this feeling, because you can sense that from their conversations.
>
> (L6)

> Sometimes it's so irritating to have conversation with them. It looks seemingly fine; inside, you may want to slam him so many times … why no collaboration with them? (I'm) well annoyed even just talking with them!
>
> (T6)

Even the earlier interviewee who believed that the two groups could get along, still stated that "we returnees are much more professional and efficient," and that "life would have been much easier if everyone in the college worked like us" (L2). One interviewee vividly described the returnees as an "isolated land of excellence" surrounded by administrative interference and academic corruption in the current higher education institutional environments in China (T3). The next two sections will elaborate how this economic, social, and cultural divide is fundamentally related to the university environment and society at large.

The Evaluation System and the Role of Higher Education

The following conversation happened in almost every interview:

A: "What's your future plan or agenda?"
B: "Survive—this is the upmost goal—to get tenure and promotion."
A: "What's the key to survive?"
B: "Papers (*lunwen*), of course."

Following the conversation, the majority of returnees would quickly tell us how academic peer-reviewed journals are rigidly classified into different tiers as a "publication list." For instance, *American Economic Review, Annals of Statistics*, and *Econometrica* are rated as "top tier"; *Journal of Finance, Annals of Probability*, and *The Accounting Review* are rated as the next tier, "first tier." Under each tier, the journals are further ranked into A or B or different zones (cited from ERU

Criteria for Tenure and Promotion 2010). In order to survive, they have to publish a certain number of articles in the top-tier and first-tier journals. Likewise, the domestically trained faculty members on the other evaluation track also have to publish a certain number of articles in top-tiered Chinese journals for promotion. As a common practice in many other Chinese universities, the university and colleges provide the domestically trained faculty members different amounts of financial awards for publications in the top journals. Interestingly, publications in Chinese journals, top or not, do not provide similar financial rewards to the returnees; nor do they count much for the returnees' tenure and promotion. "It's useless to publish in Chinese." Several returnees made such comments. For them, only the first-authored publications in ISI (The Institute for Scientific Information) or SSCI (Social Sciences Citation Index) indexed journals count.

On one hand, about one third of interviewees commented that publishing in listed journals as the first author is necessary in China, which they term as a "first-author rule." Many of them like it, as commented like this, "there are too many 'honored authors' in China. People may 'make a deal' with each other by co-authoring on everything if without the 'first-author' rule. … it is not scientific enough if without (such) uniformed criteria" (T5; Tp2-2). Further, they believe such a rule can reduce the unfairness caused by *guanxi* or nepotism. "With the current culture and academic situation, *guanxi* is very complicated. So it's necessary to have a quantifiable standard which is more scientific and subjective; otherwise, everything will be messed up" (Tp2–7).

Therefore, these quantifiable standards were favored by many returnees who are generally young and have fewer social connections. Some interviewees also believed that the uniform standards indicate that the university is gearing itself with the international conventions, since "Taiwan, Hong Kong, and other places do the same" (Lp2–12). For them, these standards are believed to help build a fair and scientific institutional environment.

On the other hand, almost everybody complained about the rigidity of the journal list and its being "overly harsh." For instance, many top journals in their respective disciplines are not rated as "top tier" in the entire college. Such a classification especially marginalized the smaller disciplines. Some international top journals are treated as "inferior" by the university, which is perceived to impede faculty's professional development. Under this evaluation system, many returnees feel undervalued. "I hope to be respected. It's not about money. We'll be very disappointed if the situation won't improve. Everything will be faked if the evaluation system goes wrong" (Lp2–2).

Some of them are much more explicit by commenting in the following way (e.g. T3):

A: "What's the most important for the current evaluation system?"
B: "It values 'garbage'."
A: "Why?"
B: "It doesn't understand each discipline at all but still has the authority to evaluate. … (the university) doesn't know what it's doing. Why do you want

> someone tenured here? The ultimate goal is to enhance your institutional reputation and academic ranking, and to cultivate more top-tiered talents. Each college has many different disciplines and each discipline is diversified. How can you use *one* journal list to evaluation everyone in the college? It's stupid."

More commonly, interviewees believe the problem is not about the ERU itself. Instead, it is closely related to how the State evaluates the higher education institutions and how, further, such evaluation determinates resource allocation. "It's unfortunate that our field favors much 'academic GDPism'" (T3). Such "academic GDPism" refers to the practice in higher education that everything is measured by publications, impact factors, and citations in English ISI or SSCI indexed journals. "China could be very shortsighted because all these quantifiable evaluation standards directly impact your (economic) interests. Everyone racks his brain to publish and doesn't really care about the quality of the work" (Lp2–5). So, they were worried that academic research is focused on something "short (*duan*), shallow (*ping*), and quick (*kuai*)" which only cares about quick profits. Someone commented that "This is a common issue across this country" (L4).

"What's the role of the university?" Several interviewees raised this question. They are concerned that the academic profession is becoming more like a profession of "making money." When the entire academic evaluation system forces one to publish journal articles, the goal of these papers are only to meet the university's desire to become a "world class" university and bring more resources associated with that status. In effect, although national development is claimed as the primary goal for the State to recruit these talents, research and development, now, are actually unrelated. They reflected that, "this type of research and papers will never be transformed into real productivity … then our profession is becoming more self-entertaining" (L2).

Challenges and Barriers

The majority answered "survival," "no plan," or "not positive" when asked about their future plans. The most common concern is "uncertainty." The first is about how long the "double track" evaluation system can exist. While these evaluation systems are perceived to bring a relatively "purer" intellectual environment for research, the returnees are concerned that the leadership could change any time. As some of them have commented, the management systems in the university, and probably anywhere else in China, are not run by "standard rules" but by "people." When people change, the rules could instantly change as well. Some people complained that the criteria have been changing all the time and "it's scary that you don't know what it is at all by the end" (Lp2–1). When asked about prospects for professional development, "unsure," "puzzled" and "not very positive" are frequent sentiments. In essence, the returnees believe that the uncertainty and noncontinuity reflect that the management system is short-sighted without a long-term goal. "That is why this system is not stable. It's ever changing once a dean, or any leadership, is replaced. It is just because it lacks the concept of sustainability and development" (L2).

Indeed, right before our project, the university president who started the "dual-track" evaluation system stepped down; following his departure, one dean, who used to be supported strongly by the president, had also just left. The dean's leave had caused tremendous concern, uncertainty, and further departures among the returnees. In fact, several participants of our project had already left the university after our interviews were conducted. Salt (1997) used to point out that the departure of a few top-level specialists in certain sectors of basic research "could lead to the collapse of national scientific schools" (22). For our case, due to a lack of shared long-term development plans within the programs and a highly centralized management system (and strategies), the change in leadership of even one person could have very serious negative effects on talent recruitment and retention.

Another common concern is with the "intellectual environment" in China. As criticized earlier, when the overall evaluation system is short-sighted by focusing on the quantity of publications and economic interests, fewer people are concerned with quality research. Such a concern is not unique for the university in the study, but perceived as "common" for the entire academic environment in the country. They commented that the academic environment in China have improved especially with increasing investment on funding and hardware from the central and local governments. However, the fundamental institutional environments are still not conducive to foster the "real" research. Participants particularly pointed out that bureaucracy has significantly impeded the formation of a constructive intellectual environment. A couple of them even used the phrase of "bureaucratic harassment" to describe the negative impacts from bureaucracy and their struggle with the conflicts between academic freedom, public interference, time management, and individual professional development.

A further discussed concern is about personal social networks and resource allocation in higher education. First, the former social connections of returnees have been broken by the years of study abroad. Quite a few people cited "lacks of connections" as a major disadvantage compared to Ph.Ds trained in China. The academic environment is rated as "clique-ish" which values social connections with officials at higher rank and established "Big Figures" (*Da Lao*) in academia. The junior faculty generally does not have power over resource allocation. Nor do they have the opportunity to participate in decision-making. So the limited academic resources are controlled by a small number of "big figures" in the field. In order to get the resources, some junior faculty members have to "please" these established researchers, try to connect with them through social networks, or join the projects under control or even slaved by these *Da Lao*. Some of them are excluded.

> With so many different parties and small inner circles, it is extremely hard for the young researchers to break in and get a piece of the pie. The returnees, who lack the necessary connections and know little about local contexts, are often excluded and hard to integrate themselves.
>
> (Tp2–6)

One last commonly cited challenge is related to family and household conditions. Even when they are provided with a high salary, the high housing price and cost of living are still a huge pressure for many of the interviewees. Different from the domestically trained faculty members on the other evaluation track who are paid less but have much freedom to teach and do projects outside universities for "extra bonus," these returnees have committed much time to research and missed other opportunities to "make extra money." In addition, women often mentioned childcare and family roles as a factor to "slow down" the research agenda or simply give up certain opportunities for professional development.

Conclusion

With a thriving knowledge-based new economy, many countries are implementing new initiatives to encourage their citizens trained overseas to return to their home country. Traditional migration theories provide valuable insights into understanding the patterns, rationales, and consequences of population movement across the borders of countries in general. However, our knowledge of the highly skilled migration occurring in the higher education institutional settings still remains limited; the experiences of post-return migration are even less known. This study investigated the factors associated with return migrants' decision-making and their experiences after returning to the home country, through a case study in one Chinese research university.

As for the decision to return, economic incentives play a significant role. Due to the extremely high housing prices and cost of living in the city where the university sits, salary level is regarded as a "precondition"; it is also a kind of "compensation" for their overseas training—as an individual investment of human capital. Economic condition as a pull factor is certainly not enough. A cluster of overseas returnees, proactive recruiting from its leadership, and a "dual-track" faculty evaluation system at the institutional level are most responsible to successfully draw the overseas returnees to the university. In this process, social networks at both individual and the institutional level are weaving people through a web of information and opportunity. Furthermore, although to a lesser degree, nonpromising prospects in the host countries, quality of life on both sides, family and household factors, and the geographic location of the city are also important. Overall, the decision to return is made based on factors at the individual, household, and institutional level, as well as the ever-changing environments in the returning place and the home country.

The forces and dynamics at multiple scales have also impacted the post-return migration experiences. At the individual level, a much higher salary and better economic package for the returnees have distinguished them from the domestically trained faculty members. More subtly, the economic disparity is accompanied by a social divide between the two groups. This divide originates from different ways of doing research, training backgrounds, research interests, and an "elite" status of the returnees perceived by both sides, consciously or unconsciously. Furthermore, these returnees' international connections and better ability to publish in English journals are much needed by the institutional endeavor to become a top world-class university in the nation and the world. Thus, personal level differences between returnees and domestically trained group are further amplified by the institutional practices through the evaluation and reward systems.

Nevertheless, it is too simple to divide the returnees and the domestically trained faculty into two different camps. Similar to their domestic counterparts, the returnees have been under significant pressure from the university, undergone continuous adjustment, and painstakingly searched the means to survive—publish, and publish in English, SSCI journals. They are fully aware what they have experienced is not simply a problem within the current university; instead, their frustration is closely related to the macro academic environment in the higher education sector in China. The rigid, quantified evaluation criteria are regarded as "unreasonable" but necessary under the reality of China. Their experiences actually reflect the issues related to the overall academic environment, the bureaucratic academic management system, and the practices of the higher education sector in the nation.

We did not find much evidence of knowledge transfer or "brain circulation" between the returnees and the domestic group. While knowledge transfer can still happen through teaching or other mechanisms, the expected or claimed benefits brought by the government's intellectual recruitment policies are not prominent in our case. Nor has the nexus between return migration and development claimed in these talent recruitment policies appeared to exist. On the contrary, both returnees and domestic faculty are concerned about Chinese universities' frenetically chasing publications in globally high-ranked English-language journals, and further questioned the role of higher education in China. With this said, we must acknowledge that these overseas returnees are actively collaborating with people in their former overseas academic networks, and such collaborations have produced significant results as indicated by the number of high-ranked English journals. It warrants further studies to examine how the collaboration possibly expands over time.

This case study provides an angle to bridge the factors at multiple scales to understand the formation of international skilled migration—here, namely, return migration, and the experiences of these migrants. Existing literature has provided significant insights into the role of human capital, social capital, and cultural capital in shaping transnational and return migration. Our case extends this literature by arguing that different types of capital are further transformed by institutional practices and policies and have reshaped the process of highly skilled migration. Furthermore, while the nexus between highly skilled migration and development are often aggregated at the national or regional level, our case study suggests that the impacts of highly skilled migration are more nuanced, multi-scaled, and multidimensional. The often claimed connections may not easily be detected, or even exist at all; instead, there are many unintended consequences at both individual and institutional level.

Further research should be conducted to explore the impacts, intended or unintended, at the personal, institutional, regional, and national level. For example, how knowledge transfer through the highly skilled migration happens (or not), and how that is related to (im)migration policies and practices. As the current study is highly constrained by the case study of one university, more studies using larger data samples, from a variety of disciplines or occupations, and in different cities and countries are much needed.

Notes

1. Due to confidentiality, we cannot release the exact name of the ranking index, nor the name of the particular field.
2. We contacted all the returnees in this college at stage one. However, four were not approachable due to either personal reasons or schedule conflicts.
3. The difference does not consider other financial sources, such as different types of allowances, benefits from teaching extra classes and research projects, and different types of rewards that are very common in China. These can provide half of the total income of domestically trained faculty members.
4. Indeed, when we interviewed the domestically trained faculty members who were of prime working age (30–45), quite a few expressed their "despair" and "hopelessness" to be promoted to full professor.

References

Ackers, H. L. 1998. *Shifting spaces: Gender, citizenship and migration in the EU*. Bristol: Policy Press.

———. 2001. *The participation of women researchers in the TMR programme of the European Commission: An evaluation.* Brussels: European Commission (DG Research).

———. 2005. *Academic career trajectories: Identifying the 'early stage' in research careers*. CSLPE Working Paper 2005–1. Leeds: University of Leeds.

Altbach, P. G. 2004. Globalisation and the university: Myths and realities in an unequal world. *Tertiary Education & Management* 10 (1): 3–25.

Beine, M., F. Docquier, and H. Rapoport. 2001. Brain drain and economic growth: Theory and evidence. *Journal of Development Economics*, 64 (1): 275–289.

Borjas, G. 1990. *Friends or strangers: The impact of immigrants on the U.S. economy*. York: Basic Books.

Boyd, M. 1989. Family and personal networks in international migration: Recent developments and new agendas. *International Migration Review* 23 (3): 638–670.

Cantwell, B. 2011. Transnational mobility and international academic employment: Gatekeeping in an academic competition arena. *Minerva* 49 (4): 425–445.

Cao, C. 2008. China's brain drain at the high end. *Asian Population Studies* 4 (3): 331–345.

Davenport, S. 2004. Panic and panacea: Brain drain and science and technology human capital policy. *Research Policy* 33 (4): 617–630.

Dill, D. D., and F. A. van Vought. 2010. *National innovation and the academic research enterprise: Public policy in global perspective*. Baltimore, MD: The Johns Hopkins University Press.

Dunn, K. 2000. Interviewing. In *Qualitative research methods in human geography*, ed. I. Hay, 50–82. Ontario: Oxford University Press.

Findlay, A. M., R. King, F. M. Smith, A. Geddes, and R. Skeldon. 2012. World class? An investigation of globalisation, difference and international student mobility. *Transactions of the Institute of British Geographers* 37 (1): 118–131.

Gmelch, G. 1980. Return migration. *Annual Review of Anthropology* 9: 135–159.

Hall, S., and L. Appleyard. 2011. Trans-local academic credentials and the (re)production of financial elites. *Globalisation, Societies and Education* 9 (2): 247–264.

Jonkers, K., and R. Tijssen. 2008. Chinese researchers returning home: Impacts of international mobility on research collaboration and scientific productivity. *Scientometrics* 77 (2): 309–333.

Jöns, H. 2011. Transnational academic mobility and gender. *Globalisation, Societies and Education* 9 (2): 183–209.

Jöns, H., and M. Hoyler. 2013. Global geographies of higher education: The perspective of world university rankings. *Geoforum* 46: 45–59.

Kim, T. 2010. Transnational academic mobility, knowledge, and identity capital. *Discourse: Studies in the Cultural Politics of Education* 31 (5): 577–591.

Kofman, E. 2007. The knowledge economy, gender and stratified migrations. *Studies in Social Justice* 1: 122–135.

Koser, K., and J. Salt. 1997. The geography of highly skilled international migration. *International Journal of Population Geography* 3 (4): 285–303.

Leung, M. W. H. 2013. Read ten thousand books, walk ten thousand miles: Geographical mobility and capital accumulation among Chinese scholars. *Transactions of the Institute of British Geographers* 38 (2): 311–324.

Lewis, W. A. 1954. Economic development with unlimited supplies of labour. *The Manchester School* 22 (2): 139–191.

Ley, D., and A. Kobayashi. 2005. Back to Hong Kong: Return migration or transnational sojourn? *Global Networks* 5 (2): 111–127.

New York Times. 2010. Fighting trend, china is luring scientists home. Available at: www.nytimes.com/2010/01/07/world/asia/07scholar.html? r=0 (accessed November 11, 2015).

People's Net (人民网). 2015. Zhenjiang University overseas-returned doctorate committed suicide. Who were waken up from their dreams? (浙大海归博士自杀 惊醒谁的梦?) Available at: http://scitech.people.com.cn/GB/25509/56813/171792/ (accessed November 11, 2015).

Robertson, S. L. 2010. Critical response to special section: International academic mobility. *Discourse: Studies in the Cultural Politics of Education* 31 (5): 641–647.

Salt J. 1997. *International movements of the highly skilled.* OECD Social, Employment and Migration Working Papers. No. 3. Paris: OECD Publishing.

Saxenian, A. 2005. From brain drain to brain circulation: Transnational communities and regional upgrading in India and China. *Studies in Comparative International Development* 40 (2): 35–61.

ScienceNet (科学网). 2013. "The thousand talent plan" recipient Guan Min Xin was fired for investigation ("千人计划"入选者管敏鑫"被解聘"调查). Available at: http://news.sciencenet.cn/htmlnews/2013/12/285941.shtm (accessed November 11, 2015).

Simon, D. F., and C. Cao. 2009. *China's emerging technological edge: Assessing the role of high-end talent.* Cambridge: Cambridge University Press.

Strauss, A., and J. Corbin. 1998. *Basics of qualitative research* (2nd ed.). Newbury Park, CA: Sage.

Solimano, A., and D. Avanzini. 2010. *International circulation of elites: Knowledge, entrepreneurial and political.* Working Paper No. 2010/113. Helsinki: United Nations University-World Institute for Development Economics Research (UNU-WIDER).

Tremblay, R., and S. Hardwick, S. 2014. *Transnational borders transnational lives: Academic mobility at the borderland.* Québec: Presses de l'Université du Québec.

Wang, H. 2010. *China's national talent plan: Key measures and objectives*. Washington, DC: Brookings Institution.

Wang, H., and L. Miao. 2013. *Annual report on the development of Chinese returnees* (no. 2). Beijing: Social Sciences Academic Press.

Waters, J. L. 2005. Transnational family strategies and education in the contemporary Chinese diaspora. *Global Networks* 5 (4): 359–377.

———. 2006. Geographies of cultural capital: Education, international migration and family strategies between Hong Kong and Canada. *Transactions of the Institute of British Geographers 31* (2): 179–192.

———. 2009. In pursuit of scarcity: transnational students, 'employability', and the MBA. *Environment and Planning A* 41 (8): 1865–1883.

Williams, A. 2009. *International Migration and Knowledge.* London: Routledge.

Xiang, B. 2011. A ritual economy of 'talent:' China and overseas Chinese professionals. *Journal of Ethnic and Migration Studies* 37 (5): 821–838.

Yang, R., and A. R. Welch. 2010. Globalisation, transnational academic mobility and the Chinese knowledge diaspora: An Australian case study. *Discourse: Studies in the Cultural Politics of Education* 31 (5): 593–607.

Yi, L. 2011. Auditing Chinese higher education? The perspectives of returnee scholars in an elite university. *International Journal of Educational Development* 31 (5): 505–514.

Zweig, D. 1997. To return or not to return? Politics vs. economics in China's brain drain. *Studies in Comparative International Development* 32 (1): 92–195.

15 Diverging Experiences of Work and Social Networks Abroad

Highly Skilled British Migrants in Singapore, Vancouver, and Boston

William S. Harvey and Jonathan V. Beaverstock

Introduction

This chapter introduces some of the contemporary literature on highly skilled migration across a range of social science disciplines. We draw upon evidence from four separate research projects on highly skilled migrants working in Singapore, Vancouver, and Boston. Despite the fact that these workers have similar levels of education, skills, training, and backgrounds, we show that they vary significantly in their experiences of migration, work, and social networks in the different host countries. Theoretically, this is important because we show that highly skilled migrants are far from homogeneous in their experiences of migration and integration, and significantly, that they produce and reproduce what Smith (1999, 12–124) refers to as "transnational social space" within the city. The idea of exclusive migrant or expatriate spatialities within cities is not new (see King 1976). However, what we show is that the production of expatiates' social networks in particular transnational spaces within the city, in close proximity to the home, workplace, and downtown area, creates a distinctive agency of place, which are crucial territories for migrant social network formation and practice, as also argued by Ley (2004) and Waters (2006). As Beaverstock (2011, 712) noted, "an important social cultural trait of the expatriate is the tendency to be dotted around the city in distinctive separated, transnational spaces." Practically, we argue that the skills of these groups have generally been recognized locally in the host country, but there are major untapped international opportunities for British organizations and its government to more actively engage with them for business networking, foreign direct investment, and talent mobility purposes. We also argue, importantly, that there remains a dearth of research which understands the "translocality" (Smith 1999, 121) or agency of place of highly skilled migrants' social networks in the city, particularly in an age of Castells (2000) *The Network Society*.

The chapter is organized into six main parts. In part one we briefly discuss the major organizational mechanisms that create the condition for the demand for highly skilled migrants in the world economy, drawing on writers from across the social sciences and International Human Resource Management. In part two we move on to reviewing the current approaches to highly skilled international migration and specifically the role of nation states in attracting such workers to "win the war" for global talent. Part three focuses on the agency of migrant networks, both social and business, and formal and informal, in supporting highly skilled migrants in new host countries. Importantly, we also build upon Smith's (1999) ideas of transnational social spaces to illustrate the significance of the agency of place in the formation and sustainability of migrant social networks. Parts four and five introduce and report the major findings from the four case study surveys of the role of networks in integrating British highly skilled migrants in Singapore, Vancouver, and Boston. Finally, in part six we report several conclusions and highlight the contribution of our research to extant debates on highly skilled international labor migration, the production of transnational social spaces, and the agency of place in a rapidly globalizing world and city-system.

Organizational Corporate Highly Skilled Migration

A significant driver for the demand of highly skilled international migrants, of all nationalities, are those firms which engage in international production outside their home country. The multinational corporation, across primary, secondary, and tertiary sectors, is one of the key actors in the world economy that facilitates the migration of highly skilled persons across national borders. By 2014, it has been estimated that there could be upward of 50 million expatriates worldwide (Finaccord). Since the establishment of the US and European multinational corporations from the 1920s onwards, such firms have engaged in transferring highly skilled labor to international locations. The purpose of this has been to manage and fill vacancies in new and established subsidiaries, offices, and other foreign investments (e.g. oil fields, agricultural plantations, mineral mining). In the modern day, multinational corporations, and also small and medium-sized firms, continue to seek highly skilled labor of all nationalities from outside their national labor markets in order to engage in the production of goods and services in a highly competitive globalized world. Multinational firms have effectively become "transnational communities" (Morgan 2001) and these organizations provide essential places for migrants to successfully build and sustain social and business networks, as discussed later. From the late 1970s, scholars in business and management have examined these processes in a newly formulated discipline, International Human Resource Management (Bach 2011; Tung 1988). Human geographers and migration specialists have sought to theorize and measure such migration flows as "transient" highly skilled international migration (Appleyard 1991; Beaverstock 1996, 2004; Cormode 1994; Findlay 1990; Salt and Findlay 1989; Salt 1988). Such studies also encompassed the strategic role of the firm, an individual's career path aspirations, and state immigration regulatory change. They also contextualized such migration in the rapid structural changes occurring in the world economy and resultant spatial reorganization and restructuring of production—deindustrialization and the rise of the service sector. Significant territorial changes include the strategic dominance of world cities and "clusters" of high-value production and innovation, like Silicon Valley (Castells

1989; Sassen 1991; Saxenian 2006), and more recently the relative opening up of the former communist countries, including China, and the neoliberalization of the formerly so-called "First World" economies.

Today, the international migration and mobility of highly skilled labor within and between the global internal labors of multinational corporations is a *normalized* process for organizing work on a transnational scale (Beaverstock 2007). The foundational text by Edstrom and Galbraith (1977, 252–253) noted that managers were transferred within the international internal labor markets of multinational firms, across borders, for three main reasons:

> First, many transfers are made to fill positions when qualified local individuals are not available or easily trained … The second motive for transfer is to develop managers for positions of responsibility in organizations doing significant amounts of international business; that is even if there were qualified local individuals available … the third reason for transfer was … to use transfer of organizational development … as a means of modifying and sustaining its structure and decision making processes.

This landmark paper remains the benchmark for theorizing firms' international human resource management systems. In essence, and drawing upon the work of Sparrow et al. (2004), firms trigger the demand for a highly skilled migrant, or an "expatriate" (known as an intercompany transfer) because such workers are required to plug local vacancies; exchange and transfer codified and tacit knowledge and expertise; train and manage the local labor force and other assets; provide leadership and ensure that there is best practice; and to ensure that the corporate strategy of the firm is being adhered to in terms of production, quality control, and strategy. Sparrow et al. (2004) also acknowledge that highly skilled international migration stimulated by firms is an essential strategy for developing the career paths of their employees and for establishing an international cadre of global staff for the organization. Several examples of multinational corporations generating highly skilled migration has been examined in detail across a number of sectors, including accounting (Beaverstock 2007), aerospace and extraction (Millar and Salt 2008), legal services (Beaverstock 2004), and pharmaceuticals and biotechnology (Harvey 2008, 2011).

Since the late 2000s the theorization and practice of highly skilled international migration has shifted from a discourse of migration to one of mobility and global talent mobility. Firms now compete for talent on a global scale. Such talent has to be captured and, significantly, retained. Global talent is intrinsically, globally mobile and composed of a migratory cadre of hyper-mobile labor. Expatriation and other forms of organizational-driven labor migration remains formalized into two-, three-, or four-year secondments and transfers within and between the subsidiaries of companies. However, these highly skilled migration flows are now complemented with new forms of mobilities, like regular three- to six-month rotations and extended international business travel (Faulconbridge et al. 2009; Millar and Salt 2008). In the next section of the chapter we will examine more closely the recent conceptual changes in considering highly skilled international migration, particularly associated with economic competitiveness and the discourse of global talent.

Current Approaches to Highly Skilled International Migration

The "war for talent" is now a well-known phenomenon among academics and practitioners and has been discussed across a range of disciplines (Chambers et al. 1998; Beaverstock and Hall 2012; Vaiman et al. 2012; Harvey 2014). In terms of highly skilled migrants, much of the literature has focused on the loss of talent from developing countries to developed countries under the banner of the "brain drain" (Rapaport 2002). However, more recently scholars have recognized that many of the highly skilled migrants who left their developing home countries are now moving back to and/or investing in these countries (Saxenian 2006; Tung 2008). There is also an established literature on highly skilled migrants who move between developed countries, particularly, but not exclusively between global cities (Beaverstock 2005; Ewers 2007; Harvey 2011). Nation states, firms, and other organizations, like intergovernmental organizations (IGOs) and non-governmental organizations (NGOs), are now competing for talent from across the globe as highly skilled labor is seen as a prized asset to create economic, social, and cultural capital in an ever globalizing and expanding world economy. Global talent is now viewed as a prime ingredient for cities to aspire to "world city status" (see Beaverstock 2016; Sassen 2013) and/or a top-ranking global financial centre (Z/Yen 2014). For example, London's labor market for highly skilled workers is now functioning at a global level and organizations seek the most skilled and qualified labor, of all nationalities, in direct competition with cities from within the European Economic Area (EEA), like Amsterdam, Berlin, Brussels, Frankfurt, Milan, Paris, and Zurich, but significantly from much farther afield, like Dubai, Hong Kong, Los Angeles, New York, Shanghai, Singapore, Toronto, and Tokyo (Beaverstock 2016; Corporation of London 2011; Jones 2010; Kochan 2014). The race to capture and retain highly skilled migrants not only involves so called "free-movers" (Favell 2008), but also, and of strategic significance, inter- and intra-company transfers. These are people who move between and within the internal labor markets of transnational corporations, and more often than not these migrants reside in world cities, in close proximity to their places of work (Beaverstock 2016; Millar and Salt 2008; Salt 2011).

A number of countries have recognized the value of attracting highly skilled migrants. The Australian government, for example, regularly updates its "Consolidated Sponsored Occupation List," which outlines a number of priority areas such as actuaries, cardiologists, engineers, pathologists, and barristers, to name only a few examples (Australian Government, 2014). New Zealand has recognized that its own talent may reside abroad, but has adopted a network approach to engage with its diaspora for business purposes through Kea New Zealand (Larner 2007): "Kea helps the one million Kiwis living offshore connect with home and with one another, enabling them to share and leverage global experience, knowledge and opportunities" (Kea New Zealand 2015: n.p.).

The Chinese government has taken a further step to try to attract its overseas talent to return to China. In 2008, for example, it introduced its "Thousand Talent Program," which aimed to attract 2,000 Chinese-born scholars, entrepreneurs, and experts to return to China through major government funding and resources (Zhang 2012). In short, there is a range of national government initiatives to engage with and attract talent, whether these are for highly skilled migrants or domestic talent who have left a country to study or work abroad. This has often been framed as a means of growing a country's knowledge-based economy, as has been documented in Singapore (Ho 2011).

Singapore's government has actively pursued a policy of attracting "Foreign Talent" since the early 1990s. The "Foreign Talent Program" has been designed to entice and ease the movement of highly skilled labor into the city-state's many high-value knowledge intensive sectors, like academia, banking and financial services, biosciences, engineering, high technology, and medicine and science (Beaverstock 2011; Sim et al. 2003; Yeoh 2004). Yeoh (2004, 2006) specifically interprets Singapore's overtly competitive talent-seeking strategy as a key policy to build the nation's cosmopolitanism and world city credentials. At the latest count, there were over 175,000 foreign "expatriates" in Singapore with an "Employment Pass" (Singapore Ministry of Manpower, 2015), drawn primarily from Europe, North America, and the Asia-Pacific region (Australia, China, India, Japan, and New Zealand; Lewis 2008).

However, not all countries have sent positive signals to the global labor market around attracting talent. The H-1B visa, for example, is used by US companies to attract expertise in specialist fields such as engineering, science, and medicine, but it has received a lot of criticism in the country—for example, for not offering enough visas for global talent. This has led to major business leaders such as Microsoft's Chairman, Bill Gates, and News Corporation's Executive Chairman, Rupert Murdoch, warning of the major damage that a reduction in H-1B visas could cause to the economic competitiveness of the United States (Broache 2008; Murdoch 2014). The United Kingdom's Points Based System (PBS) for controlling (and tightening) highly skilled immigration and the issuing of work visas from outside of the EEA has been interpreted by many commentators, drawn from commerce, industry, and the political establishment, as being significantly detrimental to the UK's competitiveness on a global scale (*Financial Times* 2014a). *The Economist* (2012) boldly stated that the City of London's status as the premier financial centre was "under threat … [as] … migration rules are off-putting and the political rhetoric unwelcoming." The UK government's target to reduce the entry of Tier 2 PBS migrants (with a sponsor, including Inter-Company Transfers) across the information technology and banking, financial and professional services sectors especially, adds great weight to fear that the UK will lose out in the race for talent. This is aptly summed up by this recent headline in the *Financial Times* (2014b): "Visa curbs on highly-skilled migrants hit UK talent pool."

Country and city survey rankings play an important role in shaping the migration decisions of highly skilled migrants. Although this is not the only source of information that migrants are likely to use—its high circulation suggests that it is influential. HSBC's Expat Explorer Survey (2014), for example, provides information on the economy, and work and social experiences as well as the environment for raising children. InterNations (2014) highlights the best and the worst places to live in terms of quality of life, ease of integrating and working, family life, personal finance, and broad satisfaction. Highly skilled migrants are not only attracted by countries, but also by particular cities where they will live and work. There are a number of notable annual rankings of cities, including *The Economist's* (2014) annual livability survey, which looks at safety and environmental factors in 140 cities, and Mercer's (2015) quality of living survey which looks at a number of variables such as climate, disease, sanitation, communication, the political and social environment, and crime. The above surveys of countries and cities, which are targeted at expatriates and their employers, are important because their outcomes will likely determine migration and talent deployment decisions. Given their wide availability and circulation among global organizations and professionals, these surveys are arguably an important means for highly skilled migrants to form impressions of destination countries and cities, which may be positive, negative, or ambivalent, and will shape migration decisions.

The literature suggests that many types of skilled migrants with high levels of skills and training who are in high demand from governments and organizations (e.g. in healthcare) face labor market barriers. Some of this literature has focused on challenges based on gender (Iredale 2001), language (Alarcón 1999), skin color (Mogalakwe 2008) and class (Khadria 2001). Williams (2007) suggests that it is less about language ability and more about assumptions of ability based on where a person received his or her qualification. Similarly, van Riemsdijk (2013) found in the context of Polish nurses in Norway that there is a particular ethnic valuation of skill. Moriarty et al. (2012) agree that stereotypes are made about particular migrant groups and their suitability for certain types of work. Zulauf (1999, 685) finds that the reputation of the secondary school and university play an important role in employment selection criteria in the City of London, and particularly in the banking sector. In the context of migrant groups, Walsh (2006) finds that British migrants in Dubai occupy a higher social status among the local Emirati population compared to other migrant groups, particularly from South Asia, as evidenced by their occupations. All of this suggests a privileged position of certain groups compared to others, which we aim to explore in greater depth below through focusing on three groups of British migrants located in different global locations to understand their experiences of network participation and employment.

There is an emerging literature on the importance of reputation and skilled migration. Harvey and Groutsis (2015), for example, argue that the reputation of home and host countries will affect whether talent stays in their current country of residence or move to another country. In particular, the reputation of countries among skilled migrants for economic opportunities, lifestyle, quality of life, and other factors will influence their migration decisions. Florida (2007) makes a similar argument where talented workers in particular economic sectors such as the creative industries are attracted by lifestyle characteristics of countries and cities (e.g. aesthetics, openness to diversity, and the presence of good universities). Although there are constraints such as the sector, labor market regulation, and language, reputation still plays an important role in influencing migration decisions among talented workers. Other forms of reputation are also important for attracting and retaining highly skilled migrants. The positive reputation of Samsung, for instance, has helped attract highly skilled migrants to work in South Korea, including Indian software developers, who have been targeted by Samsung and the South Korean government (Kim and Lee 2012). Similarly, Harvey (2011) found that many British scientists talked about acquiring their "BTA" (Been To America), which referred to gaining experience of working in top universities, pharmaceutical, and/or biotechnology companies in the United States in order to advance their careers. Here, the positive reputation of US scientific institutions was an important magnet for attracting highly skilled British migrants. In addition to reputation, various forms of social networks are important for experiences of migration and integration.

Migrant Networks, Clubs and Associations, and the Agency of Place

For the highly skilled, the production of migrant networks *within* their host country is an essential strategy for socialization, both within the workplace and domestic sphere. Such migrant networks can be composed of work colleagues and their families, neighbors and friends, and acquaintances through participation in clubs, societies, and/or more formal professional associations or trade bodies (e.g. Chambers of Commerce). These networks can be composed of similar nationality groups or an array of different nationalities and ethnicities, depending on an array of local factors, including occupation groups, family status, and different cultural traits of host countries. Most of the literature focused on highly skilled international migrants or expatriates in both Global South and North contexts do acknowledge that migrant networks, formal or informal, are important aspects of everyday living *within* the city (for example, Beaverstock 1996, 2002, 2005; Larner 2007; Ley 2004; Scott 2007; Walsh 2006).

As we have already noted, there is agreement in the literature that the workplace is a vital transnational community and place for the production of migrant networks, within and between firms, usually composed of work colleagues and wider communities (e.g. clients, members of competing firms). However, there is some disagreement in the academic literature around the degree to which skilled migrants participate in face-to-face social networks in host countries. Scott (2007) argues that skilled British migrants living in Paris tend to participate in such social networks, but in differentiated ways: some participate in formal immigrant associations whereas others prefer more informal gatherings in bars and cafes. These are the transnational spaces for skilled British workers in Paris. Meyer (2001) finds that many migrants from both of his Colombian and South African sample, who are working in developed countries, do not tend to participate in migrant networks. He argues that Columbian migrants are more likely to participate in migrant networks for job and professional purposes than South African migrants because Colombians experience greater differences in the education, job, and cultural (including linguistic) environment in the host developed countries. In contrast, South Africans experience greater similarities when they move to countries such as the United States, the United Kingdom, Canada, Australia, and New Zealand, meaning they are less inclined to forge networks with other migrants compared to their Colombian counterparts (Meyer 2001, 9).

Beaverstock's (1996, 2005) in-depth interview surveys of British highly skilled migrants working in New York's financial district found that there were mixed views concerning participation in same-nationality social networks for social and professional purposes. Many of these migrants were dispersed across Manhattan Island in terms of residency (i.e. no British enclaves were identified). They socialized mainly with co-workers, who were composed of both US and Canadian nationals and many other nationality groups, from mainland Europe, Australasia, and South America. A common thread that emerged from these two surveys was that almost all the British migrants wanted to blend into the melting pot of Manhattan life and did as much as possible to distance themselves from any sort of "expatriate" lifestyle or closely knit sole British migration networks, whether formal or informal. Unlike in Singapore and other Asian cities like Kuala Lumpur, the "expatriate" club scene was nonexistent in New York (Beaverstock 2011). For these British migrants, Manhattan Island was the manifestation of their transnational space, from the workplace and bars of Wall Street and Midtown, to the key socialization spaces dotted around the Up- and Midtown areas of the borough.

Migrant networks are also vital for migrants who move from countries with different social norms to the host country because it helps with sharing common beliefs, values, and interests (Hardwick 2003). Saxenian (2006) found a challenge for both Chinese and Indian skilled migrants moving to Silicon Valley. Immigrants in her sample experienced differences in social and professional norms from the host population and often faced difficulties with finding jobs and progressing their careers. She also found that the shared experience of migration, language, education, culture, and history among first-generation migrants forged strong ties and trusted relationships within the migrant community. These networks have meant that both groups have had great success with starting up companies in Silicon Valley and with initiating high levels of business outsourcing to China and India.

Migrant networks are not exclusively from the same country. Beaverstock (2002, 532–533), for instance, finds that expatriates from predominantly North America, Europe, Australia, and New Zealand tend to interact with each other in social clubs, and tend not to socialize with local Singaporeans unless they are clients, potential clients, or potentially useful contacts. Two main reasons were cited as accounting for the lack of local Singaporeans in the British expatriates social networks. First, expatriates tended to socialize outside work around alcohol and sporting events (e.g. rugby union and cricket) with other expatriates, frequenting social spaces that did not necessarily attract local Singaporeans who were not associated with relevant business interests. Second, many of these expatriates lived in expatriate enclaves such as Holland Village and socialized together, with their families and friends of different nationalities—i.e. those who lived in the same condominiums, around specific social and cultures events, or just by "hanging out" around the pool or at barbecues. Socializing also was centered around the networks of children at international schools, which invariably reproduced the interaction with other expatriates of all nationalities. What is unclear from both cases discussed above is what drives migrants to participate in migrant networks and whether they participate in such networks when they do not feel marginalized from the mainstream host society. Hagan (1998, 65) and Saxenian (2006, 63–64) argue that although migrant networks are important for helping migrants to settle, they need to expand their network beyond such networks to take advantage of weak ties from other networks.

An important form of social networks is immigrant associations, which are institutions that provide professional and social support for migrants, particularly those who have recently arrived in the host country. They can provide a range of information on professional contacts, job information, schooling, housing, and social activities. Hence, they are more than migrant networks because they do not merely provide contacts for migrants, but provide important resources which can have significant benefits for migrants (Kanas et al., 2009). Larner (2007) argues that transnational and expatriate networks, such as those associated with the New Zealand diaspora, are becoming more formalized and organized through organizations such as Kea, which is a global network that helps one million New Zealanders abroad connect with each other and with New Zealand.

In other parts of the world such as the United States, a number of important and powerful immigrant associations have been formed such as the Chinese Institute of Engineers (CIE) and the Indus Entrepreneurs (TiE), which have become powerful business conduits for transferring talent and resources between Silicon Valley and China and India, respectively. TiE, for example, was started by Indian entrepreneurs in Silicon Valley who wanted to help other Indian migrants start businesses. This association has helped highly skilled Indian migrants connect in the region as well as other like-minded business professionals in India. Beaverstock (2002, 533) found that skilled migrants in Singapore were encouraged and paid by their organizations (often multinational corporations) to join key business associations because of the recognition that valuable tacit knowledge can be acquired through such networks. Although in theory non-migrants are able to join the above immigrant associations, the research evidence suggests that few in practice have done so because of a lack of shared social and cultural experiences (Beaverstock 2002; Saxenian 2006).

Finally, we return to the agency of place, and the ideas of Smith's (1999) transnational urbanism and the functioning of migrants' social networks. These social networks produce particular spaces within the city that are confined to extremely small geographical areas like a particular bar, club, or recreational park, but are constantly frequented by migrants of all nationalities. As the empirical studies above illustrate, such transnational social spaces, which could also be referred to as migrant glo-cal *enclaves*, are in a continuous flux, constantly being nourished by the business–social–cultural practices and performativity of highly skilled migrants in the city. Work by Ley (2004) and Waters (2006) bring on to the agenda the role of the transnational elite, highly skilled migrant, in making transnational social spaces within the city, augmented by similar writings of authors like Beaverstock (2002, 2005) and Conradson and Latham (2005). The remainder of this chapter explores the labor market experiences, social networks and agency of place, or spatialities, of four groups of highly skilled British migrants in three global cities.

Methods

The data for this chapter derive from four large separate research projects on highly skilled British migrants in Singapore (two surveys; Beaverstock 2002, 2011), Boston and Vancouver, all of which analyzed their labor market experiences and social networks. These groups and settings are important because much of the literature on highly skilled migrants has focused on groups who have faced historical barriers in host country labor markets, particularly in terms of forming networks and finding jobs (e.g. Saxenian 2006; Hakak et al. 2010), whereas there is little recent history of highly skilled British migrants confronting major integration difficulties in Singapore, Boston, and Vancouver. Hence, we were interested to explore more deeply what experiences of labor market integration, if any, this group faced. We were also curious to explore how these different highly skilled migrants build and reproduced social networks, in particular transnational social spaces in the three cities of settlement: Singapore, Boston, and Vancouver.

Interviewees were selected and conducted with British-born migrants with high levels of education and training (typically a minimum of a university degree or equivalent and at least three years of paid or unpaid employment). Interviewees varied in age from early twenties to seventies, but typically they were in their forties and in the middle of their careers. Interviewees worked in a range of sectors, but most were working in finance and professional services, including, but not limited to investment banking, hedge funds, law, management consulting, accounting, engineering, health science, and architecture. Interviews lasted for forty-five minutes to one hour and were conducted by at least one of the authors with forty-eight interviewees in Singapore (1999 and 2004), 101 interviewees in Boston (2006) and sixty-four interviewees in Vancouver (2009). Interviewees across the three locations were a broad mixture of inter-company transfers (sometimes referred to as "assigned expatriates") and self-initiated skilled migrants (sometimes referred to as "self initiated expatriates"). There was a stronger emphasis on inter-company transfers in Singapore compared to Boston and Vancouver, but this was not stark enough to infer any relationship between the type of migrant and his or her networking behavior. A number of avenues were pursued for gaining access, including employers, personal contacts, expatriate websites, government sources, and local sports and social clubs. This broad range of avenues ensured that a cross-section of highly skilled migrants were interviewed rather than a particular subgroup. The majority of interviews were conducted in person in the cities, but a small number of interviews were conducted over the telephone when interviewees were unable to attend face-to-face interviews. We use pseudonyms below to protect the identities of participants and their employers.

A number of open-ended questions were asked around individual experiences as inter-company transferees, finding work, social networking, and conducting business in the host country, and the importance of particular places for migrant socialization. Certain a priori themes such as work opportunities, challenging work, social networks, immigrant associations and social clubs, and place were explored before analyzing the data, although these were limited to avoid issues of biasing the analysis of the interviews (Brooks and King 2014). We analyzed and categorized our data manually following the above themes. Our themes were formulated through identifying recurring features during interview accounts of their work and networking experiences.

The following section focuses on the integration experiences of highly skilled British migrants working in three different global cities: Singapore, Vancouver and Boston.

Work and Socialization in Singapore

As discussed above, Singapore's political establishment is pro-talent and actively seeks foreign workers within its "Foreign Talent Program" to fill vacancies across a range of commerce, industry, and public services. All the migrant interviewees were referred to as "expatriates" by themselves and the state, and they were issued Employment Pass visas. Interviewees entered Singapore as either intra-company transfers (i.e. moving with the firm on defined expatriate programs and resettlement packages) or inter-company transfers (i.e. moving between firms, but mostly receiving expatriate programs and resettlement packages). The dependents interviewed—the so-called, "trailing spouses" (Yeoh and Khoo 1998)—were more often than not female. Ten "trailing spouses" were interviewed from the total of forty-eight (all in 2004), of which eight were female. A common denominator for all these migrant workers was that they lived privileged lifestyles in Singapore. They received relatively high incomes in a very low personal taxation regime. They lived in exclusive condominium developments or, for the more affluent, large detached houses, all with facilities such as swimming pools and gyms. Their children were enrolled in the best international schools in Singapore, and they maintained very strong social networks with their peer groups, most often other British or Australian/New Zealand or other European nationalities. In almost all cases, these highly skilled British migrants were associated with clubs and other formal entities linked to both social and working environments. All these expatriate territories, the home, workplace, and recreational space, were classic forms of transnational social spaces, where migrant networks were produced, replenished, and articulated in tightly bounded geographical localities within the city.

Thirty-seven of the forty-eight interviewees were employed in both domestic and foreign firms in Singapore, and predominantly in the banking, and financial and professional services sectors (the remainder were dependents and interviewed as participants in The British Club). Thirty-four of these thirty-seven (92 percent) were men, further reinforcing the gender bias in highly skilled migration, and global financial centers where business networks have been significantly gendered (Kofman and Raghuram 2006; McDowell 1977). Upward of three-quarters of these migrants were married and had their families in Singapore, which is important because a lot of socialization in this group were in expatriate clubs, which were important conduits for both social and professional networking. From an organizational perspective, these migrants had so-called transnational career paths. They had often experienced working and living in other world cities outside the United Kingdom, most notably in Europe and elsewhere in Asia. For these migrants, a key motivation to be an expatriate and working in Singapore was the ability to accumulate new knowledge, both codified and tacit, transfer existing knowledge to the Singaporean workplace, and use their "softer" socialization skills to build both social and cultural capital, within and outside of the workplace in particular transnational spaces within the city (Beaverstock 2002). All these migrants had very few problems with respect to entry into Singapore, dealing with the government, and organizing day-to-day activity like living and schooling, and working in the downtown business district.

A significant aspect of migrant socialization and network building in Singapore was participation in both informal and formal activities, which also became very important transnational social spaces for knowledge accumulation. At one level, the bars and restaurants in proximity to the downtown financial center and business district were vital transnational spaces for social interaction, particularly with work and nonwork colleagues, mainly those who had been "western educated." Specific events, like the Singapore Rugby Sevens, Formula 1 Grand Prix, were vital moments in time and sites for networking and building social contacts and future knowledge streams, when mixing with other nationalities, often corporate clients and competitors. Membership of prestigious clubs and societies, also frequented by the Singaporean local elites, like the Singapore Cricket Club, The Tanglin Club, and The British Club, became, and still are, key transnational social spaces for migrant network building, for business and social purposes. As Beaverstock (2011) found, membership of a club was a vital asset for migrants to socialize with other transnational elites, of all nationalities, but mainly "Western." Such clubs had strong membership numbers among Western expatriates and represented an important space where interviewees built trusted relationships with other expatriates through shared experiences, including with family members and friends. In many ways, all the British expatriates interviewed in Singapore had highly successful working, household, and social lives because of their propensity to get embedded in Singapore's transnational spaces, both the workplace and those expatriate bars and restaurants down on the Waterfront. To forge a successful transnational career in Singapore, therefore, was not only linked to a fruitful and positive working experience in the firm, but also the ability to develop and sustain strong social networks in particular transnational spaces of the city.

Moving on to the club scene in Singapore—a vitally important place for the articulation of migrant social networks—the establishment of social and recreational clubs in Singapore can be traced back to the 1850s onwards, linked most closely to the city's colonial infrastructure and position as a vital merchant port for the British Empire (Sharpe 1993; Walsh 1991). Post-independence in the 1970s, the established clubs like the Cricket Club (1852), Tanglin Club (1865), Hollandse Club (1908), were joined by new entrants like the American Club, The British Club and specialist business clubs, like the Tower Club. By the late 2000s there were over 100 clubs in Singapore (www.cmas.org.sg). Many of these clubs became highly popular with both Singaporean local elites, from a range of sectors of the economy, and Singapore's expatriate workers. These clubs performed two main functions for the British migrants: first, they provided recreational facilities and served as transnational "meeting places" for families and thus assisted with social acclimatization in Singapore; second, they acted as places for business-related networking, alongside the formal workplace. By the turn of the 21st century, these clubs and recreational spaces were very much *transnational* in scope and no longer "badge" or labeled as solely places for "expatriates" to socialize and network (Beaverstock 2011).

Following the global financial crisis, Singapore has gained significant economic status in the Asia-Pacific, and it remains a highly prized world city location for British highly skilled workers and those of other nationalities. It is considered an important place to advance careers particularly in leading global transnational corporations across a range of industrial sectors, particularly given its proximity to China. Data from Singapore's Ministry of Manpower (2015) shows that the number of Employment Passes issued to "expatriate" workers has increased by +55 percent (+62,300) from 114,300 to 176,600 between December 2009 and June 2014.

Challenging Work and Professional Practice in Vancouver

The experiences of highly skilled migrants in Vancouver were much more integrated into mainstream Canadian social and business life compared to the experiences of highly skilled British migrants in Singapore. Nonetheless, British migrants in Vancouver said that their experiences of working in Vancouver were often different from the experiences of the local population (see Harvey 2012). Some interviewees, for example, argued that they received greater opportunities in the workplace. For instance, over 40 percent of interviewees were provided with greater levels of responsibility and expectation compared to their previous job roles in the UK. In particular, because British workers had prior experience of working in the United Kingdom and in Canada, they were often asked to work with clients and customers in both locations because of their business and cultural knowledge of both countries. In some instances, the reputation of British business played an important role in providing highly skilled migrants with additional opportunities. Briony Barker, for example, worked for one of the major UK publishers before moving to Canada and she found that she received a much higher level of responsibility because the reputation of her previous employer was a proxy for her own capabilities. In short, many Canadian employers valued British qualifications and experience, which provided highly skilled migrants with greater labor market opportunities than their Canadian counterparts. In the words of David Nelson, Partner of an architecture firm, "Years ago I think British architects were held in pretty high esteem … that's still the case, but not as much as in the eighties. British-educated people have a good experience, with parliamentary effect." This has parallels with the work of Walsh (2006) who found that British expatriates in Dubai often received greater professional opportunities than other migrant groups.

The literature on the labor market experiences of highly skilled migrants has tended to emphasize the challenges that many migrant groups have faced (Saxenian 2006; Liversage 2009; Hakak et al. 2010). In general, British migrants in Vancouver were satisfied with their Canadian employers, with the mean British migrant stating that they felt highly valued by their employer (8.3 out of 10). British migrants were also satisfied with their salaries, scoring this as 7.3 out of 10.

Despite the generally positive picture of working in Vancouver, 29 percent of interviewees said that they had faced problems obtaining work in Vancouver, which included having their skills recognized. One problem that was faced in certain sectors was protectionism from professional bodies with a lack of transferability of qualifications required to practice. As Ian Piper stated: "The issue is there is a certain amount of protectionism of professions. They don't want foreigners; it's never far under the surface." The implication here was that in certain professions such as law and engineering, it was irrelevant what prior experience highly skilled migrants had because they needed to gain the requisite qualifications in Canada. This links closely to the argument of Zulauf (1999, 683) who argues that employers and professional bodies have a high degree of discretion when it comes to recognizing different credentials to enable individuals to practice in their profession.

There was sometimes a lack of alignment between the rhetoric of the Canadian government, which sought to attract highly skilled migrants through open-door immigration policies, and labor market policies, which restricted many of these migrants from working in Canada in their field. This has short-term implications for the retention of highly skilled migrants and long-term implications for the attraction of highly skilled migrants. Potential workers will be discouraged from moving if they face problems finding work in an area commensurate with their training and skills. Salaff et al. (2002) also refer to this tension between immigration policy and institutional conditions and the importance of both aligning.

Some British migrants (22 percent) said that they were expected to prove themselves before they were treated equally. In the words of Lionel Myler, a design engineer, "Basically I think for the first eighteen months I had to prove myself, and not just professionally, but in my long-term intentions." He went on to say how he was expected to gain permanent residency and become an accredited professional engineer locally. This experience, which was similar to a number of highly skilled British migrants, serves to show some of the major labor market challenges that migrant workers faced. Simon Beech, a lawyer, went further describing the "insular environment" which did not recognize "international experience," which he found highly frustrating given his extensive international experience of practicing law abroad.

In summary, the experiences of British migrants in the workplace across a wide range of age groups and economic sectors in Vancouver were far from homogeneous. This suggests that there was not one common narrative (i.e. positive, negative or ambivalent) which encapsulated this group's experience. Nor was there a particular place or space that this group occupied professionally or socially in the city, which was evident among British migrants in Singapore, with perhaps the exception of the formal workplace, and surrounding bars and restaurants. In short, British migrants in Vancouver tended to be comfortable occupying business and social spaces with the local population rather than spaces that were predominantly or exclusively occupied by migrant groups.

Lack of Migrant Networks in Boston

Highly skilled British scientists in Boston, like highly skilled British migrants in Vancouver, showed a general lack of participation in social networks (see Harvey 2008). Despite the fact that there are a large number of British scientists in Boston, there was a general lack of participation in migrant networks, either British or other nationalities for professional or social purposes. The median British interviewee, for instance, attended only one British-related networking event a year and 44 percent of British interviewees said that they did not attend any business-related events with people from the United Kingdom. Some scientists actively recoiled from networking with other British migrants as Rory Greig, CEO of a small biotechnology company, argued: "I actively avoid networking with the Marmite brigade. I believe when in Rome do as the Romans do." The implication here was that British migrants did not wish to network with other British migrants when living abroad because they wanted to interact with other groups. Other British migrants did not see what they would benefit from interacting with other British migrants per se. These findings are in contrast to British expatriates in Singapore's financial district where interviewees considered their participation in such networks in particular transnational spaces with the city as integral to their "survival" in Singapore (Beaverstock 2002, 535). One explanation for this might be cultural and environmental differences between Singapore and the United Kingdom where British migrants found certain social spaces like expatriate clubs, bars, and residential areas a safe haven compared to other spaces of the city where cultural challenges and tensions were more pronounced. Saxenian (2006) argues that Chinese and Indian engineers in Silicon Valley formed immigrant associations as a strategy to overcome biases in the labor market, which through organizations such as the Chinese Institute of Engineers and the Indus Entrepreneurs have subsequently become sources of competitive advantage for skilled migrants.

Outside socialization in the formal workplace, professional events were organized in Boston for highly skilled British migrants. The Science and Technology Department of the British Consulate held a range of events around Boston. These typically targeted migrants who held highly senior positions. Murray Lake, Vice-President of a global strategy and consulting firm, said that although these events were important for networking, he would like to have seen more of these events when he first moved to the United States: "There was no social club, no outreach with the British government … I would like to have seen more of that when I was a grad student." Indeed, it was telling that junior scientists cited a lack of such networking events in the region. Niall George, CEO of a small biotechnology company, was highly disappointed with the lack of engagement and commitment from the UK government, stating: "I have had some of my passions whittled away from me in terms of my government treatment." Although there were British associations that were organized independently of the UK government, they had varying success in terms of participation.

There was generally little demand for British immigrant associations among highly skilled migrants, but it was not clear whether this was because existing opportunities were absent or ineffective, or whether there was simply little demand from British migrants for such associations. A number of British interviewees, for example, said that they would like to have more participation from the British Consulate in terms of communicating to them relevant opportunities in the United States and the United Kingdom, particularly when they first arrived in the US and had had limited social networks around Boston. British Expats in Life Sciences (BELS), which had some informal, but no official links with the UK government, was the only British association in the life sciences sector in Boston. There was a small number of British scientists who attended BELS events regularly (10 percent of British interviewees in Boston). Even those people who did attend BELS events said that they were more useful for consolidating social contacts than for forging new contacts. There was also a recognition that the British tended to network with other British migrants in a more limited capacity than other migrant groups. Cameron Timpson, scientist at a large biotechnology company, found the BELS events tended to have fewer attendees compared to other migrant associations, which was indicative of national-specific networking within his company: "There is quite a large Chinese group, quite a large Russian group and Indians in the company. They tend to bunch together more than the British …. Maybe it's the national language thing." In the words of Charles Watkins, Chief Scientific Office of a medium-sized biotechnology company, "As a general rule, I don't think the British group are particularly nationalistic." However, this does not explain the varying networking patterns between British migrants in different global locations. The above findings are in contrast to other migrant groups such as the British in Singapore (Beaverstock 2002), Paris (Scott 2007), and Dubai (Walsh 2006) where there are extensive networks and use of transnational social spaces among the British. This arguably may be explained by more marked differences in language and/or culture between Britain and the host country compared to the context of British migrants in Boston. In other words, British migrants in Vancouver and Boston felt closer linguistically and culturally to the host population than British migrants in Singapore, Paris, and Dubai where there were stronger linguistic and cultural divides, which led to migrants forging closer connections with other British or expatriate groups. In short, place is important in determining participation in social networks. However, it not so much geographical distance that seems to determine participation in migrant-specific networks, but more linguistic, cultural, or social distance (Neeley 2015).

A sizable proportion of British interviewees in Boston (43 percent), all of whom worked in the life sciences sector, had heard of British associations such as BELS. However, only 16 percent of interviewees said that they were important to them for professional networking such as hearing about new trends in the field or new job or professional development opportunities. The data suggest that there were both British migrants who were not aware of immigrant associations and those who were aware, but chose not to participate in such organizations. Paul Lyons, director of a small biotechnology company, recognized that there were many people in Boston from the UK, but questioned the business value of BELS: "BELS, it's great for a social get-together, but I'm not sure it helps necessarily with your networking because you don't necessarily need people from the UK in the same room." James Churt, Vice-President of a large pharmaceutical company, made a similar observation of his own experience: "I guess I wasn't just interested in getting together with expats per se." Participation in such associations were entirely at the discretion of migrants, whereas clubs in Singapore were discretionary for migrants, but often encouraged and paid for by their employers because of the recognition of their business value for sourcing talent, clients, and investment (Beaverstock 2002, 535).

In summary, despite the fact that British migrants in Singapore, Vancouver, and Boston were similar in terms of their social and professional characteristics, there were marked differences in their networking experiences with other British migrants. British migrants in Singapore actively engaged in migrant networks that were practiced and performed in particular transnational social spaces, where an agency of place was reproduced both through expatriate clubs and directly with other "Western" migrants. This was driven by both personal desire to forge social networks and by the expectations of multinational employers for expatriates to professionally network with other expatriates for establishing and maintaining business relationships, which were often spatialized outside the workplace in the wider financial district and downtown area (in, for example, bars, restaurants, and clubs). In contrast, British migrants in Boston and Vancouver tended to engage significantly less in both formal migrant associations as well as in forging networks with other British migrants, whether these were for professional or social purposes. There was not only less appetite on an individual basis, but employers of British migrants in Boston and Vancouver did not encourage or provide any incentives for participation in formal migrant associations. Many of the highly skilled British migrants in Boston and Vancouver had no concrete affinity to particular transnational social spaces with the city like the British in Singapore, except the formal workplace and particular bars and restaurants. Moreover, salient findings from the Boston and Vancouver studies actually suggest that these migrants did everything in their decision making to avoid what many of them saw as the "cringing" experiences of socializing with other expatriate communities in designated spaces, whether that be bars or social and recreational clubs.

Conclusions

This chapter has provided an overview of the main theoretical literature and practices of highly skilled migration. We began by showing that countries, regions, and organizations are increasingly seeking to attract highly skilled migrants from a range of different countries. Importantly, it is not only countries and cities that have historically sourced highly skilled migrants, but emerging economies as well, which is increasing competition between countries for this finite resource. At the same time, we are seeing a greater trend towards mobility than migration, meaning that highly skilled migrants are moving across the globe more frequently, requiring governments and organizations to be more active in both attracting and retaining talent. Surprisingly, we observe some national governments such as the United States and the United Kingdom adopting lukewarm approaches to attracting highly skilled migrants as a response to concerns in both countries around high volumes of immigration, despite strong business pressure to attract greater numbers of highly skilled migrants. This is occurring at a time when countries such as China and Singapore are actively seeking out highly skilled talent, including engaging with their own talent who are working abroad. All of this is important because these different government approaches send very strong reputation signals to potential talent looking to work in different countries. We also highlight the importance of country and city surveys, which rate and rank different destinations based on a range of criteria, again signaling the importance of reputation for influencing migration decisions. This is significant because such reputational indicators are important for a sizable number of potential migrants who are seeking to live and work abroad, but have yet to apply for specific job opportunities.

An important conclusion to note is that our comparative study of British highly skilled migrants in Boston, Singapore, and Vancouver offers mixed perspectives in conceptualizing the agency of place and transnational social spaces in the wider theories regarding highly skilled labor migration. At the macro-scale, the city and prefix of the global/world city are well known as the key sites where highly skilled migrants want to work and live, to enhance career paths and personal income, and enjoy unparalleled opportunities for social and culture living, and consumption. In our studies, all three cities are highly attractive locations for highly skilled migrants, lured by the prospects of their corporate and high-value economies and opportunities for developing both social and cultural capital. However, we begin to discover divergence in the (re)production of social networks and use of distinctive transnational social space by our highly skilled migrants at the micro level. On one hand, the migrants in the North American cities do their utmost to "go it alone" and shy away from participation in same or other nationality social networks and socialize in well-known transnational social spaces because they want to, as one participant noted, "when in Rome do as the Romans do." On the other hand, all the British expatriates working in Singapore relied on participation in social networks, both formal and informal, made up of same and like-minded nationalities (Australians, New Zealanders, South Africans) which were practiced and performed in distinctive transnational social spaces like the bars and restaurants on Clarke and Boat Quays, at expatriate clubs, and various sporting events. This is not out of place with other studies of British people in non-Western contexts, like the British in Dubai (Walsh 2006). From our studies we would conclude that the agency of place for these British highly skilled workers is much stronger in a non-Western context, where households tend to live in same nationality enclaves, and workers tend to socialize with similar ethnic groups in distinctive "Western" spaces like bars, clubs, and sporting clubs, than in a Western context like North America where residential preferences are one of dispersion in the city and membership of same or similar nationality social networks are very weak. Both Boston and Vancouver do not have the equivalent of expatriate enclaves like Holland Village in Singapore. In Asian and other non-"Western" contexts, the practice and performance of migrant social networks in exclusive transnational social spaces remain significant relational territories for both business, and social and cultural activities within the city. Some "Western" examples exist such as the British networking with other migrant groups in Paris (Scott 2007), but again these may be explained by linguistic and cultural differences between the migrant group and the local population, as is typically found with "Western" migrants living in non-"Western" countries (and vice versa).

The literature on highly skilled migration highlights the importance of social networks for both migration and integration into the host country. We show across four studies in three different global cities that the experiences of working and socialization can vary significantly geographically even among migrants who share similar social and professional characteristics. Highly skilled British migrants in Singapore, for example, painted a positive picture of working in Singapore where the government and organizations were keen to attract and retain these types of workers. British migrants in Vancouver, however, found that although the government was keen to attract them to work in Canada, the experience of work was quite divided, with some workers clearly receiving greater opportunities and responsibility, whereas others found themselves having to prove themselves or in some sectors reaccredit with little recognition of their prior education, training, and international experience. British migrants in Boston generally experienced positive signals and opportunities from their employer, but more recent migrants faced difficult immigration policies, which included the time lag from converting from immigrant status to permanent resident to citizen.

We also found variation in the use of social networks and frequenting of particular transnational social spaces within the city among different highly skilled migrant groups. British migrants in Singapore, for example, tended to strongly socialize with other expatriates from the UK and other countries, with limited socialization with Singaporeans. This was because of socio-cultural differences in work-related leisure activities focused around downtown bars and specific sporting and other social events. In addition, these expatriates tended to live in "expatriate enclaves" with families, which tended to reproduce expatriate socialization, as discussed above. This is similar to the experiences of British migrants in Paris and Dubai, where there is a production and reproduction of expatriate social networks in distinctive transnational social spaces like bars, restaurants, sporting and recreational sites, as well as "expatriate" clubs. However, this is in contrast to highly skilled British migrants in Vancouver, Boston, and New York where people were dispersed across the cities, with very little affinity to migrant transnational social spaces like the British in Singapore. In addition, in our studies in these cities, there was some social and professional interaction with other British expatriates, but it was much less common because interviewees found it limiting to their social and professional lives. This is an important finding because highly skilled British migrants, although fairly homogeneous in their education, skills, and background, varied markedly in their engagement in expatriate social networks and transnational social spaces. Some groups such as the British in Singapore rely on both social networks and participation in transnational social spaces to "survive" in the host country, while other groups such as the British in Boston strongly "recoiled" and looked down on such social behavior and sites for the articulation of transnationalism in the city.

Theoretically, this chapter raises important questions around why some highly skilled migrant groups engage and others disengage with such networks and transnational social spaces. In particular, we suggest that wider differences in cultural norms between the host country compared to the home country will increase the propensity of migrants to participate in migrant associations, networks, and transnational social spaces, and for their multinational employers to support such participation. Practically, we suggest that there are potentially important strategic opportunities for the UK government and organizations to foster and engage with highly skilled migrant business networks in host countries, which are largely privately organized, to help forge business ties, foreign direct investment, and talent flow opportunities. These have hitherto been underutilized in the context of British migrants in Singapore, Boston, and Vancouver, and yet have proved highly fruitful for other skilled migrant groups in other places such as New Zealand, China, Taiwan, Israel and India (Saxenian 2006; Larner 2007). Having said this, we would suggest that in a similar function to effective alumni networks, such ties need to be proactively formed at the early stages of a highly skilled migrant's mobility, rather than reactively waiting until that migrant has become successful in his or her career. Finally, we have found that sometimes there was a disconnect between immigration policy (i.e. national approaches to attracting skilled migrants) and labor market policy (i.e. the ability of skilled migrants to work in the host country, particularly in certain professions where there were high levels of labor market protectionism imposed by professional bodies). We would argue that greater alignment would help to ensure that the expectations of highly skilled migrants are met, which will have important long-term future implications for both the attraction and retention of global talent.

References

Alarcón, R. 1999. Recruitment processes among foreign-born engineers and scientists in Silicon Valley. *American Behavioural Scientist* 42 (9): 1381–1397.

Appleyard, R. 1991. *International migration: Challenge for the nineties.* Geneva: IOM.

Australian Government. 2014. Consolidated sponsored occupations list. Available at: www.immi.gov.au/Work/Pages/skilled-occupations-lists/csol.aspx (accessed August 5, 2014).

Bach, S. 2011. Migration and international HRM. In *International human resource management: Globalization, national systems and multinational companies,* eds. T. R. Edwards and C. Rees, 272–293. Harlow: FT Prentice Hall.

Beaverstock, J. V. 1996. Re-visiting high-waged labour market demand in the global cities: British professional and managerial workers in New York City. *International Journal of Urban and Regional Research* 20 (4): 422–445.

———. 2002. Transnational elites in global cities: British expatriates in Singapore's financial district. *Geoforum* 33 (4): 525–538.

———. 2004. Managing across borders: Transnational knowledge management and expatriation in legal firms. *Journal of Economic Geography* 4 (2): 157–179.

———. 2005. Transnational elites in the city: British highly-skilled inter-company transferees in New York City's financial district. *Journal of Ethnic and Migration Studies* 31 (2): 245–268.

———. 2007. World city networks from below: International mobility and inter-city relations in the global investment banking industry. In *Cities in globalization: Practices, policies, theories*, eds. P. J. Taylor, B. Derudder, P. Saey, and F. Witlox, 52–71. London: Routledge.

———. 2011. Servicing British expatriate 'talent' in Singapore: Exploring ordinary transnationalism and the role of the 'expatriate' club. *Journal of Ethnic and Migration Studies*, 37 (5): 709–728.

———. 2016. Global mobility and knowledge management in professional service firms. In *Spatial mobility of knowledge*, eds. P. Meusburger, H. Jöns, and M. Heffernan. Springer: Berlin (in press).

Beaverstock, J. V., and S. Hall. 2012. Competing for talent: Global mobility, immigration and the City of London's labour market. *Cambridge Journal of Regions, Economy and Society* 5 (2): 271–287.

Broache, A. 2008. Bill Gates to Congress: Let us hire more foreigners. CNET. Available at: www.cnet.com/news/bill-gates-to-congress-let-us-hire-more-foreigners/ (accessed August 5, 2014).

Brooks J., and N. King. 2014. Doing template analysis evaluating an end of life care service. Sage Research Methods Case.

Castells, M. 1989. *The informational city.* Oxford: Blackwell.

——— 2000. *The rise of the network society.* Oxford: Blackwell.

Chambers, E. G., M. Foulon, H. Handfield-Jones, S. M. Hankin, and E. G. Michaels. 1998. The war for talent. *McKinsey Quarterly* 1 (3): 44–57.

Conradson, D., and A. Latham. 2005. Transnational urbanism: Attending to everyday practices and mobilities. *Journal of Ethnic and Migration Studies* 31 (2): 227–233.

Cormode, L. 1994. Japanese foreign direct investment and the circulation of personnel from Japan to Canada. In *Population migration and the changing world order*, eds. A. Findlay and W. T. S. Gould, 67–89. Chichester: Wiley.

Corporation of London. 2011. Access to global talent: The impact of migration limits on UK financial and professional business services. London: The Corporation of London.

Economist, The 2012. Immigration and business – A harder road. October 20. Available at: www.economist.com/news/britain/21564895-government%E2%80%99s-policy-students-and-skilled-migrants-threatens-do-long-term-damage (accessed August 5, 2014).

———. 2014. The best places to live. Available at: www.economist.com/blogs/graphicdetail/2014/08/daily-chart-13 (accessed February 18, 2016).

Edstrom, A., and J. Galbraith. 1977. Transfer of managers as a coordination and control strategy in multinational corporations. *Administrative Science Quarterly* 22 (June): 248–263.

Ewers, M. C. 2007. Migrants, markets and multinationals: Competition among world cities for the highly skilled. *GeoJournal* 68 (1): 119–130.

Faulconbridge, J., J. V. Beaverstock, B. Derudder, and F. Witlox. 2009. Corporate ecologies of business travel: Working towards a research agenda. *European Urban and Regional Studies* 16 (3): 295–308.

Favell, A. 2008. *Eurostars and Eurocities: Free movement and mobility in an integrating Europe*. Oxford: Oxford University Press.

Finaccord. Press release. Global expatriates: Size, segmentation and forecast for the worldwide market. www.finaccord.com/press-release_2014_global-expatriates_-size-segmentation-and-forecast-for-the-worldwide-market.htm (last accessed June 11, 2015).

Financial Times. 2014a. Visa curbs on highly-skilled migrants hit UK talent pool. Available at: www.ft.com/cms/s/0/1019b05a-0202-11e4-9af7-00144feab7de.html#slide0 (accessed July 30, 2014).

———. 2014b. New York ousts London as top financial centre. Available at: www.ft.com/cms/s/0/9a8fbf6a-ab89-11e3-aad9-00144feab7de.html#axzz39Wp11Cgw (accessed July 30, 2014).

Findlay, A. 1990. A migration channels approach to the study of high level manpower movements: A theoretical perspective. *International Migration* 28 (1): 15–23.

Florida, R. 2007. *The flight of the creative class*. New York: Harper Business.

Hagan, J. M. 1998. Social networks, gender, and immigrant incorporation: Resources and constraints. *American Sociological Review* 63 (1): 55–67.

Hakak L. T., I. Holzinger, and J. Zikic. 2010. Barriers and paths to success: Latin American MBAs' views of employment in Canada. *Journal of Managerial Psychology* 25 (2): 159–176.

Hardwick, S. W. 2003. Migration, embedded networks and social capital: Towards theorising North American ethnic geography. *International Journal of Population Geography* 9 (2): 163–179.

Harvey, W. S. 2008. The social networks of British and Indian expatriate scientists in Boston. *Geoforum* 39 (5): 1756–1765.

———. 2011. British and Indian scientists moving to the United States. *Work and Occupations* 38 (1): 68–100.

———. 2012. Labour market experiences of skilled British migrants in Vancouver. *Employee Relations* 34 (6): 658–669.

———. 2014. Winning the global talent war: A policy perspective. *Journal of Chinese Human Resource Management* 5 (1): 62–74.

Harvey, W. S., and D. Groutsis. 2015. Reputation and talent mobility in the Asia Pacific. *Asia Pacific Journal of Human Resource Management* 53 (1): 22–40.

Ho, E. L. E. 2011. "Claiming" the diaspora: Eite mobility, sending state strategies and the spatialities of citizenship. *Progress* l*in Human Geography* 35 (6): 757–772.

HSBC 2014. Expat Explorer Survey. Avalable at: https://expatexplorer.hsbc.com/survey/?HBIB_dyn_lnk=hme_nav_t4_col1_lnk_1 (accessed July 30, 2014).

InterNations. 2014. The Best & Worst Places for Expats. Available at: www.internations.org/expat-insider/2014/the-best-and-worst-places-for-expats (accessed July 30, 2014).

Iredale, R. 2001. The migration of professionals: Theories and typologies. *International Migration* 39 (5): 7–26.

Jones, A. 2010. Immigration and the UK labour market in financial services: A case of conflicting policy challenges? In *A need for migrant labour? Labour shortages, immigration and public policy*, eds. M. Ruhs and B. Anderson, 259–289. Oxford: Oxford University Press.

Kanas, A., F. van Tubergen, and T. van der Lippe. 2009. Immigrant self-employment: Testing hypotheses about the role of origin- and host-country human capital and bonding and bridging social capital. *Work and Occupations* 36 (3): 181–208.

Kea New Zealand. 2015. Kea. New Zealand's global network. Available at: www.keanewzealand.com/what-is-kea/

Khadria, B. 2001. Shifting paradigms of globalisation: The twenty-first century transition towards generics in skilled migration from India. *International Migration* 39 (5): 45–71.

Kim Y-H., and J. A. Lee. 2012. To outdo rivals in mobile software, Samsung turns to outside talent. *Wall Street Journal*. Available at: http://online.wsj.com/article/SB10001424052702303877604577381601758850814.html

King, A. 1976. *Colonial urban development*. London: Routledge.

Kochan, B., ed. 2014. *Migration and London's growth.* London: London School of Economics Books.

Kofman, E., and P. Raghuram. 2006. Women and global labour migrations: Incorporating skilled workers. *Antipode* 38 (2): 282–303.

Larner, W. 2007. Expatriate experts and globalising governmentalities: The New Zealand diaspora strategy. *Transactions of the Institute of British Geographers* 32 (3): 331–345.

Lewis, L. 2008. The "little red dot" intent on becoming the hub that Asia cannot live without. *The Times*, Saturday, October 11, 64–65.

Ley, D. 2004. Transnational spaces and everyday life. *Transactions of the Institute of British Geographers* 29 (2): 151–64.

Liversage A, 2009. Vital conjunctures, shifting horizons: High-skilled female immigrants looking for work. *Work, Employment and Society* 23 (1): 120–141.

McDowell, L. 1997. *Capital culture: Gender at work in the city of London*. Oxford: Blackwell.

Mercer. 2015. Newsroom. Vienna tops latest Quality of Living rankings. Available at: www.uk.mercer.com/content/mercer/europe/uk/en/newsroom/2015-quality-of-living-survey.html (last accessed February 18, 2016).

Meyer, J. B. 2001. Network approach versus brain drain: Lessons from the diaspora. *International Migration* 39 (5): 91–110.

Millar, D., and J. Salt. 2008. Portfolios of mobility: The movement of expertise in transnational corporations in two sectors – aerospace and extractive industries. *Global Networks* 8 (1): 25–50.

Mogalakwe, M. 2008. The making of a foreign "labour aristocracy" in Botswana. *Employee Relations* 30 (4): 422–435.

Morgan, G. 2001. Transnational communities and business systems. *Global Networks* 1 (1): 113–130.

Moriarty, E., J. Wickham, T. Krings, J. Salamonska, and A. Bobek 2012. "Taking on almost everyone?" Migrant and employer recruitment strategies in a booming labour market. *The International Journal of Human Resource Management* 23 (9): 1871–1887.

Murdoch, R. 2014. Immigration reform can't wait, *Wall Street Journal*. Available at: http://online.wsj.com/articles/rupert-murdoch-immigration-reform-cant-wait-1403134311 (accessed February 18, 2016).

Neeley, T. 2015. Global teams that work: A framework for bridging social distance. *Harvard Business Review* 93 (10): 75–81.

Rapaport, J. 2002. Who is afraid of the brain drain? Human capital flight and growth in developing countries. Palo Alto, CA: Stanford Institute for Economic Policy Research.

Salaff, J., A. Greve, and X. L. Ping. 2002. Paths into the economy: Structural barriers and the job hunt for skilled PRC migrants in Canada. *International Journal of Human Resource Management* 13 (3): 450–464.

Salt, J. 1988. Highly-skilled international migrants, careers and internal labour markets. *Geoforum* 19 (4): 387–399.

———. 2011. Migration to and from the UK. In *Global migration, ethnicity and Britishness*, eds. T. Modood and J. Salt, 14–39. Basingstoke: Palgrave Macmillan.

Salt, J., and A. Findlay. 1989. International migration of highly-skilled manpower: Theoretical and developmental issues. In *The impact of international migration on developing countries*, ed. R. Appleyard. Paris: OECD Publications.

Sassen, S. 1991. *The global city: New York, London, Tokyo*. Princeton, NJ: Princeton University Press.

———. 2013. *Cities in a world economy.* London: Sage (4th ed.).

Saxenian, A. 2006. *The new Argonauts: Regional advantage in a global economy.* Cambridge, MA: Harvard University Press.

Scott, S. 2007. The community morphology of skilled migration: The changing role of voluntary and community organisations (VCOs) in the grounding of British identities in Paris (France). *Geoforum* 38 (4): 655–676.

Sharpe, I. 1993. *Singapore Cricket Club 150th Anniversary (1852–2002)*. Singapore: The Singapore Cricket Club.

Sim, L. L., S. E. Ong, A. Agarwal, A. Parsa, and R. Keivani. 2003. Singapore's competitiveness as a global city: Developing strategy, institutions and business environment. *Cities* 20 (2): 115–127.

Singapore Ministry of Manpower. 2015. Foreign workforce numbers. Available at: www.mom.gov.sg (last accessed February 18, 2016).

Smith, M.P. 1999. Transnationalism and the city. In *The Urban Movement*, eds. R. Beauregard and S. Body-Gendrot, 119–139. London: Sage.

Sparrow, P., C. Brewster, and H. Harris. 2004. *Globalizing human resource management.* London: Routledge.

Tung, R. L. 1988. The new expatriates: Managing human resources abroad. Cambridge, MA: Ballinger.

———. 2008. Brain circulation, diaspora, and international competitiveness. *European Management Journal* 26 (5): 298–304.

Vaiman, V., H. Scullion, and D. Collings. 2012. Talent management decision making. *Management Decision* 50 (5): 925–941.

van Riemsdijk, M. 2013. Everyday geopolitics and the valuation of labor: International migration and socio-political hierarchies of skill. *Journal of Ethnic and Migration Studies* 39 (3), 373–390.

Walsh, B. A. 1991. Forty good men: The story of the Tanglin Club in the Island of Singapore 1865–1990. Singapore: The Tanglin Club.

Walsh, K. 2006. "Dad says I'm tied to a shooting star!" Grounding (research on) British expatriate belonging. *Area* 38 (3): 268–278.

Waters, J. L. 2006. Geographies of cultural capital: Education, international migration and family strategies between Hong Kong and Canada. *Transactions of the Institute of British Geographers* 31 (2): 179–192.

Williams, A. M. 2007. International labour migration and tacit knowledge transactions: A multi-level perspective. *Global Networks* 7 (1): 29–50.

Yeoh, B. S. A. 2004. Cosmopolitanism and its exclusions in Singapore. *Urban Studies* 41 (12): 2431–2445.

———. 2006. Bifurcated labour: The unequal incorporation of transmigrants in Singapore. *Tijdschrift voor Economische en Sociale Geografie* 97 (1): 26–37.

Yeoh, B. S. A., and L. M. Khoo. 1998. Home, work and community: Skilled international migration and expatriate women in Singapore. *International Migration* 36 (2): 159–186.

Zhang, Y. 2012. Thousand Talent Program brings more pros. Available at: www.chinadaily.com.cn/bizchina/2012-04/28/content_15168335.htm (accessed July 30, 2014).

Zulauf, M. 1999. Frontier-free Europe: A study of female migrants in the banking sector. *International Journal of Human Resource Management* 10 (4): 672–688.

Z/Yen. 2014. The global financial centres index 15 (www.zyen.com)

16 Conclusion

Themes, Gaps, and Opportunities for Rethinking International Skilled Migration

Harald Bauder

Introduction

International skilled migration has long been a focus of policy and decision-making in government and among corporations and knowledge institutions, whose call for the "best and brightest" is echoing around the world (Cerna and Chou 2014; Bauder 2011). In fact, over recent decades, courting highly skilled migrants has become a trend among nation states and institutions that are competing in an international "race for talent" (Shachar 2006). As a consequence, highly skilled migrants are today among the populations that are globally most highly mobile. The international mobility of the highly skilled and the associated state and institutional policies and practices have also captured the attention of outstanding scholars from a range of disciplines, as this volume attests. In this concluding chapter, I outline particular themes, gaps, and opportunities for scholars to rethink skilled migration.

The chapter has its origin in the discussion that followed the paper presentations in the final of the three sessions on "Rethinking Skilled Migration," which Micheline van Riemsdijk and Qingfang Wang organized for the 2014 Annual Meetings of the Association of American Geographers in Tampa, FL. This session ended with a moderated open discussion to which many of the participants in all three sessions as well as members of the audience contributed. The discussion was guided by a set of predetermined questions, including: What are key themes represented in the presentations in all three sessions? Are there particular gaps in the literature that point towards setting future research agendas? Can we identify opportunities for innovative research areas and novel research questions?

The text below draws on and expands upon the fascinating discussion we had in Tampa. The ideas presented in this chapter are for the most part not my own, but emerged from a discussion that involved multiple participants. I do offer, however, my own interpretation of this discussion and the comments made by the participants; in some cases, I expanded the below narrative considerably beyond the discussion in Tampa to provide additional context. In addition, I did not adhere strictly to the sequence in which the discussion in Tampa progressed but reorganized parts of the narrative to better summarize particular ideas. Thus, there is a possibility—albeit unintentional—that my interpretation does not correspond perfectly with the intention of the participant who may have made a comment in the context of a particular part of the discussion.

Key Themes

Several important themes appear in the contemporary study of skilled migration. The first theme links to the accumulation of various *forms of capital*. Skilled migration often occurs in pursuit of some kind of economic, social, or political benefit by both the migrant and the society or institution enabling (or preventing) migration. For example, some skilled migrants move to a different country to accept a job offer or through interfirm transfers that yield higher wages and thus an increase in economic capital. Similarly, immigration policies of receiving countries often seek to attract migrants who can fill labour market gaps and increase a nation's competitiveness in the global economy. Migration can also occur in an effort to increase human capital, in the form of acquiring skills and education (see Chapter 6 by Wan Yu). A significant amount of scholarly attention in migration research has been paid to the role of social capital, which relates to a literature on professional, personal, and family networks and ties of migrants. For lower skilled migrants, social capital in the form of networks has been shown to be essential for gaining access to jobs, not only in the formal labor market but also to the informal economy where migrants may be exploited as housekeepers, caretakers, and manual labor. In the context of skilled migration, social networks can provide access to jobs. For example, expatriate British and Indian scientists in Boston can find jobs in the pharmaceutical and biotechnology sector by mobilizing their social networks and personal ties (Harvey 2008). Similarly, networks of expertise are important in the way transnational corporations move employees to different places within their internal labor markets (Millar and Salt 2008). Another important form of capital in skilled migration scholarship is cultural capital. Migration can be motivated by the acquisition of institutionalized cultural capital in the form of international degrees and credentials; it can also lead to obtaining embodied cultural capital in the form of language skills and accents, and internalizing corporeal practices and styles (Ong 1999).

Moreover, the various forms of capital can be exchanged with each other. For example, the social capital which some skilled migrants possess by belonging to a professional or personal network can be converted into economic capital when these networks enable a migrant to find a high paying job. Likewise, skilled English-speaking workers from Western countries who migrate to Taiwan are able to convert their linguistic capital into economic and social capital (Lan 2011). Conversely, economic capital can buy access to immigration status and citizenship (e.g. through investor or business immigration programs), social capital can be converted into immigration status through family reunification programs, and human capital can qualify a person for skilled immigration programs or produce a foreign job offer and in this way facilitate international migration.

This focus on various forms of "capital" and the manner in which these forms interlink prevents researchers from compartmentalizing individual aspects of the migration process into seemingly independent areas of inquiry (Bauder 2006). In addition, this focus permits integrating multiple aspects of international skilled migration into an overarching logic of accumulation, distinction, and reproduction (Bourdieu 1984). For example, social capital involves not only networks and ties, but also practices of identity and group formation that are enacted for the purpose of distinction and social reproduction. Similarly, cultural capital may be accumulated and deployed for strategic gain, but it also excludes migrants, who are unable to acquire or perform it. This Bourdieusian logic also highlights the strategic nature of the migration process, where not only migrants exercise their agency in pursuit of accumulating various forms of capital, but also states and institutions enact migration, recruitment, and citizenship policies strategically in order to acquire and mobilize human, economic, and other forms of capital in an effort to reproduce themselves and the social order and hierarchies they protect.

Current scholarship also unveils important *contradictions* related to skilled migration. For example, different stakeholders, including sending societies, receiving countries, and transnational migrant families may have very different interests and motivations that often conflict with each other. For example, state immigration and citizenship policies that affect migrants are typically designed in the interest of a nonmigrant population of citizens. In particular in the context of skilled migration, state policies are designed to capitalize on the infusion of human capital through migration and maximize the benefits for the receiving societies' national economies and public coffers. These policies and practices of attracting skilled migrants in the economic interest of their own citizens may have been pioneered by "traditional" immigration counties, such as Australia and Canada, but are now emulated by nontraditional immigration countries—including European countries—with varying degrees of success (Cerna and Chou 2014; Triadafilopoulos 2013). And yet, despite the desirability of skilled migrants, policies are not designed with the best interest of the migrants in mind. Rather, national temporary and permanent migration programs impose more or less rigid criteria upon migrants. The practice of one group of people (i.e. citizens) deciding matters affecting another group (i.e. migrants) is not only undemocratic (Dauvergne 2005, 53), but the two groups also possess very different interests, motivations, and contradicting objectives in the migration process. In many cases, state policies seek to attract migrants' human capital but these same states are reluctant to accommodate the migrants' cultural identities.

Policies and practices related to skilled migration produce further contradictions. For example, the possession of skills does not always translate into employment conditions for migrants commensurate with these skills, segmenting skilled migrants into undesirable and low-wage work (Lowell 2005; Bauder 2006). In an effort to resolve the contradiction of migrants who were selected for their human capital not being able to apply this human capital in the national labour market, countries such as Australia and Canada implemented policy changes that emphasize employment and employability. These changes can be interpreted as a rescription of the policy narrative from seeking "talent" and "the best and brightest" towards seeking the most effective worker and labor.

Further contradictions occur between the discursive representation of skilled migrant and the material roles these migrants perform. Advanced economies have long grown structurally dependent on migration (Cohen 1987; Piore 1979). Skilled migrants are an especially important resource in increasingly knowledge-driven economies. Nevertheless, in the context of skilled migration, racialized images continue, for example, to penetrate studies of international student mobility of "Chinese" and "Indian" students in the United States. Although the very concept of "migrant" has long been challenged as a construct subordinating racialized groups based on notions of national belonging and home (Sharma 2006), the iconic image of the racialized "migrant" continues to be reproduced in many studies of migration. These subordinating racialized images of skilled migrants often contradict the material roles these migrants increasingly play in global capital accumulation.

Contradictions are also entrenched in transnational family networks and ties in which migrants are embedded. In these networks and ties, the acquisition of various forms of capital through migration occurs in highly gendered ways. In this context, the benefits and burdens of migration are highly unevenly distributed between men and women. There is no singular model of skilled migration that captures the experiences across social categories.

A final key theme that was identified in our discussion relates to geographical *scale*. Despite an established literature acknowledging the problem of methodological nationalism (Beck 2000; Wimmer and Glick Schiller 2002), many studies of skilled migration continue to frame the migration process at the national scale and as a phenomenon that occurs between nation states. Yet, the migration of the highly skilled at the subnational scale is also important, as exemplified in studies of the migration of skilled workers within China (e.g. Liu and Shen 2014). Also established in the literature is research on the role of the urban scale in the context of skilled, professional, entrepreneurial, and wealthy migrants (Mitchell 2003; Beaverstock 2012; Meier 2014). Part II of this book illustrates very effectively how highly skilled migrants are transforming cities such as London, Stavanger, Kongsberg, Dortmund, or Dubai. Furthermore, an emerging literature draws attention to the way regions and provinces enact their own policies to shape the flow of international skilled migration (Flynn and Bauder 2015).

Gaps in the Literature

Several gaps exist in the way the scholarly literature currently treats these key themes. The approach to skilled migration through various forms of capital is now well established (e.g. Bauder 2006; Nohl et al. 2014; Ryan et al. 2015). Nevertheless, the overarching logic of distinction and reproduction still gets lost sometimes in the research assuming this approach. Social and political practices of distinction and reproduction may be particularly relevant in a skilled migration context, in which migrants may possess relatively high levels of pre-migration social, cultural, economic, and/or other forms of capital and are seeking to increase (or at least retain) their combined capital endowments (Lan 2011). Families rich in economic capital, for example, can mobilize this form of capital to gain access to countries where their members can acquire institutionalized cultural capital (e.g. a degree from a prestigious North American or European university), embodied cultural capital (e.g. American or British accents) and/or social capital (e.g. membership in elite networks) that can eventually be converted back into economic capital in the form of wages or profits. Nation states, businesses, corporations, universities, colleges, international school, and other institutions, strategically participate in this process of accumulation in pursuit of gaining competitive or other advantages. In this way, a perspective of forms of capital can be integrated into a political economy framework of "globalization," in which skilled labor mobility, and state and institutional policies and practices toward skilled migration, play key roles in the production and reproduction of privilege (Bauder 2006). Paying close attention to this perspective enables researchers of skilled migration to frame cultural, social, and other forms of capital in a critical manner, and helps scholars to make sure that their research is not used to affirm the neoliberal ideology but rather unveils the important role that skilled migration plays within the neoliberal project of accumulation (Jessop 2002; Harvey 2005).

Bourdieu's concept of the social field can be useful in this respect, but remains underdeveloped in exploring the relationship between migration, capital accumulation, and "globalization." Nina Glick Schiller and Ayse Çağlar (2009, 185) draw on this concept when they suggest that there is a need to "theorize the relationship between the neoliberal restructuring and rescaling of specific cities and the formation, maintenance and dynamics of migrants' transnational social field and imaginaries." In particular, the geographical nature of social fields and the associate imaginaries can offer important insights into the scale-particular connections between skilled migration, accumulation, and neoliberal restructuring (Kelly and Lusis 2006).

Contradiction is another key theme identified in the previous section. There is a rich tradition in Geography and the social sciences to grapple with contradiction through dialectical frameworks (Dixon et al. 2008; Ollman and Badeen 2015). Such frameworks are less often applied to the exploration of skilled migration. A common feature among dialectical frameworks is that contradiction is seen as a productive moment in the way social and spatial relations develop and the way researchers can understand these relations. For example, contradicting models explaining aspects of skilled migration may assume different vantage points, but these models are therefore not necessarily incompatible with each other. Rather than favoring one model over another, it may be more productive to bring contradicting models in conversation with each other. In fact, a comprehensive understanding of the political economy of skilled migration may require such a polysemic approach.

A dialectical tradition reaching back to Hegel, Feuerbach, Marx, Engels, and many others also permits scholars of skilled migration to connect imagination and structure, discourse and materiality. For example, a Canadian-focused literature has recently examined the dialectic between migration and the national imagination (Bauder 2011; Mensah 2015; Pottie-Sherman and Wilkes 2014). In this context, the request by employers from skilled migrants to possess "Canadian" labor market experience illustrates how migrants' skills are valorized in relation to imaginations of nationhood and race (Chatterjee 2015). In a similar way, exclusionary discourses of nation and national belonging continue to shape the experiences of highly educated British Arabs in London—an otherwise welcoming city where immigrants "find communality in their difference" (Nagel 2012, 402). A dialectical approach to identity formation is useful to understand these issues.

Currently, a dialectical framework does also not play a strong role in the way that scholars of skilled migration approach and theorize geographical scale. Yet, such an approach could be productive in understanding the contradictions between the policies and practices related to skilled migration occurring at various scales, the scale-particular representations of skilled migration, and the framing of migration and migrants by researchers.

Our discussion in Tampa identified additional important gaps in contemporary scholarly debate of skilled migration. A *comparative perspective* would provide nuanced understanding of the migration process. Contemporary empirical studies rarely "surprise" the scholarly community with findings derived from unconventional contexts. Rather, existing research seems to be limited to relatively restricted sets of empirical contexts, disproportionately focusing on the situation of skilled migrants in receiving countries. Especially research comparing contexts that are beyond the beaten path of current research with research in more conventional settings may provide novel insights and open new perspectives of how the migration process can be understood in the context of a global political economy of accumulation.

In a related vein, more research involving sending and receiving countries would enrich current understandings of the skilled migration process. While research on "brain circulation" and the impact of skilled migration on development in the countries of origin may be increasingly on the radar of researchers, governments, and development agencies, there is still a gap in our understanding of the interconnections between the impacts of skilled migration at the places of origin, at the places of destination, and in contexts that may not appear to be directly impacted by the skilled migration from one country to another. The need for research on such impacts at variable localities and scales may be illustrated in relation to the migration of international students (Alberts and Hazen 2013; Robertson 2013, and Part 1 of this book), in which case human capital is removed from a particular society, enhanced in another society, but then also shapes the way in which both societies as well as other communities engage in the global economy. The lack of research assuming such a perspective is not only an empirical but also a theoretical gap that needs to be bridged through conceptual frameworks that enable researchers to connect forces and impact of the skilled-migration process across various contexts. Theorizations ranging from World Systems

Theory to the international segmentation of labor and global neoliberalism may provide points of entry into advancing such frameworks.

The comparative perspective is also important to the continued exploration of scale and the theorization of the relationship between skilled migration and cities, regions, neighborhoods, and transnational spaces and fields (Meier 2015). In particular, a comparative perspective promises to provide further insights into the complex and geographically varied working of global neoliberalism through the differential incorporation of skilled migrants at different localities and at various scales (Glick Schiller and Çaglar 2009).

Opportunities

The gaps in the contemporary literature on skilled migration identified above provide opportunities to develop research agendas that address these gaps. One particular opportunity exists in theorizing skilled migration from a comparative—including cross-national—perspective beyond the notions of brain drain, brain gain, and brain circulation, and beyond the neoliberal logic that valorizes migrants as workers possessing human capital (Docquier and Marfouk 2006; Adamuti-Trache 2015). Carefully designed empirical case studies could connect various economic, social, political, and cultural aspects of skilled migration in multiple contexts, including at the places of origin, destination, and other localities and at various scales. These studies could potentially assume a forms-of-capital perspective and, in this context, develop an understanding how the concept of the social field and its geography applies to skilled migration. Such case studies could have a broader impact on the theorization of skilled migration within the political economy of global neoliberalism.

A related opportunity lies in connecting skilled migration and the mobility of international students with theorizing the development process. Over the past decades, theories of development have assumed various neoclassical, structuralist, neoliberal, neo-Marxist, and other perspectives that often contradict one another in their philosophical assumptions, their interpretations of the migration process, and the practical policy solutions they propose. For example, international student mobility—say, from the Caribbean or Africa to Europe or North America—can be construed as reinforcing global core-periphery relations, or stimulating the circulation of knowledge and capacity that fosters development. Empirical evidence is pointing towards the heterogeneous and contextualized nature of the relationship between migration and development (de Haas 2010). More comparative empirical case studies especially on skilled migration would be useful not only to illustrate the complexity of this relation but also to provide an empirical foundation for theorizing this relation. International student mobility, in particular, is an area that remains understudied and underrepresented in theories of development.

In light of the existing multiplicity of conceptual approaches towards the migration-development nexus (e.g. Piper 2009), it will be important to maintain a comprehensive perspective and avoid the "danger that ignorance or neglect of previous empirical and theoretical work leads to uninformed and, hence, naïve optimism" (de Haas 2010, 258) that celebrates migration uncritically as a self-help, bottom-up development approach. Concepts like "development" should also be framed critically and in a way that is cognizant of the dialectic between the material underpinnings of global economic, political, and social relations and the way we imagine and understand broader processes of economic, political, and social transformation.

A similar dialectic applies to the production and imagination of scale. Geographers may be especially well positioned to contribute to linking skilled migration and development by paying close attention to scale. Contemporary research exploring this link often continues to fall into the trap of methodological nationalism when it interprets phenomena, such as brain gain, brain drain, or brain circulation. Exploring these impacts at urban, regional, and other scales as well as in the context of spatial networks and flows could provide novel insight in the ways that skilled migration could be incorporated into development theories. In fact, future research could highlight the role of skilled migrants as "scale makers" (Glick Schiller and Çaglar 2009, 2011) in the context of the development process. At the same time, researchers need to reflect on the epistemological nature of scale and the way they themselves imagine how and where skilled migration creates and exchanges "talent," value, and human and other forms of capital.

The accumulation of various forms of capital through the migration process is generally relevant to a research agenda that examines multiple empirical contexts and that links skilled migration and development. For example, while economic capital can be amassed by migrants and remitted to their families and communities at the places of origin, other forms of capital can also be transferred through "social" remittances that transform economic, social, political, and cultural practices and values at the places of origin. A future research agenda on skilled migration could build on and expand upon these ideas and explore further the transnational, scalar, and dynamic nature of the social field.

The popularity of the topic of skilled migration in scholarly debate derives from the important role this topic has played in recent decades in policy and decision-making outside academia. It is therefore especially important for scholars to assume a critical perspective of the policies and practices revolving around skilled migration. Approaching this topic not only in a critical and reflective way but also from multiple perspectives and by exploring various geographical contexts and scales will be vital for rethinking international skilled migration.

Acknowledgments

I thank Micheline van Riemsdijk for providing me with the notes she took of the discussion in Tampa. In addition, I thank Wei Li, Heike Jöhns, Binod Khadria, Russell King, and Jackal Tanelorn for raising important points during the discussion. The views expressed by these individuals are represented in the narrative. Any possible misrepresentations of these views and/or other participants' contributions to the discussion are unintended.

References

Adamuti-Trache, M. 2015. Experiences of highly educated immigrants. In *Immigrant experiences in North America: Understanding settlement and integration*, eds. H. Bauder and J. Shields, 185–203. Toronto: Canadian Scholars Press.

Alberts, H., and H. Hazen, eds. 2013. *International students and scholars in the United States: Coming from abroad.* New York: Palgrave Macmillan.

Bauder, H. 2006. *Labor movement: How migration regulates Labor markets.* New York: Oxford University Press.

———. 2011. *Immigration dialectic: Imagining community, economy and nation.* Toronto: University of Toronto Press.

Beaverstock, J. V. 2012. Highly skilled international labour migration and world cities: Expatriates, executives and entrepreneurs. In *International Handbook of Globalization and World Cities*, eds. B. Derudder, M. Hoyler, P. J. Taylor, and F. Witlox, 240–250. Cheltenham: Edward Elgar Publishing.

Beck, U. 2000. The cosmopolitan perspective: Sociology and the second age of modernity. *British Journal of Sociology* 51 (1): 79–105.

Bourdieu, P. 1984. *Distinction: A social critique of the judgement of taste.* Trans. Richard Rice. Cambridge, MA: Harvard University Press.

Cerna, L., and M. H. Chou. 2014. The regional dimension in the global competition for talent: Lessons from framing the European Scientific Visa and Blue Card. *Journal of European Public Policy* 21 (1): 76–95.

Chatterjee, S. 2015. Skills to build the nation: The ideology of 'Canadian experience' and nationalism in global knowledge regime. *Ethnicities* 15 (4), 544–567.

Cohen, R. 1987. *The new Helots: Migrants in the international division of labour.* Aldershot: Avebury.

Dauvergne, C. 2005. *Humanitarianism, identity, and nation: Migration laws in Canada and Australia.* Vancouver: UBC Press.

de Haas, H. 2010. Migration and development: A theoretical perspective. *International Migration Review* 44 (1): 227–264.

Dixon, D. P, K. Woodward, and J. P. Jones. 2008. Guest editorial: On the other hand … dialectics. *Environment and Planning A* 40: 2549–2561.

Docquier, F., and A. Marfouk. 2006. International migration by education attainment, 1990–2000. In *International migration, remittances and the brain drain*, eds. C. Özden and M. Schiff, 151–199. Washington, DC: World Bank and Palgrave Macmillan.

Flynn, E., and H. Bauder 2015. The private sector, institutions of higher education, and immigrant settlement in Canada. *Journal of International Migration and Integration* 16: 539–556.

Glick Schiller, N., and A. Çağlar. 2009. Towards a comparative theory of locality in migration studies: Migrant incorporation and city scale. *Journal of Ethnic and Migration Studies* 35 (2): 177–201.

———. eds. 2011. *Locating migration: Rescaling cities and migrants.* Ithaca, NY: Cornell University Press.

Harvey, D. 2005. *A brief history of neoliberalism.* New York: Oxford University Press.

Harvey, W. 2008. Strong or weak ties? British and Indian expatriate scientists finding jobs in Boston. *Global Networks* 8 (4): 453–473.

Jessop, B. 2002. The political economy of scale. In *Globalization, regionalization, and cross-border regions*, eds. M. Perkmann and N. Sum, 25–49. Basingstoke: Palgrave Macmillan.

Kelly, P., and T. Lusis. 2006. Migration and the *transnational habitus*: Evidence from Canada and the Philippines. *Environment and Planning A* 38 (5): 831–847.

Lan, P-C. 2011. White privilege, language capital and cultural ghettoization: Western high-skilled migrants in Taiwan. *Journal of Ethnic and Migration Studies* 37 (10): 1669–1693.

Liu, Y., and J. Shen, 2014. Spatial patterns and determinants of skilled internal migration in China, 2000–2005. *Papers in Regional Science* 93 (4): 749–771.

Lowell, L. B. 2005. *Policies and regulations for managing skilled international migration for work*. New York: United Nations Secretariat, Population Division.

Meier, L., ed. 2015. *Migrant professionals in the city: Local encounters, identities, and inequalities*. London: Routledge.

Mensah, J. 2015. The Black, continental African presence and the nation-immigration dialectic in Canada. *Social Identities* 20 (4–5): 1–20.

Millar, L., and J. Salt. 2008. Portfolios of mobility: The movement of expertise in transnational corporation in two sectors – aerospace and extractive industries. *Global Networks* 8 (1): 25–50.

Mitchell, K. 2003. *Crossing the neoliberal line: Pacific Rim migration and the metropolis*. Philadelphia, PA: Temple University Press.

Nagel, C. 2012. Cultural diasporas. In *International Handbook of Globalization and World Cities*, eds. B. Derudder, M. Hoyler, P. J. Taylor, and F. Witlox, 398–307. Cheltenham: Edward Elgar Publishing.

Nohl, A.-M., K. Schnittenhelm, O. Schmidtke, and A. Weiβ. 2014. *Work in transition: Cultural capital and highly skilled migrants' passages into the labour market*. Toronto: University of Toronto Press.

Ollman, B., and D. Badeen. 2015. Preface to the special issue: Dialectics and the Gordian knot. *Capital & Class* 39 (1): 3–5.

Ong, A. 1999. *Flexible citizenship: The cultural logics of transnationality*. Durham, NC: Duke University Press.

Piore, M. J. 1979. *Birds of passage: Migrant labor and industrial societies*. Cambridge: Cambridge University Press.

Piper, N. 2009. Guest editorial – The complex interactions of the migration-development nexus: A social perspective. *Population, Space and Place* 15 (2): 93–101.

Pottie-Sherman, Y. and R. Wilkes. 2014. Good code bad code: Exploring the immigration-nation dialectic through media coverage of the Hérouxville 'Code of Life' document. *Migration Studies* 2 (2): 189–211.

Robertson, S. 2013. *Transnational student-migrants and the state: The education-migration nexus*. Basingstoke: Palgrave Macmillan.

Ryan, L., U. Erel, and A. D'Angelo, eds. 2015. *Migrant capital: Networks, identities and strategies*. Basingstoke: Palgrave Macmillan.

Shachar, A. 2006. The race for talent: Highly skilled migrants and competitive immigration regimes. *New York University Law Review* 81: 148–206.

Sharma, N. 2006. *Home economics: Nationalism and the making of 'migrant workers' in Canada*. Toronto: University of Toronto Press.

Triadafilopoulos, T. 2013. *Wanted and welcome? Policies for highly skilled immigrants in comparative perspective*. New York: Springer.

Wimmer, A., and N. Glick Schiller. 2002. Methodological nationalism and beyond: Nation-state building, migration and the social sciences. *Global Networks* 2 (4): 301–334.

Index